W9-AZF-475

What are people saying about *Theology in the Context of World Christianity*

This book is a great idea, executed well—offering a vital complement to traditional, "Western" doctrinal categories. There is much instruction here for theological students and teachers alike. Tennent asks important questions, providing answers that are often insightful and always biblically thoughtful.

Daniel J. Treier, associate professor of theology, Wheaton College, and author of *Virtue and the Voice of God: Toward Theology as Wisdom*

This volume masterfully demonstrates that listening to theological reflection from around the globe yields fresh contributions to discussions of Christian faith and practice. It contains new insights, new challenges, yet all the while interwoven with Christian history and thinking past and present. May Tennent's work be the first of many stimulating conversations!

M. Daniel Carroll R. (Rodas), Earl S. Kalland chair of Old Testament, Denver Seminary (USA); adjunct professor, El Seminario Teológico Centroamericano (Guatemala)

For a long time the systematic theology developed by the church has been generally deficient because it did not take into account the approaches of Christians from "the rest of the world" and of people of other faiths. This book by Tim Tennent shows us how to do this. He has taken samplings of some crucial issues and done an admirable job in showing how they should influence our theological formulations. The added benefit of this book is that it is easy to read—something that cannot be said of most theology books!

Ajith Fernando, national director, Youth for Christ, Sri Lanka

This book is a must-read for all people who are interested in a new and exciting way of doing theology at a time when Christianity is already a post-Western and global religion. Truly fascinating!

Sung Wook Chung, associate professor of theology, Denver Seminary

This is the book we have waited a long time for. We have all sampled selections from the growing menu of theological reflection in the Majority World church, but so often these have been viewed by scholars and students in the West as the theological equivalent of ethnic restaurants — exotic and interesting but not to be taken too seriously in the dining hall of real (Western) theology. Meanwhile Philip Jenkins, Andrew Walls, Lamin Sanneh, and others have thrust the staggering realities of Majority World Christianity into the forefront of Western Christian consciousness. Theologians are now at last grappling with what missiologists have been saying for years: theology is a cross-cultural team game with global players. And the referee is no longer the Western academy, but the Scriptures themselves.

Tim Tennent engages all his experience in mission and theology to argue that it is not just the outer forms of Christianity that are culturally translatable, but theology itself. No part of the global body of Christ can say to any other part, "I have no need of you." Every part is enriched — theologically too — by every other part. Theology, like mission, has to be "from everywhere to everywhere." This book, organized in the systematic way that Western theology likes, offers teacher and student alike a representative, thorough, constructively critical compendium of some of the key contributors to the task of global theology. The point is not whether we will *like* everything we read here, but whether we are willing to *listen.* These are the voices we must increasingly engage with in the global conversation of Christian theology.

REV DR CHRISTOPHER J H WRIGHT, international director, Langham Partnership International

THEOLOGY
in the context of
WORLD CHRISTIANITY

THEOLOGY
in the context of WORLD CHRISTIANITY

how the global church is influencing the way we think about and discuss theology

Timothy C. Tennent

Theology in the Context of World Christianity

Requests for information should be addressed to:

Zondervan, *Grand Rapids, Michigan 49530*

Library of Congress Cataloging-in-Publication Data

Tennent, Timothy C.
Theology in the context of world Christianity : how the global church is influencing the way we think about and discuss theology / Timothy C. Tennent.
p. cm.
Includes bibliographical references and indexes.
ISBN-13: 978-0-310-27511-4 (alk. paper)
ISBN-10: 0-310-27511-3 (alk. paper)
1. Theology—Methodology. 2. Globalization—Religious aspects—Christianity. I. Title.
BR118.T44 2007
230.09—dc22 2007014651

Interior design by Mark Sheeres

Printed in the United States of America

12 • 23 22 21 20 19 18 17 16 15 14 13 12 11 10 9 8 7 6 5

Dedicated to the memory of my father,
Robert W. Tennent Sr. (1925–2005),
who always encouraged me to
reach for God's highest

Table of Contents

Acknowledgments

I am indebted to the trustees and faculty of Gordon-Conwell Theological Seminary for granting me a sabbatical to write this book. My long-standing academic pursuit has been dedicated to finding new ways to reconnect the disciplines of theology and missiology. I can think of no better place to engage in this task than Gordon-Conwell. I would like to extend special thanks to my colleague Jack Davis, who read the manuscript and provided many helpful suggestions.

I am also indebted to the students, staff, and faculty of the Luther W. New Jr. Theological College in India, where I have had the privilege of teaching for the last twenty years. My interaction with students, both at GCTS and at NTC over the years, has been a continual source of insight and joy. Many of the ideas for this book arose out of stimulating discussions with students in classrooms in the USA and in India. I am particularly grateful for the friendship and mentoring I have received from my dear friend George Chavanikamannil, who opened up the door of India to me.

Although I explore this more in chapter 10, I also want to thank Andrew Walls for pointing out to me that "theological scholarship needs a renaissance of mission studies." It is this spark that was fanned into a flame and eventually became this book.

Most of my sabbatical was spent at the Overseas Ministries Study Center in New Haven, Connecticut, where I served as Senior Scholar in Residence. I am indebted to Jonathan Bonk, the director of OMSC, and his wonderful staff for their encouragement and support during the many months it took to write this book. Being able to walk across the street to the Day Missions Library of Yale Divinity School, arguably the finest missions collection in the world, is one of those great treasures I will always cherish.

I am deeply appreciative of the hard work and dedication of my research assistant, Lou Ann Stropoli. She spent many hours on my behalf tracking down that illusive book or article. Throughout the past year I have observed her growth as a budding scholar, and Lou Ann stands as a testimony to the abiding value of the Byington program at the seminary. There is no doubt that this book is stronger, and was able to be completed on time, due in no small part to her efforts on my behalf.

I am grateful for the capable assistance of Katya Covrett, Verlyn Verbrugge, and Moisés Silva from Zondervan. I commend Zondervan for their foresight and long-term commitment to helping the church understand more about the emergence of global Christianity.

I will always be grateful to my wife, Julie, for her constant encouragement and love. She faithfully read every word of the manuscript and provided invaluable feedback and thoughtful advice. I am blessed to be married to someone with such a keen interest and facility in theology and global Christianity.

Because of the beauty and breadth of world Christianity, no single person can do justice to the burgeoning theological discourse around the world. But I am reminded of Basil's wisdom when he said, "The athlete does not so much complain of being wounded in the struggle as of not being able even to secure admission into the stadium" (*On the Holy Spirit* 3.29; trans. in *NPNF*, ser. 3, 8:48). I am so thankful to God that I have been allowed entrance into this stadium and the privilege of engaging in issues that are relevant to our better understanding of what it means to be part of a global Christian community.

TIMOTHY C. TENNENT
August 2007

Foreword

The publication of *Theology in the Context of World Christianity* happens at a time when we are becoming increasingly aware that Christianity is truly a global faith because it is rooted in the multiple local realities of humankind. In our time, as in generations past, Christians need theology so that they can live wisely in the world. How should Christians go about the task of developing sapiential theology today? Tennent's book invites the reader to answer this question by investigating selected themes of Christian theology from the viewpoints of Christians from Africa, Asia, and Latin America.

In this book Christians in the West are called to think of church life in Africa, Asia, and Latin America (usually considered the "mission fields") as an important factor in the formulation and practice of theology. Tennent contends that Christians in these continents matter theologically because they are the majority of Christians in the world today. While he is aware that Western theological hegemony endures and theology is not determined by demographics alone, the author focuses on the potential for theological renewal and vitality if Christians in the West listened more attentively to those of the Majority World. So, instead of viewing theological developments in Africa, Asia, and Latin America as strange, exotic, and peripheral, Western Christians are provided with specific examples of how these theologies are really mainstream.

Theological students, especially those in the United States, are the primary audience Tennent addresses. These students need to understand the interdisciplinary and cross-cultural nature of Christian theology because they will be engaged in Christian work in a world where Christians from the Majority World will be more visible. *Theology in the Context of World Christianity* is a powerful apologetic for interdisciplinary and cross-cultural Christian theology. It is a valuable tool, especially for theological students. Here the doctrines of God, Scripture, humanity, Christ, salvation, the Holy Spirit, the church, and the last things are examined broadly from Asian, African, and Latin American perspectives.

Christians beyond the Western world will also benefit from reading this book. For them its value is its liberating power because it legitimizes the theological endeavors from their continents.

The day is coming when there will be no need to make a case for the influence of Majority World Christians on theology. Until then, the ideas put forth in this book are necessary. For this reason I commend my colleague Timothy C. Tennent for his excellent contribution.

Tite Tiénou, dean and professor of theology of missions,
Trinity Evangelical Divinity School, Deerfield, Illinois

FOREWORD

Behind Dr. Tennent's valuable book lies the important but often neglected fact that the stimulus or creative force in making theology is Christian mission. Indeed, it is Christian mission that most often creates the need for fresh theological activity.

The true matrix of theology is not the study or the library. Theology arises from situations—social situations, intellectual situations—where one must make Christian choices, and previous Christian experience offers no clear precedent. Christian theology is the attempt to think in a Christian way; it is about making the right choice intellectually. When the gospel crosses a cultural frontier or when Christians encounter those alternative formulations of spiritual reality that we call the other world faiths or religions, new situations arise that require Christians to make a Christian choice and to formulate the reasons for that choice.

Theology already existing may help to clarify the issues, but it does not have the resources to make the final decision. It was shaped for other purposes, under the conditions of another time and place. Paul's letters—the Corinthian correspondence is a good example—are full of questions (and answers to them) that reflect the life situations of Gentile Christians in Hellenistic pagan society. Nothing in the experience of even the best believers of the church in Jerusalem, safe behind the perimeter fence of the Torah, could provide guidance for such situations.

What was true of Hellenistic social and family life was also true of Hellenistic metaphysical activity and the Greek intellectual tradition. The great creeds came into existence as a result of asking Greek metaphysical questions in the Greek language, using Greek styles of argument and Greek categories of thought. The process led to new discoveries about Christ, a new shared clarity of view about his identity. Those discoveries have remained the possession of the whole church. The crossing of the frontier of Israel's heritage into the Hellenistic-Roman universe, with all the translation, linguistic and conceptual, that this process involved, made the early Christian centuries particularly active and creative theologically. The theologizing of those years (strenuous, for theologizing is hard, painful work) has blessed the church ever since.

Subsequent crossings of cultural frontiers have also produced theological advance. How the encounter with the traditional cultures of northern and western Europe has enriched the doctrine of atonement. The great religious fact of our time, as Dr. Tennent makes abundantly clear, is the deepening Christian engagement with the cultures and religions of Africa, Asia, and Latin America. He demonstrates some of the theological issues that are thrown up in interaction between Christians and Buddhists, Christians and Hindus, Christians and Muslims, and with the traditions of Africa and Asia as a whole. These encounters raise theological issues for which existing theological formulae, developed within frameworks designed for Western use, are inadequate. As with the Torah-keeping Jerusalem believers facing issues in the context of the social and intellectual ferment of the Hellenistic world, the frameworks provide no answers, because they have no questions.

Dr. Tennent puts such issues in the context of contemporary mission, points to ways of approaching them opened by some African and Asian Christians, and suggests others himself. To these ways different people will react differently. But the more important issue is that we may be on the verge of a theological renaissance. The deepening penetration of Christian thinking of the cultures of Africa and Asia could open the most active and creative period of Christian theology since the deepening penetration of Greco-Roman thought brought about the great creeds, and with them the classical formulations of the doctrines of the Trinity and the incarnation.

ANDREW F. WALLS, Centre for the Study of Christianity
in the Non-Western World, University of Edinburgh

PREFACE

Whenever a book appears that intentionally seeks to bridge two separate disciplines, it is inevitably fraught with peculiar challenges. This book seeks to integrate the fields of theology, especially systematic theology, with missiology, the study of missions. Its purpose is to show how the expansion of global Christianity (a vital missions theme) can serve as a positive influence on the way we think about and discuss God, his revelation, and his work in the world (vital themes in theology). There are a number of themes and concepts in this book that find a more natural home in either the discourse of theologians or the discourse of the missionary. Also the natural dispositions of the two groups tend to go in different directions. Missions, by nature, is a bold, activist, imprecise, and even experimental work. Theology, by nature, is a more precise, analytical, and reflective work.

Insights into the disciplines can be gained by remembering how they are often caricatured. The missionary is pictured standing in the middle of a group of fancifully dressed dancing "natives" with painted faces on some remote island of the "heathen world." The theologian is pictured sitting in a lofty "ivory tower" bent over a desk quietly reading some large tome, while jotting down notes in Latin! Neither caricature reflects what either missionaries or theologians mostly do, but it does reveal something of our history, projected perceptions, and tendencies. However, I cannot shake the fact that the apostle Paul was simultaneously the church's greatest theologian and its greatest missionary. I remain convinced that a better conversation between the two disciplines can help to reinvigorate both.

Theological students entering seminary today are, by disposition, more contextually based learners than the generations that preceded them. They want to see how theology works in authentic, real-life contexts. Today's missionaries who are observing the dramatic growth of Christianity and the increased complexity of second-generation church growth are seeing the need for theological reflection as never before. This book is designed to help bring these two disciplines together for a mutually beneficial discussion. Before we begin, however, I want to set forth my main goal for the book, along with two brief clarifications.

THE GOAL: EXPANDING OUR "ECCLESIASTICAL CARTOGRAPHY"

Maps of the world produced by Europeans during the medieval period reveal much about their worldview. Europe and the Mediterranean (from *medius terra*, meaning "middle earth") are situated at the center of the map. The maps were filled with striking details of Europe and the Mediterranean beautifully adorned with various Christian images. However, most of Africa and Asia is not even represented, and the few distorted land masses that vaguely represent the southern continents tend to blend hazily into the margins amidst drawings of savages, dog-headed kings, and grotesque demons.

These maps reveal as much about European theology as about their cartography. In fact, it was Jonathan Bonk, director of the Overseas Ministries Study Center, who first introduced to me the phrase "ecclesiastical cartography" as a reference to how the church views the world.[1] Undoubtedly, our cartography has improved dramatically over the years, but it seems that our theological analysis of the world has not kept pace. We still see the West as the ecclesiastical center of the world, even though the vast majority of Christians in the world today are located elsewhere. What African or Asian Christians are doing and writing seems so marginal to us, and it penetrates our own theological discussions only in a vague, ephemeral way.

We as Westerners continue to vastly overestimate the role of our trained theologians, missionaries, denominations, and mission agencies in the actual task of global evangelism and church planting. We continue to talk about church history in a way that puts Europe at the center, and church history outside the West is reserved for those preparing for the mission field or church historians pursuing specialist studies. We continue to think that our theological reflections are normative and universally applicable to all people from all cultures. In short, the Western church has not yet fully absorbed how the dramatic shifts in global Christianity are influencing what constitutes normative Christianity. In fact, many of the hottest and most passionate cultural and theological debates currently going on in seminaries and in denominational assemblies across the country seem trite from the perspective of Asian or African Christianity. We must learn to think bigger, listen more, and look at the church from a wider vista.

My goal in this book is to expand our "ecclesiastical cartography" by highlighting within each of the major themes of systematic theology various studies that are engaging the global church. These issues I have chosen are, of course, a mere sampling of what is emerging as a dynamic, global discourse from Christians around the world who are becoming "self-theologizing." This book is not intended to take the place of the traditional systematic theologies used in classrooms in the West. Rather it is designed to stand alongside them in a supportive way, helping our students to think more globally about the formation of theology and to expand our own understanding of what it means to be a Christian in the twenty-first century.

However, before we begin these studies, let me make two further clarifications.

Terminology in Referring to Asia, Africa, and Latin America

A word about terminology is in order. There has not yet emerged a single term to refer to Latin America, Africa, and Asia that does not involve some difficulty. Probably the most common term is still the phrase "the non-Western world." The main problem

1. Jonathan J. Bonk, "Ecclesiastical Cartography and the Invisible Continent," *International Bulletin of Missionary Research* 28, no. 4 (October 2004): 153–58.

with this phrase is that it defines the peoples from these parts of the world by what they are *not* rather than what they are. When the church in these regions of the world is called "the non-Western church," it implicitly carries the connotation that the Western world continues to represent normative Christianity, which African Christians or Asian Christians take as their point of departure.

There are times when the expression is helpful, especially when referring, for example, to *theology* that is *intentionally* non-Western, i.e., not aligned with traditional Western thinking on a particular topic. So, I occasionally use this expression when I am specifically seeking to contrast a particular theological perspective with the West, but I do not use it in the broader, geographic sense. When I am speaking in a geographic way, I sometimes speak about the church "outside the West" in the same way that I have heard Africans or Chinese speak about what goes on "outside Africa" or "outside India."

The expression "Third World" or (*Tiers Monde*) was coined in 1952 by the French demographer Alfred Sauvy. It quickly entered English as a helpful phrase to speak collectively about Africa, Asia, and Latin America. It was originally articulated in the context of the Cold War, when the world was polarized by the two "worlds" of the capitalistic, industrialized West and the communist, state-controlled East. It began as a *political* expression. Later, in the 1960s and 1970s, the expression "Third World country" began to be used in an *economic* sense to refer to underdeveloped countries marked by poverty and disease.

With the collapse of the Soviet Union and the emergence of economic prosperity in places like Singapore and the oil-rich Middle East, the phrase has become increasingly dated, and this book does not employ the phrase.[2] Later, the phrase "Two-Thirds World" emerged to counteract what was incorrectly perceived to be the statistical origin of the expression "Third World." This expression emphasized the sheer geographic size of Latin America, Africa, and Asia, though sometimes refers to the demographic size of the church in these continents.

The expression "Two-Thirds World" is helpful, but it has been superseded more recently by the simpler phrase "Majority World." The 2004 Lausanne Forum for World Evangelization, which I attended in Pattaya, Thailand, dedicated an entire working group to the theme, "The Two-Thirds World Church." It included participants from across the world, and one of their formal actions was to vote *unanimously* that the phrase "Majority World Church" be used.[3] This is the best phrase currently available. It is to be preferred because it is simpler and less confusing to students just entering

2. Although I refrain from using the phrase, I concede that it continues to be widely used in the literature. This is justified by arguing that although the phrase is frequently used in negative and unhelpful ways, its origin was based on an extension of the idea of the "Third Estate" or *Tiers État* in pre-Revolutionary France whereby the common people were seeking a voice over against the privileged voices of the clergy and the nobility. Thus, its original meaning carried the idea of newly emerging voices demanding to be heard. In this sense, the phrase is now used and applied to churches outside the ecclesiastical hegemony of the West.

3. David Claydon, ed., *A New Vision, a New Heart, a New Call*, vol. 2, Lausanne Occasional Papers from the 2004 Forum for World Evangelization hosted by the Lausanne Committee for World Evangelization in Pattaya, Thailand (Pasadena, CA: William Carey Library, 2005), 118. The full report found on pages 117–169 contains a full discussion about the various connotations surrounding the terms "Third World" and "Two-Thirds World."

this discussion for the first time, and it helps to highlight the basic point that Africa, Asia, and Latin America are where the majority of the world's Christians are now located. The studies in this book use this expression, especially when referring to Christians found in these regions as a whole.

The words "north" and "south" or "northern Christianity" and "southern Christianity" are also used regularly in contemporary missions literature. As I explore in the first chapter, Christian demographics is changing dramatically from peoples in the traditional heartland of Christianity in the north to peoples who occupy the southern continents. Thus, Latin America, Africa, and Asia are often referred to as "the South" or the "Global South," and Christians from North America and Europe are referred to as "the North." These terms are helpful, but they are difficult to apply without some qualification now that we are seeing such a rapid expansion of the church in China, which is difficult to refer to as the "South."

Finally, the term post-Western is also used in a descriptive manner to refer to Christians and theological developments that are "beyond" the West. This phrase, however, seems to unnecessarily diminish the growing partnerships and connectedness between Christians throughout the world; it also ignores the ancient churches in the East as well as some of the newer indigenous movements that have not been significantly influenced by the West and, therefore, cannot be accurately described as "post" anything. Thus, this expression will not be used unless I am specifically referring to a theological movement or trend that has moved "beyond" the West in some intentional way.

Be Irenic, not Irate

It is dangerous to talk about theological shifts with theologians. Evangelicals in particular have learned well how to play theological defense against the onslaught of attacks from liberal theologians who seem determined to "deconstruct" every central claim of historic Christianity, only to "reconstruct" a new theology far more reflective of the latest cultural trends than anything that remotely reflects the faith of the apostles. Evangelicals have been slow to learn how to engage in constructive theological discussions with African or Asian Christians who fully share in the apostolic faith, but who do not share the history of our own theological skirmishes. Sometimes our brothers and sisters in Christ from Asia, Africa, and Latin America do not understand the history behind certain words and phrases that have become the shibboleths of theological discourse in the West. Terms like *ecumenical*, *inerrant*, *liberal*, and *fundamentalist* are just a few of dozens of terms carrying theological and historical associations that do not easily translate when one suddenly finds oneself talking with a Christian from Nepal or Borneo.

If this book is read from any one of a range of sectarian theological positions, I am sure there is something in almost every chapter that some might find disquieting or even startling. But we must recall that the church is pictured not as a corporation or business, but as a great family or household, with Christ as our head. As with any household, it can sometimes be a raucous place that exhibits both unity and diversity in many surprising and unexpected ways. When adolescents are in a household, special patience and more enhanced listening skills are required! Sometimes if we listen carefully, we discover that our children have insights and perspectives on issues that can serve to enrich our experience.

I have had the opportunity of helping to train North Indian Christians (mostly first-generation converts from Hinduism) in theology and missions for nearly twenty years. Throughout this process I have been frequently amazed at how much I learn from them about the Christian faith. I trust that they also have benefited from my background and experience as a Western Christian. When Peter brought the gospel to Cornelius's household, there is no doubt that Cornelius was transformed, but so was the apostle Peter as he went away with some of his theological categories shaken; but in the process he became a more globally minded Christian. So, I encourage every reader of this book to approach these studies in global theology with an irenic disposition. If we do, we will be in a better position to be full participants in the emergence of a global Christian movement that increasingly looks like that joyous eschatological banquet awaiting us all.

Chapter 1

The Emergence of a Global Theological Discourse

On October 31, 1517, a relatively unknown Augustinian monk named Martin Luther nailed ninety-five theses of protest against abuses in the church to the door of the Castle Church in Wittenberg. This Latin document was quickly translated into German and, within weeks, had spread like wildfire across Europe, sparking what has become known as the Protestant Reformation. When Pope Leo X first heard about the ninety-five theses, he reportedly dismissed Luther as a "drunken German" who "when sober will change his mind." Later, as the movement grew, he still dismissed the growing discontent and calls for reform as a mere "squabble among monks."[1] However, before too many years had passed, everyone realized that, in fact, Christianity, and indeed Europe itself, was undergoing profound changes that would alter the entire course of Western civilization.

Today, many new changes are transforming the church and the world in ways unprecedented since the Reformation. For four hundred years Protestantism was essentially a Western cultural movement, with few African or Asian actors on the Christian stage. For example, when William Carey, the humble cobbler who was later called the father of the modern missionary movement, arrived in India in 1793 to preach the gospel, 98 percent of the entire world's Protestants lived in the Western world.[2] Even one hundred years later, at the close of the "Great Century" of foreign missions and the dawn of the twentieth century, 90 percent of all Protestants still lived in the Western world. Is it any surprise that nineteenth-century Africans often referred to Christianity as the "white man's religion"? After all, most Africans had never met a nonwhite Christian.

Is it any wonder that the most common description of a missionary in China was a *fan-kwei* or "foreign devil"? A Christian was as strange and foreign to a Chinese

1. Roland Bainton, *Here I Stand: A Life of Martin Luther* (New York: Abingdon, 1950), 85.

2. David B. Barrett and Todd M. Johnson, *World Christian Trends, AD 30–AD 2200: Interpreting the Annual Christian Megacensus* (Pasadena, CA: William Carey Library, 2001), 331.

as a Buddhist would have been to my grandmother, who lived her whole life in the United States and, I am confident, never met a Buddhist in her life. For much of the world, Christianity seemed inextricably bound up with the rise and fall of Western civilization.

We are now in the midst of one of the most dramatic shifts in Christianity since the Reformation. Christianity is on the move and is creating a seismic change that is changing the face of the whole Christian movement. Every Christian in the world, but especially those in the West, must understand how these changes will influence our understanding of church history, our study of theology, and our conception of world missions. This book focuses on the shift in theological discourse, whereby the universal truths of the gospel are being revisited and retold in new, global contexts, a process I am calling *theological translatability*. However, before the fruits of these new conversations can be heard, we must begin with a brief history lesson in the historical, geographic, and cultural translatability of the Christian faith.

CHRISTIANITY SURVIVES THROUGH CROSS-CULTURAL TRANSMISSION: KEY MOMENTS IN CHRISTIAN HISTORY

Advance and Recession

The cross-cultural transmission of the Christian faith has always been integral to the survival of Christianity. Andrew Walls, among others, has pointed out the peculiar nature of Christian expansion through history, that it has been one of serial, not progressive, growth.[3] In other words, Christianity has not had an even, steady growth beginning with a central, cultural, and geographic center from which it subsequently spread to its present position as the largest, most ethnically diverse religion in the world. Instead, Christian history has been one of advance and recession. Christian history has witnessed powerful penetrations of the gospel into certain geographic and cultural regions, only to experience later a major recession in that region and, sometimes, even to wither away almost to extinction. Yet just as Christianity was waning in one quarter, it was experiencing an even more dramatic rebirth and expansion in another.

This advance-and-recession motif is such a major theme in Christian history that the imminent church historian Kenneth Scott Latourette uses it as a major organizing motif for his famous multivolume work, *A History of Christianity*.[4] The important point is to recognize that despite what it feels like when a Christian is living in the midst of a particular cultural and geographic advance, if you step back and look at the whole picture of Christian history, you must conclude that there is no such thing as a particular Christian culture or Christian civilization.

---

3. Andrew Walls, *The Missionary Movement in Christian History: Studies in the Transmission of Faith* (Maryknoll, NY: Orbis, 1996), 22–25.

4. Kenneth Scott Latourette, *A History of Christianity*, vols. 1 and 2 (Peabody, MA: Prince Press, 2000). Latourette uses as his heading for AD 500–AD 950 the following: "The Darkest Hours: The Great Recession." The next section for AD 950–1350 he titles, "Four Centuries of Resurgence and Advance." Then comes, for 1350–1500, "Geographic Loss and Internal Lassitude, Confusion, and Corruption, Partly Offset by Vigorous Life." Many of the subheadings also reflect this theme as, for example, chapter 28, "Western Europe: Decline and Vitality," and chapter 40, "Stagnation and Advance: The Eastern Churches."

This picture is in stark contrast to what one observes, for example, in Islam or in Hinduism, the next two largest religions after Christianity. Islam initially emerged in Saudi Arabia, and from that geographic and cultural center has spread throughout the world. Today, there are far more non-Arab Muslims than Arab Muslims. Yet, despite its diversity, Islam retains a distinctly Arab orientation. Devout Muslims insist that the Qur'an is untranslatable into any language other than Arabic. The call to prayer goes out in Arabic, regardless of the national language of the surrounding Muslims. All Muslims face Mecca when they pray. These are important indicators that Islam has had a progressive, not serial, growth. It has always enjoyed a single cultural and geographic center in Saudi Arabia and has never been forced to fully embrace cultural or geographic translatability.

Hinduism emerged in the Gangetic plain of North India over three thousand years ago, making it one of the oldest religions in the world. Yet Hinduism has never lost its cultural and geographic center in North India. Just as Islam can hardly be imagined apart from Saudi Arabia, the home of the holy city of Mecca, the Ka'aba, the black stone, and the tomb of Muhammad in Medina, so it is difficult to imagine a Hinduism that withers away in India but finds a new center in, say, sub-Saharan Africa. But this is precisely what has happened repeatedly in the history of the Christian movement. Dozens of examples could be highlighted throughout the history of the church, but I have chosen three "snapshots" taken at different points in church history to illustrate the cultural and geographic translatability of the Christian faith.

Snapshots of Geographic and Cultural Translatability in Christianity

Snapshot #1: From Jewish Birth to Gentile Home

Christianity began as a Jewish movement fulfilling Jewish hopes, promises, and expectations. Indeed, the continuity between Judaism and Christianity seemed so seamless to the earliest believers that they would have never thought of themselves as changing their religion from Judaism to something else. They understood Christianity as the extension and fulfillment of their Jewish faith. Yet, right in the pages of the New Testament we read the story of those unnamed Jewish believers in Antioch who took the risky—and controversial move—to cross major cultural and religious barriers and share the gospel with pagan, uncircumcised Gentiles.

Acts 11:19 begins by recounting how, after the persecution in connection with Stephen, these scattered believers began to share the gospel "as far as Phoenicia, Cyprus and Antioch, telling the message only to Jews." The next verse records one of the most important missiological moments in the entire New Testament: "Some of them, however, men from Cyprus and Cyrene, went to Antioch and *began to speak to Greeks also*, telling them the good news about the Lord Jesus" (italics added). This is the beginning of a new cultural frontier, which, though radical at the time, became so prominent that it was considered normative Christianity.

At the time these unnamed believers from Cyprus and Cyrene began to preach the gospel to Gentiles, the church was comprised of Jewish believers and a few Gentile God-fearers like Cornelius and the Ethiopian eunuch, who had accepted the Torah.

In other words, the Gentile God-fearers had accepted the Jewish messiah as their messiah and were living out their new faith on Jewish terms. The cultural center of this young, fledgling movement, known simply as "the Way" (Acts 9:2; 19:23; 24:14), was based in Jerusalem under apostolic leadership. Jerusalem was the first geographic center of the Christian movement and Judaism was its first religious and cultural home.

The importance of Jerusalem is underscored by what happened when news got back there about this surprising turning to Christ among Gentiles. The apostles in Jerusalem sent Barnabas down to Antioch to investigate this new movement. Later, Paul and Barnabas entered into such a sharp disagreement with some Judaizers who strongly opposed the Gentiles coming to Christ apart from Judaism (circumcision, submission to the Torah, dietary restrictions, etc.) that Paul traveled to Jerusalem to make his case before the apostles (see Acts 15).

The Jerusalem Council met to debate and discuss the basis for accepting Gentiles into the church. The group decided that Gentiles did not need to come to Jesus Christ on Jewish cultural and religious terms. They were not asked to submit to or to keep the many intricacies of the Jewish law, but only to respect a few broad guidelines that would clearly separate the Gentiles from their pagan past, while still affirming that sinners are saved not by keeping the law but by faith in Jesus Christ. The Jewish "center" formally recognized the presence of Christ in these new Gentile brothers and sisters. Since this "Way" now included Gentiles on their own cultural terms, it could no longer regard itself as a curious subset of Judaism. The faith had successfully traversed its first major cross-cultural transmission.

Snapshot #2: The Fall of the Empire and the Birth of "Barbarian" and Byzantine Faith

The turn of the fourth century in the Roman empire was marked by the most brutal persecution the church had ever experienced. Emperor Diocletian ordered the destruction of church buildings and Bibles, and he imprisoned many Christian leaders. All of this changed, however, when his successor, Constantine, issued an edict of toleration in 313. In the following decades, Christianity experienced dramatic expansion among Hellenistic Gentiles until Christianity soon became the "professed faith of the overwhelming majority of the population of the Roman empire."[5] In fact, Christianity became almost coterminous with the empire.[6] Greek-speaking peoples with a Hellenistic culture and a pagan background were now the best example of *representative* Christianity. Indeed, by the fourth century, Jewish Christians represented only a tiny percentage of the church.

Throughout the fourth century the Roman empire increasingly showed signs of weakness and disintegration. Tragically, the moral and spiritual climate of nominal

5. Ibid., 1:97.

6. Ibid., 1:269. Stephen Neill tentatively estimates that the number of Christians in the empire on the eve of the Edict of Toleration (AD 313) was approximately five million (10 percent of the population). By the time Emperor Justinian officially closed the School of Athens in 529 the number of Christians was closer to 25 million. See Stephen Neill, *A History of Christian Missions* (London: Penguin, 1990), 39, 41.

Christianity generally mirrored that of the declining empire.[7] Looking back, Christianity might have shared the same demise as the empire, symbolized best by the famous sacking of Rome by the Goths in 410.[8] Remarkably, however, Christianity found new vitality outside the empire, among new people groups moving westward into Ireland and Scotland and eastward into Arabia, Persia, and beyond.[9] Many of the invading Germanic peoples were also brought to faith in Jesus Christ. In a matter of a few decades the church was facing another new cultural shock with the entrance of Visigoths (Spain), Ostrogoths (Italy), Franks (Northern Gaul), Burgundians (Southern Gaul), Vandals (North Africa), and Angles and Saxons (Britain) all entering the church in significant numbers. Centuries later, this pattern repeated itself. The relatively stable Carolingian empire, which had substantially been Christianized, eventually disintegrated, and a new wave of invasions began with the arrival of the Scandinavians, who were also, in turn, evangelized.

Not only was Christianity continually making cultural gains on one hand while suffering losses on the other hand, but the geographic center was also shifting. By the end of the second century, Rome, as capital of the empire, was the most important city for Christians. Indeed, even in the structure of Acts, we already see the strategic and cultural importance of Rome for Christians. However, in AD 330 Constantine relocated the capital to Byzantium (modern-day Istanbul), which he renamed Constantinople. By the time Rome was sacked in 410, Constantinople was the undisputed geographic center of the Christian faith.

Christianity experienced some remarkable advances in the East during this time, including important progress among the Slavic peoples. During the ninth and tenth centuries, when Christianity in the West had reached dangerously low levels of faith and practice, Constantinople represented the most vibrant expression of Christianity in the world. In fact, the Russian ruler Vladimir was so moved by what he experienced in Constantinople that he sponsored the propagation of Eastern Christianity throughout Russia. Christianity, it seems, was becoming accustomed to reinvigorating its vitality and inner life through cross-cultural transmission to new people groups and adapting to new cultural and geographic centers.

Snapshot #3: A Faith for the World: Missionaries and Migrations

The Protestant Reformation led by Luther (1483–1546), along with the Roman Catholic Counter-Reformation led by Ignatius Loyola (1491–1556), represent renewal movements that helped to stimulate new vitality among previously Christianized peoples who had become largely nominal. Christianity in the Middle Ages was still confined primarily to Europe, which remained the geographic center. However, a revitalized European Christianity eventually led to dramatic missionary endeavors

7. During this period the church was either focused on internal, doctrinal disputes as reflected in the ecumenical councils or they had become part of monastic communities that were not interested in revitalizing Roman civilization.

8. The official conquest of the empire is generally dated as 378, the year the Goths killed the emperor in the battle of Adrianople.

9. St. Patrick arrived in Ireland around AD 432, Columba founded his famous monastery in Iona in 563, and Aidan founded Lindisfarne in Northumbria in 635.

that brought the gospel to many new people groups, including most of Latin America but also Asia. Fueled by missionary activity in the wake of the *Padroado* (1493),[10] the Roman Catholic Church founded the *Sacra Congregatio de Propaganda Fide* in 1622 to assist in training new missionaries, to oversee all Roman Catholic missionary work, and to coordinate major new missionary initiatives in non-Roman Catholic regions of the world.

Eventually the Protestants, beginning with the Moravians and later through the creation of dozens of new mission-sending societies, followed with their own missionary initiatives. The nineteenth-century missionaries planted the seeds for a future twenty-first-century Christian harvest beyond anything they could have imagined during their lifetimes. However, apart from missionaries committed to sharing their faith across cultural and geographic lines, Europe itself was engaged in the largest ocean-based migration in the history of the world. From 1500 until the middle of the twentieth century millions of Europeans relocated to the New World, bringing their faith with them and spawning the birth of massive new populations, largely Christian. The gospel, once again, proved it was culturally and geographically translatable. Soon the English-speaking world, including Britain and North America, became the most important new center of vibrant Christianity.

Living on the Seam of History

The purpose of these brief snapshots is to underscore the fact that the lifeblood of Christianity is found in its ability to translate itself across new cultural and geographic barriers and to recognize that areas that once were the mission field can, over time, become the very heart of Christian vitality, while those areas that were once at the heart can lose the faith they once espoused. Jerusalem, Antioch, North Africa, and Constantinople were all at one time at the center of Christian vibrancy. Yet all of these places have only a tiny remnant of Christianity remaining and, with the exception of Jerusalem, are almost completely Islamic.[11] In contrast, places like Lagos, Nigeria, and Seoul, South Korea, where the presence of Christianity at one time seemed almost unimaginable, are today vibrant centers of the Christian faith.

If you happen to live in the middle of one of these great cultural expansions, it is easy to be left with the impression that your experience and expression of Christianity is somehow normative for all Christians everywhere. It is also clear from the writings of Christians who happened to live in places that, in their day, were at the center of global Christianity, that they fully expected Christianity would always be dominant where they lived. The mission field would always be in *other* places and with *other* people.

Indeed, during the height of such a major cultural and geographic expansion it is difficult to imagine the day when Christianity might wither away in such a place.

---

10. The *Padroado* was the papal decree that divided the world between Spain and Portugal, initially giving Spain exclusive rights to the New World in the West and Portugal the rights to the East. Later the line was moved to give Portugal access to the New World (modern-day Brazil).

11. For an excellent study of the decline of Christianity in the East see, Bat Ye'or, *The Decline of Eastern Christianity under Islam: From Jihad to Dhimmitude* (London: Associated University Press, 1996).

One hundred years ago it would have seemed incredulous if someone told you that before the end of the twentieth century the historic William Carey Memorial Church in Lester, England, would be a Hindu temple. One hundred years ago it would have seemed highly unlikely that by the dawn of the twenty-first century there would be more evangelicals in Nepal than in Spain.[12] One hundred years ago few would have believed that on a typical Sunday in the year 2000 only around one million Anglicans would attend church in Great Britain compared to over seventeen million Anglicans in Sunday worship in Nigeria.[13]

Many people believed that the presence of these new Christians was only an unfortunate by-product of Western, imperialistic colonialism and that in the wake of colonialism it would wither and die.[14] Others agreed, insisting that the forces of globalization would secularize the world, and religion would become marginal to twenty-first-century life. In fact, precisely the opposite is unfolding. During the post-colonial period the church outside the Western world is experiencing the most dramatic growth in history. The modern world has not turned into a secular city and modernization has not led to the predicted collapse of religious faith. Indeed, the eminent sociologist Peter Berger has noted that "secularization theory is essentially mistaken" because "the assumption that we live in a secularized world is false." Berger goes on to say that the key assumption of secularization theory, which insisted that "modernization necessarily leads to a decline of religion, both in society and in the minds of individuals ... turned out to be wrong."[15]

It is a special opportunity to live during a period in history when you are able to witness firsthand one of these great cultural and geographic transmissions of the gospel. Since I hold a faculty position in two seminaries, one in the USA and one in India, I have had the privilege over the last twenty years to teach every year in India as well as in the USA. My constant movement back and forth between North America and Asia has been very instructive for me. Despite the tiny percentage of Christians in North India, I always leave that country with a sense of excitement and encouragement, because I see many signs that they are experiencing the sunrise of a major move of God in their land.

It is true that a number of my Indian students have been beaten and even imprisoned for their faith in Jesus Christ, but I cannot shake the impression that India is moving toward a more profoundly Christian future. In contrast, despite the large

---

12. According to David Barrett, there were 120,000 evangelicals in Spain in 2000, whereas Nepal had 185,000. By the year 2025 Spain is projected to have 131,000 evangelicals compared with Nepal's 405,000; this figure does not count the 1.3 million Pentecostals in Nepal. David B. Barrett, George T. Kurian, and Todd M. Johnson, *World Christian Encyclopedia*, 2nd ed. (New York: Oxford Univ. Press, 2001), 527, 687.

13. Bill Bowder, "Worship Numbers Fall Again," *Church Times*, found at http://churchtimes.co.uk/templates/NewsTemplate_1 ; Ruth Gledhill, "Archbishop Thanks Africa for Lessons on Faith," *The Times* (London) (July 26, 2003), 20; Charlotte Allen, "Episcopal Church Plays Russian Roulette on the Gay Issue," *Los Angeles Times* (August 10, 2003), M–1; Dianne Knippers, "The Anglican Mainstream: It's Not Where Americans Might Think," *Weekly Standard* (August 25, 2003).

14. Dana Robert, "Shifting Southward: Global Christianity since 1945," *International Bulletin of Missionary Research* 24, no. 2 (April 2000): 53.

15. Peter L. Berger, "The Desecularization of the World: A Global Overview," in Peter L. Berger, ed., *The Desecularization of the World: Resurgent Religion and World Politics* (Grand Rapids: Eerdmans, 1999; and Washington, DC: Ethics and Public Policy Center, 1999), 2–3.

percentage of Christians in North America, I always leave the USA with the troubling impression that apart from a new Great Awakening, Christianity in North America is in the throes of a precipitous decline. I see many signs of the erosion of authentic Christian life and vitality in the West. In Western Europe, where I also lived for three years, the situation is even more beleaguered.[16]

All of this inevitably has the effect of stimulating theological reflection about what it means to be a Christian in the West and how we are to live out our faith within the context of the new realities of global Christianity. Augustine witnessed the barbarian invasions, realized their significance, and produced his classic *City of God*. William Carey lived at one of these seams of history and produced his influential *Enquiry*, which inspired hundreds of missionaries to relocate to the ends of the earth. They put up with being called "foreign devils" and being derided as representing a "white man's religion" because they had the insight to recognize that the gospel is intrinsically for all peoples and does not belong to any particular language or culture.

THE SEISMIC SHIFT IN THE CENTER OF CHRISTIAN GRAVITY

We live at another one of these important transitions in the history of Christianity as we experience the rise of the Majority World church and the signs of the possible, although once unthinkable, demise of Western Christianity. Evidence of this development is seen, for example, when we observe where the majority of Christians are now located around the world. This is often referred to as a shift in the "center of gravity" of the world Christian movement. The statistical center of gravity refers to that point on the globe with an equal number of Christians living north, south, east, and west of that point.

After its birth in Asia, Christianity had its most vigorous growth as it moved steadily westward and northward. As more and more people in the West embraced Christianity, the statistical center of gravity moved north and west. However, beginning in 1900, the statistical center began to shift dramatically southward, and in 1970 it began to move eastward for the first time in 1,370 years! (See Figure A). Today, the statistical center of Christianity is located in Timbuktu! This means that for the first time since the Reformation, the majority of Christians (approximately 67 percent) are now located outside the Western world.

Some specific examples of how the church is changing will, perhaps, help to illustrate this shift better. At the turn of the twentieth century the Christian church was predominately white and Western. In 1900, there were over 380 million Christians in Europe and less then 10 million on the entire continent of Africa.[17] Today there are over 367 million Christians in Africa, comprising one fifth of the entire Christian church. Throughout the twentieth century a net average gain of 16,500 people were coming to Christ every day in Africa. From 1970 to 1985, for example, the church in

16. See George Weigel, *The Cube and the Cathedral: Europe, America and Politics without God* (New York: Basic Books, 2005).

17. The World Christian Database notes that there were 380,641,890 Christians in Europe and 9,938,588 Christians in Africa. See worldchristiandatabase.org.

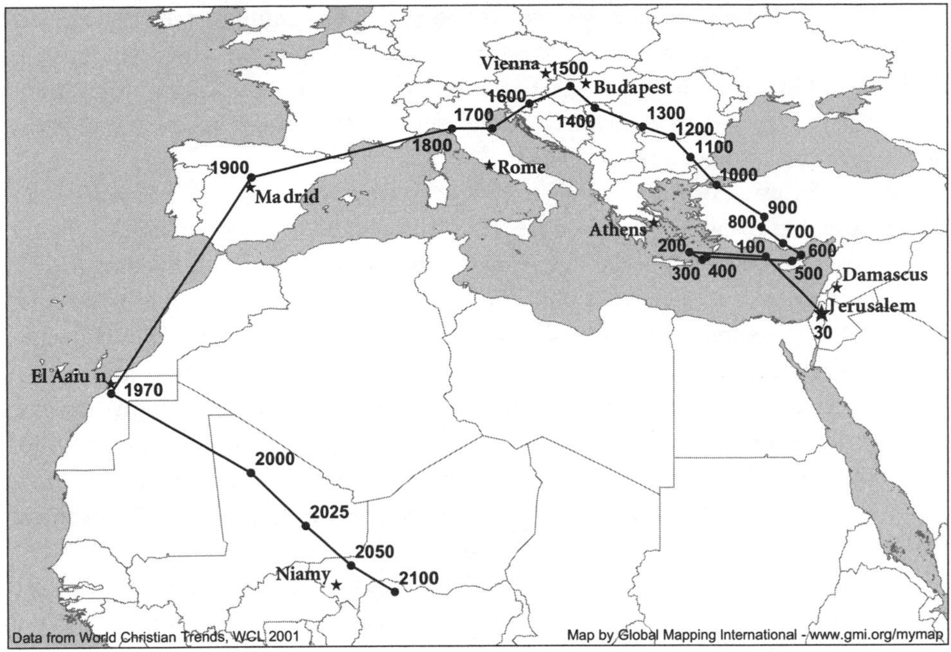

Figure A[18]

Africa grew by over six million people. During that same time, 4,300 people per day were leaving the church in Europe and North America.[19]

The church is not just moving southward, it is also moving eastward. In Korea, for example, despite the fact that Christianity was not formally introduced within that country until the eighteenth century, it is staggering to realize that today there are over 20 million Christians in South Korea alone. In fact, South Korea is widely regarded as the home of the modern church growth movement, which is exemplified by the remarkable story of the Yoido Full Gospel Church pastored by Dr. David Cho. Founded in 1958 with only five people in a small living room, the church now claims over 700,000 members, making it easily the largest church in the world.

India has been called the cradle of the world's religions, having given birth to Hinduism, Buddhism, Jainism, and Sikhism. Yet today, this land of exotic eastern religions is also the home of over 60 million Christians.[20] Church planting in India, particularly in the traditionally Hindu north, is taking place at a blistering pace so that many missiologists are predicting that by the year 2050 India will have over

18. Map found in David Barrett and Todd Johnson, *World Christian Trends* (Pasadena, CA: Willian Carey Library, 2003). Used by permission. www.missionbooks.org.

19. Lamin Sanneh, *Whose Religion Is Christianity? The Gospel beyond the West* (Grand Rapids: Eerdmans, 2003), 15. Elizabeth Isichei says that the number leaving the church in the West was 7,500 per day (see *A History of Christianity in Africa* [Grand Rapids: Eerdmans, 1995], 1).

20. Todd M. Johnson, Sarah Tieszen, and Thomas Higgens, "Counting Christians in India, AD 52–2200," unpublished research report from the Center for the Study of Global Christianity, the research center at Gordon-Conwell Theological Seminary, which produces the *World Christian Encyclopedia*. This represents 6.15 percent of the population of India, far above the official 3 percent figure given by the government. However, the official figures disenfranchise millions of Christians who are counted as "tribals" or who are remaining within Hindu communities.

126 million Christians.[21] However, even Korea and India cannot match the dramatic rise of the Chinese church. Even as recently as Mao Zedong's (Tse-tung) famous Cultural Revolution in China (1966–1976) there were only about one million Christians in China. Today, the Chinese church comprises over 90 million believers and is the fastest growing church on the planet.[22]

Samuel Huntington, in his respected analysis of global trends, *The Clash of Civilizations*, predicts that in the twenty-first century Islam will become the largest religion in the world. He bases this prediction primarily on the disparity in population growth between the West and the rest of the world, concluding that since Islam spreads primarily through reproduction, "in the long run, Muhammad wins out."[23] But Huntington dramatically underestimates the growth of Majority World Christianity. Growth is occurring in the regions that, unlike the Western world, are experiencing a dramatic rise in population. Philip Jenkins has pointed out that "today half of the inhabitants of this planet are under twenty-four, and of those, almost 90% live in the global South."[24] Thus, even if Western Christianity continues its precipitous decline, by 2050 there will still be nearly three Christians for every two Muslims in the world.[25]

Western scholars and liberal Christians have long predicted the demise of historic Christianity and the rise of the "secular city."[26] Their solution has been to call the church to abandon faith in the supernatural and the historic confessions of the Christian faith. They have argued that doctrines such as the deity of Christ, the Trinity, and the authority of the Bible are no longer credible or believable in the modern world. Therefore, Christianity should conform to the norms of Western secularism. However, it seems that rather than saving Christianity, secular, relativistic forces are quickly turning twenty-first-century mainline liberal Protestantism into a curious aberration, a mere footnote, in the larger story of the advance of global Christianity.

In contrast, the dramatic rise of Majority World Christianity is to a large extent morally and theologically conservative. These new Christians believe the Bible, are Christ-centered, and are supernaturalistic. Philip Jenkins' study of Majority World Christianity found, in contrast to their Western counterparts, that they have a "much greater respect for the authority of scripture" and "a special interest in supernatural elements of scripture, such as miracles, visions, and healings." They also believe in the

21. This is the current projection of the Center for the Study of Global Christianity. This will represent 8 percent of the projected 1.6 billion population of India.

22. Barrett, Kurian, and Johnson, *World Christian Encyclopedia*, 191.

23. Samuel Huntington, *The Clash of Civilizations and the Remaking of World Order* (New York: Simon & Schuster, 1998), 65.

24. Philip Jenkins, *The New Faces of Christianity: Believing the Bible in the Global South* (New York: Oxford Univ. Press, 2006), 27.

25. Barrett, Kurian, and Johnson, *World Christian Encyclopedia*, 4. Johnson and Barrett predict that in the year 2050 there will be 3.051 billion Christians and 2.229 billion Muslims.

26. John Spong carefully outlines his understanding of the slow demise of historic Christianity in a section of his book entitled "Exile of the Present" (*Why Christianity Must Change or Die* [San Francisco: HarperCollins, 1999], 29–42). Harvey Cox advocated the demise of traditional faith and the rise of the "secular city" (*The Secular City: Secularization and Urbanization in Theological Perspective* [New York: MacMillan, 1966]). Cox later courageously admitted he was wrong. Indeed, he said, "before the academic forecasters could even begin to draw their pensions, a religious renaissance of sorts is under way all over the globe." See Harvey Cox, *Fire from Heaven: The Rise of Pentecostal Spirituality and the Reshaping of Religion in the Twenty-First Century* (Reading, MA: Addison-Wesley, 1995), xvi.

"continuing power of prophecy."[27] As Peter Berger has said, "To put it simply, experiments with secularized religion have generally failed; religious movements with beliefs and practices dripping with reactionary supernaturalism have widely succeeded."[28] The French writer Gilles Kepel has aptly called this dramatic turnaround the "revenge of God" (*la revanche de Dieu*).[29] According to Harvey Cox, "if God really did die, as Nietzche's madman proclaimed, then why have so many billions of people not gotten the word?"[30] There is a global Christian revolution happening outside the Western world, and most Western Christians are only gradually beginning to realize the full implications of this shift.

MOVING FROM CULTURAL AND GEOGRAPHIC TRANSLATABILITY TO THEOLOGICAL TRANSLATABILITY

Understanding the "Universal" and the "Particular" in the Christian Gospel

The purpose of this book is to explore the implications these shifts are having in the formulation of theological discourse. One of the fascinating things about observing the current geographic and cultural shift in the center of Christian gravity is that despite the dramatic growth of the Majority World church, the center of theological education and Christian scholarship remains in the Western world. In fact, despite the growth of Majority World Christianity and the corresponding decline in the vitality of Western Christianity, there remains the view that Western theological writings and reflection somehow represent normative, universal Christian reflection whereas non-Western theology is more localized, ad hoc, and contextual.

The view is held that while the rise of non-Western theological reflection may have some limited usefulness in particular local contexts, it remains irrelevant to and is largely absent from Western theological discourse, which seems to carry a kind of universal validity. Having taught or spent time in several theological seminaries and Bible colleges around the world, I have observed the dominant role of Western curriculum and theological textbooks in these institutions. Even materials that are occasionally published in the national languages of vibrant, growing churches are often either written by Westerners or are merely translations of Western texts that are received, read, and studied as if they hold some kind of universal status.

I want to make it clear that my intention is not to be critical of the many wonderful and insightful contributions of Western theologians. Furthermore, I want to be equally firm in my deep appreciation for the whole field of systematic theology. A systematic theology is surely better than a random and haphazard one. I am not part of those who argue that all theological discussion in today's context must only be local,

27. See Jenkins, *The New Faces of Christianity*, 4. Jenkins makes several remarkable discoveries about some of the differences in how Majority World Christians read the Bible as compared to their Western counterparts. For example, African believers venerate the Old Testament as an ongoing, living source of authority in a way that far exceeds the way it is used in the West. Furthermore, the book of James appears to be the most quoted book of the New Testament (53, 54, 60–62).

28. Berger, *The Desecularization of the World*, 4.

29. As quoted in Cox, *Fire from Heaven*, xvii. See Gilles Kepel, *The Revenge of God* (Cambridge, MA: Polity Press, 1994).

30. Cox, *Fire from Heaven*, 103.

provisional, experimental, and hypothetical.[31] There are far too many questions that should be common to all theological discourse regardless of time or space for us to adopt a hermeneutic of suspicion about all theological enquiries.

But there is a fine line between confidence and arrogance. Indeed, most Western theologians now recognize that it would be arrogant to believe that one or more of the theologies our culture has produced have somehow managed to raise and systematically answer all questions, for all Christians, for all time. Every culture in every age has blind spots and biases that we are often oblivious to, but which are evident to those outside of our culture or time. Every culture has universal questions we all share in as members of Adam's fallen race. Every culture also has questions and challenges peculiar to their particular context. Furthermore, as will be explored in more detail in chapter 10, there is a need for a reintegration of the various disciplines of theology such that systematic theology, historical theology, and practical theology are in better dialogue with each other and all theology is done with a greater sensitivity to its universal and particular aspects.

Andrew Walls has called this tension between the universal and the particular the "pilgrim" principle and the "indigenizing" principle.[32] The pilgrim principle is the *universal* force of the gospel that transcends all the particulars of our own cultural background and gives us what Walls calls a common "adoptive past," whereby we are "linked to the people of God in all generations."[33] The pilgrim principle emphasizes our common identity in Jesus Christ, quite apart from our particular language, culture, or background. In contrast, the indigenizing principle is the *particular* force of the gospel that reminds us that the gospel really does penetrate and become rooted in the specific particularities of our cultural life. We live out our Christian lives within specific contexts, each of which has its own peculiar challenges and opportunities.

Indeed, one of the enduring lessons of the Jerusalem Council is that the apostles did not command the early Gentile believers to forsake their cultural background, but to remain in it as devoted followers of Jesus Christ. They, like us, were called to serve as agents of transformation *within* a particular cultural group rather than being extracted from that group. The indigenizing principle emphasizes our identity as members of a particular culture into which Christ is extending his Lordship and reign.

Problems arise when we unduly emphasize one of these principles over the other. An undue emphasis on the pilgrim principle assumes that all the issues we face in our culture are the same faced by every culture. In other words, our own theological reflection is universalized for the entire world. Because our issues must surely be the same as theirs and we are confident in our own theological and exegetical abilities, there is no point in humbly listening to the insights of Christians outside of our cultural sphere. By contrast, an undue emphasis on the indigenizing principle assumes that every issue the church faces is, in the final analysis, so contextualized

31. David J. Bosch, *Transforming Mission: Paradigm Shifts in Theology of Mission* (Maryknoll, NY: Orbis, 1996), 427.

32. Walls, *The Missionary Movement in Christian History*, 7–9.

33. Ibid., 9.

and conditioned by the particularities of the local setting and the time in which we live that we become skeptical of the ability of any theologian to speak with authority or confidence about the claims of the gospel on someone outside his or her own cultural arena. An overly weighted emphasis on the indigenizing principle fails to recognize our common identity as sinners in need of the grace and redemption offered freely in the Lord Jesus Christ for all peoples, regardless of language or culture.

I am arguing for a proper balance between these two principles. On the one hand, I want to clearly affirm the magnificent universal truths of the gospel that are true for all peoples, of all cultures, throughout all of time. On the other hand, I also affirm that there is much we can learn from the particular insights of the emerging global church. I also believe there is much that we can offer the newer churches outside the West because of our background and years of sustained theological reflection. Likewise, they can help to fill in the gaps in our own theological reflection, especially by exposing areas where our reflection has been biased and resistant to the actual teachings of Scripture.

Indeed, I believe that there is a growing realization that the Majority World church may play a crucial role, not only in revitalizing the life of Western Christianity, but in actually contributing positively and maturely to our own theological reflection.[34] The day of regarding the theological reflections of the Majority World church as something exotic or ancillary, or as the object of study only for a missionary or area specialist, is now over.

The positive role our Majority World brothers and sisters might play in our own theological formulation has become particularly evident in recent years as Western scholarship has focused increasingly on issues related to gender, sexual standards, and homosexuality. Philip Jenkins recounts the story of a meeting between several Anglican African leaders and their Episcopalian counterparts to discuss homosexuality and other related issues. After several hours of heated discussions between the conservative Africans and the liberal Episcopalians, the African bishop asked his Episcopalian colleague, "If you don't *believe* the Scripture, why did you bring it to us in the first place?"[35]

It is thrilling to see those who once were the object of our missionary endeavors now bringing the gospel back to us and reminding us of that which we have largely forgotten. There is an African proverb that comes from the Akan in southern Ghana: "The mother feeds the baby daughter before she has teeth, so that the daughter will feed the mother when she loses her teeth."[36] Perhaps there is a lesson here for us. The growing and developing church in the Majority World is producing a number of important theological insights that, if heeded, could help stimulate Christian renewal in the West.

34. It is beyond the scope of this book to explore how the immigrant populations of North America represent the fastest growing segments of Christian growth in the West. In Boston, for example, more people have quietly come to Christ in the many ethnic churches in Boston than during the entire Great Awakening in Boston. Doug Hall has called it the "quiet revival." This immigrant revival can be observed in many of the large urban areas of America and Europe. For example, the largest church in Britain is a Pentecostal church led by a Nigerian pastor.

35. Jenkins, *The New Faces of Christianity*, 1.

36. Diane B. Stinton, *Jesus of Africa: Voices of Contemporary African Christology* (Maryknoll, NY: Orbis, 2004), 252.

While it would be a mistake to underestimate the corrosive influence Western liberal theology has had in the Majority World church and in some of the well-established seminaries, many hopeful, promising trends abound. There are five broad trends in the lives and witness of the Christians in these newly emerging churches that I find encouraging.

Five Trends in the Theology of Majority World Christians

First, these believers accept the authority of Scripture and hold a theology that, by Western standards, is considered conservative, orthodox, and traditionalist.[37] The sheer numbers of Majority World Christians who affirm the authority of the Scripture stands as a powerful bulwark against the winds of skepticism that have swept across much of the Western academy and church.

Second, Majority World Christians are more likely to be morally and ethically conservative. The fresh voices of the global South on issues such as homosexuality and abortion provide some needed relief for Western conservatives who are exhausted from the seemingly never-ending conflict these issues have produced in many Western denominations today.[38]

Third, these new, younger churches are more likely to be sensitive to the Christian responsibility to address issues related to poverty and social justice.[39] Evangelicals in particular have sometimes drifted from a more holistic integration between spiritual and social issues that characterized much of evangelical theology and experience. After all, evangelicals played a major role in such important social movements as health care, putting an end to slavery, child labor, and promoting female suffrage. In more recent years evangelicals have been less engaged in issues such as poverty, environmentalism, ethnic reconciliation, AIDS, prison reform, and the ethics of war. Majority World Christians often live in worlds characterized by such widespread corruption, poverty, disease, and oppression that these issues cannot be conveniently ignored as they often are in our large, seeker-driven, and entertainment-oriented middle-class churches.

Fourth, these younger churches are experienced at articulating the uniqueness of the gospel in the midst of religious pluralism. Many of the younger churches are springing up within the larger context of the sometimes dominating presence of some non-Christian religion, such as Islam, Hinduism, or Buddhism. In my experience, because of their own backgrounds as well as their close proximity to other living faiths, Majority World Christians understand more profoundly the relationship of

37. Berger, *The Desecularization of the World*, 6. This also explains my disappointment in Ninian Smart and Steven Konstantine's *Christian Systematic Theology in a World Context* (Minneapolis: Fortress, 1991). Despite the title, the result is neither Christian nor systematic. Their notion of global theology is to embrace what they call a neotranscendentalism that discards all fidelity to the Bible (see pp. 47–48) and replaces it with an emphasis on human experience and the common phenomenology of world religions. Their book neither reflects the actual faith of Majority World Christians nor is faithful to historic Christian confessions.

38. I am particularly mindful of how these issues have dominated the discourse of the PC (USA), the United Methodist, the American Baptist, and the Episcopal churches in recent years. These issues have, at times, so dominated the agenda of the church's national meetings that many other important and global concerns have been neglected.

39. Jenkins, *The New Faces of Christianity*, 62–63.

FIVE TRENDS IN THE THEOLOGY OF MAJORITY WORLD CHRISTIANS

1. These believers accept the authority of Scripture and, by Western standards, hold a theology considered conservative, orthodox, and traditionalist.
2. Majority World Christians are more likely to be morally and ethically conservative.
3. These new, younger churches are more likely to be sensitive to the Christian responsibility to address issues related to poverty and social justice.
4. These younger churches are experienced at articulating the uniqueness of the gospel in the midst of religious pluralism.
5. Majority World Christians are more likely to grasp the corporate (not just individualistic) dimensions of the teachings of the New Testament.

Christianity to non-Christian religions. They often approach the continuities with less defensiveness while, at the same time, are surprisingly frank and candid about the glaring discontinuities that inevitably arise when other religions fail to recognize the true dignity of Jesus Christ.

Finally, Majority World Christians are more likely to grasp the corporate (not just individualistic) dimensions of the teachings of the New Testament. This is, perhaps, one of the most glaring blind spots in traditional Western theological reflection. The social arrangements of these Christians are far closer to the dynamics present in the first century than to the dynamics of modern Western societies. This factor has certainly influenced the direction of theological discourse in the West.

If these five trends continue to be present in the lifeblood of these new southern Christians, then I am convinced that these Christians will emerge as the new great hope for the sustenance and transmission of the Christian faith in the twenty-first century.

Theological Translatability: A Definition

The premise of this book is that the theological reflections of the Majority World church need to be heard as a part of the normal course of theological study in the West. Certainly *our* theological discourse is being widely and carefully studied by Christians outside the West. It is time that we enter into a more mutual exchange of ideas.

John Mbiti, considered one of the pioneers of African Christian theology, once lamented how Africans had dutifully traveled to the eminent European and North American theological institutions for higher studies without finding any corresponding interest in their own theological reflections. He said, "We have eaten theology with you; we have drunk theology with you; we have dreamed theology with you. But it has all been one-sided; it has all been, in a sense, your theology.... We know you theologically. The question is, 'Do you know us theologically? Would you like to know us theologically?' "[40]

The answer up to now is that we really haven't wanted to know much about the theological reflections of Majority World Christians. Mbiti went on to stress how "utterly scandalous" it is for students of Western theology to know more about the theology of heretics long dead than they do about the living theology of hundreds of millions of living Africans today.[41] Clearly, the borders of theological discourse can no longer afford to stay within the familiar perimeter of Western discourse.

This chapter has already demonstrated that the gospel is culturally and geographically translatable—that is, it has found new homes in a vast number of cultures and places. The Christian faith successfully penetrated Jews, Romans, Greeks, Armenians, Copts, Ethiopians, Berbers, Syrians, Persians, and Indians. Within a short period the feat was repeated with Vandals, Goths, Celts, Angles, Saxons, Scandinavians, Slavs, Turks, Russians, and Chinese. This pattern has been repeated over and over throughout church history. Today the worship of Jesus Christ is as likely to be heard from a Swahili-speaking Bantu as from a Spanish-speaking Bolivian. It is clear that the gospel has the potential of being infinitely translatable.

What we further need to recognize is that the Christian faith is not only *culturally* translatable, it is also *theologically* translatable. I am defining theological translatability as *the ability of the kerygmatic essentials of the Christian faith to be discovered and restated within an infinite number of new global contexts.* Today, theologies are being written in Creole as well as in Korean and in dozens of other languages. To be frank, some of these new theologies are too particularized and isolated from historic Christian confessions to be useful for nurturing the faith of the worldwide church. However, many of these theological reflections have the potential of shedding new light on the gospel and helping to correct blind spots and biases that have developed in our own theological reflections.[42]

What is unique about this particular time in Christian history is that today we are not observing a geographic or cultural shift to *one* new center, but a more complex, multifaceted emergence of what Mbiti calls multiple "centers of universality."[43] The problem is that even while many in the West are acknowledging the rapid globalization of the church, we remain theologically provincial. As Mbiti has pointed out, even though the center of gravity has shifted from the North to the South, there does "not seem to be a corresponding shift toward mutuality and reciprocity in the theological task facing the universal church."[44]

40. John Mbiti, "Theological Impotence and the Universality of the Church," in *Mission Trends No. 3: Third World Theologies*, ed. Gerald H. Anderson and Thomas F. Stransky (New York: Paulist; Grand Rapids: Eerdmans, 1976), 16–17.

41. Ibid., 17.

42. An excellent example of a theological work written from an African perspective can be found in Wilbur O'Donovan's excellent volume, *Biblical Christianity in African Perspective* (Carlisle, UK: Paternoster, 1992, 1996). For more on this, see chapter 10.

43. As quoted in Kwame Bediako, *Christianity in Africa: The Renewal of a Non-Western Religion* (Maryknoll, NY: Orbis, 1995), 157.

44. Ibid., 154.

Implications of Theological Translatability in the New Global Context

This book is a call for a whole new generation of Christian leaders to take up the challenge to approach the theological task from a more global perspective. What are some of the practical implications of this?

First, it is vital that we become more informed and conversant with the growing theology from the Majority World church. The global myopia is illustrated well by the 1991 publication of *Doing Theology in Today's World*.[45] Despite the auspicious title, the book is primarily an exploration of the diversity within Western theological traditions by Western writers.[46] More important, the voices of Majority World theologians from Africa, India, China, and Korea are not heard. One of the more helpful books published in recent years is William Dyrness's *Learning about Theology from the Third World*.[47] This book is an excellent introduction to theological contributions of Majority World Christians.

In short, we can no longer afford to ignore the *theological* implications inherent in the demographic reality that Christianity is currently experiencing a precipitous decline in the West and that the vast majority of Christians now live outside the West. The typical Christian is no longer an affluent, white, British, Anglican male about forty-five years old, but a poor, black, African, Pentecostal woman about twenty-five years old. This reality will inevitably shape and form the development of theology since new questions are being posed to the text within the larger context of poverty, powerlessness, pluralism, and the inevitable challenges that occur when vernacular languages begin to wrestle with theological issues.

Second, it is important to realize that, while we may live and work within certain well-defined theological systems such as the Reformed or dispensationalist traditions, none of these systems is universal, even though the kerygmatic truths they seek to organize and reflect are. This fact should not lead us to abandon the important task of writing systematic theologies that seek to reflect a consistent system that best reflects our understanding of the whole of the biblical data. Furthermore, this should not lead us to abandon our commitment to teach from a particular theological perspective. Nor should entering a broader, global theological discourse lead us into some nefarious world of theological relativism.

Nevertheless, certain adjustments must be made. We must recall that the Scriptures, the creeds, and the ecumenical councils did not seek to establish any particular overarching theological system. The majority of the teeming millions of new Christians coming into the church are part of independent and indigenous churches that have no clear historical connection to the Reformation. In fact, most of these new Christians cannot be easily categorized under any of the traditional and familiar headings of Roman Catholic, Eastern Orthodox, or Protestant. These Christians had no part in the European "protest," so it is difficult to call them Protestant. They are not

45. John D. Woodbridge and Thomas E. McComiskey, eds., *Doing Theology in Today's World* (Grand Rapids: Zondervan, 1991).

46. There is one chapter dedicated to Eastern Orthodoxy, but this does not reflect the locus of the growth of Majority World Christianity.

47. William A. Dyrness, *Learning about Theology from the Third World* (Grand Rapids: Zondervan, 1990).

related to the pope or the magisterium in Rome, so it is difficult to call them Roman Catholic. They are not submitted to the authority of any of the Eastern patriarchs, so it is difficult to call them Eastern Orthodox.

Many belong to independent Pentecostal movements. Others cannot even fit under this broad heading. This is why in the 1982 edition of the *World Christian Encyclopedia* several new categories were added, including "non-white indigenous" and "crypto-Christian." The 2001 edition of the same work changed the name of the "non-white indigenous" category to "independent" and added an additional category of "hidden" believers. The encyclopedia also reclassified millions of believers from the "Protestant" category to this new "independent" category.[48] We must find new ways—which may actually be a recovery of more ancient ways—of engaging in a more globally informed discourse with committed Christians from around the world. Hopefully, not only will this effort help enrich our own theological perspectives, but, more important, it will lead us to a deeper understanding of the *depositum fidei*, that ancient apostolic faith that forms our common confession.

Third, this open and honest exchange will help us to recognize some of our own, less obvious, heresies and blind spots. I have already criticized the misguided tendency within most of Western, mainline Protestantism to secularize Christianity and abandon the historic confessions of the Christian faith. I have expressed a sincere hope that the global church may help to gently, but firmly, guide mainline Protestantism back into the mainstream of historic orthodoxy.

However, the evangelical churches have their own set of problems. Evangelicals have been guilty of turning the gospel into a market commodity, all in the name of evangelism. Far too often the gospel is handled as something to be packaged, popularized, and marketed to various identifiable niches. The call to repentance, the certainty of final judgment, and the reality of hell are seldom mentioned lest it lead to a decline in our "market share." Evangelicals would rather be a respected "acolyte in the Temple of the Global Market God" than a prophetic voice in a culture that revels in using religious, even Christian, language to baptize the autonomous self.[49] So as we evangelicals in Western churches enter into a more sustained dialogue with many poor and persecuted Christians from around the world who are eagerly reading the Bible and living faithfully for Jesus Christ, it may help to expose our own deep heresies and revitalize our connection to historic Christian faith.

As we engage in this important, although somewhat painful, task we will come to realize that the Christian gospel is translatable not only on the linguistic, cultural, and geographic levels, but also on the theological level. At each of the crucial junctures in the ongoing story of the recession and advance of the church, the theological

48. The 1981 edition (p. 6) projected 154 million Christians in the "non-white indigenous" category. In the 2001 edition, this category was changed to "independent" and the figure was revised to 385 million "independent" believers. The *World Christian Encyclopedia* also found "hidden" believers within Hinduism in seven countries and within Islam in fifteen countries.

49. The phrase and metaphor originates with Harvey Cox in "Pentecostalism in Global Market Culture," in *The Globalization of Pentecostalism: A Religion Made to Travel*, ed. Murray W. Dempster, Byron D. Klaus, and Douglas Petersen (Irvine, CA: Regnum, 1999), 393.

translatability of the church was tested. Frequently, as in the Protestant Reformation, the newly emerging Christians were forced to restate the *kerygma* in ways that enabled them to clarify for their own time the crucial issues of the day necessary to keep the church faithful to Christ and the gospel "once for all delivered unto the saints." Today, as we are in the midst of another major period of recession and advance, it should not surprise us when, during the emergence of these Christian movements, new forms of theological discussions emerge.

The point of this book is to demonstrate that these new conversations demand our full and undivided attention. The theological discussion emerging in these new global contexts is not a "mere squabble" among a bunch of new Christians with strange faces from even stranger places, but rather the voices that are transforming the Christian church and changing the trajectory of human history.

Structure of the Book

This book is structured, without apology, along the traditional lines of systematic theology in the West. Since this structure has been largely followed around the world, it should not appear unfamiliar to Majority World readers. I am seeking intentionally to come alongside those students who are studying systematic theology and supplement their learning by inserting, along the way, examples from the global theological discourse that are relevant to each area of traditional theological enquiry. The purpose is to stimulate theological students to think more globally about the theological task and to hear firsthand about some of the issues and theological explorations that are emerging today.

This book will also help students preparing to serve cross-culturally to have a broader, more globally aware, theological training. Any seminary that wants to remain at the forefront of theological and ministerial training today must recognize that in today's context we must be better prepared not only to train people *from* around the world, but also to put far more emphasis on training people to serve within the many newly emerging, cross-cultural ministries, both here in the West and around the world.

In the past, such global exposure and intentional cross-cultural preparation was generally afforded only to those preparing for the mission field, and that often took place in separate degree programs. Today, all of our academic and vocational preparation must train with a deeper sensitivity to the larger global context in which Christian ministry takes place. Christianity has always been a faith for the world. Therefore, even students preparing to pastor white, clapboard churches in the plains of the Midwest or in rural hills of Georgia cannot escape the forces of globalization and religious pluralism they will meet there.

Finally, I also hope this book will be an encouragement to the thousands of Majority World students who enroll each year in the many hallowed institutions of theological learning in the West. It will be one way of letting them know that we are listening to them and that we value the contributions they will be making in our midst as they study here and, through their presence, enrich our life and faith.

This book will introduce the reader to many of the new, emerging voices in the Majority World church. Each of the eight studies in this book will highlight a particular region of the Majority World and focus on a particular issue where theological translatability is being tested. Chapter 2 is dedicated to the doctrine of God (theology proper) and examines how Muslim background followers of Jesus from the Arab world understand the continuity and discontinuity between their former faith in Allah as proclaimed by the Qurʾan and their new faith in the God of Christian proclamation. Is the Father of Jesus the same as the God of Muhammad?

Chapter 3 explores the doctrine of revelation (bibliology). The reader will enter into a theological discourse dominated by Indian Jesuits who are exploring how followers of Jesus with a background in Hinduism regard the sacred texts that formed part of their pre-Christian past. The reader will learn how the other major world religions understand the concepts of inspiration and revelation and how that has influenced Christian discourse about these issues in the Indian context. Can God use Hindu sacred texts like the Upanishads to prepare someone to receive the revelation of the Christian gospel?

Chapter 4 highlights anthropology, with a special focus on how human identity in shame-based cultures in the Far East can help us understand the full scope of human alienation from God that is marred by both guilt and shame.

Chapter 5 focuses on Christology. This chapter brings the reader into the middle of a theological conversation that has been going on in Africa for decades about how to best communicate the doctrine of Christ in an African setting. How do these new, distinctively African Christologies fit in with the historic Christological confession formulated at Chalcedon?

Chapter 6 on soteriology highlights Christians from China and Japan who have come to Christ out of a background in Pure Land Buddhism (a major expression of Mahayana Buddhism). It is important for Christian discourse because Pure Land Buddhism has a strong doctrine of salvation by grace through faith. How do Christians from this background understand and interact with that well-known doctrine that lies at the heart of the Reformation, the doctrine of *sola fide*, salvation by faith alone?

Chapter 7 examines pneumatology, the doctrine of the Holy Spirit. During the last fifty years, Latin America has experienced a dramatic rise in Pentecostal expressions of Christianity. This development, in turn, has led to a renewed interest in the doctrine of the Holy Spirit and an insistence that the person of the Holy Spirit has received insufficient attention in Western systematic theologies. Has Western theology neglected the role of the Holy Spirit? And if so, how can our Latin American brothers and sisters in Christ help us strengthen our understanding of pneumatology?

Because of the heightened interest in Islam today, chapter 8 returns the reader to the Islamic world with a focus on ecclesiology. Because of fear of reprisals or negative associations with the Christian church as being overly tainted by Western culture, many Muslims who profess faith in Jesus Christ are seeking to follow him, but choose to not call themselves Christians or join the church.[50] Can Muslim background

50. The danger involved in becoming a Christian from an Islamic background was underscored recently by the international reporting of the Afghan Abdul Rahman, who converted to Christianity from Islam. This is a violation of Islamic law. Rahman

believers follow Jesus Christ while remaining in the Islamic mosque and retaining their identity as Muslims?

The last study, chapter 9, investigates how the doctrine of eschatology plays a vital role in the emergence of the Chinese missionary movement, especially the recently popularized Back to Jerusalem Movement. In what ways are Chinese Christians contributing to a deeper understanding of eschatology in the West?

Finally, a concluding chapter explores the emerging contours of this new global discourse and the larger implications this has for classical theological discussions in the Western world.

As is evident in this brief preview, the book takes the reader on a virtual journey to various continents outside the West, where we will examine one or two examples to illustrate how theological translatability is being tested by the newly emerging church. I have chosen examples that represent, in my estimation, success stories, which should positively inform and challenge our own theological discussions, as well as instances where I remain unconvinced that this particular initiative fully resonates with historic Christian faith. The reader will, of course, ultimately decide for himself or herself.

In several of the chapters I have made an intentional effort to listen to Christians who have come to Jesus Christ out of a background in Islam, Hinduism, or Buddhism. Since most non-Christians in the world today are already members of one of these three religions, it seems imperative that we engage in a more sustained understanding of these particular contexts.[51] We must also examine how the newly emerging, mostly Pentecostal, and independent church in Latin America is negotiating its emergence against the backdrop of a whole history of church-state affiliations that are characteristic of Christendom. It is as if the sixteenth-century Reformation has finally arrived in Latin America, and the dialogue and debates among Christians there are following themes well known to those familiar with European church history. In all likelihood (as with the European Reformation) the newly emerging churches as well as the Roman Catholic Church may both be strengthened by the encounter.

CONCLUSION

Some of the issues explored in these chapters are ones that have generated extensive, and sometimes heated, debate among missionaries and missiologists, but they have received little attention from trained theologians. Conversely, some of the theological issues raised in this chapter have been written about by theologians but have not captured the attention of missiologists or field missionaries.

In fact, many missionaries do not have formal theological education. They have gained many of their insights from the invaluable laboratory of actual field experience

would have faced the death penalty if not for the strong international reaction. The prosecutor in the case said that because Rahman had converted to Christianity he was "a microbe who should be killed" (see *New York Times* [March 23, 2006]: A16). Cleric Abdul Raoulf joined the chorus of clerics who said Rahman should die. Raoulf said that by converting to Christianity, Rahman had "committed the greatest sin" and is an "apostate." Therefore, he concluded, "this man must die."

51. See my *Christianity at the Religious Roundtable: Evangelicalism in Conversation with Hinduism, Buddhism and Islam* (Grand Rapids: Baker, 2002).

working with new churches in the Majority World. This is why missions literature, as a rule, often has a far more sustained interest in anthropological issues than in theological issues. In contrast, many Western theologians have virtually no actual, face-to-face experience with the Majority World church. Sometimes theological writings seem to be completely ignorant of major on-the-ground realities in the world. Entire courses on ecclesiology can be taken in Western seminaries with no mention of Kanzo Uchimura's famous "non-church church" movement in Japan or the emergence of churchless Christianity in India. Frequently, theologians can all too easily discount the insights of the social sciences.

In short, with a few notable exceptions, the theologians and the missiologists often have a rather uneasy relationship. Each group knows that it needs the other, but neither has the background or the technical language of the other that enables a fully mutual exchange. One of the most important and strategic needs today is a positive and mutually beneficial relationship between missiology and theology. This book is an attempt to bring these two worlds together for a positive exchange.

As a missiologist, I am keenly aware of my indebtedness to the sustained reflection of theologians who have so patiently helped me to understand the universals of the Christian proclamation. Yet, as I write about various theological points, I am equally aware of my indebtedness to the sacrifice of so many missionaries who have given their lives to nurture the gospel in specific contexts. One keeps me focused on the universal message of the church, the other on the down-to-earth realities of a gospel that always must be rooted in real, particularized contexts. In the end, I hope all of us recognize the truth that culture really is, after all, the best workplace for theology.

BIBLIOGRAPHY

Allen, Charlotte. "Episcopal Church Plays Russian Roulette on the Gay Issue." *Los Angeles Times* 10 (August 10, 2003): M–1.

Associated Press releases (March 23, and March 24, 2006).

Bainton, Roland. *Here I Stand: A Life of Martin Luther.* New York: Abingdon, 1950.

Barrett, David B., and Todd M. Johnson. *World Christian Trends, AD 30–AD 2200: Interpreting the Annual Christian Megacensus.* Pasadena, CA: William Carey Library, 2001.

Barrett, David B., George T. Kurian, and Todd M. Johnson. *World Christian Encyclopedia.* 2nd ed. New York: Oxford University Press, 2001.

Bediako, Kwame. *Christianity in Africa: The Renewal of a Non-Western Religion.* Maryknoll, NY: Orbis, 1995.

Berger, Peter L. "The Desecularization of the World: A Global Overview." In *The Desecularization of the World: Resurgent Religion and World Politics.* Edited by Peter L. Berger. Grand Rapids: Eerdmans, 1999; Washington, DC: Ethics and Public Policy Center, 1999.

Bonk, Jonathan J. "Ecclesiastical Cartography and the Invisible Continent." *International Bulletin of Missionary Research* 28, no. 4 (October 2004): 153–58.

Bosch, David J. *Transforming Mission: Paradigm Shifts in Theology of Mission*. Maryknoll, NY: Orbis, 1996.

Bowder, Bill. "Worship Numbers Fall Again." *Church Times*. Available at http://churchtimes.co.uk/templates/NewsTemplate_1 (June 15, 2006).

Claydon, David, ed. *A New Vision, a New Heart, a New Call: Lausanne Occasional Papers from the 2004 Forum for World Evangelization*. 2 vols. Pasadena, CA: William Carey Library, 2005.

Cox, Harvey. *Fire from Heaven: The Rise of Pentecostal Spirituality and the Reshaping of Religion in the Twenty-First Century*. Reading, MA: Addison-Wesley, 1995.

_____. "Pentecostalism in Global Market Culture." In *The Globalization of Pentecostalism: A Religion Made to Travel*. Edited by Murray W. Dempster, Byron D. Klaus, and Douglas Petersen. Irvine, CA: Regnum, 1999.

_____. *The Secular City: Secularization and Urbanization in Theological Perspective*. New York: MacMillan, 1966.

Danby, Herbert, trans. *Mishnah*. Oxford: Oxford University Press, 1933.

Dyrness, William A. *Learning about Theology from the Third World*. Grand Rapids: Zondervan, 1990.

Gledhill, Ruth. "Archbishop Thanks Africa for Lessons on Faith." *The Times* (London) (July 26, 2003), 20.

Huntington, Samuel. *The Clash of Civilizations and the Remaking of World Order*. New York: Simon & Schuster, 1998.

Isichei, Elizabeth. *A History of Christianity in Africa*. Grand Rapids: Eerdmans, 1995.

Jenkins, Philip. *The New Faces of Christianity: Believing the Bible in the Global South*. New York: Oxford University Press, 2006.

Johnson, Todd, and Sun Young Chung. "Tracking Global Christianity's Statistical Centre of Gravity, AD 33–AD 2100." *International Review of Mission* 95 (2004): 167–81.

Johnson, Todd M., Sarah Tieszen, and Thomas Higgens. "Counting Christians in India, AD 52–2200," unpublished research report. Center for the Study of Global Christianity.

Kepel, Gilles. *The Revenge of God*. Cambridge, MA: Polity Press, 1994.

Knippers, Dianne. "The Anglican Mainstream: It's Not Where Americans Might Think." *Weekly Standard* (August 25, 2003).

Latourette, Kenneth Scott. *A History of Christianity*. Vols. 1–2. Peabody, MA: Prince, 2000.

Mbiti, John. "Theological Impotence and the Universality of the Church." Pages 6–18 in *Mission Trends No. 3: Third World Theologies*. Edited by Gerald H. Anderson and Thomas F. Stransky. New York: Paulist; Grand Rapids: Eerdmans, 1976.

Neill, Stephen. *A History of Christian Missions*. London: Penguin, 1990.

New York Times (March 23, 2006), A16.

O'Donovan, Wilbur. *Biblical Christianity in African Perspective*. Carlisle, UK: Paternoster, 1992, 1996.

Robert, Dana. "Shifting Southward: Global Christianity since 1945." *International Bulletin of Missionary Research* 24, no. 2 (2000): 50–58.

Sanneh, Lamin. *Whose Religion Is Christianity? The Gospel beyond the West*. Grand Rapids: Eerdmans, 2003.

Smart, Ninian, and Steven Konstantine. *Christian Systematic Theology in a World Context*. Minneapolis: Fortress, 1991.

Spong, John. *Why Christianity Must Change or Die*. San Francisco: HarperCollins, 1999.

Stinton, Diane B. *Jesus of Africa: Voices of Contemporary African Christology*. Maryknoll, NY: Orbis, 2004.

Tennent, Timothy C. *Christianity at the Religious Roundtable: Evangelicalism in Conversation with Hinduism, Buddhism and Islam*. Grand Rapids: Baker, 2002.

Walls, Andrew. *The Missionary Movement in Christian History: Studies in the Transmission of Faith*. Maryknoll, NY: Orbis, 1996.

Weigel, George. *The Cube and the Cathedral: Europe, America and Politics without God*. New York: Basic Books, 2005.

Woodbridge, John D., and Thomas E. McComiskey, eds. *Doing Theology in Today's World*. Grand Rapids: Zondervan, 1991.

World Christian Database. worldchristiandatabase.org (June 19, 2006).

Ye'or, Bat. *The Decline of Eastern Christianity under Islam: From Jihad to Dhimmitude*. London: Associated University Press, 1996.

Chapter 2

THEOLOGY

IS THE FATHER OF JESUS THE GOD OF MUHAMMAD?

Hindus are fond of a well-known tale about a man who spent his entire life as a kind of theistic census taker. He went from village to village, house to house, occupation to occupation, caste to caste, inquiring at every location about which deities were worshiped at that place by those people. After traveling throughout India and recording the names of all the deities who were worshiped, he chronicled the list in a great book. The number is traditionally held to have been 330 million. When the weary traveler finally returned to his home village, exhausted and in his ninety-third year, he was asked to count how many gods were in his book. According to the tale, he spent seven years counting the gods, and at the end of the book he wrote the grand total—one. He declared in his dying breath that there is "one God worshipped in India."[1]

The story symbolizes one of the big differences between theological reflection about God in the pluralistic East and traditional writings about God in the "Christian" West. In India, theological affirmations about God resemble more of a semipermeable membrane than a high wall of clear delineation. Particular gods such as Viśnu or Shiva may be known for particular deeds or certain attributes or character traits; yet, in the end, every god is related to all other gods. In fact, all the gods may be simply different names for the One Divine Reality.

In contrast, theological reflection about God in the West has traditionally been a part of a systematic study of scriptural revelation within the context of an unassailable Christian "plausibility structure"[2] that has never really contemplated how the God revealed in the Bible relates to anyone else's claims about God. Without a doubt there has always been a group of dedicated scholars interested in interreligious dialogue, but, frankly speaking, it never gained much traction among mainstream Christians—especially evangelicals.

1. L. J. Baillas, *World Religions: A Story Approach* (Mystic, CT: Twenty-Third Publications, 1991), 158.

2. Sociologists use the expression "plausibility structure" to describe the "canopy of meaning" and purpose that undergirds a society. See Peter Berger, *The Sacred Canopy* (Garden City, NY: Doubleday, 1967).

Then came September 11, 2001. Suddenly, everything seemed to change. I remember driving to Connecticut in early October of 2001, less than a month after the attack on the World Trade Towers, to engage in a public dialogue with several Muslim leaders about the biblical view of God versus the Qurʾanic view of Allah. I had engaged in many dialogues like this over the years and was accustomed to tiny gatherings of a few missionaries or enquiring laypeople. On this occasion, however, I was stunned to see the entire parking lot filled. When I walked into the church not only was every seat in the auditorium filled, but the local media was there with their cameras, and even the city's mayor was in attendance. Suddenly, it seemed, Christians all across America were keenly interested in learning more about Allah and the Islamic faith. That evening, as it turned out, was just the beginning of a whole new phase of my life.

Over the next several years I was invited to participate in public dialogues across the country, from Boston to Indianapolis to Spokane. We can now look back and say with some certainty that September 11, 2001 changed many things in America—but one of the most fascinating changes is a new, widespread interest in learning more about Islam. Many of our carefully formulated doctrinal discussions about God, which had been faithfully discussed and learned in our seminaries, had to be put out on the table of public discourse in a fresh way, because "Allah" had showed up at the table—and we were not quite sure what to do about it.

Probably one of the most commonly asked questions in this new climate was this: *Do you believe that Christians and Muslims worship the same God?* I had been asked this question for years by mission-minded students in my classes, but, once again, I realized a new day had dawned when even President Bush was asked this question during a press conference in November 2003. In an ABC exclusive interview, Charles Gibson asked the president if he believed that both Christians and Muslims worship the same God. Bush replied, "I think we do," adding that we just have "different routes to get to the Almighty."[3] Bush's favorable and generous (some said, "politically correct") reply created a firestorm of reactions from both sides of the question, leading *Christian Century* to dedicate a five-part series to the question and to publish replies from Christian, Jewish, and Muslim scholars.[4]

This question, which serves as the focal point of the present chapter, was captured well by a small monograph published in 2002 by Timothy George entitled, *Is the Father of Jesus the God of Muhammad?*[5] Traditional systematic theologians have written tens of thousands of pages about the God revealed in Scripture, yet such a question is rarely, if ever, addressed in such volumes. But today's theological reflection is more contextual and mission oriented. We are returning to a "pre-Christendom" world

3. http://abcnews.go.com/Politics/story?id=1937468&page=1 (accessed May 1, 2007).

4. This series of five articles appeared over five months beginning in the April 20, 2004 issue and concluding with the August 24, 2004 issue. The articles are by Jon Levenson (Jewish), Lamin Sanneh (Roman Catholic), Dudley Woodberry (Evangelical), Wesley Ariarajah (Mainline Protestant), and Umar F. Abd-Allah (Muslim). I specifically say that it was in response to the outcry after George Bush's press conference statement because the editors of *Christian Century* retell the account of the news conference in a prominent editorial box at the center of the first page of all five issues.

5. Timothy George, *Is the Father of Jesus the God of Muhammad?* (Grand Rapids: Zondervan, 2002).

where no Christian statement is accepted at face value. Like the patristic writers of long ago, today's theologians must be engaged apologists with a stronger mission focus and global orientation. Indeed, today's students preparing to be tomorrow's pastors and church leaders can no longer afford to study the doctrine of God in a vacuum, apart from these new global realities.

I intend in this chapter to explore this question, which, unfortunately, has all too often drawn more heat than light. As will become evident, how we respond to the question is largely determined by understanding precisely what is meant in the first place.

DEFINING THE QUESTION

Do Christians and Muslims worship the same God? Are the terms "*Allah*" and "*God*" interchangeable? Is the Father of Jesus the God of Muhammad? Are these all just different ways of asking the same question? What strikes me about these questions is not their *similarity*, but the fundamental *differences* that lie behind each of the questions. For some, it is really a matter of linguistics. They simply want to know if the English word "God" and the Arabic word "Allah" are interchangeable. Others are naturally drawn to a more philosophical bent and really want to know if, *ontologically* speaking, the subject of sentences that begin "God is ..." and "Allah is ..." have the same referent. Furthermore, how similar or contradictory are the predicates that Christians and Muslims use to complete these sentences?

Still others are more practical and are interested in neither philosophy nor linguistics, but are Christians living in personal relationship with Muslims and are grasping for how to talk about their faith with their new friends. For them, it is as practical as asking, "Is it OK if I tell my Muslim friend that Allah became incarnate in Jesus Christ?" There are several other subtexts and insights that lie behind the main text of these questions. Indeed, sometimes the way a question is posed reveals far more than we might suppose. The point is, it is important that we wrestle with a number of separate issues that must be considered before we can really understand both *what* is being asked and *how* best to answer.

This chapter will have three main parts. First, we will begin with an examination of the etymology of the word "Allah" and its use by pre-Islamic and later non-Islamic monotheistic peoples in Arabia. Second, we will explore the ontology of monotheism and how this relates to the many ways God is spoken of in the Qurʾan and in the Bible. This part of the chapter will necessitate a careful study of several key texts in these documents that give us predicates for the subjects God and Allah. Finally, we will survey several pastoral and practical considerations crucial to the question at hand.

ETYMOLOGY, PRE-ISLAMIC AND NON-ISLAMIC HISTORY, AND USAGE OF THE WORD "ALLAH"

The etymology, history, and usage of the word "Allah" is an important place to start for two reasons. First, we need to know if there are etymological links between the Hebrew words for God (*ʾel, ʾeloah, ʾelohim*) and the Arabic word *ʾallah*. Second, we need to know if the Arabic word has a history that predates the rise of Islam and if the rise of Islam influenced how the term was used by non-Islamic monotheists. Did the word "Allah" serve as a general concept of God, a specific title for God, or a specific, personal name designating God?

Etymology of Allah/God

There is overwhelming historical, textual, and archaeological evidence to substantiate that the word "Allah" as a designation of deity was in use before the time of Muhammad. There are differences of opinion, however, regarding the original meaning and precise usage of the word prior to the rise of Islam. One popular notion is that the word "Allah" originally was the name of a moon god worshiped in Arabia at the time of Muhammad. It is true that moon worship was widespread in the ancient Near East. A crescent moon was also a common symbol of the moon god, known in Arabia as *ʾilah*. Since the crescent moon is a key symbol for Islam, appearing regularly on signs, mosques, flags, and so forth, this is thought to give added weight to the connection between the moon god and Allah.

According to this view, the word for the moon god, *ʾilah*, gradually became used as a generic word for god—literally, "*a* god." Others argue that an originally generic term was specifically applied to the moon god. In either case, with the rise of Islam, Muhammad took this generic word for god (*ʾilah* or "a god") and put a definite article on the front to make it *ʾal ʾilah*, meaning "*the* god."[6] Then, by contraction and usage the two words were joined to produce the term *ʾalilah*, eventually becoming Allah.[7] This theory essentially understands Muhammad as taking a general, pagan word for deity and upgrading it to the sovereign, exalted creator as revealed in the Qurʾan.[8]

There are several problems with this theory. First, it does not explain the pre-Islamic use of the term by *Christians* and *Jews*, who would not have tolerated any association of their God with a moon god.

Second, there are several lexicographic difficulties with the notion that the two words *ʾal* and *ʾilah* could have become conflated to form the word "Allah." For example, it is difficult to imagine the partial loss of the syllable *il* through conflation when that is the most crucial syllable in the entire construction. Indeed, *ʾil* or *ʾel* is the ancient Semitic word for God, which, in turn, appears in the Hebrew Old Testament.[9]

Third, there are historical problems that make it difficult to reconcile its origin as a pre-Islamic moon god for Arabs. For example, the Kaʿbah, the central shrine of pilgrimage in Mecca that predates Muhammad, was known as the "house of Allah" (*Beit Allah*). Since the Kaʿbah is traditionally believed to contain 360 Arabian deities, it is highly unlikely that the entire shrine would be named after the moon god.

6. Arthur Jeffery, *The Foreign Vocabulary of the Qurʾan* (Baroda: Oriental Institute, 1938), 66.

7. Robert Morey, *Islamic Invasion* (Eugene, OR: Harvest House, 1992).

8. This would not be dissimiliar to what happened with the Hebrew *ʾel*, the Greek *theos*, and even the English word "God."

9. According to Imad Shehadeh, the doubling of the "l" in Allah is irrelevant to the discussion since this is a development in Arabic orthography that occurs after the time of Muhammad. Yet, many scholars, including Timothy George in *Is the Father of Jesus the God of Muhammad?* rely upon this double "l" to make their case for two words that have been conflated (p. 70). See Imad Shehadeh, "The Triune God and the Islamic God," *Bibliotheca Sacra* 161 (January–March 2004): 19.

Furthermore, there was an Arabian monotheistic tradition not formally identified as a part of Judaism or Christianity.[10] By the Qurʾan's own testimony, these monotheists, known as *hanifs,* used the word "Allah" for the One True God, clearly demonstrating that this term was not associated with a moon god.[11]

A more plausible explanation is that the word "Allah" did not emerge as the conflation of two separate words, but is actually derived from the Aramaic and Syriac word for God, *ʾelah* (Aramaic) and *ʾalah* (Syriac) or *ʾelahaʾ* and *ʾalahaʾ,* meaning "the god."[12] Aramaic was the lingua franca of the ancient Near East, so it is reasonable to assume that this word for God could gain currency. Furthermore, we should not underestimate the numbers of Christians and Jews migrating to Arabia, thereby providing a living witness to monotheism in Arabia.

Christian and Jewish Presence in Arabia and Use of the Word "Allah"

In response to persecution, Jewish people migrated into Arabia long before the birth of Christ.[13] In fact, major settled Jewish communities were present in places like Yathrib/Medina, where Muhammad first took refuge after the Hejira in 622.[14] The numerous references to Jewish scriptures, practices, and even dietary practices that appear in the Qurʾan are ample proof that Muhammad had ongoing and sustained contact with Jewish groups throughout his life.

Christian presence in Arabia may date back as early as a brief visit on the way to India by the famous Alexandrian scholar Pantaenus in AD 180.[15] By the third century there were bishoprics among the Arabs to serve the growing number of ascetics seeking solitude and Christians fleeing persecution, both finding refuge in the vast deserts of Arabia.[16] Indeed, one of the bitter ironies of Arabian Christian expansion is that it is largely fueled by persecuted refugees, initially from the Roman empire and, later, from Persia. Prior to 313, when Constantine legalized Christianity, the persecution of Roman emperors like Diocletian had led to thousands of Christians fleeing the empire.

The first mission specifically targeting southern Arabia dates back to the fourth century, when Constantius (son of Constantine the Great) sent the Arian deacon Theophilus "The Indian" to the southwest corner of Arabia, known today as Yemen.[17]

10. See Surah 3:67. The Arabic word *hanif* means "one who turned away from paganism." Sheikh Ibrahim Al-Qattan and Mahmud A. Ghul note that these hanifs may have been henothesists, worshiping one God but not necessarily denying that other gods exist. This preserves the unique role of Muhammad in lifting the henotheism of the hanifs to pure monotheism. See Sheikh Ibrahim Al-Qattan and Mahmud A. Ghul, "The Arabian Background of Monotheism in Islam," in *The Concept of Monotheism in Islam and Christianity,* ed. Hans Köchler (Wien, Austria: Wilhelm Braumüller, 1982), 26–29. J. Spencer Trimingham notes that three of the four hanifs specifically named in the Qurʾan eventually become Christians. See J. Spencer Trimingham, *Christianity among the Arabs in Pre-Islamic Times* (London: Longman Group, 1979), 263.

11. See, for example, Surah 3:67. For a full discussion of these problems, see Shehadeh, "The Triune God and the Islamic God," 16–22.

12. Kenneth J. Thomas, "Allah in Translations of the Bible," *Technical Papers for the Bible Translator* 52, no. 3 (July 2001): 301.

13. Heribert Busse, *Islam, Judaism, and Christianity: Theological and Historical Affiliations* (Princeton: Markus Wiener, 1988), 10.

14. The Hejira refers to Muhammad's famous "flight" or "exodus" from Mecca to Medina in 622, which marks the beginning of the Islamic calendar.

15. Ian Gillman and Hans-Joachim Klimkeit, *Christians in Asia before 1500* (Richmond, Surrey: Curzon, 1999), 77–78. Paul's sojourn in Arabia (Gal. 1:17) refers to an area not considered part of Arabia today.

16. Ibid., 78.

17. Samuel Hugh Moffett, *A History of Christianity in Asia* (Maryknoll, NY: Orbis, 1998), 1:274.

Then, beginning in 339, Shapur II of Persia began to persecute the Christians in the East who, like their counterparts in the Roman empire, fled to Arabia for refuge. But even after official opposition to Christianity waned, persecution from within Christianity soon developed against those who held nonorthodox views. The Arab churches in Syria, for example, were persecuted by Emperor Justin I (518–527). The monks were given the choice of conforming to Chalcedonian Christology or "being turned out into the desert."[18] Many of them chose the deserts of Arabia. These migrating Christians brought into Arabia a diverse smorgasbord of Christological views, including Monophysite, Nestorian, and Arian views.[19]

Whatever the actual origin of the word "Allah" or the theological diversity of Christians in Arabia, what is clear is that by the time of Muhammad, and certainly by the time of his mission, Allah was widely used by monotheistic Arabs (*hanifs*), Jews, and Christians as the word for God. Various inscriptions with the word "Allah" have been discovered in Arabia as far back as the fifth century BC, and its use has continued among Arabic-speaking peoples ever since.[20] Although the New Testament was not translated into Arabic until the ninth century, from the beginning Arabic translators consistently used the word "Allah" to translate *ʾelohim* in the Old Testament and *theos* in the New Testament.

In fact, the oldest biblical Arabic manuscript, known as Codex 151, which contains a large portion of the New Testament, begins all but three of the books with the inscription, "In the Name of Allah, the Merciful and Compassionate," following the practice of the Qurʾan. Interestingly, the other three books (Acts, Romans, and 2 Corinthians) begin with the inscription, "in the name of the Father, Son, and Holy Spirit."[21] Likewise, Jewish commentators writing in Arabic also used Allah for *ʾelohim* in their translations of the Hebrew Scriptures and in their commentaries.[22] However, they generally did not use the word "Allah" to translate the Hebrew tetragrammaton, YHWH, since it was the personal, covenantal name for God, not the more generic word for God as *ʾelohim*. Instead, Arabic translations often either transliterated it as *Yahwah* [sic] or followed Jewish custom and inserted the title *LORD* in its place.

In summary, we have made several points.

1. There are clear etymological links between the word "Allah" and the Jewish words for God (*ʾel*, *ʾeloah*, *ʾelohim*).
2. Historical and archaeological evidence reveals the widespread use of Allah as the one sovereign God by every Arabic-speaking monotheistic group in the region.

---

18. Trimingham, *Christianity among the Arabs*, 163–64.

19. Kenneth Scott Latourette notes twenty different Monophysite sects in Egypt alone. He notes that one of the greatest Monophysite missionaries, Jacob Baradaeus, moved to Alexandria and consecrated "two bishops, eighty-nine patriarchs, and a hundred thousand priests." Also, a Yemeni merchant named Hayyan became a convinced Nestorian Christian and was the first native Arabic speaker to evangelize lower Arabia and, later, Yemen. See Kenneth Scott Latourette, *A History of Christianity* (Peabody, MA: Prince, 2000), 1:282–83.

20. Thomas, "Allah in Translations of the Bible," 302.

21. Harvey Staal, ed., *Mt. Sinai Arabic Codex 151* (Lovanii in Aedibus E. Peeters: Corpus Scriptorum Christianorum Orientalium, 1983), Vols. 1–4.

22. Thomas, "Allah in Translations of the Bible," 302.

3. The use of the word "Allah" in Christian and Jewish Arabic translations of Scripture has a long history that continues to the present day. This practice actually includes not only Scripture, but also hymns and poetry and other expressions of worship produced by Arabic-speaking Christians over the last nineteen centuries.
4. The word "Allah" was used to translate the broad *concept* of God; it was not used to translate the personal, covenantal name revealed to Moses, YHWH. The Jews, in turn, applied *ʾelohim* to both their covenantal God, Yahweh, as well as to false gods, using *ʾelohim* in much the same way as we use the generic English word "god." In contrast, "Muslims never use Allah to refer to a false god, but is used only of the one true God."[23]

The Ontology of Monotheism and the Predicates of Revelation

If monotheism, by definition, affirms that (ontologically speaking) there is one, and only one, God over the entire universe, then, as Jon Levenson has observed, "no monotheist can ever accuse anyone—certainly not another monotheist—of worshiping *another* God, only (at most) of improperly identifying the one God that both seek to serve."[24] In other words, no true monotheist can hold, without contradiction, that more than one Supreme Being exists. This is what Kenneth Cragg means when he points out that Muslims and Christians "are obviously referring when they speak of him, under whatever terms, to the same Being."[25] The real difficulty lies not in identifying the ultimate referent of the word "God," but knowing how to respond to the dizzying array of predicates *about* God that sometimes seem contradictory.

It is here that the ephemeral world of philosophy must meet the real world of faith and confession. No Muslim or Christian I have ever met worships a *generic* God or the mere *concept* of God in some vague, philosophical mist. We worship God as he has been revealed in his particulars, whether in Jesus Christ through the Bible or through Muhammad's recitation of the Qurʾan. When Pascal made his famous observation that the God of Abraham was not the God of the philosophers, he was not suddenly becoming some kind of Zoroastrian dualist, affirming two ontological beings, one for the philosophers and another for the rest of us. Rather, he was pointing out that the predicates that the philosophers ascribe to God through reason and the predicates that the biblical narratives ascribe to God through revelation are so different that we cannot properly equate the two subjects.

Linguistically speaking, the fideist and the rationalist may both use the word "God" but the common predicates that both can affirm are far more limited than one

23. Joshua Massey, "Should Christians Use 'Allah' in Bible Translation?" *Evangelical Missions Quarterly* 40 (July 2004): 284. This is why even the *Shahadah* begins with the phrase *lā-ilāha-illā-allāh* ("There is no *god* but Allah").

24. Jon D. Levenson, "Do Christians and Muslims Worship the Same God?" part 1 of five-part series in *Christian Century* 121, no. 8 (April 20, 2004): 32. The Muslims make the same observation with the humorous saying, *dalîl al-tamânoᶜ*, which means, "Every God will prevent the other from being a real God."

25. Kenneth Cragg, *The Call of the Minaret*, 2nd ed. (Maryknoll, NY: Orbis, 1985), 30.

might think.[26] The result is that even a common word, because of usage and context, may have very different meanings to different groups who use it. This is why the etymological argument examined earlier cannot be used to fully settle the issue of the interchangeability of the words "God" and "Allah."

Is Allah the Same as Allah?

Thankfully, both Muslims and Christians alike reject any vague "God of the philosophers" known only through human reason and speculation. Both Islam and Christianity claim to be based on specific, divine revelation. Thus, we have specifically revealed predicates about Allah found in the Qurʾan and specifically revealed predicates about God found in the Bible. The point is, even though the word "God" in English has wide, generic application, when a *Christian* uses the word "God," it is normally used in reference to an assumed body of predicates about God as revealed in the Bible. In the same way, even though Allah may have been used in a broad, generic sense for God, when a *Muslim* speaks of Allah it can only be understood in reference to a received body of predicates about Allah revealed in the Qurʾan.

Lamin Sanneh opens his article on "Do Christians and Muslims Worship the Same God?" by posing the question, "Is the 'Allah' of Arabian Islam the same as the 'Allah' of pre-Islamic Arab Christianity?"[27] (I would add, or pre-Islamic Judaism or the pre-Islamic *hanifs*, etc.). This is, I think, a better way to grasp the central issue, rather than asking if God and Allah are the same. The way it is traditionally posed all too easily derails the whole issue into a discussion about etymology. Instead, it is more illuminating to ask the question, "Are 'Allah' (as used by pre-Islamic and non-Islamic monotheists) and 'Allah' (as used by Muslims) the same?"

Posing the question in this way effectively shifts the discussion beyond the obvious shared etymological heritage to the more important examination of the predicates (shared or otherwise) of which Allah is the subject. No one seriously questions the shared etymology of the word "Allah" as it appears in the Arabic Bible and the word "Allah" as it appears in the Qurʾan. The point, however, is that the word "Allah" *as used by Muslims* is now tied to a particular religious community that holds to the text of the Qurʾan as sacred and revelatory. The exact same word "Allah" as used by Arabic-speaking *Christians* is also tied to their own religious community and traditions that hold the Bible as sacred and revelatory.

Classes of Revelatory Predicates

Most everyone agrees that the predicates about Allah in the Qurʾan and the predicates about Allah in the Arabic Bible have important similarities as well as crucial

26. It should be noted that while figures like Tertullian are cited as being fideist, most Christians have rejected the complete separation of faith and reason. See, for example, the encyclical *Fides et ratio* issued by the late Pope John Paul II on September 15, 1998. This same tension is present in Islam. For example, the famous Iranian theologian al-Ghazzali wrote *Talafut al-falasafa*, *the Incoherence of the Philosophers*, which sought to downplay the role of reason despite his impressive use of philosophical argumentation. (See M. al-Ghazzali, *Tahafut al-falasifah: A Parallel English-Arabic Text* (Provo, UT: Brigham Young Univ. Press, 1997). Other figures, such as the twelfth-century Islamic philosopher/theologian Averroes, openly accepted the important role of reason.

27. Lamin Sanneh, "Do Christians and Muslims Worship the Same God?" part 2 of five-part series in *Christian Century* 121, no. 9 (May 4, 2004), 35.

differences.[28] If someone poses the question, "Is the Allah as revealed in the Qur'an identical to the Allah as revealed in an Arabic Bible?" the answer is obviously "no." There is an important difference between asking the question from a philosophical/ontological perspective, "Are Allah and God references to the same *being?*" (clearly, yes), and asking the same question with an eye to all of the revealed predicates of particularity to determine if the common word identification is helpful, misleading, or even wrong. Suddenly, what seemed so clear now has us befuddled and we grope for words of clarification and qualification. This is particularly evident when reading the series of five articles published by *Christian Century* on the question. It should not go unnoticed that all of the writers from either a Jewish or a Christian perspective refused to give a categorical "yes" or "no" to the question, "Is the God of Muhammad the Father of Jesus?" whereas the Muslim writer was able to give a categorical "yes."

The Jewish representative, Jon Levenson, writes, "In the last analysis, the Christian and Muslim conceptions of the one God have enough in common to make a productive comparison possible, but as in any responsible comparison, the contrasts must not be sugared over."[29] The Roman Catholic Lamin Sanneh says that the identification of Allah and God "is adequate insofar as there is only one God, but inadequate with respect to God's character, on which hang matters of commitment and identity, the denial of which would sever our ties to God."[30] The evangelical Dudley Woodberry's entire article hinges on distinguishing between what he calls "the Being to whom we refer" and "what we understand about the *character* and *actions* of that Being in the two faiths."[31] In other words, Woodberry is making the distinction, as I am in this chapter, that ontologically there is only One True God, but affirming this solidarity with Muslims and other monotheists in the world should not cause us to forget the significant differences in the predicates we apply to the subject, God or Allah. Mainline Protestant Wesley Ariarajah points out that in Asian tradition a question can be answered in one of four ways: "yes," "no," "I don't know," and silence. He insightfully points out that "the question, 'Do Christians and Muslims worship the same God?' raises the possibility of a fifth kind of answer: yes and no."[32]

Contrast the ambiguity of the Christian and Jewish replies to the clear and unequivocal reply made by the Muslim author, Umar Abd-Allah. He begins his article by declaring that he can say "unequivocally that Christians and Muslims worship the same God."[33] When faced with what he calls "the diversity of religious predicates," he dismisses it by saying, "Does anyone worship the same God?" He points to the

28. It is worth noting that the reverse is also true. The God of the anglicized English Qur'an has a different set of predicates than the God of an English Bible. The point is, whether you ask if God is the same as God or is Allah the same as Allah, the argument shifts from an etymological discussion to a look at *usage*, which is derived from the revealed predicates.

29. Levenson, "Do Christians and Muslims Worship the Same God?" 33.

30. Sanneh, "Do Christians and Muslims Worship the Same God?" 35.

31. Dudley Woodberry, "Do Christians and Muslims Worship the Same God?" part 3 of five-part series in *Christian Century* 121, no. 10 (May 18, 2004): 36.

32. S. Wesley Ariarajah, "Do Christians and Muslims Worship the Same God?" part 4 of five-part series in *Christian Century* 121, no. 11 (June 1, 2004): 29.

33. Umar F. Abd-Allah, "Do Christians and Muslims Worship the Same God?" part 5 of five-part series in *Christian Century* 121, no. 17 (August 24, 2004): 34.

internal theological battles between Hillel and Shammai in the Jewish tradition, or between the Alexandrian and Antiochian schools within early Christianity, or the ongoing debates between the rationalists and the Sufi in the Islamic tradition. For Umar Abd-Allah this only reveals that "religion is unpredicated" and that "definitions and propositions delimit numinous reality."[34] Instead he says, "From a Muslim perspective, the premise that Muslims, Jews and Christians believe in the same God—the God of Abraham—is so central to Islamic theology that unqualified rejection of it would, for many, be tantamount to a repudiation of faith."[35]

Umar Abd-Allah says this because, unlike the Bible, the Qurʾan itself declares not just an *ontological* continuity between the Allah of the Qurʾan and the God of Scripture, but a vital continuity between the *revelations* and *dispensations* beginning with Abraham, through Moses and Jesus, and finally to Muhammad (see Surah 2:136; 6:83–89; 29:46). This is why in Surah 29:46 Allah instructs Muhammad to say the following to both Jews and Christians: "We believe in what was revealed to us and what was revealed to you. Our God and your God is one."[36] Of course, the Islamic affirmation of the continuity of all the particulars of monotheistic revelation (Torah, Injil, and Qurʾan) must be tempered by the realization that wherever the Jewish or Christian revelation diverges from the Qurʾan, Muslims believe it is because of either willful or transmissional corruption in the non-Islamic texts.[37]

The Islamic doctrine of corruption (*tahrif*) originally claimed that the Jews and Christians distorted the *meaning* of the text without necessarily altering the text itself. However, as knowledge of the actual text of Scripture became known, adherents of this doctrine began to teach that Christians and Jews had actually altered the original text.[38] Christians and Jews, on solid historical and textual grounds, cannot accept the baseless charge that our sacred texts have experienced such drastic corruption. In fact, there is overwhelming evidence that the current text of both the Old and New Testaments is based on existing manuscripts that predate the rise of Islam by centuries.[39]

This is important because it underscores the fact that despite the many similarities Christianity and Judaism share with Islam, there are also honest differences that are based not just on animosity, jealousy, or resentment over the rise of Islam but also on what has been revealed about God in our respective sacred texts. Therefore, despite our ontological agreement that there is only one subject, known by Muslims and Arabic-speaking Christians alike as Allah, the predicates associated with the Christian and Muslim doctrine of God have remarkable convergences and divergences that must be taken seriously.

34. Ibid., 35.

35. Ibid., 36.

36. Throughout this book, unless otherwise noted, I am using the IFTA edition of the Qurʾan. See, Mushaf Al-Madinah and An-Nabawiyah, eds., *The Holy Qurʾan: English Translation of the Meanings and Commentary* (Mecca, Saudi Arabia: IFTA, n.d.). It should be noted that the Arabic word for "one" used in this passage is not *ahad*, which is linguistically similar to the Hebrew word for "one" in the Shema, but "*wahid*," which means "one and the same." This supports Umar Abd-Allah's understanding of the text.

37. See, for example, Surah 2:79 or 3:75–78.

38. Norman Geisler and Abdul Saleeb, *Answering Islam: The Crescent in the Light of the Cross* (Grand Rapids: Baker, 1993), 209.

39. For a more detailed discussion, see Morris Seale, *The Qurʾan and the Bible: Studies in Interpretation and Dialogue* (London: Croom Helm, 1978); Bruce M. Metzger and Bart D. Ehrman, *The Text of the New Testament: Its Transmission, Corruption and Restoration*, 4th ed. (New York: Oxford Univ. Press, 2005).

How do we assess this without falling into either an overly optimistic assessment that "sugarcoats" the differences or being so overwhelmed with the irreconcilable discrepancies that we despair of any meaningful dialogue? The key is to embark on the work of a systematic theologian, but with an added feature crucial to the thesis of this entire book. The task begins by rereading the Bible and making a long list of every predicate attributed to God. Thankfully, this kind of work has been done countless times by systematic theologians and is the basis for building a proper biblical theology of God. When this task is finished, the result is a long list of over a thousand predicates, such as "God is creator," "God is just," "God became incarnate in Jesus Christ," and so forth.

Today's theologians must then take the next step and engage in a similar exercise with the Qurʾan. This is seldom done by Christian theologians who tend to operate in a theological vacuum. However, today's global context demands that theologians understand not just the biblical doctrine of God, but the biblical doctrine of God vis-à-vis the Islamic doctrine of God, the Hindu views of God, and so forth. This is not only because globalization and immigration have made our world smaller, but also because the Christian faith is now growing in areas where non-Christian religions remain predominant. Once this systematic task through the Qurʾan is complete, a second list of predicates emerges, which include such things as "Allah is the creator" (*al-khaliq*), "Allah is merciful" (*al-rahim*), "Allah is the avenger" (*al-muntaqim*), and so forth.

The European Islamic scholar J. W. Redhouse did this work and found at least 550 different predicates of God noted in the Qurʾan.[40] This long list is largely reflected in the ninety-nine beautiful names of Allah that Muslims regularly recite and which serve to reinforce the basic parameters of the Islamic doctrine of God. As A. K. Brohi has noted, "the concept of God in Islam is spellable by focusing attention on His beautiful names (*Asmaul Husna*)."[41]

A comparison of the two lists reveals several important things. First, Islamic theologians, like Christian theologians, have had to wrestle with the fact that some of God's attributes (*sifāt*) seem to relate to his nature or *essence* whereas others seem to relate to his *actions*. Because of the strong emphasis in the Qurʾan on the absolute pure unity and simplicity of the divine essence (*tawhīd*), many Islamic thinkers taught that an emphasis on the attributes of God would imply either divisions and distinctions within the divine essence or undue comparisons between God's attributes and human attributes. Mohamed Ridah sums this perspective up well when he writes, "If God is unique, it follows logically that He does not resemble His creatures, neither in essence, nor in attributes nor in actions, so that *laysa kamithlihi shay* (nothing is like Him) is a principle of Islamic faith."[42] This school of thought became known as the Muʿtazilah school.

40. See Kenneth Cragg, *The Dome and the Rock* (London: SPCK, 1964), 84. Redhouse's work also included the Hadith, which Muslims regard as sacred.

41. A. K. Brohi, "Some Random Reflections on the Concept of Monotheism in Islam and Christianity," in *The Concept of Monotheism in Islam and Christianity*, ed. Hans Köchler, 108. It should be noted that according to Kenneth Cragg, only about two-thirds of the 99 beautiful names actually appear in the Qurʾan, but all do reflect and undergird the doctrine of God as understood by Muslims.

42. Mohamed A. Abou Ridah, "Monotheism: Its Interpretations and Social Manifestations within Islam and Christianity," in *The Concept of Monotheism in Islam and Christianity*, ed. Hans Köchler, 47.

Another school of thought, known as the Ashᶜarites, affirmed seven essential attributes of God: life, will, omnipotence, omniscience, speech, vision, and hearing. The Ashᶜarites were even willing to distinguish between those predicates that relate to Allah's essence (*al-dhāt*) and those that relate to his actions (*afʾāl*)—or his absolute versus his relative attributes.[43] Allah's existence, immutability, and infinity, for example, are clearly related to his essence, whereas Allah as creator or forgiver relate to his actions. The Ashᶜarite system has generally prevailed as the dominant and orthodox view among Sunni Muslims.[44]

Second, our lists of biblical and Qurʾanic predicates would reveal that there are quite a few on the biblical list that do not readily seem compatible with the Qurʾanic list. Likewise, there are several on the Qurʾanic list that are difficult to reconcile with the biblical list. This is represented by the following diagram (see Figure B).

This diagram is not meant to be precise, but rather to make the general point that much of what the Qurʾan proclaims about Allah does not directly contradict biblical revelation about God.[45] A Christian can fully affirm, for example, the Qurʾanic affirmation that Allah is the creator (Surah 57:4), that Abraham is a great example of faith (Surah 16:123), that Jesus was born of the virgin Mary (Surah 3:45–47), or that Jesus was without sin (Surah 19:19). Dozens of additional examples can be cited.[46]

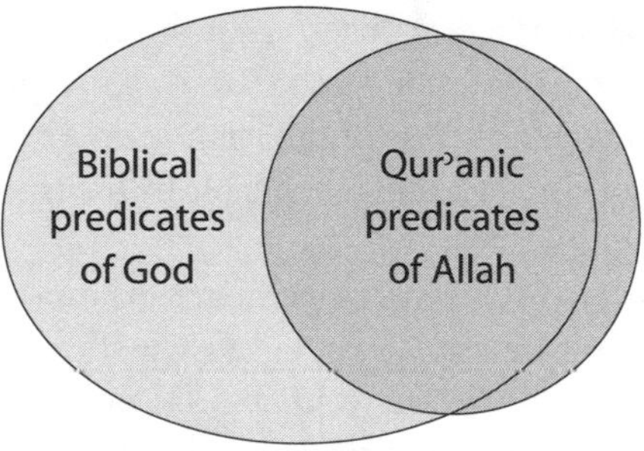

Figure B

43. Ibid., 46.

44. Caesar E. Farah, *Islam*, 6th ed. (Hauppauge, NY: Barron's Educational Series, 2000), 208. This debate is also relevant because the Muᶜtazilites believed that the Qurʾan was created, lest there be two eternal realities in the universe. However, since the Ashᶜarites affirmed speech as one of the seven essential attributes of God, they affirm an eternal Qurʾan that represents the eternal speech of Allah.

45. See my *Christianity at the Religious Roundtable: Evangelicalism in Conversation with Hinduism, Buddhism and Islam* (Grand Rapids: Baker, 2002) for a full discussion of how Christians have often read into the Qurʾan more hostility and incompatability about Christ than is actually there.

46. Other well-known parallels include Allah creating the earth in six days (Surah 25:59) and Adam and Eve eating a forbidden fruit and becoming aware of their nakedness (20:115–122). In the Qurʾan Allah sends Moses to confront Pharoah, inflict the plagues on Egypt, and lead the Israelites out of Egypt by parting the Red Sea (26:9–75). Allah gives Moses the Ten Commandments on two tables of stone, which are subsequently broken (Surah 7:143–150). Many of the Ten Commandments are repeated in the Qurʾan, including the command "to serve no other gods" (24:55), the prohibition against making idols (4:116), the commands to not covet (4:32) or murder (6:151), and the command to honor your father and mother (6:151). In the Qurʾan, one can read about familiar Old Testament stories such as Noah building the ark (11:25–49), King David's adultery with Bathsheba (28:21–25), the Queen of Sheba's visit to Solomon (27:22–44), and Jonah's being swallowed by the great fish (37:139–148). There is little doubt that the Qurʾan fully identifies Allah with the biblical God of the Old Testament.

However, as the Bible explores themes such as the Trinity (implied in the doctrines of the deity of Christ and the deity of the Holy Spirit), the incarnation of God in Jesus Christ, God in Christ suffering on the cross, and so forth, these predicates clearly lie *outside* the teaching of the Qurʾan. Likewise, some Christians have raised objections to several of the ninety-nine beautiful names of Allah because they are thought to be incompatible with biblical revelation. For example, the affirmation that Allah is the deceiver (*al-mudill*) who wills to lead some people astray is felt by some to fall outside of the biblical revelation of God.

It is important to note, therefore, that quite apart from traditional ways of dividing and discussing God's attributes, we must make a distinction between those predicates of Allah affirmed in both the Qurʾan and the Bible and those predicates that the Bible affirms but the Qurʾan does not. It has already been noted that from the Islamic perspective, it is precisely these predicates that lie outside of the Qurʾanic conception of God that are identified by Muslims as the texts that have been corrupted or changed from the pure *injil* (gospel) they technically accept.

It is becoming clear that how one poses the question will determine the response to the question. If someone asks, "What is the Arabic word for God?" then it is clearly a question of linguistics, and some explanation of the common etymological origin and historical uses of the Arabic *ʾallah* and the Hebrew *ʾel* will be reassuring to the questioner. If someone asks, "Do Allah and God refer to the *same* God?" they may be asking an ontological question, which, once again, should be answered in the affirmative by any true monotheist.

However, if someone asks, "Is the Father of Jesus the God of Muhammad?" then the question is much larger than mere linguistics and far too particularized to be a reference only to ontology. This question seems to be asking whether or not Muhammad and all of the Muslims who follow his prophetic message worship the same God as the one whom Christians are called upon to worship and to adore. The question is now being tied to two specific communities of faith with two separate and distinctive texts about God. It is at this point—and because of this point—that the Christian and Jewish writers noted earlier begin to equivocate. Yet, it is precisely this area which needs more scrutiny and reflection.

Is the Father of Jesus the God of Muhammad?

While affirming that the words *ʾallah* and *ʾel* share the same linguistic heritage and that ontologically Allah and God refer to the same being, I am not as convinced that an equally affirmative answer can be given to the question, "Is the Father of Jesus the God of Muhammad?" There are three main reasons for my hesitation. First, there is the distinctive nature of the predicates about which Islam and Christianity differ—a matter that also has dramatic implications even for those predicates about which we are in agreement. Second, there is a fundamental difference in the way the word "Allah" functions in its contemporary usage by Arabic-speaking Christians and Arabic-speaking Muslims. Third, I have an evangelistic and pastoral concern for anyone who is not in relationship with the "God and Father of our Lord Jesus Christ." Each of these three will now be explored.

1. Predicates of Christian Identity

The predicates about Jesus Christ found in the biblical revelation are central to our identity with God and with one another as followers of Jesus Christ. It is precisely those areas where the biblical and Qurʾanic texts differ that are so crucial to our identity as Christians. This is why, as noted earlier, Lamin Sanneh wrote that the identification of Allah and God "is adequate insofar as there is only one God, but inadequate with respect to God's character, on which hang matters of commitment and identity, the denial of which would sever our ties to God."[47] His point is clearly that our very identity as Christians and, indeed, our redemptive relationship with God hinges on our understanding that "God was reconciling the world to himself in Christ, not counting people's sins against them" (2 Cor. 5:19 TNIV).

It is not as if the texts of the Qurʾan and the Bible differ on minor points of eschatology or the precise nature of the soul. They differ on central doctrines of identity such as the Trinity, the deity of Christ, the doctrine of the incarnation, the redemptive power of the cross, and the resurrection of Jesus Christ from the dead. All of these doctrines are central to what we as Christians mean when we say, "We worship God." For the Christian, the doctrine of God cannot possibly be separated from Christology.

When we say, "We worship God," what we *mean* is that we worship the God who revealed himself and became incarnate in Jesus Christ. We worship the Triune God. We worship the God and Father of our Lord Jesus Christ. We worship Jesus Christ, the Word made flesh, who, as God incarnate, suffered on the cross for our sins. We worship Jesus Christ who said, "I and the Father are one" (John 10:30). We worship our Lord Jesus, about whom the apostle Paul declared, "For in Christ all the fullness of the Deity lives in bodily form" (Col. 2:9). All of these proclamations are central to our identity as Christians; without them the term *Christian* means nothing. Without them the term *God* itself is transformed in meaning beyond recognition.

There is a famous story told by Muslims that dates back to the year 614, seven years before the Hejira. Several dozen families of Muhammad's embattled followers fled across the Red Sea to Abyssinia (modern-day Ethiopia) and were granted refuge under the protection of the Christian king, Ashabah. During this remarkable encounter between emerging Islam and a Christian kingdom, Muhammad's uncle, Abū Tālib, gave an exposition of Islam based on a chapter in the Qurʾan known as *Mary* (after the mother of Jesus) and explained to the king why they were being persecuted. After hearing him, the king reportedly picked up a stick, drew a line in the sand, and said, "As God is my witness, the difference between your position and ours is not as wide as this line."[48]

Many modern-day writers have followed the king of Abyssinia's lead and emphasized the continuity between Islam and Christianity. I was in a dialogue a few years ago with a Muslim who was eloquent in his masterful survey of all of the similarities and common ground shared by Muslims and Christians. However, he concluded his

47. Sanneh, "Do Christians and Muslims Worship the Same God?" 35.

48. Suwar min Hayat Muhammad, *Images from the Life of Muhammad* (Dar al-Maʾarif, Egypt: Amin Duwaidar, n.d.), 185.

survey by turning to me and saying, "You and I could find complete agreement if you would just give up this notion of the Trinity and the Deity of Jesus Christ." That, of course, strikes at our very identity as Christian worshipers of God. Muslims, however, see these doctrines as corrupted baggage, which should be discarded so that we might recover the original, pure monotheism. As one Islamic writer put it, "the theology of the Qur'an ... stands off from Christianity in that it detects in the doctrine of the Trinity, God the Father, God the Son and God the Holy Ghost, an erosion of the purity of monotheism in Islam."[49]

Thus, although the number of differences between Christianity and Islam may not seem wider than the line drawn by the king of Abyssinia, the theological significance stemming from those few issues is deeper than the Red Sea that separated Arabia from Abyssinia. While terms like *theism* or *monotheism* are generic and freely embrace both Islam and Christianity, *Christian* theism or *Christian* monotheism is unintelligible apart from Christ. Without him we lose our identity and find ourselves talking about some vague "God" of philosophical enquiry or abstract thought, not the God who became fully enfleshed in Jesus Christ. Indeed, the apostle John clearly teaches that for the Christian, theism can be seen only through the lens of Christ. He declares, "No one who denies the Son has the Father; whoever acknowledges the Son has the Father also" (1 John 2:23). To deny the full dignity and deity of the Son is to sever our identity with the Father. John was simply exploring what Jesus himself said when he declared, "No one knows the Father except the Son and those to whom the Son chooses to reveal him" (Matt. 11:27).

Once we fully grasp the implications of Christology on Christian monotheism, we begin to see how difficult it actually is to separate all of the texts of the Qur'an and the Bible into "shared predicates" and "unique predicates." Indeed, Christ has a way of transforming even the most basic biblical predicates about God. For the Christian, Christ is central to both the old and the new covenants. This is why the Christians who may struggle over the question "Is the Father of Jesus the God of Muhammad?" do not hesitate to affirm that the Father of Jesus is the God of *Abraham*.[50] The only Scripture the early Jewish followers of Christ had was what Christians now call the Old Testament.

Christians do not just recognize Christ as a novel feature of the New Testament. The entire Christian gospel, including the specific proclamation of Christ's birth, death, and resurrection, were all proclaimed by early Jewish believers from their sacred texts (Old Testament).[51] However, a similar Christocentric reading of the Qur'an would be both irresponsible and disingenuous to the Qur'anic message. Indeed, because the Qur'an fails to accord Christ his proper status and dignity, even the most basic predicates we share with Islam must be accompanied by some further explanation or

49. G. I. A. D. Draper, "The Historical Background of the Concept of Monotheism," in *The Concept of Monotheism in Islam and Christianity*, ed. Hans Köchler, 38.

50. See, for example, Origen's treatise entitled "The God of the Law and the Prophets, and the Father of Our Lord Jesus Christ, Is the Same God," *De Principiis* 2.4 (see Alexander Roberts and James Donaldson, eds., *Ante-Nicene Fathers* [Peabody, MA: Hendrickson Pub., 1999], 4:275–78).

51. See, for example, New Testament applications of Psalm 16:10; 22:1–18; Isaiah 9:6; Daniel 7:13–14; Micah 5:2. The importance of this will be explored in more detail in chapter 3.

clarification. Two examples will be given to illustrate this point: Allah/God is One and Allah/God is powerful.

Allah/God is One

Islam, Judaism, and Christianity all affirm that God is One. This is the most basic shared predicate of all monotheists. Judaism, along with Christianity, wholeheartedly affirms the *Shema*, "Hear, O Israel: The LORD our God, the LORD is one" (Deut. 6:4; Mark 12:29).[52] A similar confession occurs in the Qurʾan, especially in the opening lines of Surah 112, which is one of the most often quoted texts in Islam: "Say, 'He is Allah, the One'" (Surah 112:1).[53] The Jewish understanding of *ʾeḥad* ("One") in the context of Deuteronomy 6 is about the uniqueness and unrivaled sovereignty of Yahweh rather than any reflection about his metaphysical unity.[54] In other words, it is a statement of monotheism and a rejection of polytheism, not a metaphysical speculation about the internal essence of God or his indivisible nature.[55]

However, Islamic interpretation of Allah's Oneness is far more than an affirmation of monotheism and the sovereignty of Allah over all false gods. It is also used to buttress the Islamic doctrine of *tawhid*, which affirms the uncompromising unity of Allah's nature. In fact, it is this metaphysical interpretation of God's Oneness in Islam that forms the basis for the dispute about God's essence and attributes between the Muʿtazilites and Ashʿarites discussed earlier. The Muʿtazilites taught that Allah's attributes have no "independent or hypostatic existence, but were merged in the unity of God's being."[56] The Ashʿarites accepted distinctive attributes of Allah, but still strongly objected to any notion of separate, personal hypostases in God. Thus, the doctrine of *tawhid* interprets Allah's absolute, indivisible unity in a way that cannot permit either descriptive attributes that try to break down God's Oneness into individual parts or any notion of personal distinctions (*hypostases*) inherent in the Christian doctrine of the Trinity.

The Islamic understanding of Allah as "One" is interpreted in light of the doctrine of divine simplicity. This means that Allah cannot even be spoken of as knowing himself, "since self-knowledge implies a distinction between knower and known."[57] In an earlier book I sought to demonstrate how all unity contains plurality. The idea of undifferentiated unity is only a theoretical construct of the mind or a mathematical abstraction and, ultimately, is no different from nonbeing.[58] For our purposes here it

52. The confession is known as the *Shema*, so named because this is the opening word in the confession as found in the Old Testament, translated "Hear."

53. See also Surah 20:8, 14; 37:4; see also Isaiah 45:22; 44:8.

54. The use of the word "one" as an anti-Christian polemic does eventually emerge in rabbinic writings, e.g., Midrash VIII Ruth and Ecclesiastes.

55. This also explains why Jesus as the second person of the Trinity could so wholeheartedly confess the *Shema* in Mark 12:29.

56. W. Montgomery Watt, *Islamic Philosophy and Theology* (Edinburgh: Edinburgh Univ. Press, 1985), 49. In other words, it is impossible to distinguish between Allah's essence (*dhāt*) and his attributes (*sifāt*).

57. Geisler and Saleeb, *Answering Islam*, 263.

58. See Tennent, *Christianity at the Religious Roundtable*, 138 (for the full discussion, see 148–67). The Islamic view of divine simplicity is based on the reasoning of Plotinus, who argued that God's Oneness cannot even allow for self-knowledge, because that would imply a distinction between the knower and the known. God, Plotinus concluded, must be beyond knowing or consciousness or even being itself. Thus, God must be nonbeing. See also W. H. T. Gairdner, *God as Triune, Creator, Incarnate, Atoner* (Madras: CLS, 1916), 9.

is only necessary to point out that even a simple affirmation of God's Oneness can be understood in such a way as to preclude the possibility of Trinitarian monotheism, the deity of Jesus Christ, or the incarnation, all of which are central to the Christian faith. Thus, even if a Muslim and a Christian stand side by side and confess in Arabic, "Allah is One," underneath the perceived unity lie fundamental differences in how the predicate "One" is understood and applied to the subject, Allah.[59]

Allah/God is Powerful

The Qurʾan regularly affirms that Allah is all-powerful (Surah 2:20; 59:23). Furthermore, several of the ninety-nine beautiful names of Allah are related to his omnipotence, such as the powerful (*al-muqtadir*), the mighty (*al-aziz*), and the most strong (*al-qawi*). The Christian Scriptures also affirm that God is all-powerful. The psalmist declares, "Proclaim the power of God" (Ps. 68:34). Jeremiah revels in God's great power in creation and declares that "nothing is too hard for you" (Jer. 32:17). In Matthew 19:26 Jesus himself declares that "with God all things are possible." God is known as the "Lord God Almighty" (Rev. 19:6), and this concept is reflected in the opening words of the Apostles' Creed, "I believe in God the Father, *Almighty*, maker of heaven and earth." Unquestionably, the omnipotence of God/Allah appears to be a predicate shared by both Muslim and Christian understandings about God.

However, in the New Testament it is clear that God's greatest expression of his power is manifested through "weakness," which God displayed by sending his Son to the cross in order to defeat the powers of Satan. The apostle Paul, for example, declares that Christ, "having disarmed the powers and authorities ... made a public spectacle of them, triumphing over them by the cross" (Col. 2:15). Such an understanding of God's power is clearly unintelligible according to traditional Islamic teaching regarding Allah's power.[60] Thus, even the shared predicate that God is all-powerful requires further explanation and clarification when the texts of the Qurʾan and the Bible are closely examined.

Clarification concerning Muhammad's Prophethood

My strong affirmation of the unique message of the New Testament concerning Christ and the role of Jesus Christ in shaping our understanding of God, our identity before him, and our identity with one another should not be construed as encouraging an overly negative or hostile attitude towards the Qurʾan, the Islamic religion, or Muhammad. Indeed, further clarification concerning the Christian assessment of the nature of Muhammad as a prophet of Allah is in order.

59. This explains why Islamic scholars such as Nassir El-Din El-Assad, President of the Royal Academy for Islamic Civilization Research, prefer to speak of the unisation or unisity of Allah rather than monotheism. El-Assad sees unisity as a more adequate understanding of *tawhid* than monotheism, since monotheism is normally used only to deny polytheism, whereas *tawhid* makes a positive statement about Allah's nature. See his "The Concept of Monotheism in Islam and Christianity," in *The Concept of Monotheism in Islam and Christianity*, ed. Hans Köchler, 23.

60. While the notion of Allah's power manifested in weakness is incomprehensible to Muslims, the Shiʿa tradition extols the passion and martyrdom of Hussayn. Hussayn's suffering is extolled as a virtue that ultimately overcomes, thus providing a potential bridge for understanding the redemptive power of suffering.

It is true that Christian theism is unintelligible apart from our proclamation concerning Christ. It is also true that Islamic theism is unintelligible apart from an acceptance that Muhammad is the prophet of Allah. In short, Islamic identity concerning Allah is not integrally linked to the mission of Jesus, but it is to the prophetic mission of Muhammad. Nevertheless, just as Muslims need to grow in their understanding of the true significance of Christ for the Christian, so Christians need to grow in their understanding of the place of Muhammad in Islam. The Qurʾan repeatedly declares that Muhammad is the prophet of God and equates obedience to Allah with obedience to his messenger (Surah 24:54). Indeed, the *shahadah*, the central confession of the Islamic faith, links the two together when it declares, "There is no god, but Allah, and *Muhammad is the prophet of Allah*." This confession links faith in Allah with faith in the prophet. How should Christians respond to this?

In February 2006 the Western world was captivated by worldwide riots and angry demonstrations by Muslims throughout the Islamic world because of several cartoons that had been published in the *Jyllands-Posten*, a popular Danish newspaper. The controversy surrounded twelve editorial cartoons depicting the prophet Muhammad in an unfavorable light.[61] The shock of the Western world at the riots highlights how the West continues to underestimate the importance of Muhammad in the faith and identity of Muslims around the world. In fact, the church has been guilty of helping to perpetuate many of these negative stereotypes that portray Muhammad as a bloodthirsty, deceived, mentally deranged charlatan. So, how should Christians respond to the prophethood of Muhammad?

Christians have been deeply divided over how to talk to Muslims about their prophet. Martin Luther often spoke of Muhammad and Islam abusively, referring to the Turks, the pope, and the devil as "the three enemies of God."[62] While this kind of attitude was typical in the Middle Ages, over the long span of Christian history attitudes have ranged from open denunciation of Muhammad as a false prophet and an agent of Satan himself to well-known modern writers like Montgomery Watt, who openly declare that "Muhammad was truly a prophet."[63] There have also been those who tried to find the way to some middle ground, such as Thomas Carlyle (1795–1881), who famously said that he considered Muhammad "by no means the truest of Prophets, but I do esteem him a true one."[64]

61. The prohibition of creating any pictorial representation of Muhammad is based largely on the Hadith (see *Bukhari*, vol. 4, Book 54:447–450; vol. 9, Book 93:646; *Sahih Muslim*, 3:5268, 5271).

62. Jean-Claude Basset, "New Wine in Old Wineskins: Changing Protestant Views of Islam," in *Islam and Christianity: Mutual Perceptions since the Mid–20th Century*, ed. Jacques Waardenburg (Leuven: Peeters, 1998), 80. Medieval exegesis routinely identifies Islam with the Beast and Muhammad serves as a type of the Antichrist. The Franciscans were particularly ingenious in working out various ways in which the number 666 referred to the rise of Islam and the prophethood of Muhammad. See John Victor Tolan, ed., *Medieval Christian Perceptions of Islam* (New York: Garland, 1996), especially 94–100, 134–47, 246–51.

63. William M. Watt, *Muhammad's Mecca: History in the Qurʾan* (Edinburgh: Edinburgh Univ. Press, 1988), 1. For a fuller discussion of this theme, see David A. Kerr, "'He Walked in the Path of the Prophets': Toward Christian Theological Recognition of the Prophethood of Muhammad," in *Christian-Muslim Encounters*, ed. Yvonne Yazbeck Haddad and Wadi Z. Haddad (Gainesville, FL: Univ. Press of Florida, 1995), ch. 26.

64. Thomas Caryle, "The Hero as Prophet," in *On Heroes* (London, 1841) as quoted by Lyle L. Vander Werff, *Christian Mission to Muslims: The Record* (Pasadena, CA: William Carey Library, 1977), 21.

As tempting as it may be to sidestep such a controversial question, we cannot adequately reflect on the identity of Allah for Muslims without asking the question: Was Muhammad a prophet of God? The answer is largely determined by how one understands the meaning of the term *prophet.* Louis Massignon, the famous French Islamicist, introduced the distinction between the "positive" and "negative" attributes of authentic prophecy. By "positive" prophecy he referred to the declaration of a prophet that "challenges and reverses human values which are prone to weakness and sin."[65] A "negative" prophecy for Massignon was one that bore witness to "the final separation of the good from the evil." The former is more socially oriented, the latter more eschatological. Massignon sees Muhammad as fulfilling both of these functions and therefore is worthy of being called a prophet by Christians.

Islamicist Charles Ledit, a contemporary of Massignon, rightly felt that this distinction between "positive" and "negative" prophecy was too vague and not sufficiently Christocentric to be accepted by Christians. Instead, drawing from Thomas Aquinas's teachings on prophecy, Ledit identified two aspects of the prophetic office. The first he calls "theological prophecy," defined as "that which receives and communicates faith in Christ's incarnation."[66] Ledit believed that all true prophets prior to Christ pointed to the coming of Jesus Christ and that, therefore, this use of "theological prophecy" ended abruptly with the coming of Christ, who fulfilled all of these prophetic expectations.[67] However, Ledit also recognized what he called "directive prophecy," whereby God, in his sovereignty, uses people outside of the covenant to further his will, to direct people, and even, at times, to rebuke his own people. Ledit was seeking to apply to Muhammad and seventh-century Arabia what Aquinas meant when he wrote that "at all times there have not been lacking persons having this spirit of prophecy."[68]

While I do not agree with all of the particulars of Ledit's proposal, I nevertheless find his distinction a helpful application of Aquinas and a good example of the challenges of cross-cultural and cross-religious theological reflection. Since Muhammad appeared on the world scene after the time of Christ, he cannot stand in the long line of prophets who prepared the way for the coming of Christ. However, does this automatically render him a false prophet? Could God have used Muhammad to further his work in the lives of the Arab people? In a broad sense, Muhammad does seem to engage in "directive prophecy" by pointing people away from idolatry towards monotheism, away from social disintegration to a more unified society, and away from paganism towards a more consistent theism.

Thus, Muhammad's prophecies, at least in the early years, seem to be pointing the Arabs in the right direction, even though, in the final analysis, unfortunate animosities

65. Kerr, "He Walked in the Path of the Prophets," 429.

66. Ibid., 430. The full discussion of this is found in Thomas Aquinas, *Summa Theologica*, Part 2, sec. 2, question 174, "Of the Division of Prophecy." See Thomas Aquinas, vol. 2, *Summa Theologica* (New York: Benziger Brothers, 1947).

67. Aquinas argued that John the Baptist was the last of this class of prophets because John "with his finger pointed to Christ actually present" (*Summa Theologica*, Part 2–2, Question 174, Article 6, Reply Obj. 3).

68. Ibid. The well-known Islamic author Muhammad ʿAbduh defines a prophet as someone sent from God who "brings to us doctrines and ordinances from God, the creator of men, who gives to them, as to other creatures, what they need for the fulfillment and satisfaction of their being in all its aspects" (see *The Theology of Unity*, trans. Ishaq Masaʾad and Kenneth Cragg [New York: Arno, 1966, 1980], 77).

developed between Muhammad and both the Jewish and the Christian communities, resulting in an increasingly more negative assessment of the Jewish and Christian messages. However, we should not let the whole history of Islam cloud our assessment of Muhammad. If it can be said that God spoke "directive prophecy" through Cyrus, who announced the end of exile (2 Chron. 36:22; Ezra 1:8), then why could God not have spoken a directive word through Muhammad?[69] Clement of Alexandria even said that the pagans were given the stars to worship so they might not fall into atheism: "It was a road given to them, that in worshipping the stars they might look up to God."[70]

Let me be clear: as Christians we strongly reject any notion of prophetic infallibility for Muhammad. We categorically reject any doctrine that posits that Muhammad is the final "seal" of all the preceding prophets.[71] Nevertheless, I am still prepared to hail the emergence of early Arabian monotheism as a positive development, a potential *preparatio evangelica*, which may yet serve as a bridge for Islamic peoples to cross over and receive the Christian gospel. In short, despite our differences, Christians need not speak disparagingly about Muhammad or Islam. Christians can celebrate with Muslims their timely rejection of idolatry and their acceptance of monotheism. Indeed, these are wonderful examples of God's grace and a fulfillment of his promise to use Abraham to bless all peoples (Gen. 12:1–3) as well as his promise to make the descendents of Ishmael a great nation (17:20; 21:11–13). However, we can still insist, along with the New Testament, that this general knowledge of God, if not united with a true knowledge of Christ, will not be salvific, and Muslims still need to hear and respond to the good news of Jesus Christ.

2. The Usage and Meaning of "Allah" by Arabic-Speaking Christians and Muslims

The second major area needing further reflection if we are to give an adequate reply to the question, "Is the Father of Jesus the God of Muhammad?" relates to the actual usage of the word "Allah" by Arabic-speaking Christians and Muslims. Because of time and usage, words are not static entities with fixed meanings. Words are the living expression of communities of peoples who are embedded in particular social, political, and religious arrangements. Words are sounds or written characters that convey the thoughts and meaning of people in those contexts.

Even words like "Allah" or "God" do not have fixed meanings. We have already discussed at some length the possible origins of the word "Allah." The English word "God" has its roots in a common Teutonic word for deity that appears in German as *Gott*, in Swedish as *Gud*, and so forth.[72] Some scholars relate its origin to the Aryan/

69. One cannot help but recall the words of E. Stanley Jones, who said, "God uses many instruments, and he used Mahatma Gandhi to help Christianize unchristian Christianity" (see his *Mahatma Gandhi*, as quoted in Andrew F. Walls, ed., *The Cross-Cultural Process in Christian History* [Maryknoll, NY: Orbis, 2002], 25).

70. Clement of Alexandria, *Stromateis* 1.28, as quoted in *Research Seminar on Non-Biblical Scriptures*, ed. D. S. Amalorpavadass (Bangalore, India: National Biblical, Catechetical, and Liturgical Centre, 1974), 231.

71. Aquinas points out that "there is nothing inconsistent if one and the same prophet, at different times, receives various degrees of prophetic revelation" (*Summa Theologica*, Pt. 2–2, Question 174, Article 3, Reply Obj. 2).

72. *Encyclopedia Britannica*, 11th ed. (New York: Encyclopedia Brittanica, 1911), 11:169.

Sanskrit word *gheu*, which means "to invoke" or "to pour," whereas others connect it to Taurus the Bull (*guth*) or to a Germanic chieftain named *Gaut* who was later deified.[73] While we are uncertain of the precise origin of the English term *God*, what is clear is that the word has changed and evolved over time as it was increasingly informed and shaped by thousands of biblical predicates that were, through regular usage, applied to it. This is precisely why a discussion of the common etymological roots of the Arabic *ʾilah* and the Hebrew word *ʾel* is not helpful. Words like *ʾilah* and *ʾel*, and later God, have been dramatically influenced by usage over time.

One of the most important changes is that the term *Allah* has come to be used by Muslims as the particular name for the God of Islam and proclaimed by the prophet Muhammad. In other words, what began by etymology to be the generic term for the Creator God derived from the Aramaic *ʾalaha* has become, through particular and sustained usage, understood primarily through the predicates applied to Allah by the Qurʾan, the Hadith, and the Islamic faithful. There are several reasons for this development.

First, Islam has become the dominant religion throughout the Arabic-speaking world, so other uses of the word "Allah" are muted by the dominant Islamic presence. Second, Islamic writers never apply the term *Allah* to a false god. The Arabic language does not have, as English does, the familiar feature of capitalization, which allows a writer to distinguish between "God" and "god." The capitalization device in English is accomplished through the Arabic definite article "the," which is understood by Muslims to be inherently present in the word "Allah," making it impossible to speak of Allah in generic, indefinite terms. This is why in the *Shahadah* the Arabic cannot say, "There is no allah, but Allah"; rather it declares that there is no *ʾilāha*, but Allah. Third, the distinctive Islamic usage and particular understanding of the term *Allah* have been reinforced in modern times through the attempts of Muslim leaders to Islamize their countries. Sometimes the process of Islamization includes banning Arabic-speaking Christians from using "Allah" in their Bible translations.

One of the most publicized examples in recent years occurred by the government of Malaysia, which since the 1980s has carried out a campaign of Islamization. The constitution of Malaysia states that "Islam is the religion of the Federation; but other religions may be practiced in peace and harmony in any part of the Federation."[74] However, under Islamization, Christians could be imprisoned or fined if they were caught "exposing a Muslim to Christian literature."[75] In 1986 the government went further by banning several words in Malay Christian literature, including the use of the word "Allah" in a Christian context. In 2003 the government decided to apply this law to the Iban language Bible used in Borneo because it had used "Allah" in the translation. The Bible was banned as "detrimental to public peace" because, the government reasoned, the use of the word "Allah" could confuse a Muslim who read the Bible.

73. The *New English Dictionary* suggests the Aryan origin from *gheu*; the *Encyclopedia Brittanica* suggests the connection with Taurus the Bull from *guth*, Wikipedia develops the notion of the Germanic chieftan named *Gaut*.

74. Article 3 (1) of the 1957 Constitution as amended in 1963.

75. Andrew Wark, "Christians in East Malaysia Fear Encroachment of Islamic Society," *News Network International: Special Report* (September 7, 1994), 3.

The Christian outcry over this act eventually led the government to reverse its ban on the Iban Bible, but the government has continued to oppose Indonesian Christian literature that uses "forbidden" words.[76] The Christians were shocked and dumbfounded by the ruling because, for them, "Allah" is a perfectly suitable translation for such words as *ʾel*, *ʾelohim*, and *theos*. Indeed, the word "Allah" is part of their own received vocabulary and usage for God dating back to the time of the Dutch missionaries who brought the gospel to Muslim peoples in Indonesia.

The clash over the use of the word "Allah" occurred because of a genuine difference in the connotation of the word by the Christians and the Muslims. This is why I pointed out earlier in this chapter that the real question is not whether God and Allah are the same (which sparks the etymological discussions) but, "Is Allah the same as Allah?" because this forces us to recognize the vital contextual reality that we have at least two distinctive uses of the word. On the one hand, Christians understand the word "Allah" as a broad term for God in the Bible, but not for the tetragrammaton YHWH, which is the covenantal name for God in the Old Testament. On the other hand, Muslims clearly use the word "Allah" in a more specific sense, almost like a name for God. This is why Norman Geisler and Abdul Saleeb state that "Allah is the *personal name* for God in Islam."[77] This also explains why Muhammad Pickthall makes the following point about his retaining the word "Allah" even in an English translation of the Qurʾan: "I have retained the word Allah throughout, because there is *no corresponding word in English*."[78]

We should not be too surprised that this subtle but important shift has occurred in the Islamic use of the term *Allah* because it is similar to what happened with the Canaanite term *Baal*. This term was previously a generic word for "lord, master," but eventually became identified with particular forms of pagan Canaanite worship. This is why the names Ish-Baal and Merib-Baal (sons of Saul and Jonathan) were later amended to Ish-Bosheth and Mephibosheth.[79] However, the best-known example of this type of change is the Christian use of the word "Christ," which is, by etymology and original usage, a generic *title* ("anointed one") but today is largely used as a *name* for Jesus.[80]

3. Evangelistic and Pastoral Concerns

The third and final major area needing reflection before we can adequately attempt to answer the question, "Is the Father of Jesus the God of Muhammad?" relates to some basic pastoral and evangelistic concerns I have about the question. Pluralists

76. "Malaysia," *News Network International: Special Edition* (June 30, 1993), 4.

77. Geisler and Saleeb, *Answering Islam*, 13, emphasis added.

78. Muhammad Marmaduke Pickthall, trans., *The Glorious Qurʾan* (Mecca: Muslim World League, 1977), 1, emphasis added.

79. The note in the *NIV Study Bible* for 2 Samuel 2:8 says that this was to avoid confusion with the increasing identity of Baal with the Canaanite god (see also 1 Chron. 8:33–34).

80. In fact, in contemporary English usage if you want to specify the *title* Christ, it is now necessary to insert a definite article to make that clear: We worship Jesus, the Christ. Kwame Bediako makes a similar point about the Ghanian "*Nana Yesu*," which means "ancestor Jesus." Bediako observed that Ghanian Christians regularly called Jesus "*Nana Yesu*," but would hardly ever use it in translation as "ancestor Jesus". He eventually realized that it was because the word "*Nana*" is both a title and a personal name, whereas in English the word "ancestor" is only a title. This will be explored in more detail in chapter 5. See Kwame Bediako, "The Doctrine of Christ and the Significance of Vernacular Terminology," *International Bulletin of Missionary Research* 22, no. 3 (July 1998): 110–11.

are fond of saying, "We all worship the same God." But what exactly is meant by this statement? Upon reflection, the context reveals that pluralists are not really making a point about either etymology or particular points of revelation found in someone's sacred text. I do not even think they are trying to make an ontological point, although for some this may be an accepted implication of the statement.[81]

On the lips of pluralists this phrase is often intended as an affirmation of theological relativism. It is a way of de-emphasizing any of the particular predicates about God/Allah as revealed in the Bible or the Qurʾan that might be offensive to another group, and trying instead to focus on our common humanity and "aspirations for the transcendent." The difficulty is that the moment pluralists begin to distance themselves from the predicates of particularity, the more they move away from *both* the God of the Bible and the Allah of the Qurʾan. Instead, they move us closer to Pascal's "God of the philosophers," whom no one actually knows or worships.[82] The living God of revelation has been traded in for the bland, generic God of rational speculation. Indeed, the specificity required for any sustained reflection on the "God of Muhammad" or the "Father of Jesus" has long since faded from view.

When someone committed to historic Christian faith asks the question, "Is the Father of Jesus the God of Muhammad?" it is not just another way of asking, "Don't we all worship the same God?" Rather, the question is posed in the larger context of "faith seeking understanding" (*fides quaerens intellectum*). The questioner is probing for a starting point or a foothold in the specificity of divine revelation. The questioner takes seriously the fact that dozens and dozens of predicates about God found in the Qurʾan are, at least on the surface, remarkably similar to what one reads in the Bible. The questioner is aware that both Christianity and Islam share a common monotheistic heritage in Abraham. Yet the very fact that the question is even raised indicates that there must be some lingering doubts about how a Christian and a Muslim can have a meaningful conversation about God while leaving the dignity and identity of Christ bracketed off.

From the Christian perspective, the question is not some etymological conundrum to be solved; it is a life-or-death question because a Muslim without Christ remains alienated from God. Muslims stand in need of a reconciliation that cannot come through human effort but has been freely offered through Jesus Christ. From the Islamic perspective, precisely because of our claims about Jesus Christ, the Christian belongs to a community that has "gone astray" (Surah 1:7). Christians are those who have refused to submit to the will of Allah.

It is now becoming clear that the question about the relationship of the "God of Muhammad" to the "Father of Jesus" has profound pastoral and soteriological implications for the communities of those who follow Christ and those communities who

81. I only say "some" because there are religious atheists who completely embed all theistic experience in personal, subjective experiences with no *necessary* correlation with an actual objective being. I am thinking of people like Feuerbach, who wrote that "there is no essential distinction whatsoever between God and man." For Feuerbach, what we call "God" is no more than a human projection, like an echo from a canyon wall (see Ludwig Feuerbach, *The Essence of Christianity* [New York: Harper & Brothers, 1957], 19, 23, 140).

82. John Hick in his *God and the Universe of Faith: Essays in the Philosophy of Religion* (London: MacMillan, 1973) attempts just this and ends up with a bland "noumenal" about whom/what one can say nothing definitive.

follow Allah and his prophet Muhammad. Is the Father of Jesus the God of Muhammad? How can that question be answered without some recognition that the Muslim does not *know* the Father of Jesus? Jesus himself declares that "no one comes to the Father except through me" (John 14:6). From the Islamic perspective, we Christians do not *know* the "God of Muhammad" because we have rejected the revelation of the Qur'an. We have turned away in unbelief. We falsely claim that Jesus is divine. For Muslims, we have committed the unforgivable sin, known as *shirk*, which means associating "partners" with God, simply by affirming the Trinity. We have put our trust in a corrupted text. In short, we are not in a position to expect Allah's favor, only his wrath (Surah 1:7). From this perspective, we cannot help but recognize that those who follow the "God of Muhammad" and those who follow the "Father of Jesus" are in a state of profound discontinuity.

Calling the Question

This study has sought to clarify many of the issues that lie behind the question, "Is the Father of Jesus the God of Muhammad?" First, I pointed out the importance of differentiating between those predicates about God that we share with Muslims and those predicates about God that are distinctively Christian. We observed not only how crucial the distinctively Christian predicates are to Christian identity, but even how a truly Christocentric perspective transforms the *shared* predicates.

Second, I attempted to demonstrate that the long and sustained use of the word "Allah" by Muslims has altered its connotation such that, for Muslims, it has become a name for the Islamic God, not just the Arabic equivalent of the English word "God" as it is used by Arabic-speaking Christians and Jews. For the Muslim, the word "Allah" is becoming more like the Islamic equivalent of the Jewish Yahweh (YHWH) than the more general words *'el* or *theos*, which, like the English word "God," have a broader application.

Finally, we reflected briefly on the pastoral and evangelistic implications of our question, since this issue has major ramifications for large communities of people who follow the "God of Muhammad" and the "Father of Jesus" respectively.

The result of this survey has concluded that although "Allah" and "God" are etymological equivalents and, as monotheists, we only believe in one God, it would fragment our very identity as Christians to accept the statement that the Father of Jesus is the God of Muhammad. The reason is that the statement is not essentially an etymological or an ontological statement, but an attempt to identify the predicates associated with the Islamic and Christian use of the words "Allah" and "God" respectively. The phrases "God of Muhammad" and "Father of Jesus" are spoken by communities of faith with important books of revelation that provide hundreds of predicates, all helping to set forth the full context for the meaning of these two phrases. From this perspective, I must conclude that the Father of Jesus is not the God of Muhammad.

Conclusion

This chapter is the first of a series of cross-cultural, interreligious theological reflections that touch upon the major themes of traditional systematic theology.

The purpose has been to widen the perimeter of theological reflection so that the theologians, church leaders, and missionaries of tomorrow will be more adequately equipped to respond to the changing global context in which we live. Why do theological students in the West continue to spend countless hours learning about the writings of a few well-known, now deceased, German theologians whose global devotees are actually quite small, and yet completely ignore over one billion living, breathing Muslims who represent one of the most formidable challenges to the Christian gospel today? We must be far more intentional about fostering a more engaged, mission-focused theology that is informed by actual global realities. The effectiveness of our global witness as the church of Jesus Christ depends on it.

BIBLIOGRAPHY

ʿAbduh, Muhammad. *The Theology of Unity*. Translated by Ishaq Musaʾad and Kenneth Cragg. New York: Arno, 1980.

Abd-Allah, Umar F. "Do Christians and Muslims Worship the Same God?" Part 5. *Christian Century* 121, no. 17 (August 24, 2004): 34–36.

Al-Ghazzali, Muhammad. *The Incoherence of the Philosophers = Tahafut al-falasifah: A Parallel English-Arabic Text*. Provo, UT: Brigham Young University Press, 1997.

Al-Madinah, Mushaf, and An-Nabawiyah, eds. *The Holy Qurʾan: English Translation of the Meanings and Commentary*. Mecca, Saudi Arabia: IFTA, n.d.

Al-Qattan, Sheikh Ibrahim, and Mahmud A. Ghul, "The Arabian Background of Monotheism in Islam." Pages 26–29 in *The Concept of Monotheism in Islam and Christianity*. Edited by Hans Köchler. Wien, Austria: Wilhelm Braumüller, 1982.

Aquinas, Thomas. *Summa Theologica*. 3 vols. New York: Benziger Brothers, 1947.

Ariarajah, S. Wesley. "Do Christians and Muslims Worship the Same God?" Part 4. *Christian Century* 121, no. 11 (June 1, 2004): 29–30.

Baillas, L. J. *World Religions: A Story Approach*. Mystic, CT: Twenty-Third Publications, 1991.

Barnhart, Clarence L., Sol Steinmetz, and Robert K. Barnhart, eds. *The Barnhart Dictionary of New English since 1963*. Bronxville, NY: Barnhart/Harper & Row, 1973.

Basset, Jean-Claude. "New Wine in Old Wineskins: Changing Protestant Views of Islam." In *Islam and Christianity: Mutual Perceptions since the Mid–20th Century*. Edited by Jacques Waardenburg. Leuven: Peeters, 1998.

Bediako, Kwame. "The Doctrine of Christ and the Significance of Vernacular Terminology." *International Bulletin of Missionary Research* 22, no. 3 (July 1998): 110–11.

Berger, Peter. *The Sacred Canopy*. Garden City, NY: Doubleday, 1967.

Brohi, A. K. "Some Random Reflections on the Concept of Monotheism in Islam and Christianity." Pages 107–11 in *The Concept of Monotheism in Islam and Christianity*. Edited by Hans Köchler. Wien, Austria: Wilhelm Braumüller, 1982.

Bukhari, Muhammad ibn Ismail. *Sahih al-Bukhari: The Translation of the Meanings of Sahih al-Bukhari: Arabic-English*, 9 vols. Translated by Muhammad Muhsin Khan. Darya Danj: New Delhi: Islamic Book Service, 2002.

Busse, Heribert. *Islam, Judaism, and Christianity: Theological and Historical Affiliations.* Princeton: Markus Wiener, 1988.

Carlyle, Thomas. "The Hero as Prophet." In *On Heroes* (London, 1841), as quoted by Lyle L. Vander Werff, *Christian Mission to Muslims: The Record.* Pasadena, CA: William Carey Library, 1977.

Clement of Alexandria. *Stromateis* 1.28, as quoted in *Research Seminar on Non-Biblical Scriptures.* Edited by D. S. Amalorpavadass (p. 231). Bangalore, India: National Biblical, Catechetical, and Liturgical Centre, 1974.

Cragg, Kenneth. *The Call of the Minaret.* 2nd ed. Maryknoll, NY: Orbis, 1985.

_____. *The Dome and the Rock.* London: SPCK, 1964.

Draper, G. I. A. D. "The Historical Background of the Concept of Monotheism." Pages 30–39 in *The Concept of Monotheism in Islam and Christianity.* Edited by Hans Köchler. Wien, Austria: Wilhelm Braumüller, 1982.

El-Assad, Nassir El-Din. "The Concept of Monotheism in Islam and Christianity (An Introduction)." In *The Concept of Monotheism in Islam and Christianity.* Edited by Hans Köchler. Wien, Austria: Wilhelm Braumüller, 1982.

Encyclopedia Britannica. 11th ed. New York: Encyclopedia Brittanica, 1911.

Farah, Caesar E. *Islam.* 6th ed. Hauppauge, NY: Barron's Educational Series, 2000.

Feuerbach, Ludwig. *The Essence of Christianity.* New York: Harper & Brothers, 1957.

Gairdner, W. H. T. *God as Triune, Creator, Incarnate, Atoner.* Madras: CLS, 1916.

Geisler, Norman, and Abdul Saleeb. *Answering Islam: The Crescent in the Light of the Cross.* Grand Rapids: Baker, 1993.

George, Timothy. *Is the Father of Jesus the God of Muhammad?* Grand Rapids: Zondervan, 2002.

Gillman, Ian, and Hans-Joachim Klimkeit. *Christians in Asia before 1500.* Richmond, Surrey: Curzon, 1999.

"God." Wikipedia, the Free Encyclopedia. http://en.wikipedia.org/wiki/God (June 16, 2006).

Hick, John. *God and the Universe of Faith: Essays in the Philosophy of Religion.* London: MacMillan, 1973.

Jeffery, Arthur. *The Foreign Vocabulary of the Qurʾan.* Baroda: Oriental Institute, 1938.

Jones, E. Stanley. *Mahatma Gandhi.* Quoted in *The Cross-Cultural Process in Christian History.* Edited by Andrew F. Walls. Maryknoll, NY: Orbis, 2002.

Kerr, David A. "'He Walked in the Path of the Prophets': Toward Christian Theological Recognition of the Prophethood of Muhammad." Pages 426–46 in *Christian-Muslim Encounters.* Edited by Yvonne Yazbeck Haddad and Wadi Z. Haddad. Gainesville, FL: University Press of Florida, 1995.

Latourette, Kenneth Scott. *A History of Christianity.* Vol. 1. Peabody, MA: Prince Press, 2000.

Levenson, Jon. "Do Christians and Muslims Worship the Same God?" Part 1. *Christian Century* 121, no. 8 (April 20, 2004): 32–33.

"Malaysia." *News Network International: Special Edition* (June 30, 1993), 4.

Massey, Joshua, [pseudo.]. "Should Christians Use 'Allah' in Bible Translation?" *Evangelical Missions Quarterly* 40 (July 2004): 284–85.

Metzger, Bruce M., and Bart D. Ehrman. *The Text of the New Testament: Its Transmission, Corruption and Restoration.* 4th ed. Oxford: Oxford University Press, 2005.

Moffett, Samuel Hugh. *A History of Christianity in Asia.* Vol. 1. Maryknoll, NY: Orbis, 1998.

Morey, Robert. *Islamic Invasion.* Eugene, OR: Harvest House, 1992.

Muhammad, Suwar min Hayat. *Images from the Life of Muhammad.* Dar al-Ma'arif, Egypt: Amin Duwaidar, n.d.

Pickthall, Muhammad Marmaduke, trans. *The Glorious Qur'an.* Mecca: Muslim World League, 1977.

Pope John Paul II. "Encyclical Letter *Fides Et Ratio* of the Supreme Pontiff John Paul II to the Bishops of the Catholic Church on the Relationship between Faith and Reason." September 15, 1998. http://www.vatican.va/holy_father/john_paul_ii/encyclicals/documents/hf_jp-ii_enc_15101998_fides-et-ratio_en.html (June 16, 2006).

Ridah, Mohamed A. Abou. "Monotheism: Its Interpretations and Social Manifestations within Islam and Christianity." Pages 40–59 in *The Concept of Monotheism in Islam and Christianity.* Edited by Hans Köchler. Wien, Austria: Wilhelm Braumüller, 1982.

Roberts, Alexander, and James Donaldson, eds. *Ante-Nicene Fathers.* Vol. 4, Origen's *De Principiis.* Peabody, MA: Hendrickson, 1999.

Sanneh, Lamin. "Do Christians and Muslims Worship the Same God?" Part 2. *Christian Century* 121, no. 9 (May 4, 2004): 35–36.

Seale, Morris. *The Qur'an and the Bible: Studies in Interpretation and Dialogue.* London: Croom Helm, 1978.

Shehadeh, Imad. "The Triune God and the Islamic God," Parts 1–4. *Bibliotheca Sacra* 161 (2004): 14–26; 142–62; 274–88; 398–412.

Staal, Harvey, ed. *Mt. Sinai Arabic Codex 151.* Vols. 1–4. Lovanii in Aedibus E. Peeters: Corpus Scriptorum Christianorum Orientalium, 1983.

Tennent, Timothy C. *Christianity at the Religious Roundtable: Evangelicalism in Conversation with Hinduism, Buddhism and Islam.* Grand Rapids: Baker, 2002.

Thomas, Kenneth J. "Allah in Translations of the Bible." *Technical Papers for the Bible Translator* 52, no. 3 (July 2001): 301–6.

Tolan, John Victor, ed., *Medieval Christian Perceptions of Islam.* New York: Garland, 1996.

Trimingham, J. Spencer. *Christianity among the Arabs in Pre-Islamic Times.* London: Longman, 1979.

Wark, Andrew. "Christians in East Malaysia Fear Encroachment of Islamic Society." *News Network International: Special Report* (September 7, 1994), 3.

Watt, William M. *Islamic Philosophy and Theology.* Edinburgh: Edinburgh University Press, 1985.

_____. *Muhammad's Mecca: History in the Qur'an.* Edinburgh: Edinburgh University Press, 1988.

_____. *Muslim-Christian Encounters: Perceptions and Misperceptions.* London, New York: Routledge, 1991.

The White House, "President Bush, Prime Minister Hold Joint Press Conference" (November 2003), http://www.whitehouse.gov/news/releases/2003/11/20031120-3.html (accessed February 25, 2006).

Woodberry, Dudley. "Do Christians and Muslims Worship the Same God?" Part 3. *Christian Century* 121, no. 10 (May 18, 2004): 36–37.

Chapter 3

BIBLIOLOGY

HINDU SACRED TEXTS IN PRE-CHRISTIAN PAST

A few years ago, *Christianity Today* reported that eighty-five percent of the members of Yale University's Campus Crusade for Christ chapter are Asian, whereas "the university's Buddhist meditation meetings are almost exclusively attended by whites."[1] It is clear that Christianity is finding a new home in Asia. This book is seeking to examine some of the theological implications of this geographic shift in the Christian center of gravity. Christianity is growing dramatically in areas that are the traditional heartlands of major non-Christian religions. How can one really talk about the rise of Indian Christianity without giving due consideration to the role of Hinduism, which for many centuries has shaped Indian thought, religious vocabulary, and cultural life? How can we grapple with the rise of Chinese Christianity without reflecting on their Buddhist and Confucian past?

I am particularly interested here in how Christians with a Buddhist, Muslim, or Hindu background regard the sacred texts in their pre-Christian past. Because of the rich textual tradition in India, I will primarily use the Hindu context to examine these questions, although our study will include references to several of the world's major religions.

UPANISHADS AS A HINDU OLD TESTAMENT? — THE CHALLENGE STATED

It is not uncommon to hear Indian Christian theologians referring to the Upanishads as *their* Old Testament. Such a statement must seem odd to an outsider, but the idea is that just as the Old Testament served to prepare the way and point people to Christ in the early Jewish context, so the Upanishads serve as a kind of *preparatio evangelica* for the gospel in the Indian context. Some Indian theologians, reading the account of Jesus on the road to Emmaus, which states that "he explained to them what was said in all the Scriptures concerning himself" (Luke 24:27), have applied the passage

1. "Go Figure," *Christianity Today* 47, no. 7 (June 2003): 13.

to Jesus' presence in India today. In their view, Jesus walks alongside Indian Christians and explains to them how the Indian scriptures point to and bear witness to him.[2]

Some Indian Christians even include readings from the Vedas or the Upanishads in Christian worship services.[3] A. J. Appasamy, a well-known Indian bishop of the Church of South India and considered one of the fathers of Indian Christian theology, published a book entitled *Temple Bells,* which was a collection of readings taken from a wide variety of Hindu sacred texts. The book was designed to be used devotionally and liturgically by Indian Christians. In his preface Appasamy sets forth several reasons why Indian Christians should become acquainted with the sacred texts of Hinduism. Although published in 1930, the reasons he gives remain essentially unchanged today.[4] First, he reminds the reader that Jesus "came to fulfill, not to destroy" (cf. Matt. 5:17). Appasamy was writing in the nineteenth-century heyday of "fulfillment" theology, so this theme struck a concordant note in his readers. He urged Christians to take special note of "the impulses, instincts, questions, longings and aspirations" reflected in these texts. Only by looking intently at the Hindu questions can we truly grasp how Jesus comes to India as the answer to, and the fulfillment of, the deepest longings of the Hindu heart.[5]

Second, Bishop Appasamy pointed out that only by reading Hindu sacred texts can Christians become acquainted with the "storehouse of terms, images and metaphors" that have become "a great charm for the Indian mind." Hindu religious and philosophical vocabulary, with all of their stock images and metaphors, continue to dominate Christian language discourse in India. For example, Krishna Mohan Banerjea, another pioneer of Indian theology, published his landmark book under the title *Christ the True Prajāpati.* The book with its strange title remains unintelligible to someone not familiar with the importance of the *Prajāpati* figure in the Hindu Vedas. *Prajāpati* is a cosmic figure who sacrifices himself to create the world. Banerjea drew on this powerful image, which resides as a stock image in the consciousness of Indians, and argued that Christ fulfills and completes the sacrificial figure of *Prajāpati* by becoming the true and final sacrifice and the progenitor of a new, redeemed world.

Third, Appasamy argued that the "loving, joyful abandon to God" conveyed through the devotion of Hindus can be an inspiration to Christians who are also called to be wholeheartedly devoted to God. Appasamy's doctoral research at Oxford

2. See, for example, Pal Puthanangady, "The Attitude of the Early Church towards Non-Christian Religions and Their Scriptures," in D. S. Amalorpavadass, ed., *Research Seminar on Non-Biblical Scriptures* (Bangalore, India: National Biblical, Catechetical, and Liturgical Centre, 1974), 222–36.

3. A. J. Appasamy, *The Gospel and India's Heritage* (New York: SPCK, 1942), 77. There are several articles on this in *Research Seminar on Non-Biblical Scriptures,* ed. D. S. Amalorpavadass (see previous note). See especially Ft. Ignatius Puthiadam, "Reflections on Hindu Religious Texts," 300–314; Sr. Vandana, "Reflections of a Christian on the Upanishads," 327–59. See also M. Amaladoss, "Other Scriptures and the Christian," *Indian Theological Studies* 22, no. 1 (March 1985): 62–78.

4. The following four reasons may all be found in A. J. Appasamy, ed., *Temple Bells* (London: Student Christian Movement Press, 1930), viii–ix. It should be noted that while Appasamy believed in the value of Christians knowing the Hindu scriptures, he did not accept the idea that these texts could in any way *replace* the Old Testament. He believed that the Hindu scriptures could "supplement, not supplant" the Old Testament. See his *Christianity as Bhakti Marga* (Madras: Christian Literature Society for India, 1930), 166.

5. A number of well-known books have been written that seek to demonstrate how Jesus is the fulfillment of Hinduism. See, for example, Raimundo Panikkar, *The Unknown Christ of Hinduism* (Maryknoll, NY: Orbis, 1994); E. Stanley Jones, *Christ of the Indian Road* (Nashville: Abingdon, 2001); J. N. Farquhar, *The Crown of Hinduism* (New York: Oxford Univ. Press, 1913).

University focused on reading John's gospel in light of the Hindu devotional movement known as *bhaktism*.[6]

Finally, Appasamy was convinced that only by reading Hindu sacred texts such as the Vedas, the Upanishads, and the Bhagavad-Gītā can someone really understand the Bible. He argued that many of the traditional Eastern emphases "inherent in Christian thought" have been lost in the long sojourn of Christianity in the Western world. Now that Christianity is coming back to its home in Asia, the Christian texts can be read with greater clarity and power, for "it is when the Bible is placed in its old environment that it can be fully understood."[7]

Appasamy's reflections raise important questions about the relationship of a Christian believer to the sacred texts of their pre-Christian past. How does a well-defined canon like the Bible relate to noncanonical sacred materials? Can noncanonical materials that form the sacred texts of other religions be used as a *preparatio evangelica*? By not acquainting ourselves with their own pre-Christian texts, are we unwittingly contributing to the promotion of a kind of spiritual amnesia, that is, assuming that when someone comes to Christ, everything in their past must be jettisoned to make room for Christ?[8] Should Christians make use of the sacred text of another religion if it helps them in communicating the Christian gospel? These are a few of the issues this chapter seeks to address—questions that are not normally reflected on in a traditional theology class when considering issues of inspiration, revelation, and canonicity.

The Canon of the New Testament and Its Relationship to Other Texts

Very early the church held a virtually unanimious opinion regarding the inspiration of the twenty-seven books that today comprise the New Testament.[9] Although there have been a few dissenting voices, the fact that Roman Catholics, Protestants, Anglicans, Pentecostals, and Eastern Orthodox Christians all agree on the extent of the New Testament canon is remarkable.

My purpose here, however, is not to focus on the canon of the New Testament per se, but rather to examine the ways in which it has come in contact with other sacred or authoritative texts. This is an issue that is largely ignored in traditional seminary training in the West and yet is becoming increasingly important in today's new global context. In the West, it is rare to find someone who has more than a cursory knowledge of the sacred texts of others religions. In contrast, because Christians in the Majority World are often in settings dominated by other religions, it is not uncommon to meet a Christian with a Muslim, Hindu, or Buddhist background who has an intimate knowledge of another sacred text.

6. A. J. Appasamy, *The Johannine Doctrine of Life: A Study of Christian and Indian Thought* (London: SPCK, 1934). Later, Appasamy published his well-known book *Christianity as Bhakti Marga*, which is a more popularized version of his doctoral research.

7. Appasamy, *Temple Bells*, ix.

8. This idea of spiritual amnesia will be developed in more detail in chapter 5.

9. For a full discussion on canonicity, see Bruce Metzger, *The Canon of the New Testament* (Oxford: Clarendon, 1987), and R. Laird Harris, *Inspiration and Canonicity of the Scriptures* (Greenville, SC: A Press, 1957, reprint, 1995).

Because there are so many facets to this issue, I will begin by setting forth the four main ways in which the New Testament canon interacts with other sacred and/or authoritative texts. I will then focus on the last two of the four because they represent the issues most neglected by evangelical scholarship.

1. Old Testament in the New Testament

The first and most obvious way that the New Testament canon interacts with another sacred text is through its extensive quotation and application of passages from the Jewish canon. The hundreds of quotations from the Law, Prophets, and Writings of the Jewish canon (what we call the Old Testament) are fully accepted and received without question as canonical within their new home in the New Testament. This is because the entire corpus of inspired writings within Judaism were accepted a priori as inspired by the newly emerging Christians since the Christian church was birthed out of Judaism. The apostle Paul alone quotes the Jewish canon over ninety times.

The most common type of Jewish text incorporated into the New Testament canon consists of passages that the early Christians believed pointed to Jesus Christ, thus demonstrating continuity between the Hebrew Scriptures and the fulfillment now being proclaimed in Jesus Christ. Texts such as Psalm 2; 16:10; 110; and Isaiah 53 are quoted in the New Testament and applied to Jesus Christ. The use of these Jewish texts is particularly interesting because the early followers of Christ quoted from the Jewish canon as a means to authenticate and bring legitimacy to their message. So, the full acceptance of the New Testament canon was, in part, contingent upon the idea that the apostolic proclamation was consistent with, and a fulfillment of, the pre-Christian sacred writings that they had already received and accepted as Jewish believers. This conviction is the source of Augustine's saying, "*Novum in vetere latet, vetus in novo patet*"—that is, "the New [Testament] is hidden in the Old [Testament] and the Old is revealed in the New."[10] This area has received considerable attention by Christian scholarship and thus does not concern us in this chapter.

2. Noncanonical "Jesus Material" Used in the Canonical Texts

A second way the New Testament canon interacts with authoritative sources is in its use of authoritative source material about the life and teachings of Jesus Christ. It has long been observed, for example, that Matthew and Luke seem to share a common source not available to Mark. This source has often been called "Q" (after the German word *Quelle*, meaning "source"). The existence of "Q" is, of course, a pure conjecture, but it remains one of the leading explanations for the structure and wording similarities between Matthew and Luke.[11]

We have other evidence that the apostolic *paradosis* ("tradition"; lit., "passing down" or "handing down") was apparently larger than what was eventually included

10. This is also the source of the saying, "*universa scriptura de solo Christo est ubique*" ("everywhere the whole of Scripture is about Christ alone").

11. For an extensive discussion concerning hypotheses regarding sources for and relationships between the Synoptic Gospels, see E. P. Sanders and Margaret Davies, *Studying the Synoptic Gospels* (Philadelphia: Trinity Press International, 1989), or almost any introduction to the Gospels.

in the Gospels. The apostle John makes his well-known statement in the last verse of his Gospel that if everything Jesus did were written down, then "even the whole world would not have room for the books that would be written" (John 21:25). The apostle Paul also quotes "the words the Lord Jesus himself said: 'It is more blessed to give than to receive'" (Acts 20:35), although that saying of Jesus never appears in any of the four canonical Gospels. Similarly, the account of the woman caught in adultery in John 8 does not appear in the earliest manuscripts of this Gospel but is widely accepted as an authentic story of Jesus. Apparently, part of the Holy Spirit's work of inspiring the writers of the Gospels was helping them in their selection of which texts to use in conveying their message (see Luke 1:1–4). This is also an area that has received considerable scholarly attention and, therefore, will not be discussed here.

3. Noncanonical, Non-Christian Texts in the New Testament

The third way the New Testament canon interacts with other sacred or authoritative texts is actually an extension of the second, but is important for our purposes here to treat separately. This is the borrowing, use, and adaptation of noncanonical sources that have no natural connection to the Christian movement (as the Jesus material has) but eventually find their way into biblical text. This is important not only because it has not received sufficient attention by evangelical scholars, but also because there are several ways it is being used and applied today by Christians in the Majority World that deserve careful scrutiny and reflection.

Every student of the Bible is familiar with examples in the Old Testament where a rather strange noncanonical text is quoted. For example, Numbers 21:14 quotes from the "Book of the Wars of the Lord," which is no longer extant but appears to be an ancient collection of war songs used to worship God in times of conflict. Other examples include Joshua's command for the sun to stand still during his conflict with the Amorites (Joshua 10:12–13) and David's mourning of Jonathan's death (2 Sam. 1:17–27); in both instances they quote from the "Book of Jashur," a text that was never received as part of the Jewish canon. These sources, although noncanonical, seem to arise out of the experience and worship of the people of God in a way similar to the "Q" document noted above.

In the New Testament we encounter several examples similar to what we have observed in the Old Testament. However, we also observe some distinctively new elements. Perhaps the best-known quotation in the New Testament of a noncanonical source occurs in the letter of Jude. Jude recounts in some detail a dispute between the archangel Michael and the devil over the body of Moses. This dispute is not recorded in the canonical texts of Judaism, but the early church fathers wrote that the account was recorded in a Jewish work known as the *Assumption of Moses,* which is no longer extant. Later in his letter, Jude quotes from *1 Enoch* as follows:

> Enoch, the seventh from Adam, prophesied about these men: "See, the Lord is coming with thousands upon thousands of his holy ones to judge everyone, and to convict all the ungodly of all the ungodly acts they have done in the

> ungodly way, and of all the harsh words ungodly sinners have spoken against him." (Jude 14–15)

First Enoch is a pseudonymous text written from the perspective of the famous patriarch Enoch, who, according to Genesis 5:24, "walked with God; then he was no more, because God took him away."[12] Jude quotes from a vision of Enoch about the blessings God has promised the righteous and the corresponding judgment on the wicked (*1 Enoch* 1:9).[13] This noncanonical book, having risen out of Jewish life and experience, enjoyed wide popularity in the first century, and Jude clearly assumes his readers are familiar with it.

In the New Testament, however, we also encounter several quotations that find their origin in sources that have no connection with the life and experience of God's people. On several occasions Paul quotes Greek poets popular in the first century. For example, Acts 17:16–34 records Paul's visit to Athens, where he is invited to the Areopagus to preach. His audience is Greek, not Jewish. Thus, rather than drawing from Jewish sources, either canonical or pseudepigraphic, Paul quotes from the Athenians' own Greek poets. In verse 28 Paul quotes from the seventh-century BC Cretan poet Epimenides when he declares, "In him we live and move and have our being." In the same verse Paul goes on to say, "As some of your own poets have said, 'We are his offspring,'" a quotation from the Cilician poet Aratus.[14]

Later, when writing to the church in Corinth, Paul quotes from a well-known Greek comedy *Thais* written by the Greek poet Menander when he says, "Bad company corrupts good character" (1 Cor. 15:33). Finally, one of the most memorable secular quotations used by Paul is from the poet Epimenides, a native of Crete, who wrote, "Cretans are always liars, evil brutes, [and] lazy gluttons" (see Titus 1:12).

The broad response to these texts, whether they are found in the Old or New Testament, or whether their original source is from religious or secular sources, has been to affirm that their presence in the canon of the New Testament in no way should be taken to imply either the authority or the inspiration of the texts from which these quotations are taken. Nevertheless, once they are part of the received text of the New Testament, they now fully share in the authority and inspiration of the Scriptures.

This trustworthy answer has served evangelical students in the West for many generations because for a long time there were no major rivals to Christianity in the West. However, in the Majority World, where preaching Christianity more closely resembles the first-century context, it has become incumbent on evangelists, pastors, and scholars alike to demonstrate how Christianity is similar to or contrasts with the major world religion(s) with which people are already intimately acquainted. In the

12. This Enoch is not to be confused with the Enoch in the line of Cain spoken of in Genesis 4:17. The Enoch quoted in Jude is in the line of Seth and is mentioned in Genesis 5:18–24 and 1 Chronicles 1:3. *The Book of Enoch*, as well as Jude, refer to him as the "seventh from Adam" (See *1 Enoch* 60:8; 93:3).

13. Jude quotes from the Greek version of the text, which was originally in Aramaic. Earlier in Jude he assumes his readers are also aware of the punishment on the fallen angels, recorded in *1 Enoch* 6–11.

14. The quote appears in Aratus's *Phaenomena* as well as in Cleanthes (331–233 BC) in his *Hymn to Zeus*.

New Testament church we observe how vital it was to demonstrate the continuity between the Jewish canon and the Christian proclamation. We accept the extensive presence of the Jewish canon in the New Testament without question. However, that Jewish connection was, in many cases, irrelevant to the Greeks, which explains Paul's quotations from Greek, rather than Jewish, sources.

Many Christians in the Majority World have taken Paul's quotation of Greek poets or John's use of *logos* as an important precedent, modeling for us how we should communicate the gospel when we are in an Islamic, Buddhist, Hindu, secular, or any other setting where people are unfamiliar with Jewish texts, prophecies, and expectations. Is this a legitimate application of Pauline or Johannine practice? Should we encourage insightful quotations from the Islamic Qur'an, the Hindu Upanishads, the Buddhist Tipitaka, or the Sikh Granth, if it will help us to communicate the gospel in the varying contexts in which Christian witness takes place today?

I raise this question because many make a strong distinction between a pastor quoting from an inspiring poem or a popular movie (which is accepted without question) and quoting from a text that is regarded as sacred by another religion. Quoting from the latter implies to some that the authority of that book in its entirety is accepted, thus unwittingly eroding confidence in the sole authority of the Bible. Is there a difference between quoting from a source that no one considers inspired and quoting from a source like the Qur'an, which is revered by the followers of Islam to be the absolute, inerrant Word of Almighty God? These are some of the questions that must be explored further in this chapter.

4. Biblical Texts Appearing in the Canon of Another Religion

The fourth and final way in which the biblical canon interacts with other sacred texts is the appearance of biblical texts (or allusions to those texts) incorporated into the sacred texts of non-Christian religions. By far the best examples can be found in the Islamic Qur'an, which contains hundreds of references to biblical texts, mostly from the Old Testament. Because the Bible was not translated into Arabic until after the death of Muhammad, we do not find many precise quotations of the Bible in the Qur'an. Nevertheless, the open use and adaptation of canonical materials is extensive.

For example, as in the biblical account, the Qur'an states that Allah created the earth in six days (Surah 25:59), culminating in the creation of the first man, Adam. He and his wife eat the forbidden fruit and become aware of their nakedness (20:115–222). Allah sends Moses to confront Pharaoh, inflict the plagues on Egypt, and lead the Israelites out of Egypt by parting the Red Sea (26:9–75). Allah gives Moses the Ten Commandments on two tablets of stone, which, as in the biblical account, are subsequently broken (7:143–150). Throughout the Qur'an, many of the Ten Commandments are repeated, including the command to "serve no other gods" (24:55), the prohibition against making idols (4:116), the commands to not covet (4:32) or murder (6:151), and the command to honor one's father and mother (6:151). In the Qur'an, one can read about familiar Old Testament stories such as Noah's building the ark (11:25–49), King David's adultery with Bathsheba (28:21–25), the

Queen of Sheba's visit to Solomon (27:22–44), and Jonah's being swallowed by the great fish (37:139–148).[15]

Examples can also be found where the Qur'an is clearly influenced by the canon of the New Testament, although like the Old Testament, mostly through oral contact with people who were acquainted with the Scriptures rather than through any intimate knowledge of the precise wording of particular texts. For example, the Qur'an affirms that Jesus was born without sin to the Virgin Mary (Surah 19:15–22). His ministry is foretold by John the Baptist, and he is a worker of many miracles (3:49–50; 43:63). Jesus is also given several honorific titles like those found in the Christian Scriptures, such as the Word (3:39; 4:171) and the Messiah (3:45).

When Muslims who have an intimate knowledge of the Qur'an come to a saving faith in Jesus Christ and begin to read the Bible, they will naturally notice many of the parallels noted above, as well as some of the striking differences between the two texts I have not taken time to highlight here.[16] But certainly the issue is raised: How do we respond to the presence of inspired, canonical material which shows up in the Qur'an? Can the Qur'an be considered a trustworthy or reliable witness to truths that are consistent with biblical revelation? Are statements in the Qur'an that, for example, affirm that the Israelites crossed the Red Sea or that Jesus was born of a virgin become in any way "less true" or "less inspired" once they appear in the larger context of the Qur'an, whose inspiration and canonicity we soundly reject? These are a few of the questions that, along with those noted above, must be considered.

CANONICITY, REVELATION, AND INSPIRATION IN OTHER RELIGIONS

Before we can adequately address the questions we have posed, it is important for students unfamiliar with non-Christian religions to recognize that terms such as *canonicity*, *revelation*, and *inspiration* have distinctively Christian connotations that sometimes do not have a clear parallel in other religious traditions. Thus, when Hindus, Buddhists, or Muslims use terms such as *revelation* and *inspiration*, they frequently understand these terms differently from how they are understood within mainstream Christian discourse. This difference, in turn, sometimes influences the way Christians with a Hindu, Buddhist, or Islamic background have understood and written about these questions. It is vital, therefore, that we begin this part of our study with an overview of how these key terms are understood among those belonging to the major non-Christian religions. This chapter assumes that the reader has a general understanding of how these terms are used within the Christian tradition.[17]

15. It is beyond the purpose of this chapter to explore many of the places where the Qur'an contradicts some of the details of the Old Testament texts or is silent about key events in Israel's history. For more on this, see my *Christianity at the Religious Roundtable: Evangelicalism in Conversation with Hinduism, Buddhism and Islam* (Grand Rapids: Baker, 2002), 177.

16. One of the differences that surprises Muslim background readers of the Bible is that Abraham offered up Isaac, rather than Ishmael, on the sacred mountain (cf. Gen. 22:1–18). For more on this, see my *Christianity at the Religious Roundtable*, 176–77.

17. For a basic introduction to these terms, see Harris, *Inspiration and Canonicity of the Scriptures*.

Hinduism

Hindus accept neither the human authorship nor the historical origin of the content of their most sacred texts. True knowledge (or what we would identity as the content of revelation) is eternally reverberating throughout the universe as a resonating sound known as *anāhata śabda* (i.e., the "unstruck sound"). This sound, which resonates eternally throughout the universe, is symbolized by the sound *OM* (pronounced AUM) and does not require, though it may not exclude, its being associated with the self-disclosure of a personal God. The way this sacred sound gets translated into textual form begins with unknown meditating sages who, at the dawn of each of the unending creation cycles, rehear the knowledge that then forms the core content of the sacred oral tradition.

This oral tradition was later written down and codified into sacred texts, such as the four Vedas (Rig, Sāma, Yajur, Atharva), and their famous philosophical/religious appendices known as the Upanishads. This represents the highest form of revelation in Hinduism and is known as *śruti* (i.e., "that which is heard"). However, there is no certainty that the sages have heard—or even that it is possible to hear—the full content of the "unstruck sound," so the resulting *śruti* canon leaves room for the possibility of further revelation as long as it does not contradict what has already been heard. That which is not yet "heard" is sometimes collectively referred to as the mysterious "fifth Veda."

Hindus also have a large collection of sacred materials that they recognize as having both human authorship and a particular historical origin. This material is known as *smriti* (i.e., "that which is remembered") and forms a lower, second-tier body of texts. This material includes such important texts as the philosophic *Sūtras*, the Law Books, the *Purānas*, and the two great epics, *Mahābhārata* (including *Bhagavad-Gita*) and *Rāmāyana*. *Smriti* is considered authoritative because it is held to be consistent with *śruti* and, indeed, much of the *smriti* material represents authoritative expositions of *śruti*. The line that separates *śruti* from *smriti*, and *smriti* from nonauthoritative texts, is not absolutely fixed, since Hindus are not in complete agreement as to what constitutes the *śruti* texts. Furthermore, there are also significant differences about what material can appropriately be considered *smriti*.[18]

From this survey, what can we conclude about Hindu views regarding inspiration, revelation, and canonicity? First, it is clear that the Christian canon is what Paul Hiebert would call a "bounded set," that is, it is fixed, whereas the Hindu canon is more of a "fuzzy set," since there is not complete agreement on whether the Vedas should be given priority over the Upanishads or even which specific Upanishads should be accepted as *smriti* and which should be rejected as sectarian documents.[19]

Second, the most sacred texts in Hinduism (*śruti*) are not regarded as the result of any acts of divine personal self-disclosure, as in Christianity. The "unstruck sound"

18. Some, for example, only include the *Samhitās*, i.e., the original Rig, Sāma, Yajur and Atharva Vedas without the Brāhmanas and Āranyaka supplementary material. There are also different views about the relationship of the Upanishads to the earliest Vedic material.

19. See Paul G. Hiebert, "The Category Christian in the Mission Task," *Anthropological Reflections on Missiological Issues* (Grand Rapids: Baker, 1994), 107–36.

is eternal, but it is nonpersonal. Indeed, most of the theistic self-disclosure forms of "revelation" occur in the lower-tier *smriti* texts. Perhaps the best example of this would be the *Bhagavad-Gītā*, which is believed to be the personal self-disclosure of Krishna to one of his devotees, Arjuna.

Third, because the highest tier of Hindu sacred texts is eternal, they are not believed by Hindus to be related to any particular historical contexts as is the case in the Christian canon.

Islam

Islamic views of canonicity, inspiration, and revelation are dramatically different from those of the Hindus, but also have several important differences with the historic Christian view. Muslims believe that revelation is rooted in the divine will, which Allah chooses to reveal to the human race. Like Christianity, Islam accepts propositional revelation. In other words, the content of the revelation has been perfectly recorded in truth statements written down in the Arabic Qurʾan (Surah 39:28; 43:3–4). The 114 chapters or surahs of the Qurʾan, comprising 6,236 verses known as *ayat*, were revealed to one person, Muhammad (48:28–29), through one mediator, the angel Gabriel (2:97), over a twenty-two year period of time (AD 610–632).

Muslims believe that all of the words contained in that revelation were fixed on a heavenly tablet since before the world was created. This heavenly tablet is called in Surah 85:22 the "Preserved Tablet," to distinguish it from earlier revelations that were not in Arabic and have become corrupted. The contents were thus recited to Muhammad, who took them down like dictation from the heavenly tablet, which is also known as the Mother of the Book:

> We have made it a Qurʾan in Arabic, that you may be able to understand. And verily, it is in the Mother of the Book, with Us, high (in dignity), full of wisdom. (Surah 43:3–4)[20]

The Qurʾan is specifically in Arabic since "the twenty-eight letters of the Arabic alphabet form the language of the Divine Breath (*Nafs-al-Rahmān*) itself."[21] The contents of the Qurʾan, therefore, represent a "bounded set."

The Arabic language makes clear distinctions between the words *ilham* (inspiration), *wahy* (prophetic rapture), and *tanzīl* (sending down).[22] *Ilham* could happen to any spiritual person, like a great theologian or cleric, whose natural insights and creativity is heightened. Many people can be said to be inspired in this way. Prophetic utterances are also widely accepted in Islam. All Muslims believe that Allah has sent many prophets into the world and, in fact, to many different nations of the world.[23] For Muslims, the important point is not that Muhammad was the *only* prophet God ever sent,

20. Cf. also footnote 37 of ch. 2.

21. Sam Bhajjan, "The Muslim Understanding of the Scripture" as found in Amalorpavadass, ed., *Research Seminar on Non-Biblical Scriptures,* 493.

22. Keith Ward, *Religion and Revelation* (New York: Oxford Univ. Press, 1994), 174.

23. Traditionally, Islam accepts 124,000 prophets.

but that he was the *last* of a long line of prophets. Muhammad is considered the "seal" of the prophets, since the highest and most complete revelation was given to him.

This is why the greatest form of revelation in Islam, known as *tanzīl*, occurs only with the Qurʾan. *Tanzīl* means "sending down" and refers specifically to that revelation directly transmitted from the Preserved Tablet into the mind of Muhammad. So, when Muslims acknowledge that the Jewish Torah or the original gospel of Jesus Christ was inspired or that Jesus is one of many prophets, it must be understood as lower tiers of revelation when compared with the concept of *tanzīl*, which applies only to the Qurʾan.[24]

Just as Hindus have two tiers of revelation, *śruti* and *smriti*, Muslims also have a second tier of revelation known as *hadīth*. Both Sunni and Shīʿite Muslims accept the idea that the example of Muhammad, known as *sunna*, is an important source for guiding the Islamic community, particularly since the Qurʾan is silent about many of the practical social and religious details essential for Islamic catechesis and for the formation of a comprehensive legal code, known as *sharīʿa*.

After Muhammad's death many stories and recollections began to circulate about events in the Prophet's life, his practice, and a number of pithy sayings of Muhammad that revealed his wit and wisdom. Eventually these were collected together into short narratives known as *hadîth*. Soon it became clear that many of the circulating *hadīth* were obviously spurious and had been invented to meet a particular religious or social need. Therefore, Islam developed an elaborate system of verifying and authenticating a *hadīth* by a careful scrutiny of the sources that trace the saying from the Prophet or one of his immediate companions to the point where it was written down as a *hadīth*. This list of sources is known as the chain of *isnād* and is the closest Muslims come to practicing a form of textual criticism, which is forbidden for the Qurʾan but was essential for establishing a reliable collection of *hadīth*.[25] Today there are six collections of *hadīth* that the Sunni accept; the oldest and most reliable is the collection by al-Bukhari containing 7,300 *hadīth*.[26] Shīʿite Muslims have five collections of *hadīth* they accept.[27]

---

24. Muslim scholars are divided between those who believe that this Tablet has been eternally in the presence of Allah and those who believe that the revelation is the creation of Allah. The Muʿtazilah believe that the Qurʾan must be created or Islam would be forced to accept that Allah is not the only eternal reality in the universe. The Ashʿarite, by contrast, affirm speech as one of the eternal attributes of Allah and, therefore, affirm an eternal, uncreated Qurʾan. Most Sunni Muslims accept a view of the Qurʾan's eternality, whereas a minority (such as the Ismāʿīl sect of Shīʿite Islam) believe that the Qurʾan is a creation of Allah. For more on this debate about the Qurʾan being created or uncreated, see W. Montgomery Watt, *Islamic Philosophy and Theology* (Edinburgh: Univ. of Edinburgh Press, 1985), 35, 48, 58–59. This debate is important because an uncreated Qurʾan would dramatically downplay the importance of the relationship of the Qurʾan to the history of the Arab peoples.

25. According to Islamic tradition, some disputes broke out among Islamic leaders about the proper reading of certain texts in the Qurʾan. The third Caliph, ʿUthmān (644–656), ordered an authentication of the text of the Qurʾan, which was eventually copied and sent throughout the Islamic realm. All textual variations were then destroyed.

26. The following six collections are accepted by Sunni Muslims: Bukhari (256 AH), Muslim (261 AH), Tirmizi (279 AH), Abu Daoaod (275 AH), An-Nasaer (303 AH), and Ibn Majaah (273 AH). The dates refer to the Islamic calendar which began in 630 AD. Although, the al-Bukhari collection contains 7,300 *hadîth*, there are many duplications or very similar *hadīth*, but with different chains of *isnâd*. Thus, al-Bukahri's collection contains 2,762 unique *hadīth*.

27. The Shīʿite accept the following five collections: Kafi (329 AH), Sheikh Ali (381 AH), Tahzib (466 AH), Istibsar (466 AH), and Ar-Razi (406 AH). Sometimes the *hadīth* in the Shīʿite collection is identical to the Sunni collection, but the *isnād* is established through respected Shīʿite leaders. However, there are some significant differences in the *hadīth* themselves since the Shīʿite place less weight on the reliability of the Companions of the Prophet than do the Sunni.

Once the Islamic community had a set number of *hadīth* verified as authentic, the *hadīth* were divided between what Muhammad did (*sunnat-el-faʿil*), what Muhammad said/commanded (*sunnat-el-kaul*), and what Muhammad allowed (*sunnat-et-takrir*). Finally, each of these categories was further separated into either sacred (*Qudsi*) *hadīth* or noble (*Sharif*) *hadīth*; the former represent *hadīth* binding on the Islamic community, whereas the latter are informative and worthy of emulating, but are not binding on Muslims. So, for example, the Qurʾan never explicitly commands Muslims to pray five times per day, but this precept is found in the *hadīth* and is considered binding on the Islamic faithful. Elsewhere, the *hadīth* tells us exactly how Muhammad tied his sandals. This particular *hadīth* is declared to be informative, but not binding on the Islamic community.[28]

With this brief overview, it should now be clear that Muslims have a two-tiered understanding of revelation. At the highest tier the text of the Qurʾan stands as the embodiment of divine revelation. For Muslims, the Qurʾan transcends human history and most believe its texts to be eternal. All faithful Muslims believe in the inerrancy of every word in the Qurʾan, the text of which is beyond question and, indeed, cannot even be translated from Arabic into any other language without a loss in the beauty, meaning, and power of the Qurʾan. At the second tier, Muslims believe in the revelatory nature of the authenticated *hadīth*.

However, these passages are different from the Qurʾan for three main reasons. First, the *hadīth* are not considered eternal since they find their origin firmly rooted in the life of Muhammad. Second, the *hadīth* is not a "bounded set" for all Muslims everywhere, since various groups within Islam accept as authoritative different collections of *hadīth*, some of which support various sectarian beliefs or practices that other groups do not accept. Third, Muhammad received the Qurʾan as the direct revelation from Allah (through Gabriel). Muhammad was merely the passive conduit through which it came. He heard it, he recited it and, eventually, it was written down. To suggest any influence from Muhammad is blasphemous. In contrast, Muhammad's life is the active and positive source of the *hadīth*. Muslims believe that because Muhammad is the greatest example of someone who fully submitted to Allah, his life, words, and actions (*sunna*) remain an important guide to Muslims throughout the world.

Buddhism

Unlike Muslims and Christians, Buddhists do not have a single sacred text that all the faithful accept as authoritative in a final sense. In fact, there are actually thousands of sacred texts, known as *sūtras*, in Buddhism. However, understanding how the diverse sacred textual traditions of Buddhism emerged requires some basic knowledge of its history.

The teaching of the Buddha is known generally as the *dharma*. The basic message of the *dharma* is to set forth a "middle way" (between extreme asceticism and materialistic

28. I am providing this overview because each of these elements is crucial for the formation of Islamic Law, known as *sharīʿa*. In fact, one of the most important differences within the four major legal traditions within Islam is the varying emphases put on these various authoritative sources.

consumption) that leads to enlightenment. The core content of the *dharma*, attributed to some early expositions by Buddha to his disciples, is known as "turning the wheel of *dharma*" and is not understood as having any reference to a sovereign, objective God. Today, these early sermons include the four noble truths, the Eightfold Path, and the doctrines of dependent arising (*pratītya-samutpāda*) and no-self (*anātman*). The content of this teaching represents the core teachings of Buddhism. This teaching is nontheistic, denies the reality of the self, and rejects all ultimate first causes.

The basic teaching or *dharma* of Buddha became codified into a canon in the years following his death (456 BC). According to tradition, one of the Buddha's closest followers, known as Mahākāśyapa, called a council of the elders to discuss the movement. He questioned several of the Buddha's disciples, who were able to recite from memory all of the discourses of the Buddha as well as the rules of the monastic life.

Eventually, these teachings, along with some early theoretical discussions, were brought together into three collections known as *pitaka*, or baskets. The Basket of Discipline (*Vinaya Pitaka*) sets forth all of the rules of monastic Buddhism. The Basket of Discourses (*Sūtra Pitaka*) records the teachings of the Buddha. The Basket of Higher Teachings (*Abhidharma Pitaka*) contains profound discussions concerning philosophy and moral psychology. These three "baskets," known collectively as the *Tipitaka*, represent the closest thing to a Buddhist canon. In fact, they are often referred to as the Pali Canon, since they were originally written down in the Pali language. The earliest Buddhist tradition, known as *Therevāda* (Way of the Elders), regards this canon as closed and final.

While most Buddhists accept the canonicity of the *Tipitaka*, the vast majority also believe that additional, and more advanced, teachings have been preserved in other *sūtras* besides those found in the *Tipitaka*.[29] This view is held by the largest branch of Buddhism, known as *Mahāyāna*. The word *Mahāyāna* means "great vehicle" and is the popular, lay form of Buddhism that represents nearly 80 percent of all Buddhists in the world. The *Mahāyāna* believe that the Buddha turned the wheel of *dharma* a second time and left teachings not found in the *Tipitaka*. In other words, the canon is effectively reopened by *Mahāyāna* Buddhists and thousands of new *sūtras* are added to the original Pali canon.

Mahāyāna Buddhists resolve the "problem" of an expanding canon in two ways. First, some groups will create a hierarchy of teachings that progressively reveals deeper and deeper insights into Buddhism, finally culminating in the particular text most revered by that group. Second, many *Mahāyāna* Buddhists will frankly admit that Buddhist teachings are dramatically different, even contradictory, but that the Buddha, like a great doctor, understood that different medicines were necessary to treat various diseases. In the same way, various teachings are tailor-made to fit various problems related to human ignorance and desire, which, according to Buddhists, must be extinguished.[30]

29. I say most because, for example, the Chinese Buddhists only accept four of the five sections of the *Tipitaka*. However, one of the most important and popular divisions of the fifth section, the *Dhammapada*, does appear as a separate *sūtra* in China.

30. This is known as the doctrine of *expedient means*.

The notion of an expanding Buddhist canon is further complicated in several ways. First, some *Mahāyāna* Buddhists believe that because a particular *sūtra* contains or surpasses all of the insights of all the other *sūtras*, there is no point in studying any other text. This effectively means that different Buddhist groups may revere totally different sets of sacred texts. Second, sometimes particular commentaries on or summaries of certain *sūtras* are revered as authoritative, thereby blurring the line between a sacred text and a commentary on a sacred text.

While a comprehensive survey of *Mahāyāna* sacred texts is beyond the scope of this study, it may be helpful and illustrative of the points made so far to introduce a few examples of how these principles work out in some of their most important texts. The earliest body of sacred literature in *sūtra* is known as the *Prajñāpāramitā Sūtras*, meaning the Perfection of Wisdom teachings. These *sūtras* date back to around the first century. However, over the next several hundred years some important summarizing works appeared that claimed to distill all the wisdom of the *Prajñāpāramitā* into condensed form. The two most famous summaries, known as the *Diamond Sūtra* and the *Heart Sūtra*, are among the most influential and famous texts within *Mahāyāna* Buddhism. They are frequently revered apart from the original texts they summarize.

Other famous *sūtras* emphasize different methods of liberation. For example, the famous *Lankāvatāra Sūtra* emphasizes the importance of meditation in achieving liberation. In contrast, the *Lotus Sūtra* emphasizes the role and assistance of certain enlightened beings known as Bodhisattvas, who dwell in a transcendent realm and who can be called upon to assist a Buddhist in his or her path toward enlightenment. For many East Asian Buddhists, the *Lotus Sūtra* is so revered that Buddhist scholar Paul Williams remarks that, for them, "it is the nearest Buddhist equivalent to a Bible."[31]

Several aspects of how terms like *inspiration*, *revelation*, and *canonicity* are understood in Buddhism must now be highlighted. First, it is clear that the textual canon of Buddhism is remarkably fluid when compared with Christianity and Islam. Indeed, even when compared against the sacred texts of Hinduism, Buddhism is far more fluid because in Hinduism all sacred texts are built on the foundation of the Vedas (*Samhitās*) and acknowledge its seminal authority. In contrast, Buddhism has developed several different lineages of textual traditions that effectively operate in isolation from one another.

Second, because Buddhism is nontheistic, whatever texts are received as authoritative are not understood as the self-disclosure of an objective, transcendent God, but rather as the enlightened teachings of a buddha.[32] Once the doctrine of God is rejected, it is not difficult to begin to grasp how dramatically this influences the understanding of revelation and inspiration. For example, the entire content of Buddhist teachings is the result of sustained discipline and meditative skills developed through self-denial by the Buddha over hundreds of lifetimes until, finally, in an extreme meditative state, he grasped the insights that form the basis of Buddhist teachings.

31. Paul Williams, *Mahāyāna Buddhism* (London: Routledge, 1989), 141.

32. Buddhism is united in its rejection of theism, but is divided over whether there was only one Buddha or many buddhas.

FOCUSING THE QUESTIONS: TWO CATEGORIES OF QUESTIONS

With this general background, we are now in a position to explore the questions raised earlier in the chapter. Essentially, all of these questions fall into two distinct categories. The first category seeks to understand how we regard those examples when our canonical texts have been incorporated into the sacred text of another religion. While there is evidence of some Christian influence in some of the texts of Hinduism and Buddhism that emerged after the Christian era, our focus is on Islam, since this is a major and undeniable feature of the Qurʾan. The second category, which we will focus on more extensively, deals broadly with whether or not we should make use of the sacred texts of Hinduism, Buddhism, or Islam in communicating the gospel to those who are already familiar with these texts. If so, can any of these texts or any portions of them be regarded as inspired or in any way arising through some kind of revelation?

The Presence of Inspired, Revelatory Material in the Qurʾan

The first category of questions relates to the relationship of biblical, canonical material to the sacred texts of other religions. Even if we reject the inspiration of the Qurʾan, we still have to reflect on how we regard those portions of the inspired texts of Christians (Old and New Testaments) that have been incorporated into the Qurʾan.

It is important to remember that Muslims do not believe that a single verse of the Qurʾan was in any way influenced or taken from either Jewish or Christian sources. The Qurʾan was verbally given to the prophet Muhammad as a kind of dictation from the Preserved Tablet in heaven. Muhammad memorized it and, later, recited it to his followers, who eventually, according to Muslims, wrote the recitations down exactly as they had heard them. It is, therefore, impossible for Muslims to accept that some of the material in the Qurʾan had been revealed earlier in the Jewish Torah and later accepted by Muhammad as authoritative. In Islam the entire text of the Qurʾan, all 6,236 verses of it, are viewed as a single unit in complete isolation from any of our texts. The Qurʾan is *tanzīl* (i.e., a sending-down of divine truth) and should not, in their view, be confused with or discussed alongside *ilham* (inspiration) or *wahy* (prophetic rapture), which may be found in the undistorted portions of the Jewish and Christian writings.

So, despite the remarkable and extensive presence of Jewish and Christian writings that are incorporated into the Qurʾan, there is no meaningful way to discuss this issue with a Muslim in an Islamic context. From the Christian point of view, since these texts have been taken out of their Christological and ecclesiological context when brought into the Qurʾan, they may no longer be spoken of as either inspired or revealed, even though those particular statements that the Qurʾan has incorporated into its text without distortion remain trustworthy and true.

Using Non-Christian Sacred Texts in a Christian Context

We are now prepared to examine the second category of questions related to the use and/or acceptance of the nonbiblical sacred texts of other religious traditions. In December of 1974 Roman Catholic scholars in India convened a week-long conference in Bangalore entitled, "Research Seminar on Non-Biblical Scriptures." The papers and official statements from the conference were eventually published in a book containing more than seven hundred pages.[33] The central question that brought the conference together was: Can we use the scriptures of other religions in our worship? This, in turn, led the conference to address a number of related questions, including whether or not the scriptures of non-Christians can be considered inspired or revealed.

Many of the papers from that conference were also published in various academic journals; these, in turn, generated considerable discussion on the topic, at least within India. In fact, it should not surprise us that the "Research Seminar on Non-Biblical Scriptures" was convened in India by Indian scholars, or that one of the most important books published on the subject, *Inspiration in the Non-Biblical Scriptures,* was published by the Indian Jesuit Ishanand Vempeny.[34] We also have already noted that it was the Indian bishop of the Church of South India, A. J. Appasamy, who as early as 1930, published a collection of readings from Hindu religious literature to be used devotionally and liturgically by Christians. The reason is that one cannot live as a Christian in India and not be aware of the presence of 700 million Hindus whose religion has permeated virtually every aspect of Indian life and culture.

Being a Christian minority in a country where some other religion is predominant was the context of the early church, just as it is the context of most Christians in Asia today. Increasingly, Western Christians must learn important lessons from our Asian brothers and sisters in Christ, who have hundreds of years of experience in facing what has become a relatively new phenomenon in the Western world. What lessons can we learn from Asian Christians? Two main lessons will be explored, which will help to prepare us to address the central questions.

Two Lessons from Asian Christians

1. Avoid broad condemnation or naïve acceptance of non-Christian texts.

Asian Christians are generally more nuanced in their attitude towards non-Christian sacred texts. In the West, Christians tend towards two extreme views. On the one side are the liberal Christians, who have drunk deeply at the well of relativism. They are content to put all the world's sacred texts on the same shelf as equal partners. For them, the Upanishads are just as likely to yield spiritual light as the Sermon on the Mount.

On the other side are the conservative Christians, who have far less exposure to the actual texts of other religions and tend to react defensively to the suggestion of any spiritual light outside of the Bible. They argue that the Qurʾan, far from yielding any spiritual insights, is a satanic book that does not acknowledge the full deity of Jesus Christ and has helped to lead millions of Muslims into condemnation. Likewise, the Hindu Upanishads are said to be full of evil, spiritual darkness, and deception and

33. Amalorpavadass, *Research Seminar on Non-Biblical Scriptures.*

34. Ishanand Vempeny, *Inspiration in the Non-Biblical Scriptures* (Bangalore, India: Theological Publications in India; Poona: Sakal, 1973). Evangelical scholarship in the West has begun to discuss these issues in more detail. See, for example, Gerald McDermott, *Can Evangelicals Learn from World Religions?* (Downers Grove, IL: InterVarsity Press, 2000).

should be discarded to make room for the salvific message of the New Testament. To be fair, there are some who accept that one or two pearls might be found in these texts in the midst of heaps and heaps of worthless rubbish, but, generally speaking, Christians tend toward these two extreme views.

Without a doubt, both of these extreme views are also found in India, but there is, comparatively speaking, a more substantial group in the middle who reject both extremes. Interestingly, both the liberal and the conservative extremes are rejected on the same grounds, namely, for being insufficiently Christocentric. The liberal view is rejected because it tends to relativize and downplay the uniqueness and centrality of Jesus Christ in the Christian message. The conservative extreme is rejected because it tends to lock Jesus Christ up inside the covers of a book and forgets that he is also "the true light that gives light to every man" (John 1:9); practically speaking, this view regards Christology as a subset of bibliology. Instead, many Indian Christians argue that there are rays of light present in the sacred texts of India, which, however dim, ultimately point to and find their fulfillment in Jesus Christ. This view leads us into the second lesson we can learn from our Christian brothers and sisters who live in Asia.

2. Christ does not arrive in any culture as a stranger.

Asians insist that Christ does not arrive in Asia as a stranger. They do not have to experience spiritual amnesia when they receive Jesus Christ as their Lord and Savior. We will hear the same message from African Christians in chapter 5, so it is a point that should demand our attention and response. Ishanand Vempeny opens his book, *Inspiration in the Non-Biblical Scriptures,* by retelling the story of the Islamic sacking of Alexandria. Reportedly, the Arab commander Amrouh did not know what to do with the Alexandrian library, which contained the literary masterpieces of the Western world and was considered the largest library in the world, even though portions of it had been destroyed by fire earlier. However, according to the Islamic legend, Caliph Umar gave the order to destroy the library because, he said, "The Qur'an contains all the truths that are worthwhile. Let every other book be reduced to ashes."[35]

Although the account is probably an apocryphal caricature, it does illustrate an attitude that conveys the idea that the only way to fully affirm the worth of Holy Scripture is to insist that all other books are worthless. This notion is rejected, not only by Vempeny, but by many Indian Christians with a Hindu background who are trying to understand how Christ not only demolished the false doctrines and evil idolatry of their Hindu past, but how, at the same time, Christ came to fulfill and complete longings and aspirations they had held as Hindus.

Having taught in India over the last twenty years and having many students, colleagues, and friends who are Hindu-background Christians, I can say that when many of them look back on their past life in Hinduism and reflect on it, they are aware of profound discontinuity as well as surprising continuity. They see not only deliverance from demonic deception, but also, quite remarkably, they see little windows of God's grace in preparing and drawing them, even while they were still Hindus, for the day

35. Vempeny, *Inspiration in the Non-Biblical Scriptures*, xvi.

when they would receive the full light and glory of the Christian gospel and live their new lives in the presence of the risen Christ.

These admonitions from our Indian brothers and sisters should at least give us grounds to consider the possibility of using nonbiblical texts in the context of Christian worship or preaching, even if we are predisposed toward rejecting it. Nevertheless, for an evangelical fully committed to the final authority of the Bible, it is important that the biblical basis for such a practice be clearly and convincingly set forth. To put the question plainly: Is it biblical for Christians to quote Hindu sacred texts when communicating the gospel to Hindus?

Biblical Basis Explored: An Imaginative Journey from Text to Context

Earlier in the chapter we examined several passages where the apostle Paul quotes from well-known Greek poets and playwrights. It was argued that he quoted from these texts because he was preaching to Greeks, who would not be easily persuaded by quotations from what they would have considered strange Jewish prophets who had anticipated the coming of a Jewish messiah. Those listening to Paul were not Jews and therefore the coming of a Jewish messiah was irrelevant to them. Even though the Old Testament is the inspired Word of God and provides the most trustworthy preparation for and anticipation of the coming of Christ, Paul, surprisingly, elected to utilize quotations from sources that he neither accepted as generally authoritative nor believed were inspired by God, but which helped to corroborate his message in the hearts and minds of his pagan audience. The challenge, of course, is making the leap from the first century to the twenty-first century. Can Paul's practice become an example for us to follow?

To answer this question, let us begin by using a bit of imagination in order to apply this biblical account to a more contemporary situation. What if the apostle Paul were preaching the gospel to Hindus in India rather than to Hellenistic pagans in the Roman empire? What if we found the apostle Paul standing in the holy city of Varanasi on the banks of the Ganges River rather than on top of Mars Hill in Athens?

In some ways the scene would be very familiar to Paul. If you are standing on top of Mars Hill, the most imposing visual site is the massive Parthenon, the great temple of the goddess Athena, which is immediately to the southeast of Mars Hill. Likewise, if Paul were in Varanasi and stood on the banks of the Ganges River, the most imposing visual site is the great Kashi Vishwanath Temple of Lord Shiva, the god of the Ganges River.[36] It is believed that the Ganges River flows from Shiva's hair and that anyone who dips in these sacred waters will have their sins washed away. For centuries Hindus have made the long and arduous pilgrimage to this city, considered the holiest city in India, and, like Athens, one of the oldest cities on earth.

In Athens, Scripture records, Paul saw dozens of altars with inscriptions to various gods and goddesses, including one with the inscription, "TO AN UNKNOWN GOD" (Acts 17:23). Likewise, if Paul were in Varanasi and walked along the banks of the Ganges,

36. Kashi is the ancient name of modern day Varanasi, a city the British called Benares. Vishwanath means "Lord of All."

he would see hundreds of shrines and temples and altars to various gods and goddesses in the Hindu pantheon. While in Athens, Paul got into a dispute with a group of Epicurean and Stoic philosophers, two of the major intellectual schools of that time (17:18). If Paul were to stay long in Varanasi, he would soon find himself in a dispute with philosophers who teach at the famous Benares Hindu University. Followers of the great philosophers Sankara and Ramanuja still debate the nature of God, the reality of the world, and the best path to salvation. Finally, Paul's Hindu audience in Varanasi would be just as ignorant of Jewish promises and prophets found in the Old Testament as were those "men of Athens" who heard Paul's message on Mars Hill.

In such a situation, would it not be just as unlikely for the apostle Paul to try to reach Hindus with the gospel by quoting from foreign Jewish prophets about whom they know nothing? If Paul were to walk around Varanasi for long, he would notice that the Hindus, like the Athenians, are very religious. They take great pride in the outward religious displays of sacrifice, self-denial, pilgrimage, and so forth. One of the most important messages for a Hindu is that outward ritual and outward religiosity has no benefit, because God looks into our hearts. Paul might quote the well-known text from 1 Samuel 16:7, "The Lord does not look at the things man looks at. Man looks at the outward appearance, but the Lord looks at the heart." But then, to corroborate this text I can certainly see the apostle Paul going on to say, "for even as your own poet Tukārām has said, 'The shell of the coconut is hard, but the inside is excellent. In accordance with this, remember, that purity inside is what we aim at ... the value of a thing depends on its inner qualities.'"[37]

Quoting Tukārām in such a context does not give an exalted or inspired status to Tukārām's poem any more than Paul's quotation of Epimenides's poem *Cretica* gave it any kind of special status. Yet it serves as a powerful indigenous corroboration of the biblical text that brings the message of Jesus Christ into the Hindus' worldview, rather than non-Indian Christians insisting that they relate to Christ as a stranger.

Guidelines for Use of Nonbiblical Sacred Texts

I do believe the biblical account in Acts 17 provides a convincing precedent for the use of nonbiblical sacred texts in certain *limited* contexts. However, I suggest three guidelines. First, the use of these texts should be limited to *evangelistic outreach*, where the audience consists predominantly of non-Christians who are acquainted with the texts being quoted. Paul's quotation of pagan poems on Mars Hill is clearly in an evangelistic context. His audience would probably not have been familiar with a Jewish prophet like Isaiah, but they were well acquainted with a text like the *Hymn to Zeus*, from which Paul quotes. The context of Paul's use of Greek texts seems to provide a good rule of thumb to follow today as well.

Second, non-Christian texts should be used only to provide a *corroborative witness* to a biblical message, rather than an independent testimony in isolation from the

37. J. N. Fraser and K. B. Marathe, *The Poems of Tukārām*, vol. 3, p. 197, as quoted in Appasamy, *Temple Bells*, 84. Tukārām was a seventeenth-century Marati, poet-saint from Maharashtra. Tukārām was a devotee of the god Krishna and his poems are filled with love and adoration to Krishna. They are used as sacred texts in the *bhakti* tradition of Hinduism.

biblical witness. As Christians, we do not accept the final authority of the Upanishads any more than Paul accepted the final authority of the *Hymn to Zeus*. However, this fact does not prevent these texts from being used in a way that serves to corroborate a biblical message.

In a courtroom, sometimes even convicted felons are called upon to testify because they heard or saw something that helps to advance the prosecution's case. In the same way, a Christian may find it advantageous to call on external witnesses outside the Bible to assist in corroborating the biblical message. For example, if one were preaching to Hindus and wanted to demonstrate the inner longing all men and women have for truth and eternity, it may help to quote what is widely believed as one of the best-known prayers in India, taken from the Upanishads:

> From the unreal, lead me to the real!
> From darkness, lead me to the light!
> From death, lead me to immortality. (Brihad-Âranyaka Upanishad 1.3.28)[38]

Such a text might well serve as a corroborative witness to Paul's point in Acts 14:17 when he declared that even among the pagans, God has "not left himself without testimony." Using a nonbiblical sacred text as a corroborative witness serves to sharpen the biblical message and helps to demonstrate that Jesus does not arrive in India as a stranger, but in answer to the prayers of Hindu hearts.

Third, any nonbiblical sacred text that is quoted should be lifted out of its original setting and clearly reoriented within a new *Christocentric setting*. Both Epimenides and Aratus were, like Tukārām, non-Christian poets committed to the worship of false gods. Epimenides's poem, cited in Acts 17, consists of words on the lips of Minos, Zeus's son, and was given in praise of Zeus. Minos declares, "But thou art not dead; thou livest and abidest forever, *for in thee we live and move and have our being*."[39] Paul clearly rejected that Zeus was alive and "abidest forever," but he boldly applied it to the Christian gospel, calling on pagans to reach out and receive God's grace in their lives.

The original quote from Aratus was also in honor of Zeus. The original line of the poem is as follows: "It is with Zeus that every one of us in every way has to do, *for we are also his offspring*."[40] However, in its new setting Paul used the quote to demonstrate that the entire human race is under the rule of the living God of biblical revelation and that he is calling the whole world to account and will judge the world by and through Jesus Christ (Acts 17:28–31). This is the basic pattern of Paul, whether he is quoting from the sacred Jewish Scriptures or from a pagan source. He imports the text out of its original context and reorients it within a new, distinctively Christian setting.

Using such texts in this limited fashion clearly conveys that they are not regarded as inspired or revelatory in the Christian sense of the word. The Christian understanding

38. S. Radhakrishnan, ed., *The Principal Upanishads* (Amherst, NY: Humanity Books, 1992), 162.

39. Richard N. Longnecker, "Acts," *The Expositor's Bible Commentary* (Grand Rapids: Zondervan, 1981), 9:476. Italics mine, to emphasize the portion which Paul quotes.

40. Ibid. Italics mine, to emphasize the portion which Paul quotes.

of inspiration and special revelation cannot be understood in isolation from the broader theological framework of Christology and ecclesiology. All inspired texts must ultimately bear witness to Christ, who is the Word made flesh. Furthermore, all inspired texts are those that have been given to serve the community of God's redeemed people, the church, which is the body of Christ. Even a partial quotation from the *Hymn to Zeus* can become part of the inspired text of the New Testament because it has been reoriented within this larger Christological and ecclesiological framework. This is an example of an inspired use of an uninspired text.

Conversely, even if John 3:16 were incorporated into the sacred text of another religion, it would be a noninspired use of an inspired text, because it would no longer be found within the larger context of Christian revelation. Therefore, the entire Christian understanding of special revelation is predicated on our larger understanding of Christ, who embodies and fulfills all other revelation, and on the purpose of that revelation, which is to call forth the redeemed community, the body of Christ.

It is, therefore, impossible to speak about Christian views of inspiration and revelation outside the larger context of Christology and ecclesiology. The Upanishads or the Qur'an or the Tipitaka do not bear witness to Christ and do not serve the church and therefore cannot be regarded as inspired. This does not mean, of course, that these texts contain only error. On the contrary, God has made certain truths about himself known universally, which is why, as noted above, Paul can declare that God has not left himself without a witness.

In fact, it seems that God has provided at least two universal witnesses to himself. The first is an external witness that is heard through the glorious proclamation of creation: "The heavens declare the glory of God" (Ps. 19:1). The second is an internal witness that is heard through the voice of conscience, which demonstrates that "the requirements of the law are written on their [Gentile] hearts" (Rom. 2:15). We should expect that insights derived from these two universal witnesses might be reflected in the world of literature, including non-Christian sacred texts. We would be surprised if it did not. Wherever such texts help to corroborate the Christian message, we rejoice, but because their overall contexts are not specifically related to either Christ or the church, we cannot consider them inspired or revealed in the special Christian sense of those words.

CONCLUSION

This chapter has sought to examine two questions. First, how should we regard the presence of material borrowed from the Bible that has been incorporated into the sacred texts of other religions, particularly Islam? Second, can Christians make use of sacred textual material from other religions in worship, preaching, and teaching in Christian settings? We have concluded that while we should not use these texts liturgically, Christians can and, indeed, *should* make use of appropriately selected materials from the sacred or secular traditions that surround us as long as certain guidelines are followed.

This chapter has also sought to establish that a doctrine of revelation and inspiration is unintelligible apart from the larger framework of Christology and ecclesiology. Therefore, even though the sacred texts of other traditions sometimes make statements that are true, insightful, inspirational, and even spiritually edifying, they cannot be regarded as inspired or revelatory since they lack the proper Christological and ecclesiological context. This principle even applies to the biblical material itself when it has been taken out of its original biblical setting and set within a non-Christian context, such as the Qurʾan. Even though these inspired texts remain true, they are being used in an uninspired way when they are taken out of the larger Christological and ecclesiological framework of the Christian Scriptures.

BIBLIOGRAPHY

Amaladoss, M. "Other Scriptures and the Christian." *Indian Theological Studies* 22, no. 1 (March 1985): 62–78.

Amalorpavadass, D. S., ed. *Research Seminar on Non-Biblical Scriptures.* Bangalore, India: National Biblical, Catechetical, and Liturgical Centre, 1974.

Appasamy, A. J. *Christianity as Bhakti Marga.* Madras: Christian Literature Society for India, 1930.

_____. *The Gospel and India's Heritage.* New York: SPCK, 1942.

_____. *The Johannine Doctrine of Life: A Study of Christian and Indian Thought.* London: SPCK, 1934.

Appasamy, A. J., ed. *Temple Bells.* London: Student Christian Movement, 1930.

Bhajjan, Sam. "The Muslim Understanding of the Scripture." Pages 489–507 in *Research Seminar on Non-Biblical Scriptures.* Edited by D. S. Amalorpavadass. Bangalore, India: National Biblical, Catechetical, and Liturgical Centre, 1974.

Farquhar, J. N. *The Crown of Hinduism.* London: Oxford University Press, 1913.

"Go Figure." *Christianity Today* 47, no. 7 (June 2003): 13.

Harris, R. Laird. *Inspiration and Canonicity of the Scriptures.* Greenville, SC: A Press, 1995.

Hiebert, Paul G. "The Category Christian in the Mission Task." Pages 107–36 in *Anthropological Reflections on Missiological Issues.* Grand Rapids: Baker, 1994.

Jones, E. Stanley. *Christ of the Indian Road.* Nashville: Abingdon, 2001.

McDermott, Gerald. *Can Evangelicals Learn from World Religions?* Downers Grove, IL.: InterVarsity Press, 2000.

Metzger, Bruce. *The Canon of the New Testament.* Oxford: Clarendon, 1987.

Panikkar, Raimundo. *The Unknown Christ of Hinduism.* Maryknoll, NY: Orbis, 1994.

Puthanangady, Pal. "The Attitude of the Early Church towards Non-Christian Religions and Their Scriptures." Pages 222–36 in *Research Seminar on Non-Biblical Scriptures.* Edited by D. S. Amalorpavadass. Bangalore, India: National Biblical, Catechetical, and Liturgical Centre, 1974.

Puthiadam, Ignatius. "Reflections on Hindu Religious Texts." Pages 300–314 in *Research Seminar on Non-Biblical Scriptures.* Edited by D. S. Amalorpavadass. Bangalore, India: National Biblical, Catechetical, and Liturgical Centre, 1974.

Tennent, Timothy C. *Christianity at the Religious Roundtable: Evangelicalism in Conversation with Hinduism, Buddhism and Islam.* Grand Rapids: Baker, 2002.

Sr. Vandana. "Reflections of a Christian on the Upanishads." Pages 327–59 in *Research Seminar on Non-Biblical Scriptures*. Edited by D. S. Amalorpavadass. Bangalore, India: National Biblical, Catechetical, and Liturgical Centre, 1974.

Vempeny, Ishanand. *Inspiration in the Non-Biblical Scriptures*. Bangalore, India: Theological Publications in India; Poona: Sakal, 1973.

Ward, Keith. *Religion and Revelation*. New York: Oxford University Press, 1994.

Watt, W. Montgomery. *Islamic Philosophy and Theology*. Edinburgh: Edinburgh University Press, 1985.

Williams, Paul. *Mahayana Buddhism: The Doctrinal Foundations*. London and New York: Routledge, 1989.

Chapter 4

ANTHROPOLOGY

HUMAN IDENTITY IN SHAME-BASED CULTURES OF THE FAR EAST

In traditional Japanese culture, it was not uncommon for a man to borrow money against his good name, promising to repay the debt by the next New Year. Lenders extended such loans without asking for any collateral because they knew that the sense of obligation to repay was so strong in Japan that a person would not risk their public reputation by defaulting on the loan. In making such a loan, the borrower would say to the lender: "I agree to be publicly laughed at if I fail to repay this sum." But underlying this statement lay a more ominous reality. If the New Year came and the person was unable to repay the debt, the debtor might be expected to commit ritual suicide to clear his name and to protect the honor of his family.[1] Certainly, people from a wide variety of cultures around the world resonate with someone who pledges on his own good name to repay a debt.

We can find many similar examples, such as the famous Japanese novelist Yukio Mushima (1925–1970), who committed ritual suicide after he failed to create a successful rebellion against the adoption of the modern Japanese constitution.[2] Likewise, public school teachers have committed suicide in Japan because they mispronounced the emperor's name in the reading of the Imperial Rescript on Education or because a school burned down and they failed to rescue the emperor's portrait.

Such stories may seem like distant images from the days of the Samurai warriors, but the role of shame and honor continues to play a dominant role in many cultures outside the Western world. In the last few years dozens of cases of murders and mutilations have been reported in the media in which the perpetrators either went completely unpunished or received extremely light sentences because their crimes were considered an act of honor to cleanse the family of shame.

---

1. Ruth Benedict, *The Chrysanthemum and the Sword* (Cambridge, MA: Riverside, 1946), 151, 156. See also Zuk-Nae Lee, "Korean Culture and Sense of Shame," *Transcultural Psychiatry* 36, no. 2 (June 1999): 187.

2. Yukio Mushima is the pseudonym for Kimitake Hiraoke. See "Yukio Mushima: A 20th Century Warrior," *New Dawn* 29, no. 1 (January–March, 1995): 21.

For example, Kifaya Husayn, a sixteen-year-old girl from Jordan, was tied to a chair by her own brother, who then proceeded to slash her throat. After her death, he ran out into the streets and waved the bloody knife, declaring, "I have killed my sister to cleanse our honor." Kifaya's crime was that she had been raped and had thereby brought disgrace to the family's honor. One twenty-five-year-old Palestinian man who hung his own sister with a rope said that he did not want to kill her, but that he "did it to wash with her blood the family honor that was violated ... and in response to the will of society that would not have had any mercy on me if I didn't."[3] Thousands of murders and mutilations using hot oil or ignited gasoline occur each year, many of which are never reported; if investigated, they are, according to many human rights organizations, officially ruled an accident or suicide.

In June 1871, the United States Marines invaded Kanghwa Do, an island off the coast of Korea. The United States prevailed in the conflict and, in the process, captured over one hundred Korean soldiers. The Marines were shocked when the captured Koreans began to throw themselves into the river and cut their own throats. Those who did not commit suicide began to beg the Marines to kill them rather than return them safely to Korea. For these Korean soldiers, the shame and loss of honor that accompanied their defeat was worse than death. If they died in battle, they would be held in honor in perpetuity by their families, but if they were returned as humiliated captives, their families would never escape the dishonor and shame.[4]

These stories underscore in dramatic fashion the importance of maintaining honor and avoiding the humiliation of public shame in cultures around the world. Anthropologists have consistently observed that the concept of shame and the maintenance of public honor is one of the "pivotal values" outside the West and can be observed in a wide variety of cultures stretching from Morocco in North Africa all the way to Japan in the Far East.[5]

The "shame-based" cultures are often contrasted with what are called "guilt-based" cultures, which are more predominant in the Western world. The purpose of this chapter is to explore this observation made by anthropologists, but from a theological perspective informed by biblical revelation. A few of the key questions that will shape this chapter are as follows: What is the role of guilt versus shame in the formation of human identity? What are the implications of this distinction for our understanding of sin and the application of the work of Christ in our lives? Should a theology of the atonement

3. Syed Kamran Mirza, "Honor Killing—Is It Islamic?" *News from Bangladesh* (July 3, 2005), available at http://bangladesh-web.com/view.php?hidDate=2005-07- 03&hidType=OPT&hidRecord=0000000000000000050641. The names of victims such as Fadime Sahindal, Rim Abu Ganem, Hatin Sürücü, Samaira Nazir, and Mariam Abu Hobzi, who all died tragic deaths, are a few of the more prominent examples who have captured international media attention in recent years. For an excellent study of honor and shame in an Islamic context see Bill A. Musk, *Touching the Soul of Islam* (Crowborough, East Sussex, UK: MARC, 1988, 1995), ch. 4.

4. Lee, "Korean Culture and Sense of Shame," 189.

5. British social anthropologist Julian Pitt-Rivers has written extensively on the role of honor and shame, particularly in the Mediterranean world (see *The People of the Sierra* [Chicago: Univ. of Chicago Press], 1961; "Honour and Shame," in J. G. Peristiany, ed., *Honour and Shame: The Values of Mediterranean Society* [London: Weidenfeld and Nicholson, 1966], 21–77; J. G. Peristiany and J. Pitt-Rivers, *Honour and Grace in Anthropology* [Cambridge: Cambridge Univ. Press, 1992]). Roland Muller has observed that the regions of the world most closely identified as having shame-based cultures roughly corresponds to the more well-known 10/40 window (see *Honor and Shame: Unlocking the Door* [Birmingham, UK: Xlibris, 2000], 18).

be formed differently when articulated within the context of a shame-based culture? However, before any of these questions can be addressed, we need a more careful understanding of what is meant by a shamed-based culture and a guilt-based culture.

GUILT/INNOCENCE AND SHAME/HONOR IN GLOBAL CULTURES

Ruth Benedict was the first anthropologist to categorize Western cultures as guilt-based and Eastern cultures as shame-based. The basic difference, she pointed out, was that "shame cultures rely on external sanctions for good behavior" whereas guilt cultures rely on "an internalized conviction of sin."[6] According to this distinction, shame arises from the pressure of external sanctions formed in the court of human opinion, whereas guilt arises from some internalized value system.

Lyn Bechtel has argued that "shame stimulates fear of psychological or physical rejection (lack of belonging), abandonment, expulsion, or loss of social position and relies predominantly on external pressure from an individual or group." In contrast, "guilt is a response to a transgression against internalized societal or parental prohibitions or against boundaries that form an internal authority, the conscience."[7] Guilt generally follows the transgression of a moral law, particularly a law that has been revealed by divine revelation. Shame generally follows any action perceived by the larger group to reduce one's standing or status within the group. The former represents a loss of innocence; the latter represents a loss of face.

Guilt leaves us with an internal sense of moral failure, even if no one else knows about our transgression. One can sense guilt without the knowledge of "the expressed scorn of other persons."[8] In contrast, shame leaves us with a sense of humiliation, defeat, and ridicule and is intricately tied to our exposure and loss of honor or status before our peers and those in authority within our social network. Shame is not inherently individualistic or private, but corporate and public; it cannot be experienced apart from the larger social context.

More recent research has been less inclined to accept the "internal-external" distinction unless it is acknowledged that in a shame-based context it is not essential that an observer be physically present, since the notion of a real or imaginary observing external audience is often internalized.[9] Nevertheless, the comparative value placed on group identity or individual freedom continues to play an important role in the formation of human identity and in social and ethical guidelines.

Significantly, the last few decades of anthropological research have also demonstrated that no known cultures of the world can be spoken of as *exclusively* guilt-based

6. Benedict, *The Chrysanthemum and the Sword*, 223.

7. Lyn Bechtel, "The Perception of Shame within the Divine-Human Relationship in Biblical Israel," in *Uncovering Ancient Stones*, ed. Lewis M. Hopfe (Winona Lake, IN: Eisenbrauns, 1994), 80.

8. Helen Merrell Lynd, *On Shame and the Search for Identity* (New York: Science Editions, 1961), 21.

9. Millie R. Creighton, "Revisiting Shame and Guilt Cultures: A Forty-Year Pilgrimage," *Ethos* 18, no. 3 (1990): 285. Earlier anthropologists, such as Julian Pitt-Rivers, argued strongly for the necessity of the "presence of witnesses" in any expression of honor and shame; public knowledge was an "essential ingredient." Later anthropologists modified this by pointing out that in shame-based cultures the perceived attitudes and reactions of the group can be internalized and influence behavior and feelings about one's own reputation. See Julian Pitt-Rivers, "Honour and Social Status," in *Honour and Shame: The Values of Mediterranean Society*, ed. J. G. Peristiany, 27.

or shame-based. Virtually every culture in the world contains concepts of both guilt and shame, including the pressure to conform to certain group expectations as well as some kind of internalized ideas about what is right or wrong.[10] The difference is not in the absence of either shame or guilt, but rather in how dominant these tendencies are. Furthermore, anthropologists have distanced themselves from some of the earlier attempts that sought to rank guilt as a superior value to shame within various theories of social evolution. Nevertheless, anthropologists continue to find the terms "conceptually distinguishable" because there is a persistent "cultural variation" in the way guilt and shame function as social mechanisms.[11] The research and accompanying literature on this theme continues to grow and demonstrates that the distinction between shame and guilt remains helpful in understanding certain cultural dynamics.[12]

The emphasis on the distinction between guilt and shame as a way to better understand cultures began to impact Christian missiology with the 1954 publication of Eugene Nida's classic *Customs and Cultures: Anthropology for Christian Missions*, where he proposed a cultural analysis scheme that examines cultures in terms of three different reactions to transgressions: fear-based, shame-based, and guilt-based cultures.[13] Other missiologists (such as Hans Kasdorf, Hannes Wiher, and David Hesselgrave) have popularized these distinctions in their missiological writings.[14]

Asian scholar Young Gweon You makes a convincing case that although these tendencies are found around the world, the shame orientation is particularly dominant in Asia. Using Korea as a model shame-based culture, he cites five major reasons why this orientation has become so dominant.[15] First, Koreans have a strong group orientation and "put high value on the harmonious integration of group members." From the earliest age one's identity and self-concept is shaped and formed within a strong reference to the larger views and needs of the group (family, clan, and lineage) to which the person belongs. The needs of the group take priority over the needs of the individual.

Second, family dynamics in Korea emphasize the importance of providing an "external authority which is present in every sphere of life." There is less emphasis on internalizing standards of conduct because the ubiquitous presence of family members embodies that authority. Children look to their parents and elders for counsel and

10. The presence of guilt and shame in all cultural systems also dispels the attempts of early anthropologists to place a value judgment on either shame or guilt as a more effective motivator for guiding ethical behavior, since the two values, though distinct, are inseparably linked to the other.

11. Takie Sugiyama Lebra, "The Social Mechanism of Guilt and Shame: The Japanese Case," *Anthropological Quarterly* 44, no. 4 (October 1971): 242.

12. Anthropologists such as J. Pitt-Rivers in *The People of the Sierrra* (quoted above) and Douglas Haring advanced the distinction considerably in the 1950s and 1960s. By the 1990s the distinction persisted, but has been rearticulated along the lines noted in this chapter. See, for example, Lee, "Korean Culture and Sense of Shame, 181–94," and Millie Creighton (see footnote 9). Compare with the earlier research of Douglas Haring, *Personal Character and Cultural Milieu* (Syracuse, NY: Syracuse Univ. Press, 1956).

13. Eugene A. Nida, *Customs and Cultures: Anthropology for Christian Missions* (Pasadena, CA: William Carey Library, 1954), 150.

14. See Hans Kasdorf, *Christian Conversion in Context* (Scottdale, PA: Herald, 1980), 111–15; David J. Hesselgrave, "Missionary Elenctics and Guilt and Shame," *Missiology* 11, no. 4 (October 1983): 461–83; Hannes Wiher, *Shame and Guilt: A Key to Cross-Cultural Ministry* (Bonn, Germany: Culture and Science, 2003).

15. The five points and the quotations are taken from Young Gweon You, "Shame and Guilt Mechanisms in East Asian Culture," *Journal of Pastoral Care* 51, no. 1 (Spring 1997): 58–61.

guidance, and they experience shame if they fail to meet the obligations expected of them by members of the family.

Third, ancestor veneration (which is reinforced by Confucian ideals) further reinforces the presence of the group, rather than an internalized code of divine law that establishes the rules of proper behavior.

Fourth, Koreans strongly emphasize the importance of maintaining the social status of the group. Any action perceived by the group as bringing disrepute to their social ranking causes them to "lose face" and is a source of great shame. Koreans frequently use expressions such as "saving one's face," "losing one's face," and "maintaining one's face." These expressions refer to the importance of maintaining the honor of the group and avoiding a situation that might bring shame to the larger collective.

Finally, the entire social matrix of Korean culture emphasizes the importance of maintaining the balance in reciprocal obligations. It is expected that in all social interactions there should be a mutual balance between "rights and duties, social assets and liabilities, dept and payment, give and take." When this balance collapses because reciprocity either is ignored or becomes impossible to fulfill, a heightened sense of shame is experienced.

While You uses Korea as a case study, these five dynamics could be applied to much of Asia; moreover, with the exception of his emphasis on ancestor veneration and the lack of a divine code in East Asia, they have also been broadly observed throughout the Islamic world.[16] These observations about the social dynamics that produce a shame-based culture are in contrast to the Western emphasis on individual autonomy. Throughout the social structures of Western societies, individual achievement is rewarded and "standing out" is valued over "blending in." Our culture is full of various proverbs, such as "different strokes for different folks" and "beauty is in the eye of the beholder," which underscore the value of individualism and personal choices and judgments. Even the United States Army, arguably an institution with the greatest need for group coordination and deference to leaders, has used surprisingly individualistic slogans, such as "Be all you can be" and the current slogan, "An Army of One." Contrast this with the well-known Japanese proverb, "The nail that sticks up gets hammered down."

In the West, independence, even from an early age, is valued over interdependence. In a highly individualistic culture the ethical values and social mores of the larger society must be reinforced through a process of internalizing codes of conduct so that the reference point is more internal and personal rather than external and public. Parents teach children what is right and wrong and expect that the internalization of those principles and guidelines will serve as a reference point throughout life. Shame-based cultures rely heavily on "public opinion, outward appearances and group pressure to enforce its norms."[17] While these reference points are also present in the West, they are outweighed by the emphasis on individualism and the early development of an internalized sense of

16. Roland Muller, who has spent much of his adult life living in the Islamic world, argues that the emphasis on honor and shame is one of the central values observed throughout the Islamic world. See his *Honor and Shame*; also Musk, *Touching the Soul of Islam*.

17. Bechtel, "The Perception of Shame," 81.

responsibility for one's own actions. E. R. Dodds argues that this is rooted in a change that took place in Graeco-Roman civilization where, to use his words, "'you will do it because I say so' gives place to 'you will do it because it is right.'"[18]

Now that Christianity has emerged as a truly global faith and the majority of Christians are located outside the West, we can no longer afford to ignore the discussion of how the traditional understanding of human sin, our guilt before God as sinners, and the redemptive work of Christ on the cross might be best understood and expressed in a shame-based context. This is an important intersection between anthropology and theology that requires further reflection. Our study will fall into three major sections. First, we will begin by exploring whether the concepts of shame and guilt as outlined above are reflected in the Scriptures themselves. Second, we will seek to apply our findings to systematic theology and determine whether our deepened understanding of human identity in a shame-based culture should influence how we understand and talk about the atonement. Finally, we will seek to demonstrate how the twin values of innocence/guilt and honor/shame relate to one another in positive, constructive ways.

GUILT AND SHAME IN THE SCRIPTURES

The emphasis on guilt in the Western world is often attributed to the presence of Christianity. The overarching authority of the Scriptures and the clear ethical guidelines set forth there, coupled with the judicial language associated with the doctrine of justification, have all helped to emphasize the legal aspect of salvation. Guilt and its corollary, innocence, are essentially legal concepts. As sinners, we have broken God's laws, and the good news of the gospel declares that we have been justified through Christ's atoning work on the cross. Christ paid the penalty for us so that when we stand at the bar of God's judgment seat, we who deserve his condemnation are declared "not guilty."

Popular expositions of the "plan of salvation" such as the Roman Road and the Four Spiritual Laws all emphasize personal guilt and the need for an individual decision to receive Christ as one's personal Lord and Savior.[19] These basic explanations of the gospel have been very fruitful, and I am grateful for the wonderful way God has used both of these plans in personal evangelism. Both of them are based on scriptural passages and are simple enough for any believer to use. The question is whether this basic approach is adequate for evangelism in the Majority World and whether the gospel story can also be approached from a shame perspective, while yet remaining fully scriptural. To answer this question we must explore the biblical evidence for the concept of shame, beginning with the very earliest reference to the entrance of sin into the world, as recorded in Genesis 3.

18. E. R. Dodds, *The Greeks and the Irrational* (Berkeley: Univ. of California Press, 1951), 48.

19. The Roman Road refers to a simple explanation of the basic gospel message using texts from Paul's letter to the Romans (using Romans 3:10; 3:23; 6:23; 10:9; and 10:13). *The Four Spiritual Laws* is the popular four-step plan of salvation developed by Bill Bright for the Campus Crusade for Christ. According to Campus Crusade for Christ, *The Four Spiritual Laws* is the most popular tool for personal evangelism in history, currently exceeding 1.5 billion copies.

Biblical Evidence for Honor and Shame in the Old Testament

The Legacy of the Fall: Guilt, Shame, and Fear

In Genesis 2:16 we read that God gave to Adam an explicit command to "not eat from the tree of the knowledge of good and evil." This command was coupled with a clear warning of divine sanction should he disobey: "for when you eat of it you will surely die." According to Genesis 3:6 Adam and Eve disobeyed God by eating the fruit from the forbidden tree. The description that follows demonstrates several consequences of sin, including feelings of guilt, shame, and fear. Adam and Eve knew that they had transgressed an explicit command of God. When challenged by the serpent, Eve was able to recount the command, even though it had been given to Adam before she was created.[20] It is clear that both Adam and Eve had internalized the command. Once they disobeyed, Adam and Eve felt guilt because they knew that they had transgressed God's command.

However, Adam and Eve not only experienced guilt, they also felt shame, as indicated by the realization of their nakedness and their attempts to hide from God. Before the fall, the text had declared, "the man and his wife were both naked, and they felt no shame [בּוֹשׁ]" (Gen. 2:25). After the fall, the man and woman "realized they were naked ... and made coverings for themselves" (3:7) and tried to hide from the Lord (3:8).

Finally, when God called to them, we have the first reference in the Bible to fear; Adam said to God, "I heard you in the garden, and I was afraid" (3:10). The account emphasizes guilt, shame, and fear as three of the consequences of the entrance of sin into the world, and all three can be traced throughout the Scriptures.

This chapter assumes that the reader is acquainted with the emphasis on guilt and divine acquittal or condemnation in the Scriptures, for this well-attested biblical theme has become an integral part of the Western theological tradition. Both the Old and the New Testaments use legal language and even draw on the imagery of a court case and trial to reinforce the idea that sin makes us personally guilty before God and that we will be held legally accountable for our actions.[21] While affirming the importance of the guilt/innocence (or guilt/forgiveness) emphasis in Scripture and the legal aspects of redemption, recent biblical scholarship has also increasingly recognized the importance of understanding shame/honor as a distinctive category from guilt/innocence.

Terms and Examples of Honor and Shame in the Old Testament

The Old Testament contains at least ten different words, occurring nearly three hundred times, to convey various aspects of shame. These words include "to shame"

20. Eve's recounting of the prohibition differs only slightly from the original. For example, there is no indication in the original prohibition about touching the fruit, only not eating it. We are left to assume that Adam recounted the prohibition to Eve, although it is possible that God also told Eve this command and it is simply not recorded in the text. The main point is that it is clear that Eve understands the command and has internalized it.

21. See, for example, the dramatic example of the Lord bringing Israel to court, calling the earth itself as a witness and declaring Israel guilty of breaking the covenant (Mic. 6).

(בוש);[22] "scorn, insult, reproach or disgrace" (החפה);[23] "to publicly humiliate/afflict" (ענה);[24] "to be slighted" or "to have no honor or weight" (קלה);[25] "to expose nakedness or make naked" (ערה);[26] "to be insulted, put to shame, chide" (כלם),[27] among others.[28] These words are often contrasted with the idea of honor (כבד), which, with its various cognates, occurs more than one hundred times.

Lyn Bechtel's "The Perception of Shame within the Divine-Human Relationship in Biblical Israel" is one among many studies that have demonstrated the role of shame and honor in the Old Testament.[29] Bechtel points out that part of God's covenantal agreement with Israel was to shame her enemies and to protect his covenantal people from being shamed. The psalmist frequently asks God to shame his enemies: for example: "May all who seek to take my life be put to shame and confusion.... May those who say to me, 'Aha! Aha!' be appalled at their own shame" (Ps. 40:14–15).[30] The psalmist worships Yahweh for shaming Israel's enemies: "He beat back his enemies; he put them to everlasting shame" (Ps. 78:66). Yahweh even shames other gods when their followers claim their god had a position of higher rank, power, or status than Yahweh.

The public shaming of other gods was also common in the ancient world. Assyria, for example, often captured the idols of opposing nations and "set them in a public place in a position of submission before the Assyrian high god, Ashur."[31] The entire ritual was designed to emphasize the honor of the superior god and to expose to public shame the vanquished god as a sign of inferiority.

---

22. Root, "to blush, to come to shame"; in Hiphil form, "to act shamefully, cover in shame" (Ps. 89:45) or "put to shame/humiliate" (2 Sam. 19:5). See Benjamin Davies, *Hebrew and Chaldee Lexicon* (Boston: Bradley & Co., 1879), 83 (hereafter referred to as *HCL*). See also בשנה ("ashamed," Hos. 10:6); see L. H. Koehler, W. Baumgartner, and J. J. Stamm, *The Hebrew and Aramaic Lexicon of the Old Testament*, trans. and ed. M. E. J. Richardson, 5 vols. (Leiden: Brill, 1994–1999), 117. Hereafter referred to as *HALOT*.

23. For example, Gen. 34:14 (for an Israelite to give his sister to the uncircumcised for marriage causes shame and reproach); Ps. 15:3 (a righteous man does not shame his neighbor); 22:6 ("I am a worm, not a man, scorned by men and despised by the people," foreshadowing Jesus' shame on the cross); 69:6–9 (the psalmist does not want to bring shame to the people of God, nor does he want his enemies' shame to fall on him). See *HCL*, 233; *HALOT*, 356.

24. See, for example, Deut. 26:6, where it is used to describe the Egyptian humiliation of the Hebrew slaves. See *HCL*, 82–83, especially in the Piel; *HALOT*, 853.

25. To be honored is to have "weight" (כבד), so to be dishonored is to be "light" (קלה). In its Piel construction it carries the idea of honor. Thus, to be considered "light" is to have no honor (Job 16:10; Ps. 15:3; 22:6; 69:7, 10). See F. Brown, S. R. Driver, C. A. Briggs, ed., *A Hebrew and English Lexicon of the Old Testament*, trans. E. Robinson (Oxford: Clarendon, 1957 [1907]), 457 (hereafter BDB). In the Niphal form it can mean "to be slighted or despised"; in the Hiphil, "to hold despicable." See *HCL*, 561–62; *HALOT*, 1102, "to shame."

26. Gamberoni provides an excellent discussion on the extended and figurative meaning of being clothed (לבש) and unclothed. See Johannes Botterweck, Helmer Ringgren and Heinz-Josef Fabry, eds., *Theological Dictionary of the Old Testament* (Grand Rapids: Eerdmans, 1995), 7:461–68. See also *HCL*, 490–91 in Piel, Hiphil, and Hithpael forms (Lev. 20:18–21; Lam. 4:21); *HALOT*, 882.

27. *HCL*, 297–98. In Niphal "to be insulted," as when Hanun shaved off half the beards and cut off the clothing of David's delegation (2 Sam. 10:5). In Hiphil, הכלים means "to reproach" (Job 19:3); "to put to shame" (Ps. 44:9); "to put on shame as a garment" (Ps. 109:29). See also *HALOT*, 480.

28. There are many positive words that, when negated or used in special constructions, are translated as "shame." For example, הלל ("shine, bright," in Piel, "to sing praises") in the Pual can be used in negation as "to put to shame" (Job 12:17).

29. Bechtel, "The Perception of Shame," 79–92. See also Gary Stansell, "Honor and Shame in the David Narratives," *Semeia* 68 (1994): 55–79; Ronald Simkins, "Return to Yahweh: Honor and Shame in Joel," *Semeia* 68 (1994): 41–54; idem, "Honor and Shame in Genesis 34 and 1 Samuel 25," in *Teaching the Bible*, ed. Mark Roncace and Patrick Gray (Leiden: Brill, 2005), 104–6; Dianne Bergant, 'My Beloved Is Mine and I Am His' (Song 2:16): The Song of Songs and Honor and Shame," *Semeia* 68 (1994): 23–40.

30. See also Ps. 6:10; 53:5; 57:3; 70:2; 71:13, 24; 78:66; 83:16–17; 109:28–29.

31. Bechtel, "The Perception of Shame," 89.

When the ark of the covenant was captured by the Philistines and brought into the temple of Dagon, it was a deliberate act intending to shame and humiliate Yahweh and all Israel. In reply, Yahweh shamed Dagon by causing him to lie prostrate and face down, bowing before Yahweh. The Philistines set Dagon back in his place, but the next morning they discovered Dagon "fallen on his face on the ground before the ark of the LORD! His head and hands had been broken off and were lying on the threshold" (1 Sam. 5:3–4). Dagon's head and hands were cut off because "the head was a symbol of superiority and the palms of the hands a symbol of physical power."[32] To lose one's head is the ultimate humiliation and shame, and to lose one's hands is a sign of the loss of power.[33]

According to 2 Kings 18, Sennacherib's delegation, sent to force Israel's surrender, publicly taunted Yahweh in the hearing of the people and declared that Israel's god had no more power to deliver them than the gods of the other vanquished nations (18:33–35). In reply, Hezekiah cried out to Yahweh saying, "Give ear, O LORD, and hear; open your eyes, O LORD, and see; listen to the words Sennacherib has sent to insult/shame/reproach [חרף] the living God" (19:16). When Yahweh defended his honor by annihilating the Assyrian forces, the Assyrian king "withdrew to his own land in disgrace" and was murdered by his own sons in the temple of his god (2 Chron. 32:21). The whole account is couched in the language of honor and shame. Assyria sought to shame Yahweh, but God's power and greatness was vindicated; therefore his public honor and reputation were upheld and Assyria was publicly shamed.

In the prophetic tradition, Zion's future glory is characterized as the end of shame and the joy of being honored by Yahweh. For example, Isaiah declares, "Do not be afraid; you will not suffer shame. Do not fear disgrace; you will not be humiliated. You will forget the shame of your youth and remember no more the reproach of your widowhood" (Isa. 54:4).

Another important feature of shame and honor, which can be traced back to the account of the fall in Genesis, is the association of nakedness with shame and the corresponding association of clothing with honor. Jacob honored Joseph by clothing him with the richly ornamented robe (Gen. 37:3). Yahweh honored the priestly office by giving the priests elaborately embroidered garments (Ex. 28:1–43). In Esther, when King Xerxes asked his official Haman what should be done to honor someone who delights the king, Haman answered that he should be clothed with the king's royal robe. Haman foolishly thought he was the one the king was going to honor, but he ended up being publicly shamed by having to put the king's robe on his Jewish enemy, Mordecai, and then placing him on a horse and leading him through the city proclaiming, "This is what is done for the man the king delights to honor" (Est. 6:11).

---

32. Ibid., 92.

33. This also helps to explain why terrorists who are up against a vastly superior military power will sometimes resort to kidnappings, followed by publicly (via television) beheading the person. It is intended to publicly shame the greater power. This is also why even a military defeat can be regarded as a victory, as long as it is publicly understood that the defeat was in the cause of defending the honor of the country.

This custom explains why the prophets portray God as wearing a great robe. When Isaiah saw the Lord on a high throne, "the train of his robe filled the temple" (Isa. 6:1). To express public shame and humiliation in the Old Testament, people tore their clothes (Gen. 37:34; 44:13; Num. 14:6; Josh. 7:6; 2 Sam. 13:31; 2 Kings 22:11).

King David's wife Michal misinterpreted David's disrobing himself and dancing before the Lord as an act of public shame. However, David's reply indicates that he did not view it as shameful since it was done "before the LORD" (see 2 Sam. 6:20–22), whose honor is beyond challenge. If, however, David had disrobed himself and danced primarily before the public (which is how Michal interpreted it), that would have, indeed, brought shame to David's public reputation. Many other examples from the Old Testament could be shown to demonstrate that public, external shame is a distinct category from guilt.[34]

Biblical Evidence for Honor and Shame in the New Testament

The Gospels

In the first century, Greeks, Romans, and Jews all highly valued public honor and status. Likewise, the avoidance of public shame was crucial. Honor was frequently attached to one's birth, family name, appointment to an important office, physical prowess, or military success. But the most common way to acquire honor was "in the face-to-face game of challenge and riposte," which was an integral part of daily life.[35] If the honor of one's name or family was offended, it was accepted that such honor could be restored only through the shedding of blood.

According to anthropologist Julian Pitt-Rivers, honor "provides a nexus between the ideals of a society and their reproduction in the individual through his [or her] aspiration to personify them."[36] In the ancient world honor was tied to the physical body, which was understood as a microcosm of the larger social context. The head and face were the most honorable parts of the body, and a person was thereby honored by being crowned. In contrast, to slap someone in the face or spit on someone's face brought shame. The less honorable parts of the body, such as genitals and buttocks, must be clothed if one's honor is to be preserved.[37]

In recent years New Testament studies have benefited from biblical scholars who have highlighted the role of honor and shame in the Scriptures. Bruce Malina's *The New Testament World: Insights from Cultural Anthropology* and Jerome Neyrey's *Honor and Shame in the Gospel of Matthew* are excellent examples of how the cultural associations of honor and shame in the Mediterranean world play an important part in understanding the New Testament. In the New Testament, as well as in the LXX, the most prominent

34. When Absalom slept with King David's concubines "in the sight of all Israel," the text does not emphasize his guilt because of unlawful sexual intercourse, but the way this act publicly shamed his father (2 Sam. 12:11; 16:21–22). When the Ammonites wanted to humiliate David, they seized David's men and "shaved off half of each man's beard, cut off their garments in the middle of the buttocks, and sent them away" (2 Sam. 10:4). These are all illustrative more of honor/shame than guilt/innocence.

35. Jerome H. Neyrey, "Despising the Shame of the Cross: Honor and Shame in the Johannine Passion Narrative," *Semeia* 68 (1994): 116.

36. Pitt-Rivers, "Honour and Social Status," 22.

37. Ibid., 116–17. See also Mary Douglas, *Purity and Danger: An Analysis of the Concepts of Pollution and Taboo* (London: Routledge & Kegan Paul, 1966), 115.

word for "shame" is αἰσχύνη.[38] There are six other Greek roots that are often translated as shame, including ἀτιμία ("dishonor, lacking honor, disgrace") and the verb ἐντρέπω ("to shame, show no honor").

To honor (τιμάω) someone is to give them public recognition, whereas to shame (αἰσχύνω) someone means a loss of respect or reputation and often involves some kind of public censure. Neyrey argues that many of the parables cannot be properly understood apart from notions of public shame, which are quite different from judicial or internalized conceptions of guilt.[39] For example, Jesus employs the social usage of someone experiencing shame in the parable of the dishonest, but shrewd, manager, who acknowledges that he is too ashamed (αἰσχύνω) to beg (Luke 16:3), or the person takes the seat of honor at a wedding feast only to be asked to suffer the humiliation and public shame of being moved to the lowest place because a more distinguished guest has arrived (Luke 14:7–11).

This latter passage is particularly significant because Jesus deliberately contrasts the two values of shame and honor in his exposition of the parable. In a powerful foreshadowing of the cross, Jesus tells his disciples to act like servants and take the lowliest seat in the house, and then, when the host arrives, he will publicly show honor by moving them to a higher place. Then, Jesus concludes, "you will be honored [lit., there will be glory, δόξα, to you] in the presence of all your fellow guests" (Luke 14:10).

One of the best illustrations of the dynamics of shame and honor in the parables of Jesus is found in the parable of the two sons asked by their father to work in the vineyard (Matt. 21:28–32). The first adamantly refused, but later changed his mind and went. The second son agreed to work, but never actually did. Most Western readers do not sense the real tension in the story. Certainly the first son, who refused to work but eventually did, is being honored by Jesus and compared with the tax collectors and sinners who initially refused to honor God, but were now repenting and entering the kingdom. Western readers find Jesus' question patently obvious and the whole construction seems to lack the tension that is so often present in parables.

However, the tension of this parable is felt when heard within the context of a shame-based culture. From an honor and shame perspective, the son who publicly agreed to work is actually better than the son who publicly shamed his father by refusing to work and telling him that to his face. Even though the one who refused to work later changed his mind and worked while the former never actually obeyed the father, the public shaming of the father is still a greater sin than not performing the task.[40] The first son may have eventually obeyed the father, but the father lost face. The second son may have not obeyed the father, but he protected the father's public honor.

In the teaching of Jesus, both guilt and shame play important roles in understanding how we are affected by sin. Conversely, both forgiveness and honor occupy central roles in understanding the nature of God's gracious work in our lives. The parable of

38. In the LXX it is used most often to translate the verb בוש ("to be ashamed") and the noun בשׁת ("shame").

39. Jerome H. Neyrey, *Honor and Shame in the Gospel of Matthew* (Louisville, KY: Westminster John Knox, 1998). See, for example, the man without the wedding garment (Matt. 22:11–15), the wicked servant (24:51), or the unprepared virgins (25:12).

40. Ibid., 31.

the prodigal son is not only about the son's receiving forgiveness for his incurred guilt (Luke 15:18, 21), but also about his shame being taken away and his being restored to a place of honor as a son. The son sought forgiveness for his guilt by confessing his sin and asking to be made like a hired servant. The father could have forgiven his son, cleansed him of any guilt, and then made him like one of his hired servants. However, the father not only forgave him for his sins, but also restored him to the place of honor as a son by kissing his face (15:20), clothing him with a robe, and putting a ring on his finger and sandals on his feet (15:22). He honored him further by ordering that the fattened calf be killed and a great celebration be held in his son's honor (15:23). The text does not indicate that the older son was angry because the father forgave his younger brother. The actual wording of the text makes it clear that he was angry because his younger brother had been shown honor, despite his having brought shame on the family, while he who had never brought shame on the family had never been so honored (15:28–31).

Pauline Usage

The apostle Paul uses the term *shame* in the broad, common sense of the word when he shames the Corinthians for having people in their midst who are apparently ignorant of the gospel. Paul declares, "I say this to your shame [ἐντροπή]" (1 Cor. 15:34). He even encourages the Thessalonians (2 Thess. 3:14) to not associate with those who refuse to obey his instruction, "that he may feel ashamed [ἐντρέπω]."

The verb καταισχύνω conveys the action "to shame, to bring to shame." In its most common usage, God acts as the subject in bringing shame through his righteous judgment.[41] Paul understands the incarnation as the way in which God shames the unbelieving world by demonstrating the wisdom of his "foolishness" and the strength of his "weakness." First Corinthians 1:27 declares that God chooses the foolish things of this world in order to shame the wise. He takes the weak things of this world in order to shame the strong. The incarnation sets God's "great reversal" into motion: those who are first (the place of honor) will be last (the place of shame), and those who are last will be made first (cf. Matt. 20:16). The "great reversal" continues at the cross. At the very hour of Jesus' public shame on the cross, he was actually in the process of shaming his enemies, disarming the powers and authorities and making "a public spectacle of them, triumphing over them by the cross" (Col. 2:15). With these new eschatological realities breaking in on the present order, the only remaining "glory" (δόξα) of the world, Paul declares, "is in their shame [αἰσχύνη]" (Phil. 3:19).[42]

It is with some irony that these words to the Philippians were written by Paul while in prison. Paul recognizes that his current position as a prisoner of Rome will be perceived by the social world of the first century as shameful. But he anticipates his deliverance and, in Philippians 1:20, he expresses his hope that he "will in no way be ashamed [αἰσχύνω]." First-century Christians were seen to share in the same shame as those captured in Roman military campaigns and paraded through the streets and exposed

41. Gerhard Kittel, ed., *Theological Dictionary of the New Testament*, trans. G. F. Bromiley (Grand Rapids: Eerdmans, 1964), 1:189.

42. Jude 1:13 describes the rebellious world as "wild waves of the sea, foaming up their shame [αἰσχύνη]."

to public humiliation. However, Paul declares that before God we are actually being "led in triumphal procession in Christ" (2 Cor. 2:14) and what appears to be the "smell of death" is actually the "fragrance of life" (2 Cor. 2:16). Likewise, the apostle John, despite his current trials and public exile, anticipates the day when Christ appears and we will "be confident and unashamed [μὴ αἰσχυνθῶμεν] before him" (1 John 2:28). When Paul and John speak of not being ashamed or of being unashamed, they mean something far more significant than a vague notion of not being embarrassed by the gospel (2 Tim. 1:8; 1:12). They realize that in the present age the gospel appears shameful because they worship a crucified Savior (1 Cor. 1:18) and they are being persecuted and imprisoned (2 Tim 1:16). However, Paul confidently declares, "I am not ashamed (ἐπαισχύνομαι of the gospel" (Rom 1:16). For him, this is an eschatological statement that Jesus has already borne our future penalty and our shame, and that the future glory and honor of our state is already being celebrated in the midst of the present evil age.

Theology of the Cross in a Shame-Based Context

From this biblical study, we can now focus on how people from shame-based cultures might understand the atonement differently than the classical Western formulations. Therefore, we must now return to the Gospels and reflect on the dynamics of guilt and shame in the crucifixion of Christ and within the larger context of the passion.

One of the opening scenes in Christ's passion is his arrest in the Garden of Gethsemane. A capture and arrest is an obvious form of public shaming and loss of honor. Interestingly, the text in various ways underscores that even though Jesus accepted this shame, it did not involve an *actual* loss of honor. Jesus stands up and exhibits control of the situation, giving directions to the Roman soldiers (John 18:8), acknowledging that this arrest took place to fulfill Scripture (Matt. 26:54, 56), healing the man's ear (Luke 22:51), and even causing the soldiers to draw back and fall to the ground while Jesus remained standing (John 18:5).

The arrest is followed by a Roman trial. A trial is a classic challenge to someone's honor since it is so closely involved with all the key elements of honor, such as one's name and reputation in the community. In the ancient world there was no legal presumption of innocence until proved guilty (John 18:30). Nevertheless, Jesus' trial has a clear forensic element whereby charges are brought forward, the accused is given the opportunity to respond, and the interrogator evaluates the two arguments. The trial and public flogging of Jesus contains a rich deposit of material that plays heavily on the ideas of rank and honor, challenge and riposte, especially in the interchange about Jesus' title ("King of the Jews"), the reference to his kingdom being from "another place," and his statement, "everyone on the side of truth listens to me" (John 18:33, 36–38).[43]

A crucifixion involves several parts, including the scourge, carrying the beam to the place of execution and, finally, the agonizingly slow death after being impaled on the beams. The scourge has all the elements of public shaming that we have examined

43. For a more detailed examination of this, see Neyrey, "Despising the Shame of the Cross: Honor and Shame in the Johannine Passion Narrative," 118–32. See also Martin Hengel, *Crucifixion in the Ancient World* (Philadelphia: Fortress, 1977).

so far. Jesus is stripped naked, his hands are bound, and he is publicly beaten, including spitting and repeatedly striking the head (Matt. 27:30). All the features of honor are brought forward in a mock coronation ritual ceremony, adding to the humiliation and shame. Jesus is given a crown of thorns for his head, a purple robe to wear, they shout "Hail, king of the Jews" as they strike him (27:29), and they mockingly bend their knees and bow to him. Everything is done to maximize the shame.

The act of carrying one's own beam to the place of execution is a form of shaming, especially since it is carried publicly through the streets and the criminal is taunted along the way by the crowds. The Scriptures emphasize that Jesus is forced to carry the cross (John 19:17), and considerable attention is given to the fact that he is publicly mocked and taunted by several different groups of people (Matt. 27:38–43; Mark 15:27–32; Luke 23:35–39). Ancient crucifixions took place in public (John 19:20), which increased the shame because the criminal was nailed to the beam and exposed naked. This is emphasized in the scriptural account, which records that Jesus is nailed to the cross and placed between two criminals. Then the soldiers take his clothes, possibly even his undergarments, and divide them among one another (John 19:23), an act explicitly mentioned as a fulfillment of Psalm 22. We should recall that the vocabulary of shame is integral to Psalm 22, which foreshadows his humiliation:

> They cried to you and were saved;
> in you they trusted and were not disappointed [בּוֹשׁ, shamed].
> But I am a worm and not a man,
> scorned [חרפּת] by men and despised [בזה] by the people.
> All who see me mock me [לעג];
> they hurl insults, shaking their heads....
> Dogs have surrounded me;
> a band of evil men has encircled me,
> they have pierced my hands and my feet.
> I can count all my bones;
> people stare and gloat over me.
> They divide my garments among them
> and cast lots for my clothing. (Ps. 22:5–7, 16–18)

As noted earlier, all the Gospel writers portray the full shame of Jesus' passion, but find subtle ways to make it clear that even in the midst of his public shaming, Jesus was, in fact, a person of the greatest honor. John is the most explicit as he records that even while on the cross Jesus demonstrated his true honor. He records Jesus' fulfilling one of the most important duties in a shame-based culture, namely, the responsibility of the eldest son to care for his mother. So, in the midst of Jesus' being publicly shamed, he makes the honorable arrangements with John to care for his mother, a provision that also serves to shield his mother from shame and to preserve her honor (John 19:27).[44]

44. Neyrey, "Despising the Shame of the Cross: Honor and Shame in the Johannine Passion Narrative," 131.

John is also the one who prepares the reader by placing the account of this public, seemingly ignominious, death of Jesus in perspective by recording Jesus' words about his life prior to the passion: "No one takes it from me, but I lay it down of my own accord. I have authority to lay it down and authority to take it up again" (10:18).

The resurrection is, of course, the great vindication that he who had been treated so shamefully was, in fact, the eternal Son of God and has been "crowned with glory and honor" (Heb. 2:9). The resurrection overturns the shame, and Jesus is restored to his former position of honor at the Father's right hand. The book of Revelation repeatedly uses the language of honor to describe Jesus Christ (Rev. 4:9, 11; 5:11–12; 7:12), finally culminating in all the glory and honor of the nations being brought to Jesus Christ in the new Jerusalem (21:25).

Even this cursory overview of the passion has demonstrated that crucifixion was deliberately designed to maximize the public shame along with the execution. In the cross Jesus bore the shame of our sins as well as our guilt. A mere execution would have atoned for guilt, but not for the shame. As sinners, the most profound shame is that of being publicly separated and judged by God. Jesus bears this judgment throughout his passion and death. Through his resurrection, we have victory not only over the condemnation we deserve at the bar of God's justice, but also the public shame of being disgraced before the world as those who are under God's curse. The author of Hebrews tells us that Jesus "endured the cross, scorning its shame [αἰσχύνη], and sat down at the right hand of the throne of God" (Heb. 12:2).

Jesus bore our shame as well as our guilt. Undoubtedly, his death accomplished a forensic act such that we who had been declared "guilty" are now declared "not guilty." The forensic aspect of the cross is clearly taught in the New Testament, particularly in Paul's letters. But the cross was also a public, social deliverance. Just as the Hebrew slaves publicly shamed Pharaoh and his mighty army when they crossed the Red Sea, so the cross of Christ was a public shaming of Satan and the principalities and powers allied with him. Satan was publicly shamed by Christ when the Lord Jesus "disarmed the powers and authorities" and "made a public spectacle of them, triumphing over them by the cross" (Col. 2:15). Through the resurrection, we who were the bearers of guilt and shame are now declared to be the recipients of justification and honor. Jesus now sits in honor, exalted at the right hand of God the Father.

Implications for Systematic Theology and Our Understanding of the Atonement

The second part of this study seeks to apply these biblical reflections to systematic theology and determine whether our deepened understanding of human identity in a shame-based culture should influence how we understand and talk about the atonement. Since Western systematic theology has been almost exclusively written by theologians from cultures framed primarily by the values of guilt and innocence, there has been a corresponding failure to fully appreciate the importance of the pivotal values of honor and shame in understanding Scripture and the doctrine of sin. Even with the publication of important works such as *Biblical Social Values and Their*

Meaning and *The New Testament World*, systematic theologies have remained largely unchanged by this research.[45]

Bruce Nicholls, the founder of the *Evangelical Review of Theology*, has acknowledged this problem, noting that Christian theologians have "rarely if ever stressed salvation as honoring God, exposure of sin as shame, and the need for acceptance and the restoration of honor."[46] In fact, a survey of all of the leading textbooks used in teaching systematic theology across the major theological traditions reveals that although the indexes are filled with references to guilt, the word "shame" appears in the index of only one of these textbooks.[47] This omission continues to persist despite the fact that the term *guilt* and its various derivatives occur 145 times in the Old Testament and 10 times in the New Testament, whereas the term *shame* and its derivatives occur nearly 300 times in the Old Testament and 45 times in the New Testament.[48]

This is clearly an area where systematic theology must be challenged to reflect more adequately the testimony of Scripture. I am confident that a more biblical understanding of human identity outside of Christ that is framed by guilt, fear, *and* shame will, in turn, stimulate a more profound and comprehensive appreciation for the work of Christ on the cross. This approach will also greatly help peoples in the Majority World to understand the significance and power of Christ's work, which has heretofore been told primarily from only one perspective.

Traditional Understandings of the Atonement

I have chosen the atonement as the application of this study on anthropology because, for the Christian, the work of Christ on the cross is the most fundamental place where our new identity is formed. In Adam we became identified with guilt, fear, and shame. In Christ we are now identified with forgiveness, confidence, and honor. The apostle Paul uses the expression "in Christ" or close equivalents (e.g., "in him") 165 times in his letters. He declares, "I have been crucified with Christ and I no longer live, but Christ lives in me" (Gal. 2:20). For Paul the cross is the place where our new identity is formed; it is the great intersection between anthropology and theology.

---

45. See Joseph Plevnik, "Honor/Shame," in John J. Pilch and Bruce J. Malina, eds., *Biblical Social Values and Their Meaning* (Peabody, MA: Hendrickson, 1993), 95–104. See also chapter 2 of Bruce Malina, *The New Testament World: Insights from Cultural Anthropology* (Louisville, KY: Westminster John Knox, 1993), 28–62.

45. See Joseph Plevnik, "Honor/Shame," in John J. Pilch and Bruce J. Malina, eds., *Biblical Social Values and Their Meaning* (Peabody, MA: Hendrickson, 1993), 95–104. See also chapter 2 of Bruce Malina, *The New Testament World: Insights from Cultural Anthropology* (Louisville, KY: Westminster John Knox, 1993), 28–62.

46. Bruce Nicholls, "The Role of Shame and Guilt in a Theology of Cross-Cultural Mission," *Evangelical Review of Theology* 25, no. 3 (2001): 232.

47. See L. Berkhof, *Systematic Theology* (Grand Rapids: Eerdmans, 1941); Henry Thiessen, *Lectures in Systematic Theology*, rev. ed. (Grand Rapids: Eerdmans, 1977); Alan Gomes, ed., *Dogmatic Theology by William G. T. Shedd*, 3rd ed. (Phillipsburg, NJ: Presbyterian & Reformed, 2003); Helmut Thielicke, *The Evangelical Faith* (Grand Rapids: Eerdmans, 1974); Wolfhart Pannenberg, *Systematic Theology*, vols. 1–3 (Grand Rapids: Eerdmans, 1991–1997); Millard J. Erickson, *Christian Theology*, 2nd ed. (Grand Rapids: Baker, 1998); James Leo Garrett Jr., *Systematic Theology: Biblical, Historical and Evangelical*, 2 vols. (Grand Rapids: Eerdmans, 1990–1995); Wayne Grudem, *Systematic Theology* (Grand Rapids: Zondervan, 1994). The only systematic theology I found with a reference to shame is a single line in volume 3 of Norman Geisler's *Systematic Theology* (Minneapolis: Bethany, 2002–), which acknowledges that Adam's sin "brought on him guilt, as well as the shame he expressed in view of it" (Gen. 3:7).

48. Nicholls, "The Role of Shame and Guilt," 235.

Theologians throughout history have offered an impressive range of theories to help Christians better understand Christ's work on the cross. They have drawn from a wide range of biblical words and metaphors that seek to understand the meaning of Christ's death. The more important metaphors include sacrifice, propitiation, justification, substitution, redemption, ransom, and reconciliation. Some of these themes, such as sacrifice, draw their primary inspiration from seeing Christ as fulfilling the Old Testament. Other themes, such as justification and substitution, focus on the righteousness of God and/or the sinfulness of humanity, which, by moral necessity, required the death of Christ if communion with God was to be restored. Other images, such as ransom, celebrate Christ's victory over Satan.

In the Middle Ages, theories concerning the work of Christ became more theologically sophisticated and were classified as "*objective* theories, which find the necessity for Jesus' death in the nature or functions of God, and the *subjective* theories, which find the necessity for Jesus' death in the situation of human beings."[49] Some of the better-known theories of the atonement include Anselm of Canterbury's satisfaction theory, John Calvin's penal substitution theory, Hugo Grotius's governmental theory, Augustus Strong's eternal atonement theory, and Peter Abelard's moral influence theory.[50]

The writings on this topic are so abundant that even a cursory survey would lead us too far astray. The point to recognize is that although these various theories of atonement are all important, we should not think that any one of them, or even all of them together, somehow exhaust the full meaning and significance of the biblical doctrine. The role of honor/shame, for example, is not emphasized in any of the well-known theories of atonement. In contrast, the role of guilt plays a prominent role in many of these theories.

There is, of course, an ongoing need for a strong emphasis on human guilt and the corresponding forgiveness that occurs through the work of Christ on the cross. Guilt is an objective result of sin. Louis Berkhof defines guilt as "the state of deserving condemnation or of being liable to punishment for the violation of a law or a moral requirement."[51] Central to biblical teaching regarding salvation from sin is that in Christ we have been justified. Through his work on the cross, we have been acquitted from guilt and punitive liability. The emphasis on guilt is central to the biblical message and cannot be lost. It should always be integral to how the gospel is proclaimed and received by people groups around the world.

The point that the present study seeks to advance is that while the cross is never *less* than a judicial act, it is certainly much *more* than a judicial act. In other words, even though as sinners the statement "we are guilty" is perfectly true, our identity as sinners transcends that particular statement. The work of Christ on the cross provides a more comprehensive response to human alienation than is sometimes reflected in our studies on the atonement. This is particularly true because the West has often understood guilt in personal, private terms. The result is that the public, social aspects of what Christ did on the cross are sometimes overlooked.

49. Garrett, *Systematic Theology*, 2:21.

50. For a survey of the major theories of atonement, see ibid., vol. 2, chs. 46–48.

51. Berkhof, *Systematic Theology*, 232.

The goal of this section is not to uproot any particular cherished theories of the atonement but rather to explore how the role of shame and honor in the work of Christ needs to be more deeply understood and carefully highlighted in global contexts where human identity is strongly shaped by the values of honor and shame. There are several important contributions to theology that a view of the atonement emphasizing Christ's work in bearing our shame and restoring our honor before God might make. As noted earlier, these contributions influence not only our ability to understand and communicate a deeper understanding of Christ's work, but also how this good news may be better received in cultural contexts where these values are so pervasive. Three contributions will be highlighted.

Contributions of an Emphasis on Honor and Shame

Public Nature of Atonement

First, the emphasis on shame and honor highlights the *public* aspect of Christ's work. Why is this important? Does it really matter whether or not Jesus died and rose again privately or publicly? Many of the best-known understandings of the atonement convey the idea that the most meaningful aspects of Christ's death were being transacted on some distant transcendent stage behind the "veil of tears." However, from the perspective of honor and shame, the public nature of the atonement is actually important. As we have explored, one of the distinctive features of a shame-based culture is that honor and shame are related to the group and these values are, for the most part, lived out and defended in the public arena. In other words, honor and shame are public values and are external, whereas guilt and innocence are more naturally thought of in private terms and tend to be interiorized.

In a normal honor and shame context, if a person of greater honor is shamed by someone of a significantly lower status, the offended party has the right to unleash public punishment on those who have offended their honor. As noted earlier, this response often involved shedding the blood of the offender.[52] The punishment must take place publicly, or at least become widely known by the larger group. Only then can the honor of the one who was offended be restored.

As sinners, we have dishonored God and brought shame on ourselves by publicly spurning his gracious call for us to live in intimate communion with him. God's holiness requires that his honor be publicly defended and that our corresponding shame be publicly exposed. Immediately after the initial human rebellion, God responds by confronting Adam and Eve and announcing his righteous judgment against them and against the human race. Adam and Eve are publicly exposed as sinners and thereafter feel the crushing burden of sin, including guilt, fear, and shame. However, the Scripture records, quite unexpectedly, that immediately after God's public judgment on Adam and Eve, he extends grace to them by making garments of skin and clothing them (Gen. 3:21).[53] As noted earlier, clothing someone is a symbol of bestowing honor.

52. In certain cases when an honorable person is shamed by someone who is significantly below their social status, they may choose to ignore the offense lest they bring some dignity to the offender just by responding to them.

53. The *NIV Study Bible* comments, "God graciously provided Adam and Eve with more effective clothing to cover their shame."

This incident is, of course, the first of many examples of the intricate interweaving of God's judgment and grace in Scripture. However, these great themes of judgment and grace all meet in the cross of Jesus Christ. In the mystery of the Christian gospel, rather than God punishing us as we deserve, Christ bears the judgment of God on our behalf and publicly bears our shame. He could have demanded the shedding of our blood to satisfy his honor (Heb. 9:22). Instead, on the cross, he publicly bears our shame and sheds his blood on our behalf. Later, in the resurrection, the full glory and honor of God in Christ is revealed and made publicly manifest (1 Cor. 15:4–8).[54]

According to the protocols of an honor and shame culture, it is essential that honor be restored in a public manner. As we have seen throughout this study, to have honor is to have "publicly acknowledged worth."[55] If it is not demonstrated publicly, there is no basis for declaring that one's honor has been truly satisfied. A survey of traditional systematic theologies reveals no proper emphasis on the public aspect of Christ's work. Yet the scriptural language makes it clear that the work of Christ in bearing our sins and his glorious victory over death represents, among other things, a public declaration of God's honor before the peoples of the world as well as the hosts of evil whom "he made a public spectacle" (Col. 2:15).

Furthermore, his triumph over the scorn, humiliation, shame, and death that he suffered on the cross is publicly declared through the resurrection. The public nature of his victory will be made fully manifest in the eschaton, when there will be universal acknowledgment of Christ's honor, glory, and power: "Then I heard every creature in heaven and on earth and under the earth and on the sea, and all that is in them, singing: 'To him who sits on the throne and to the Lamb be praise and honor [τιμή] and glory [δόξα] and power, for ever and ever!'" (Rev. 5:13).

Social and Relational Aspect of Atonement

Second, the emphasis on shame and honor underscores the social and relational aspect of Christ's work. Scholars such as J. G. Peristiany and Bruce Malina have made a convincing case that the first-century Mediterranean world was dyadistic rather than individualistic.[56] In other words, in that setting one's identity is formed by the group one belongs to and by the larger social context within which one lives. Malina argues that in the social world of early Christianity one's personality is linked to what he calls "group embeddedness."[57] This means that one's self-image is formed in terms

54. Ironically, the redeemed community who follow Christ become subject to the world's shame. Hebrews declares, "Remember those earlier days after you had received the light, when you stood your ground in a great context in the face of suffering. Sometimes you were publicly exposed to insult and persecution; at other times you stood side by side with those who were so treated" (Heb. 10:32–33).

55. Plevnik, "Honor/Shame," 96.

56. Bruce Malina, "The Individual and the Community: Personality in the Social World of Early Christianity," *Biblical Theology Bulletin* 9, no. 3 (July 1979): 127–28.

57. Ibid., 129. This also helps us to understand what Paul means when he quotes the proverb, "Cretans are always liars, evil beasts, lazy gluttons," and adds, "This testimony is true" (Titus 1:12–13a). In an individualistic culture this strikes us as a shocking example of crass stereotyping. However, in a dyadistic context Paul is merely acknowledging that this is the overall identity of the group. This does not deny that there may be a few outstanding Cretans with noble characters who live honorable lives. The point is that even if such outstanding Cretans existed, their reputation is still linked to the overall identity of the group.

of how one is regarded by the group. In a dyadistic culture, there is a powerful social mechanism whereby you are dependent on others for your psychological existence and feel shame if the image (or projected image) of yourself does not agree with the image shared and believed by others.[58]

This principle has important implications for what it means to see ourselves as sinners. In a pure individualistic guilt context, being a sinner means that we have individually transgressed God's law and therefore stand guilty before God's bar of justice. Our identity is not embedded in the group and so we think of ourselves as standing alone before God. In a pure dyadistic shame context, being a sinner means that we are collectively embedded as members of a race who together stand ashamed before God because we have corporately robbed God of his honor. We are embedded in a sinful race and stand as a race before God.

Shame-based, dyadistic cultures do not have any serious difficulty accepting our collective condemnation through Adam (Rom. 5:12–19). The Scriptures teach that in Adam, as well as through our own willful sinning, the whole human race has dishonored God. We are not merely individually or privately guilty before God. We are also corporate participants in a race that has robbed God of the honor due him. This is why Paul declares such truths as "in Adam all die" (1 Cor. 15:22) or "the result of one trespass was condemnation for all men" (Rom. 5:18).

In the contemporary West, our understanding of human guilt and salvation has, at times, become so hyperprivatized that our connectedness to the larger fallen race has become blurred. This, in turn, opens the door to the ancient Pelagian heresy that falsely understood that the human race stands condemned only because of the universal accumulation of endless individual acts of transgression. In Pelagianism, there is no recognition of the sin nature, only of the particular sinful deeds individuals have committed.[59] Shame-based cultures are not as vulnerable to Pelagianism, which, ultimately, spawns an inadequate view of both the depth of human sin and the height of divine grace. Dyadistic cultures can also more readily appreciate the beauty and power of what it means for the redeemed community to be found collectively "in Christ."

The collective, social emphasis in shame-based cultures also helps in our understanding of the atonement by revealing the inherent limitations of approaching Christ's work solely in judicial terms. From a purely legal perspective, a judge does not have a *necessary* relationship with those over whom he or she presides. Judges often declare someone guilty of a crime without personally knowing the defendant. It is simply a matter of determining the facts of the case and applying the relevant laws. In fact, personal intimacy between the judge and a defendant is considered deleterious to justice and the pursuit of impartiality. If a judge has any personal involvement or intimacy with someone who is to be judged, it is the responsibility of the judge to dismiss himself from the case.

This is, of course, neither possible nor necessary in the case of divine justice, since God is intimately acquainted with every person who stands before him and yet remains

58. Ibid., 128.

59. Pelagianism, named after the British monk Pelagius, was condemned at the Synod of Carthage in 418 and later at the Council of Ephesus in 431.

untainted by any partiality (Rom. 2:11). Nevertheless, there is no *necessary* social relationship involved in the administration of justice. Legal actions are taken almost every day by judges and members of Congress even though they have never even met vast numbers of the very people who will be directly influenced by their decisions.

In contrast, shame does involve a necessary *social* relationship between various parties. Shame-based cultures often think about sin primarily in social rather than private contexts. This explains why Western missionaries working in shame-based cultures have often been perplexed when they discovered that personal sins were not ranked as grievous as social, corporate sins. For example, Wayne Dye, who served as a missionary in Papua New Guinea, observed that the Bahinemo people did not feel acute guilt about things like polygamy, betel nut chewing, or smoking, whereas they were deeply troubled by actions that caused discord in the village such as disobedience to husbands and parents, refusing hospitality to someone, or ignoring an expected interclan payment.[60] In these contexts sinning is viewed more relationally. Sin is, of course, both personal and relational. The difference is in the existential awareness of sin by people from different cultures. Although every culture has its own hamartiological blind spots, it seems clear that as we become more active listeners at the table of global Christianity, Christians from different parts of the world can help to expose each other's blind spots.

The great contribution from shame-based cultures seems to be the reminder that the legacy of sin is far more than the objective guilt we incur because of the transgression of specific commands. We have dishonored the Triune God, brought shame on ourselves, and caused a breach in the divine-human relationship. As we become aware of God's righteousness and our sinfulness, it should be experienced not only as an internal realization of guilt, but also as an increased awareness that we collectively stand ashamed before God. In other words, God's righteousness not only declares us forensically guilty, it also places us as relationally distant and shamed before the presence of the Triune God. It is not just his Word that condemns us; it is his Triune person who shames us.

Process of Christian Conversion (Application of the Atonement)

Third, because shame-based cultures are group-oriented, the process of Christian conversion may be different from what we are accustomed to in the West. In these settings, converting to Christianity may be perceived to bring shame on the family, the extended social network, and even their identity as a people. The good news of what Christ has done on the cross is heard as bad news because of the accompanying social upheaval and disruption that acceptance of this message brings. For example, the vast majority of Muslims believe that if a Muslim converts to Christianity, it brings shame not only to his or her entire family, but on the entire Islamic religion. This is why so many Islamic countries consider conversion a capital offense, punishable by beating, imprisonment, or even death.

60. T. Wayne Dye, "Toward a Cross-Cultural Definition of Sin," *Missiology* 4, no. 1 (January 1976): 28–29.

Missionaries who have worked in shame-based cultures frequently observe that the reason most Muslims, Hindus, and Buddhists resist becoming Christians is not primarily because of specific theological objections to the Christian message. More often, there are powerful social and cultural forces that serve as the primary barrier to Christian conversion. People in a shame-based culture are more acutely aware of the surrounding opinions of the group and are constrained from taking individual action in isolation from the larger group. Our frame of reference is apologetically focused on convincing individual Muslims of the truth of Christianity. However, the major barrier is actually not theological or doctrinal, but social, cultural, and relational.[61] This larger issue is often ignored completely.

I do not mean to convey the idea that people from shame-based contexts should never be put in a situation where they are forced to sever their family and social ties and follow Christ. Certainly the message of the cross will always be a stumbling block, and Jesus repeatedly calls us to take drastic action to escape the condemnation of the world (Luke 16:1–8; 1 Cor. 1:18–25). We are exhorted to seek first the kingdom of God and to recognize that following Christ takes final priority over all other obligations, including one's own family and nation (Matt. 10:35–37; Luke 9:59–62). Nevertheless, we should rejoice when an entire family or tribe or even an entire people group comes to Christ.

The New Testament contains several examples of exhortations for entire households to be saved and, subsequently, the conversion and baptism of entire families and groups (Acts 11:14; 16:15, 34; 18:8). The households of Cornelius, Lydia, the Philippian jailer, and Crispus probably represent not only the immediate families, but also the servants and other individuals who may have been employed under their authority. This picture creates a sense of discomfort for some Western evangelical readers who want to be assured that each person has individually repented of their sins and received Christ into their lives. This discomfort is related, at least in part, to our tendency to focus on the judicial side of the atonement, which is more individualistically oriented. However, people who live within a social setting that is shame-based are more oriented toward seeing the entire social group come to Christ together or resist the message together.

In a shame-based culture it is difficult to act in isolation from others, especially those senior to you. The New Testament seems to recognize this reality and, therefore, encourages entire households to come together to minimize the social dislocation and avoid the charge that one person has brought shame on the rest of the family. We should remember that the source of the shame is not so much tied to the propositional content of the Christian message, as it is to the scandalizing notion that someone may be acting independently from the will of the larger group.

In my experience in India over the years, I have seen several remarkable examples of extended families and other larger social groups coming to Christ together. This

61. Even the majority of theological objections are formed by culturally shared agreements as to what they think Christians believe about who Christ is. These views may be strictly adhered to even after someone becomes intellectually convinced that that belief is not consistent with the actual teachings of the church.

tendency should not be viewed, as it sometimes is by outsiders, as an abandonment of the need for individual faith and repentance. Rather, whenever an extended social network comes to Christ, it should be seen as multicoordinated personal decisions.[62] This means that multiple numbers of people are deciding to follow Christ in a single movement rather than through dozens of individual decisions isolated from one another.

We now have over a century of sustained missiological research, both exegetical and field work, to support the validity of such group conversions. This research dates back to Gustav Warneck (1834–1910) and continues in major studies published by Waskom Pickett, Donald McGavran, Alan Tippett, Georg Vicedom, and Ralph Winter.[63] Orlando Costas, a missiologist from Costa Rica, sums up the research well when he writes,

> The concept of multi-individual decisions gives a sociological orientation to the experience of conversion because it affirms that conversion, which depends on a personal act of faith in Christ, can take place in a group setting, where all the members of a given group (family, clan, tribe or mutual interest group) participate in a similar experience with Christ after considering it together and deciding to turn to Christ at the same time.[64]

In short, Christian conversion is always personal, but not necessarily individualistic. The church is not just the sum total of all the individuals who have accepted Christ; the church is the people of God, the bride of Christ, the new humanity. Even in a mass conversion, each person must put his or her faith in Christ, but in a shame-based context their identity is oriented toward the group. Therefore, when they are brought into their new identity in Christ, it emerges as a part of a larger group experience. The meaning of Christ's death and resurrection is received and responded to together.

Relationship between Guilt and Shame in the Way We Identify with the Atonement

The final part of this study will briefly reflect on the relationship between guilt and shame. At the beginning of this chapter we noted that anthropologists no longer classify cultures as exclusively guilt-based or shame-based. This is an important insight, because it demonstrates the importance of our developing a deeper understanding of how both guilt and shame function together in the Scriptures and within the context of human cultures. Guilt and shame are distinct, but they are also intricately related to one another. Anthropologists have noted that "guilt is seldom entirely intrinsic," and

62. The phrase is my own, but missiologist Alan Tippet refers to these extended social conversions as "multi-individual decisions" or "multi-personal conversions." See Alan Tippet, *People Movements in Southern Polynesia: A Study in Church Growth* (Chicago: Moody Press, 1971), 123–241.

63. See Gustav Warneck, *Evangelische Missionslehre*; Bd. IIII,1: *Der Betrieb der Sendung*, 2nd ed. (Gotha: Perthes, 1902); Waskom J. Pickett, *Christian Mass Movements in India* (Lucknow, India: Lucknow, 1933); Donald A. McGavran, *Bridges of God* (New York: Friendship, 1955); Tippett, *People Movements in Southern Polynesia*; Georg Vicedom, "An Example of Group Conversion," *Practical Anthropology* 9 (1962): 123–28; Ralph Winter, "Quality or Quantity?" in *Crucial Issues in Missions Tomorrow*, ed. Donald A. McGavran (Chicago: Moody Press, 1972), 175–87.

64. Orlando Costas, *The Church and Its Mission: A Shattering Critique from the Third World* (Wheaton: Tyndale, 1974), 128.

feelings of guilt can be magnified once knowledge of one's actions become public.[65] So, what is the Christian understanding of the relationship between shame and guilt within the larger context of human identity?

Emil Brunner, in *The Scandal of Christianity*, accepts the distinction noted earlier that all theories of the atonement fall into the two basic categories of objective and subjective theories.[66] This distinction tends to separate theories of the atonement based on whether they are situated first and foremost in theology or anthropology. The objective theories are "God-centered"; the subjective theories are "man-centered."

Not surprisingly, Brunner chooses Peter Abelard's moral influence theory as the best example of a subjective theory since, according to this view, the cross is "the means by which man understands and believes God's incredible love."[67] The cross is more of a subjective experience than an objective, judicial transaction. Brunner chooses Anselm's satisfaction theory as the classic example of an objective view of the atonement: "What gives Anselm's thought its superiority is the fact that it starts from the objective fact of guilt. Guilt is a reality, even for God. Man's revolt against God's will is a fact against which God reacts with his wrath."[68]

Brunner is, of course, quite right to point out that Anselm does place great emphasis on objective guilt and the need to satisfy God's wrath, which we deserve. However, Brunner overstates his case when he says that objective guilt is the starting point for Anselm. Actually, in Anselm's famous work *Cur Deus Homo?* in which he establishes his view of the atonement, he begins with the concepts of honor and shame and then proceeds to demonstrate how humanity is objectively guilty before God. When Anselm defines sin, he argues that it is, at root, any act that robs God of his honor. Anselm argues that every rational creature owes God honor and that the only way to honor God is to fully love and obey him in all that we do. Anselm argues that "a person who does not render God this honor due Him, takes from God what is His and dishonors God, and this is to commit sin."[69]

For Anselm, sin is fundamentally a dishonoring or shaming of God because sin robs God of his honor. The specific acts of rebellion against God's will represent the objective fruits of a deeper malady rooted in our unwillingness to honor God. In short, Anselm does rely heavily on the concept of objective, judicial guilt, but roots it in relational, not merely legalistic, soil by demonstrating that objective sinful acts that render us guilty arise first and foremost out of a personal rejection of God whereby we have refused to give him the honor that is due him.[70]

As we come to the end of this study, it is helpful to recognize that Anselm has provided a helpful model that demonstrates the reciprocal relationship between guilt

65. Jackob A. Loewen, "The Social Context of Guilt and Forgiveness," *Practical Anthropology* 17, no. 2 (March–April 1970): 82.

66. Emil Brunner, *The Scandal of Christianity* (Philadelphia, Westminster, 1951), 86.

67. Ibid., 87.

68. Ibid.

69. Anselm, *Why God Became Man and the Virgin Conception and Original Sin by Anselm of Canterbury*, trans. Joseph Colleran (Albany, NY: Maji, 1969), 84.

70. Anselm utilizes the language of honor and shame throughout his argument. When Anselm argues for the need for God's justice to be satisfied (1.22), he uses the language of honor and shame. In the course of a relatively short passage Anselm uses "honor" four times, "dishonor" once, and "shame" once. See ibid., 110–11.

and shame in discussing human alienation. It is true that sin is measured against the objective, revealed will of God. God's justice must be satisfied. It is also true that sin is the fruit of a broken relationship. Sin is both objective and subjective. If we only know about guilt, there is a danger toward legalism and a depersonalization of what it means to be a human in rebellion against God and in discord with our neighbor. If we only know about shame, there is a danger of losing the clear objective basis for God's righteous judgment that transcends the changing vagaries of human culture.

CONCLUSION

This chapter has demonstrated that honor and shame are among the most important values in the ancient Mediterranean world and continue to play a vital role in the formation of human identity in much of North Africa, Middle East, and Asia. A deeper appreciation for how the gospel relates to these values will be increasingly important as the church continues to expand in the context of cultures that are predominantly shame-based. As Christians in the West interact more extensively with our brothers and sisters from the Majority World church, I trust that our appreciation for the place of both guilt and shame in shaping human identity will increase. Jesus bore our guilt and our shame, reversing the curse of the fall for all those who are in Christ. We, who once were identified by guilt and shame, now have a new identity in Christ and have become partakers of his righteousness *and* his honor.

BIBLIOGRAPHY

Anselm. *Why God Became Man and the Virgin Conception and Original Sin by Anselm of Canterbury*. Translated by Joseph Colleran. Albany, NY: Maji, 1969.

Bechtel, Lyn. "The Perception of Shame within the Divine-Human Relationship in Biblical Israel." Pages 79–92 in *Uncovering Ancient Stones*. Edited by Lewis M. Hopfe. Winona Lake, IN: Eisenbrauns, 1994.

Benedict, Ruth. *The Chrysanthemum and the Sword*. Cambridge, MA: Riverside, 1946.

Bergant, Dianne. "'My Beloved Is Mine and I Am His' (Song 2:16): The Song of Songs and Honor and Shame." *Semeia* 68 (1994): 23–40.

Berkhof, Louis. *Systematic Theology*. Grand Rapids: Eerdmans, 1941.

Botterweck, Johannes, Helmer Ringgren, and Heinz-Josef Fabry, eds. *Theological Dictionary of the Old Testament*. Translated by John T. Willis et al. 15 vols. (so far). Grand Rapids: Eerdmans, 1974–present.

Brown, Francis, S. R. Driver, and Charles A. Briggs, ed. *A Hebrew and English Lexicon of the Old Testament*. Translated by E. Robinson. Oxford: Clarendon, 1957 (1907).

Brunner, Emil. *The Scandal of Christianity*. Philadelphia: Westminster, 1951.

Costas, Orlando. *The Church and Its Mission: A Shattering Critique from the Third World*. Wheaton: Tyndale, 1974.

Creighton, Millie R. "Revisiting Shame and Guilt Cultures: A Forty-Year Pilgrimage." *Ethos* 18, no. 3 (1990): 279–307.

Davies, Benjamin. *Hebrew and Chaldee Lexicon*. Boston: Bradley & Co., 1879.

Dodds, E. R. *The Greeks and the Irrational*. Berkeley: University of California Press, 1951.

Douglas, Mary. *Purity and Danger: An Analysis of the Concepts of Pollution and Taboo*. London: Routledge & Kegan Paul, 1966.

Dye, T. Wayne. "Toward a Cross-Cultural Definition of Sin." *Missiology* 4, no. 1 (January 1976): 27-41.

Garrett, James L. Jr. *Systematic Theology: Biblical, Historical and Evangelical*. 2 vols. Grand Rapids: Eerdmans, 1990–1995.

Haring, Douglas. *Personal Character and Cultural Milieu*. Syracuse, NY: Syracuse University Press, 1956.

Hengel, Martin. *Crucifixion in the Ancient World*. Philadelphia: Fortress, 1977.

Hesselgrave, David J. "Missionary Elenctics and Guilt and Shame." *Missiology* 11, no. 4 (October 1983): 461–83.

Kasdorf, Hans. *Christian Conversion in Context*. Scottdale, PA: Herald, 1980.

Kittel, Gerhard, ed. *Theological Dictionary of the New Testament*. Translated by G. F. Bromiley. 10 vols. Grand Rapids: Eerdmans, 1964–1976.

Koehler, L. H., W. Baumgartner, and J. J. Stamm. *The Hebrew and Aramaic Lexicon of the Old Testament*. Translated by M. E. J. Richardson. 5 vols. Leiden: Brill, 1994–2000.

Lebra, Takie Sugiyama. "The Social Mechanism of Guilt and Shame: The Japanese Case." *Anthropological Quarterly* 44, no. 4 (October 1971): 241–55.

Lee, Zuk-Nae. "Korean Culture and Sense of Shame." *Transcultural Psychiatry* 36, no. 2 (June 1999): 181–94.

Loewen, Jackob A. "The Social Context of Guilt and Forgiveness." *Practical Anthropology* 17, no. 2 (March–April 1970): 80–96.

Lynd, Helen Merrell. *On Shame and the Search for Identity*. New York: Science Editions, 1961.

Malina, Bruce. "The Individual and the Community: Personality in the Social World of Early Christianity." *Biblical Theology Bulletin* 9, no. 3 (July 1979): 126–38.

_____. *The New Testament World: Insights from Cultural Anthropology*. Louisville: Westminster John Knox, 1993.

McGavran, Donald A. *Bridges of God*. New York: Friendship, 1955.

Mirza, Syed Kamran. "Honor Killing—Is It Islamic?" *News from Bangladesh*. July 3, 2005. http://bangladesh-web.com/view.php?hidDate=2005–07- 03&hidType=OPT&hidRecord=0000000000000000050641.

Muller, Roland. *Honor and Shame: Unlocking the Door*. Birmingham, UK: Xlibris, 2000.

Mushima, Yukio. "A 20th Century Warrior." *New Dawn* 29, no. 1 (January–March 1995): 21.

Musk, Bill A. *Touching the Soul of Islam*. East Sussex, UK: MARC, 1988, 1995.

Neyrey, Jerome H. "Despising the Shame of the Cross: Honor and Shame in the Johannine Passion Narrative." *Semeia* 68 (1994): 113–37.

_____. *Honor and Shame in the Gospel of Matthew*. Louisville, KY: Westminster John Knox, 1998.

Nicholls, Bruce. "The Role of Shame and Guilt in a Theology of Cross-Cultural Mission." *Evangelical Review of Theology* 25, no. 3 (2001): 231–41.

Nida, Eugene A. *Customs and Cultures: Anthropology for Christian Missions*. Pasadena, CA: William Carey Library, 1954.

Peristiany, J. G., and J. Pitt-Rivers, *Honour and Grace in Anthropology*. Cambridge: Cambridge University Press, 1992.

Pickett, Waskom J. *Christian Mass Movements in India*. Lucknow, India: Lucknow, 1933.

Pitt-Rivers, Julian. "Honour and Shame." Pages 21–77 in *Honour and Shame: The Values of Mediterranean Society*. Edited by J. G. Peristiany. London: Weidenfeld & Nicholson, 1966.

_____. *The People of the Sierra*. Chicago: University of Chicago Press, 1961.

Plevnik, Joseph. "Honor/Shame." Pages 94–104 in *Biblical Social Values and Their Meaning*. Edited by John J. Pilch and Bruce J. Malina. Peabody, MA: Hendrickson, 1993.

Simkins, Ronald. "Honor and Shame in Genesis 34 and 1 Samuel 25." Pages 104–6 in *Teaching the Bible*. Edited by Mark Roncace and Patrick Gray. Leiden: Brill, 2005.

_____. "Return to Yahweh: Honor and Shame in Joel." *Semeia* 68 (1994): 41–54.

Stansell, Gary. "Honor and Shame in the David Narratives." *Semeia* 68 (1994): 55–79.

Thielicke, Helmut. *The Evangelical Faith*. Grand Rapids: Eerdmans, 1974.

Tippet, Alan. *People Movements in Southern Polynesia: A Study in Church Growth*. Chicago: Moody Press, 1971.

Vicedom, Georg. "An Example of Group Conversion." *Practical Anthropology* 9 (1962): 123–28.

Warneck, Gustav. *Evangelische Missionslehre*. Bd. IIII,1: *Der Betrieb der Sendung*. 2nd ed. Gotha: Perthes, 1902.

Winter, Ralph. "Quality or Quantity?" Pages 175–87 in *Crucial Issues in Missions Tomorrow*. Edited by Donald A. McGavran. Chicago: Moody Press, 1972.

You, Young Gweon. "Shame and Guilt Mechanisms in East Asian Culture." *Journal of Pastoral Care* 51, no. 1 (Spring 1997): 57–64.

Chapter 5

CHRISTOLOGY

CHRIST AS HEALER AND ANCESTOR IN AFRICA

At the dawn of the twenty-first century, the typical "face" of Christianity may more likely be encountered in Lagos than in London. We in the West may live to see the day when "the phrase 'a white Christian' may sound like a curious oxymoron, as mildly surprising as 'a Swedish Buddhist.'"[1] What is emerging is the sunrise of a fourth major branch of the Christian faith, not so easily pigeonholed within the familiar categories of Roman Catholic, Eastern Orthodox, and Protestant Christianity. Andrew Walls predicts that if current trends continue, African Christianity will become "*the* representative Christianity of the twenty-first century."[2] This emerging reality is why Philip Jenkins has boldly proclaimed the emerging Majority World church as "the next Christendom."[3]

THE NEXT FACES OF CHRISTIANITY

The Rise of the Global Church

The shift from the West to the South is even more dramatic when one realizes that Western Christianity is increasingly becoming secularized, nominal, and even hostile to historic Christian confessions, whereas Christianity in the Southern hemisphere is vibrant, supernaturalist, and largely orthodox.[4] In other words, Southern Christianity is an evangelistic and reproducible faith. While Western churches are looking increasingly like either entertainment centers or politically correct corporations, the African church is busy preaching the gospel of Jesus Christ, baptizing new believers, and planting churches.

This should be a clarion call for Western Christians who are committed to historic Christianity. Hendrick Kraemer once said that "the Church is always in a state of crisis

1. Philip Jenkins, *The Next Christendom: The Coming of Global Christianity* (London: Oxford Univ. Press, 2002), 3.

2. Andrew Walls, "Africa in Christian History: Retrospect and Prospect," *Journal of African Christian Thought* 1, no. 1(June 1998): 2.

3. Jenkins, *The Next Christendom*, 4.

4. See Harvey Cox, *Fire from Heaven* (Reading, MA: Addison-Wesley, 1995).

and that its greatest shortcoming is that it is only occasionally aware of it."[5] The church in the West must wake up and recognize that not only is the *numerical* percentage of Western Christians hemorrhaging away at an alarming rate, but the *spiritual* center of Christianity has already shifted to the church in the Majority World. We are in the midst of a massive spiritual crisis in the West, which, mercifully, is coinciding with one of the most dramatic and vibrant expansions of Christianity in history taking place in Africa. Therefore, we must learn to stand shoulder to shoulder with our African brothers and sisters, who are in the bright sunrise of a great movement of God across the continent of Africa, and allow them to teach us and help us to bring renewal and revitalization back to the Western church.

We have much to learn as well as to relearn from Africa, although there is also much that our own heritage, history, and collective Christian memory have to teach Africa. It is time for a truly mutual exchange. We should recall that African proverb from Ghana cited in the introduction: "The mother feeds the baby daughter before she has teeth, so that the daughter will feed the mother when she loses her teeth."[6] Perhaps our own faith and theological reflections can be nourished by listening to the voices of our young African brothers and sisters in the faith. As Andrew Walls has said so well, "Shared reading of the Scriptures and shared theological reflection will be to the benefit of all, but the oxygen-starved Christianity of the West will have the most to gain."[7]

If African Christianity is to be the standard-bearer of Christianity for the twenty-first century, this means that "what happens within the African churches in the next generation will determine the whole shape of church history for centuries to come ... what sort of theology is more characteristic of Christianity in the twenty-first century may well depend on what has happened in the minds of African Christians."[8] In this chapter we seek to understand what is "happening in the minds of African Christians," particularly as it relates to Christology.

The Christological Puzzle

For Christians, Christological reflection is the centerpiece of all theological enquiry. Indeed, the entire Christian faith stands or falls on the person of Jesus Christ. If, for example, John Hick and the other British theologians in *The Myth of God Incarnate* are correct in their denial of the full deity of Jesus Christ, then Christianity, as Christianity, has been struck down. The new "Christianity" that emerges would be nothing more than a vacuous and ephemeral projection of relativism hiding beneath the language of devotion and piety. If such views were to gain traction in the life of the church, Christianity would soon be cast, like the broken statue of Stalin, into the dustbin of history.

5. Hendrick Kraemer, as quoted in David J. Bosch, *Transforming Mission: Paradigm Shifts in Theology of Mission* (Maryknoll, NY: Orbis, 1996), 2.

6. Diane B. Stinton, *Jesus of Africa: Voices of Contemporary African Christology* (Maryknoll, NY: Orbis, 2004), 252.

7. Andrew F. Walls, *The Cross-Cultural Process in Christian History* (Maryknoll, NY: Orbis, 2002), 47.

8. Andrew F. Walls, "Towards an Understanding of Africa's Place in Christian History," in J. S. Pobee, ed., *Religion in a Pluralistic Society* (Leiden: Brill, 1976), 183.

In contrast, if the Christians who formulated the Nicene Creed are correct in their affirmation that Jesus Christ is "very God of very God," who "for our salvation came down from heaven, and was incarnate by the Holy Spirit," then Christianity has a powerful message worthy of being proclaimed to the ends of the earth. In short, Christianity derives its life and meaning from Christ himself. Thus, Christology will always remain central to Christian reflection.

However, despite my strong affirmation of the Christology expressed in the Nicene Creed (AD 325), it would be a mistake to understand even this powerful statement as the final word on Christology as if no more conversations are either needed or desired. Indeed, the emergence of the later, more precise, Chalcedonian formula (AD 451), which finally hammered out the "two natures, one person" Christology that has become received orthodoxy, demonstrates that further, post-Nicene conversations were needed. The importance of the Nicene Creed and the Chalcedonian formulation lies in the fact that they were *ecumenical* councils. In other words, dozens of general church councils over the years have produced various Christological statements, but an *ecumenical* council is one that finds broad acceptance as "an expression of the mind of the whole body of the faithful both clerical and lay, the *sensus communis* of the Church."[9]

The proceedings of these ecumenical councils remind me of the experience of sitting down at a table before a large, thousand-piece jigsaw puzzle. Many of us know how frustrating it can be to keep trying piece after piece that looks like it should fit, but it doesn't. I have even been guilty of trying to force a piece into the wrong space, even though I know only one will be a true fit. Eventually, I find the proper puzzle piece that provides an exact fit.

Likewise, the delegates to the Council of Nicea and the Council of Chalcedon were seeking to be faithful to the hundreds of Christological "pieces" found in the texts of Scriptures. It was their unenviable task to put the whole "picture" of Christ together for the very first time in such a way as to find a perfect match for every piece. At times, various groups presented "pieces" they believed were a proper fit regarding the humanity or deity or natures or wills of Christ, but, in the end, each was declared to be improper fits. The proceedings of these councils did more to declare which pieces were *not* true pieces of the puzzle and should be discarded, than to provide a final, definitive statement of Christology that would silence all future discussions. We may know that the "Arius," "Nestorius," and "Eutyches" pieces do not fit the Christological puzzle, but this is not to say that a final and complete picture emerged.

Thus, even while fully affirming an ecumenical council like Chalcedon, we can also admit that the proceedings left several Christological questions unresolved. For example, precisely how does the *person* of Christ (which is the part of the puzzle the Council focused on) relate to the *work* of Christ? As Oscar Cullmann has pointed out, "the New Testament hardly ever speaks of the person of Christ without at the same time speaking of his work."[10] This dilemma was also felt by Wolfhart Pannenberg in

9. Philip Schaff and Henry Wace, eds., *Nicene and Post-Nicene Fathers*, vol. 14, *The Seven Ecumenical Councils*, 2nd series (Peabody, MA: Hendrikson, 1999), xii.

10. Oscar Cullmann, *The Christology of the New Testament* (Philadelphia: Westminster Press, 1959, 1963), 3.

his *Jesus: God and Man*.[11] Chalcedon seems to be focused almost exclusively on the person of Christ.

Another example is reflected in the insightful question about Chalcedon raised by Millard Erickson: "How do we integrate and understand a Christology 'from above' with a Christology 'from below'?"[12] In other words, the Council of Chalcedon was looking at the Christological puzzle from the upper side, that is, from the divine perspective of God's initiative in becoming a man. They did not deliberate or discuss how the incarnation is understood from the perspective of, for example, fifth-century Persian Christians who, at the time of this council, were being persecuted for their faith in Christ.

Even these few examples reveal two important insights about Chalcedonian Christology. First, even if we accept, as the *sensus communis* has, that every single piece Chalcedon placed into the Christological puzzle was a perfect fit and every single piece they rejected was truly worth rejecting, we must still recognize that the puzzle is much bigger than Chalcedon or any other council could fully tackle.[13] Second, as it turns out, the puzzle is more complex than an ordinary one because each piece of the puzzle seems to have two sides: an "upper side" revealing God's perspective on Christ (eternality, Trinity, Son of God, etc.) and an "under side" revealing the human perspective on Christ (teacher, healer, friend of sinners, etc.). A complete Christology (if it is even possible) must surely be the work of many generations of faithful Christians, not merely the work of a particular council.

Christological reflection must be a part of the ongoing life of the church not only because of the sheer depth and glory of Christ himself, but also because each generation produces new challenges and questions that call us back to the biblical text and the apostolic witness concerning Christ. Even though the church has already said a collective "no" to the Ariuses and the Eutycheses of the ancient world, we must find new ways to say "no" to the John Hicks and the J. A. T. Robinsons of the contemporary world. We must also be reflectively critical about our own, less obvious, deep heresics that creep into our own worldview, such as the pathology of unbridled individualism so deeply engrained in Western evangelicalism. In short, each generation must learn to recognize the heresies of its day as well as the previously rejected heresies that, from time to time, get represented for fresh consideration.

This chapter is dedicated to listening to what African Christians have been saying concerning Christology. However, it is important that any new Christological discussions be heard in the larger context of those reflections that have stood the test of time and the test of many generations of Christians now in the presence of the living Christ. G. K. Chesterton once said that "tradition is the greatest expression of democracy." What he meant was that by listening attentively to the voices of those long dead

11. Wolfhart Pannenberg, *Jesus: God and Man*, 2nd ed., trans. by Lewis Wilkins and Duane Priebe (Philadelphia: Westminster, 1968, 1977), 112, 137, 167, 186–89, 210, 279, 286–93, 300–303, 324, 360–61, 365, 397.

12. Millard Erickson, *The Word Became Flesh: A Contemporary Incarnational Christology* (Grand Rapids: Baker, 1991), 11.

13. I realize that not all of the Eastern churches accepted the language of Chalcedon. However, the signed agreement between the Pope and the Assyrian Church of the East in 1993 demonstrates that, while the Eastern Church objected to some of the language, they were in broad agreement with the theology of Chalcedon. See "Common Christological Declaration between the Catholic Church and the Assyrian Church of the East" (November 11, 1994), *Information Service* 88, no. 1 (1995): 1.

(tradition), we actually bring more people to the table who might not have our particular cultural or theological biases and who can provide a check and balance to the tendencies that tempt us to force a piece that doesn't fit into the picture.

In short, we are always enriched by those who have struggled before us. We are not the first Christians to reflect deeply on the question, "Who is Jesus Christ?" Nevertheless, the fact that millions of Christians have already devoted countless hours to Christological reflection does not relieve us of the sacred responsibility of understanding Christ in the light of the issues we face in our own time. We desperately need the input and perspective of African Christians concerning Jesus Christ. I sincerely hope that this chapter reflects this balance between honoring the past and yet being enriched by these fresh new voices from the Majority World church.

Setting the Stage for the Emergence of African Christology

Christological reflection was first stimulated by Jesus Christ himself when he posed the question, "Who do people say the Son of Man is?" (Matt. 16:13). Jesus then asked Peter and the other disciples in a more direct and pointed fashion: "Who do *you* say that I am?" (v. 15, emphasis added). At a very basic level, Christology is the answer to this question.

For many years, African Christians were not encouraged to reflect on this question for themselves. Instead, they were taught to mimic what they had been taught. They were, in effect, answering the question, "Who do the *missionaries* say the Son of Man is?" The Africans learned to faithfully repeat what they had been taught about Christ. But as the number of African Christians grew and theological reflection deepened, many Africans began to sense the Lord Jesus turning to Africans *as Africans* and asking, "Who do *you* say that I am?" This question has stimulated a whole generation of African Christians and theologians, men and women, educated and illiterate, to speak out about the meaning of Jesus Christ for the African.

However, the emergence of an indigenous African Christology has not come easily. Paul Hiebert has correctly pointed out that the marks of an indigenous church are much more than the familiar three selfs: self-governing, self-supporting, self-propagating. The most neglected and missing "self," argues Hiebert, is self-*theologizing*.[14] The central difficulty, it seems, is that the Africans arrived at the "Christological puzzle" quite late and were not entirely sure that they had their own contribution to make.

One of the best analogies that describes the African experience comes from Anselme Sanon, a Roman Catholic archbishop in the country of Burkina Faso. Sanon begins by picturing the scene of Peter and John running to the empty tomb (John 20).[15] John outran Peter and arrived first, but he didn't go inside. Peter arrived and went into the tomb and saw that the body was gone. He also noticed that the grave

14. Paul G. Hiebert, *Anthropological Reflections on Missiological Issues* (Grand Rapids: Baker, 1994), 97. The original "three-self" conception of indigeneity was articulated in 1851 by the missionary statesman and leader of the Church Missionary Society, Henry Venn.

15. The text does not explicitly say that John was running with Peter. It only says that Peter "and the other disciple, the one Jesus loved"—widely understood to be a reference to John.

clothes were carefully folded up and placed to one side (20:7). Everything seemed to be neat and in a state of order. John also entered the tomb and, the text declares, "he saw and believed." There in the empty tomb, Peter and John join the women (who had earlier become the first witnesses to the resurrection) in a new and profound Christological reflection: He is the risen Lord!

Sanon goes on to point out how generation after generation has symbolically followed the women and the disciples into the empty tomb and have also contemplated and reflected on Christ. They put various words and descriptors about Jesus Christ all over the empty tomb. Indeed, they left everything in good order, well classified, and neatly explained. The Africans are some of the last people to arrive at the tomb. When they do arrive, Sanon asks, "what can be said of Jesus of Nazareth that has not [already] been said?"[16] Those who have gone before have left behind creeds and formulations, icons and images, theology and sculptures; "everything has been tried, everything done, to transmit the best of this face, to deliver the secret of its beauty."[17]

But, as explored earlier, the full Christological puzzle will not be complete until the Africans have reflected long and deep on what it means for Christ to come into Africa. John V. Taylor once said:

> Christ has been presented as the answer to the questions a white man would ask, the solution to the needs that Western man would feel, the Savior of the world of the European world-view, the object of adoration and prayer of historic Christendom. But if Christ were to appear as the answer to the questions that Africans are asking, what would he look like? If he came into the world of African cosmology to redeem Man as Africans understand him, would he be recognizable to the rest of the Church universal? And if Africa offered him the praises and petitions of her total, uninhibited humanity, would they be acceptable?[18]

As each generation of Christians reflected on Christ, they observed different facets of his glory. Naturally, each generation is tempted to think that their particular insights into Christ are normative and represent the last word for each succeeding generation. However, as we have noted, the "Christological puzzle" is exceedingly rich and textured.

Jaroslav Pelikan, in his *Jesus through the Centuries*,[19] has carefully documented how different generations have responded to the question, "Who is Jesus Christ?" He documents eighteen different portraits of Christ over the centuries. For the early Jewish believers he was the Messiah, the fulfillment of Jewish prophetic hopes and expectations. However, this image (while completely true) was insufficient to fully capture what the Gentiles had found in Jesus. For the Gentiles, to call Jesus the Messiah would have been merely mimicking what Peter said of Jesus, "You are the Messiah, the Son of

16. Anselme T. Sanon, "Jesus, Master of Initiation," in *Faces of Jesus in Africa*, ed. Robert J. Schreiter (Maryknoll, NY: Orbis, 2005), 92.

17. Ibid.

18. John V. Taylor, *The Primal Vision: Christian Presence and African Religion* (London: SCM, 1963), 7 (in the Fortress Press ed. of *The Primal Vision*, the quote is on p. 24).

19. Jaroslav Pelikan, *Jesus through the Centuries: His Place in the History of Culture* (New Haven, CT: Yale Univ. Press, 1985).

the living God" (Matt. 16:16 TNIV).[20] The Gentiles did not share the Jewish prophetic hopes for a coming messiah. Therefore, the title *Messiah* did not carry the same meaning for Gentiles as it did for Jews. This explains why, in the book of Acts, Paul continues to preach *to Jews* that Jesus is the Messiah (Acts 9:22; 17:3; 18:5), while curiously avoiding this title in preaching *to Gentiles*. Instead, he seems to prefer to proclaim the "Lord Jesus" to Gentiles (Acts 15:11; 16:31; 19:5, 17; 20:21).[21]

Centuries later, in the post-Constantinian period of church history, Christianity became the official religion of the Roman empire. During this period Christological reflection began to emphasize that Jesus Christ is the King of kings and the Lord of the nations. Later, during the Renaissance, with the increased emphasis on human reason and autonomy, Jesus was celebrated as the Universal Man. In times of war and conflict, he is looked to as the Prince of Peace. In our own time, we have seen Jesus burst the borders of Western Christendom and become a source of comfort to those who are disenfranchised and suffering. For our time, Pelikan argues, Jesus has become the great "Liberator" and the "Man who belongs to the world."[22]

All of these images must be tested by the Scriptures and the apostolic witness to Jesus, since the Word of God provides divine revelation about Jesus Christ and the trustworthy record of the actual eye and ear witnesses to him. Each of the images that have emerged reflects genuine and helpful insights into the Lord Jesus Christ. As with all metaphors, each of these images also holds the potential to lead astray without constant vigilance and clarification. Yet, even those Christological reflections that stand the test of Scripture and time cannot be used to declare a moratorium on Christological reflection. If the gospel had stayed contained within the single ethnicity of Judaism, we would not have benefited from the Christological translatability whereby the Gentile, Hellenistic Christians reflected on the same Jesus and had new insights because of their own cultural and social context.

In the same way, as the gospel has been translated into Chinese, Indian, African, Korean, and other cultures, we gain more and more insights into the beauty and reality of Jesus Christ. I have referred to this phenomenon as the "ontic expansion of God in Jesus Christ."[23] This expression, of course, does not refer to any ontological change in the nature of Jesus Christ himself, but rather, to how our own understanding and insight into the full nature and work of God in and through Jesus Christ is continually expanding as more and more people groups come to the feet of Jesus. With this in mind we now turn to an examination of African Christology.

20. It seems clear that, despite the widespread use of the title "Christ," it was not considered mandatory. The term does not appear a single time in the Apostles' or Nicene Creeds.

21. By the time of Paul's letters, the term *Christ* was widely used (Paul uses it 270 times) by Gentiles. But, as Larry Hurtado points out, this word as used by Gentile Christians was a *name* for Jesus rather than the Jewish *title* of Jesus. See Larry Hurtado, *Lord Jesus Christ* (Grand Rapids: Eerdmans, 2003), 99.

22. Pelikan's eighteen images of Christ in *Jesus through the Centuries* are: the Rabbi, the Turning Point of History, the Light of the Gentiles, the King of Kings, the Cosmic Christ, the Son of Man, the True Image, Christ Crucified, the Monk who Rules the World, the Bridegroom of the Soul, the Divine and Human Model, the Universal Man, the Mirror of the Eternal, the Prince of Peace, the Teacher of Common Sense, the Poet of the Spirit, the Liberator, and the Man who Belongs to the World.

23. Timothy C. Tennent, "The Challenge of Churchless Christianity," *International Bulletin of Missionary Research* 29, no. 4 (October 2005): 174–75.

Key Themes in African Christology

As late as 1967 John Mbiti, widely regarded as one of the leading pioneers of African theology, bewailed the fact that Africa is "a church without a theology, without theologians, and without theological concerns."[24] What he meant was that despite the presence of hundreds of African theologians and various theological institutions, African theology was "imported" from the outside. Bolaji Idowu articulated the same frustration in 1965 when he said that all Africa had was "a prefabricated theology, a book theology ... what she reads in books written by European theologians, or what she is told by Europeans is accepted uncritically and given out undigested in preaching or teaching."[25] John Pobee has characterized this situation as the "North Atlantic Captivity of the Church," whereby Christianity in Africa begins "with an assumed definition of the Christian faith which is definitely North Atlantic—intellectually, spiritually, liturgically [and] organizationally."[26]

At the dawn of the twenty-first century, such statements cannot now be made without serious qualification. While there are still signs of Africa's "theological captivity" to the West, the last forty years have seen the rising tide of genuine African reflection and theological contributions represented by dozens of landmark books and articles by African theologians. The center of Christian gravity has now shifted to Africa, giving it a prominence hardly imaginable forty years ago. In 1967 Mbiti had declared that "African concepts of Christology do not exist."[27] By 2005 Tanzanian theologian Charles Nyamiti declared that "Christology is the subject which has been most developed in today's African theology."[28]

Today's student has the opportunity to become acquainted with several important works on Christology written by Africans. Yet, curiously, the insights of these thinkers are largely ignored by Western theologians writing in the area of Christology. However, if we truly aspire to think and live as globally oriented Christians, we must become acquainted with the reflections and insights of Africans concerning Jesus Christ. Furthermore, it is important to reflect on how these newer, African indigenous Christological works relate to the traditional Western Christological formulations of Nicea (325), Chalcedon (451), Constantinople II (553), and Constantinople III (680). It is only with this context that we can then examine some of the specific Christological contributions by African theologians.

1. A Theology from Below

A survey of the major works on African Christology reveals at least four distinctive features that African writers tend to emphasize. First, as noted earlier, the starting point and main concern of African Christology is "from below," not "from above."

24. John Mbiti, "Some African Concepts of Christology," in *Christ and the Younger Churches*, ed. Georg F. Vicedom (London: SPCK, 1972), 51.

25. Bolaji Idowu, *Towards an Indigenous Church* (London: Oxford Univ. Press, 1965), 22–23.

26. John S. Pobee, "Jesus Christ—the Life of the World: An African Perspective," *Ministerial Formation* 21 (January 1983): 5, quoted in Stinton, *Jesus of Africa*, 25.

27. Mbiti, "Some African Concepts of Christology," 51. Even as late as 1982 Aylward Shorter spoke of the "failure to produce a convincing African or Black Christology" (see "Folk Christianity and Functional Christology," *Afer* 24 [1982]: 134).

28. Charles Nyamiti, "African Christologies Today," in *Faces of Jesus in Africa*, ed. Robert J. Schreiter, 3.

Two implications result from this perspective. The first is that African thinkers are not as focused on the ontology of Christ and the relationship of his deity and his humanity as Western theologians have been. Africans do not invest a lot of time discussing precisely how the two natures of Christ become united into one theanthropic person. They rarely discuss how the two wills of Christ confirm him as the God-Man without confusion or compromise. Yet, these were all central concerns of the ecumenical councils that tended to focus on the person of Christ.

In contrast, African Christology tends to be more holistic in the way it integrates the person and work of Christ. Its view of the person of Christ is constantly informed by what Christ has accomplished in history and what he continues to do in the world. There is a deep concern in African Christology to demonstrate that Christ is no stranger to the practical realities of poverty, illiteracy, ethnic tensions, colonialism, dictatorship, illness, disenfranchisement, and suffering, all of which Pobee and Akinade have aptly called, Africa's "multiheaded hydra."[29] Africans tend to examine the "Christological puzzle" from the underside, not from the upper side. Therefore, their Christologies tend to focus more on Jesus' work than on his person in isolation. As John Pobee has noted, "Christology is not only the person of Christ, but also what he does."[30]

The second implication of Africans' starting their Christology "from below" is that its overall approach is more holistic and integrative in explaining how the person and work of Christ apply to the whole of African life. This inevitably means that African Christology is almost unintelligible apart from soteriological, ecclesiological, and even eschatological themes. Many Africans' early exposure to Western, missionary-borne Christianity left the impression that Jesus Christ was the expert in protecting the individual from punishment in the afterlife and vouchsafing the African's safe passage into heaven, a place of joy and bliss. While this emphasis is true, it tended to ignore the traditional African worldview, which did not recognize any fundamental distinction or clear demarcation between the visible and the invisible worlds.

The early preaching about Jesus Christ did not, for example, point out that Jesus was Lord of the crops or the one who provided protection during dangerous journeys or who assisted in the safe birth of a new baby. The nineteenth-century missionaries did not generally come from Christian traditions that practiced casting out demons or were accustomed to praying for God to bring in the crops, except perhaps during times of extreme drought. In short, the Jesus Christ who was preached was often a truncated Christ, not measuring up fully to the biblical picture of Jesus' life, work, and ministry.

John Mbiti tells the story of one of the first Africans to go to Europe to study for the ministry. He learned German, Latin, Greek, and Hebrew and learned about the writings of Bultmann, Barth, Küng, and Niebuhr, among others. He carefully studied church history, systematic theology, homiletics, and biblical exegesis. He was eventually awarded a degree and returned to Africa. The relatives and neighbors in

29. Akintunde Akinade, "Who Do You Say that I Am?—An Assessment of Some Christological Constructs in Africa," *Africa Journal of Theology* 9, no. 1 (April 1995): 191. See John S. Pobee, "In Search of Christology in Africa: Some Considerations for Today," in *Exploring Afro-Christology*, ed. John S. Pobee (New York: Peter Lang, 1992), 10.

30. Pobee, "In Search of Christology in Africa," 10.

his home village were so excited about his newly acquired knowledge (he was the first to ever receive a higher theological degree from his village) that upon his return after several years away, they planned a large celebration to welcome him home.

However, during the festival the man's older sister suddenly shrieked and fell to the ground. Everyone gathered around her and called her brother to come and help. He came and insisted that she be taken immediately to the hospital. They reminded him that the hospital was over fifty miles away. Someone else pointed out that she was possessed by a demon and the hospital would not be able to help her anyway. The village chief insisted that since the brother had studied the Bible and theology for all these years, he should be able to help her himself. Despite his great learning, Mbiti concluded, the man was not able to help his sister because "Bultmann has demythologized demon possession."[31] Mbiti acknowledges that the story is fictional and caricatures Western Christianity within a narrow band of Protestant liberalism, but it is still important that we listen to this story because it gives an important insight into how Western Christianity is *perceived* and into the real disconnect that many Africans sense between the Jesus Christ of Western Christianity and the real life issues and needs facing Africans.

2. Conscious Awareness of Traditional Christological Formulations

The second distinctive feature of African Christology is its conscious awareness of traditional Christological formulations from the West. Unlike Western theologians who often write in isolation from the wider global context, African theologians are keenly aware of the historic Western Christological focus on precise philosophical and metaphysical questions concerning the person of Christ. It is true that some African theologians are critical of the way the councils produced "metaphysical rather than biblically functional images of Jesus,"[32] or complain that the historic formulations are "static"[33] and fail to "touch the souls" of Africans or relate to the "concrete lives of people."[34] But the overall tenor of African Christology is marked by a profound respect for historic Christian confessions.

In fact, John Pobee encourages emerging African theologians to listen carefully to those who have gone before us so that we "do not go hopelessly wrong." He reminds Africans that they are not "starting from scratch," but that they must write in the context of the *depositum fidei* that should inform all African Christology.[35] John Onaiyekan calls the classical formulations "valid reference points" and argues that every African Christian should "consider this classical Christology part of the common theological patrimony of the Church, of which we are full-fledged members."[36] In

31. To read the full story, see John Mbiti, "Theological Impotence and the Universality of the Church," in *Mission Trends, #3: Third World Theologies*, ed. Gerald Anderson and Thomas Stransky (New York: Paulist; Grand Rapids: Eerdmans, 1976), 6–8.

32. This comment by John Pobee is reported in Akinade, "Who Do You Say that I Am?" 186.

33. Akinade, "Who Do You Say that I Am?" 181.

34. Robert J. Schreiter, "Jesus Christ in Africa Today," in *Faces of Jesus in Africa*, ed. Robert J. Schreiter, ix.

35. Pobee, "In Search of Christology in Africa," 10–11.

36. John Onaiyekan, "Christological Trends in Contemporary African Theology," in *Constructive Christian Theology in the Worldwide Church*, ed. William R. Barr (Grand Rapids: Eerdmans, 1997), 362.

this regard, rather than reading African Christology as an *alternative* to the ecumenical confessions, a student should read these writers as looking at Christology from an *additional* vantage point. To continue with the puzzle analogy, the Africans are not seeking so much to take out past pieces that fit well and have served the church. Rather, they are simply seeking to add some additional pieces that have not yet been properly accounted for in Christological discussions to date.[37]

3. Connecting Christ to Africa's Pre-Christian Past

Third, African Christology is deeply interested in understanding better how Christ connects with the pre-Christian past of Africa. One of the most prominent criticisms of the nineteenth-century missionaries is that they approached Africa as if it was a spiritual *tabula rasa*. African culture in all of its particulars was widely condemned by missionaries and described in the most degrading terms. African religion was regarded as no more than a pagan array of witch doctors, fetishism, and superstition. In the nineteenth century, the "Great Chain of Being" placed the peoples of Africa at the very bottom—ethnically, culturally, and religiously.[38]

Thus, Christ was presented to Africa as a foreign stranger in complete discontinuity with its own past. For an African to become a Christian was to step into a world of spiritual amnesia whereby everything in the African past was to be jettisoned to make way for their newly found faith in Christ, which was firmly hinged to a European worldview. Andrew Walls has described the resulting situation as the "crisis of African identity," whereby Africans live in a state of spiritual schizophrenia, not knowing how "to be truly Christian and authentically African."[39] Therefore, the task of integrating Christian faith with authentic African identity becomes a central theme in the emergence of African Christology.

4. An Emphasis on the Power and Victory of Christ

Fourth, despite the diverse Christological images developed by African writers, a common underlying theme is an emphasis on the power and victory of Christ. All of the major African Christological images, such as Christ as Liberator, Chief, Ancestor, Healer, Master of Initiation, and so on, tend to portray Christ in terms of power as *Christus Victor*. Harold Turner, in his *Profile through Preaching*, has documented this emphasis in the popular preaching of African independent church leaders.[40] He discovered that African preachers often focus on Jesus' victory over the devil, his works

37. This is not only because Africans, in general, have a healthy respect for the past, but most of the leading theologians of Africa are either Roman Catholic or Anglican—traditions that hold the ecumenical councils in high regard.

38. The chain ranked races as follows: White, Red, Yellow, and Black. This was also linked to a religious chain that was ranked as follows: Trinitarian monotheism, Jewish and Islamic monotheism, polytheism, and base fetishism. See *Encyclopedia Britannica* (1797), under "Religion," as quoted in Kwame Bediako, *Christianity in Africa—The Renewal of a Non-Western Religion* (Maryknoll, NY: Orbis, 1995), 194.

39. Diane Stinton, "Africa, East and West," in *An Introduction to Third World Theologies*, ed. John Parratt (Cambridge: Cambridge Univ. Press, 2004), 112. See also Andrew Walls "Africa and Christian Identity," in *Mission Focus: Current Issues*, ed. Wilbert Shenk (Scottdale, PA: Herald Press, 1980), 212–21. This is one of the important distinctions between "inculturation," which inserts Christianity into a new culture, and "indigenization," which involves, in part, a Christianization of the religious past.

40. See John Mbiti's discussion of this study in "Some African Concepts of Christology," 53.

of healing and demonic deliverance, his announcement of deliverance for the captives, his triumphal entry into Jerusalem, and his resurrection.

These findings are entirely consistent with African colonial history, the legacy of slavery, the traditional African emphasis on the presence of spiritual powers, the active belief in the demonic, and the presence of devastating physical maladies such as AIDS. Mbiti points out that Jesus draws attention "first and foremost as the Victor over the forces which have dominated African life from time immemorial." Jesus is portrayed as the one who fought victoriously over the "multiheaded Hydra" of Africa. He is the Victor, the Great Conqueror, the one who has emerged victorious from each of the battles that frame much of the African existence. Thus, Mbiti concludes, "the greatest need among African peoples is to see, to know, and to experience Jesus Christ as the victor over the powers and forces from which Africa knows no means of deliverance."[41] It is evident that African Christology is influenced and shaped by the physical, sociopolitical, cultural, and economic realities of the African context. With this general background in mind, it is now time to examine more closely several of the Christological images that have been utilized by sub-Saharan Africans.

Images of Christ in Africa

The Jesuit scholar Avery Dulles, in *Models of the Church*, served us well by demonstrating how "extremely luxuriant" the New Testament is in producing ecclesiological imagery.[42] Images such as the body of Christ, the vine, the temple, the bride, God's field, or the flock all provide unique perspectives in understanding the reality of the church, which transcends any simple or singular description.

Ian Ramsey calls each of these images a "disclosure model."[43] Each one discloses certain truths about the mystery of the church, but each can only illuminate in part and needs all of the other images to bring out a fully biblical picture of the church. Some of the images are intended to inspire hope and courage in the face of persecution. Others emphasize the importance of purity, our continuity with God's past acts, or our connectedness to Jesus Christ. If this is true of ecclesiology, how much more so must this be true of the mystery of Christ himself! Thus, our task is to gaze at the images of Christ being presented to the global church by our African brothers and sisters and to reflect deeply on what these images mean for them and for us.

Four Pillars for Building an African Christology

In the rest of this chapter I have selected two prominent Christological models that emphasize different tendencies within African scholarship. Both models will be described and then evaluated according to four points of reference that Mbiti has suggested as the guide for constructing African theology, especially Christology. I have found these guidelines to be a helpful measuring rod for assessing and discussing the contours of African Christology.

---

41. Ibid.

42. Avery Dulles, *Models of the Church* (Garden City, NY: Doubleday, 1974), 17. Dulles notes that Paul Minear, in his *Images of the Church in the New Testament*, explores ninety-six different images of the church.

43. Dulles's use of the term *model* is similar to the more familiar language of *paradigm* by Thomas Kuhn, which frequents missiological literature.

First, a biblical, exegetical standard must be applied to all African Christologies. Is the proposed image of Christ consistent with what we know about Christ from the biblical revelation? Second, we must take seriously the Christology of what Mbiti calls the "older churches." How do these new Christological images relate to, expand, contradict, or contrast with the historic, ecumenical confessions of the ancient church? Third, we must reflect on how effectively this particular Christological proposal resonates with or responds to the traditional African worldview. Finally, any authentically African Christology must somehow connect with the living experience of Africans, including the Church in Africa. As the AACC (All-Africa Conference of Churches) once said, "We must try to rescue theology and therefore Christology from the shelves of universities ... and make it a living, dynamic, active and creative reality in our communities and among our people."[44] While there is considerable divergence in how much weight various African writers put on each of these four pillars, they remain important in all of their major Christological images.

A survey of the key publications on African Christology reveals six major images that have been proposed: Christ as Healer and Life-Giver, Christ as Liberator, Christ as Chief, Christ as Mediator, Christ as Master of Initiation, and Christ as Ancestor/Elder Brother. There are some variations on these themes and there is considerable overlap. For example, similar emphases are brought out in the images of Christ as Healer and Christ as Liberator. Likewise, there is considerable overlap between Christ as Mediator and Christ as Ancestor.

There is also a distinction between those images that are more universal and draw on language explicitly found in Scripture and those images that do not utilize explicitly biblical language but are rooted more naturally in the particularity of the African context.[45] To illustrate the spectrum I have chosen to examine two of the six major Christological images: (1) Jesus as Healer and Life-Giver, which is drawn quite intentionally from biblical language used to describe Christ, and (2) Jesus as Ancestor, which draws on language never explicitly used of Christ in the Bible, but which deeply resonates with the African religious worldview.

CASE STUDY IN TWO AFRICAN CHRISTOLOGIES

Jesus as Healer and Life-Giver

The influence of the Enlightenment on the worldview of many of the nineteenth-century Western missionaries, coupled with the dramatic rise in health care in the nineteenth-century West, had several important effects. As noted above, the missionaries tended to de-emphasize the supernatural aspect of Christ's healing ministry. Furthermore, they also tended to attribute illness to solely physical causes, calling more for a physician (even an unbelieving one) than a pastor. In light of the strong emphasis in the Gospels on Jesus' healing and deliverance ministry, it is justifiable that the Africans felt that the Christology they had been taught was, upon reflection, inadequate.

44. Akinade, "Who Do You Say that I Am?" 184. Mbiti appears to be adapting John Wesley's famous quadrilateral (Scripture, tradition, reason, and experience) to the African setting, but with a deeper respect for tradition.

45. For a general survey of African Christologies, see Schreiter, ed., *Faces of Jesus in Africa*, or Stinton, *Jesus of Africa*.

It seemed to be lacking both in its honest accounting of the scriptural evidence regarding Christ's work and in its sensitivity to many of the cultural and spiritual realities of Africa regarding suffering and illness.

The Imagery of Christ as Healer and Life-Giver

The imagery of Christ as Healer and Life-Giver should be understood as containing several circles of meaning, each linked with the next and each carrying deeper understandings of Christ. The Christological picture begins with a recognition that Jesus spent a considerable amount of time in his earthly ministry reaching out to people with various infirmities. Christ as Healer and Life-Giver emphasizes that Jesus cares about Africa's suffering and malnutrition and the AIDS pandemic. This is an important starting point. It is a picture of a Christ fully connected to the suffering of Africa.

This is the Christ we meet in the Gospels. He who was "despised and rejected by men" comes as the Life-Giver to those who, more than any other races on earth, have also been despised and rejected by others. Jesus Christ enters Africa not as a stranger but as one who is "familiar with suffering" (Isa. 53:3). Jesus comes as the Great Physician. A key verse that summarizes this image may be found in John 10:10, "I have come that they may have life, and have it to the full." Indeed, John's Gospel is filled with metaphors that provide grounding for this image. Christ is the bread of life (6:35), the living water (4:10), the light of the world (8:12; 9:5), and the resurrection and the life (11:25). These are all images of a life-giving Christ.

The Christological image of Christ as Healer is not limited to his meeting physical needs. In the second link one should picture Christ's role in *spiritual* healing. However, this role should be seen not as a separate work of Christ but as an extension of the first. This is why the various dimensions of the African understanding of Christ as Healer should be viewed as links in a chain rather than separate spheres of action. Africans simply do not maintain a sharp demarcation between physical healing and spiritual healing, as often occurs in Western writings. Even the traditional healers in African cultures served as bridges between the physical and the spiritual.

For the African Christian, this integration is exemplified in Acts 3, which records the story of a crippled beggar being healed through the name of Jesus. This physical healing provides public, tangible evidence to support Peter's claim to the onlookers that Jesus is "the author of life" (Acts 3:15). Thereupon, Peter applies Christ's healing power to his work in healing sinful hearts (3:19).

This holistic view of Christ's healing work is central to African Christology. For example, a Ghanaian pastor named Aboagye-Mensah says that "Jesus is the healer, [the] one who heals not only our sicknesses, but our deeply wounded souls."[46] A Kenyan laywoman named Marcy Muhia also finds great comfort in Jesus as Healer. He not only heals our broken bodies, she declares, but we are "broken in our sinfulness, broken in our relationships because of that sinfulness ... and I think Christ is able to heal that, to heal very completely."[47]

46. As quoted in Stinton, *Jesus of Africa*, 71.

47. Ibid., 72.

In light of our study in chapter 4, it is interesting to observe how Africans seamlessly link the spiritual healing that Jesus brings with the rebuilding of a broken *community.* The work of Christ, for the African, implies not just the restoration of an individual into a right relationship with God, but also the spiritual healing of our relationships one with another. Jesus extends his healing within the larger context of social reintegration into the community. Healing is both physical and spiritual; it is both individual and corporate.

Because the starting point of African reflections about Christ is the work of Christ, African Christology is closely linked with both soteriology and ecclesiology. In other words, Christ as Healer is part of his larger work of soteriology—Christ saves his people. Christ as Healer is also part of his larger work of ecclesiology—Christ is bringing restoration to the community by building his church. Of course, none of this work would be possible apart from the person of Christ, so African Christology largely presupposes the prior Christological formulations regarding Christ's person.

The third link in the image of Christ as Healer and Life-Giver exemplifies the full cosmic dimensions of the African worldview. Christ comes not only to heal our diseased bodies and to spiritually restore our communities, but he also comes as the one who grants us victory over Satan. The enemy has come to "kill, steal and destroy," whereas Jesus has come so that his sheep "may have life" (John 10:10). Therefore, the life of Jesus must be extended into the whole cosmos, overturning Satan and the principalities and powers that rule in "the present evil age" (Gal. 1:4). The Ghanaian pastor Aboagye-Mensah, quoted above, goes on to say that Jesus is the "one who is victorious over the spiritual forces," including the "powers of darkness" and the "principalities and powers."[48]

From a cosmic perspective, it is clear that the Christological image of Christ as Healer and Life-Giver is understood in the larger context of *Christus Victor*, giving an eschatological emphasis to African Christology. The following diagram demonstrates the holistic, threefold understanding of healing and life-giving in African Christology. (See Figure C.)

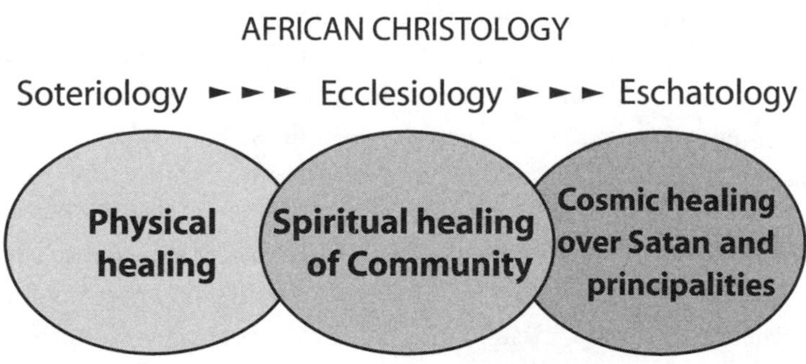

Figure C: Christ as Healer/Life-Giver

48. Ibid., 74.

Evaluation of Christ as Healer and Life-Giver

Let us now evaluate the image of Christ as Healer and Life-Giver utilizing the four criteria suggested by Mbiti.

1. Biblical criteria. There are no serious objections to the general recognition that healing was a regular component of the earthly ministry of Jesus. Even a casual survey of the New Testament reveals dozens of verses portraying Jesus Christ as Healer and Life-Giver. The only major objection on biblical grounds to this particular image of African Christology has come from those who argue that too much emphasis on physical healing will serve to diminish the deeper, spiritual significance of Christ's ministry and, possibly, create a movement to Christ for the wrong motives.

Some have argued that African Christianity lacks depth and that its superficiality is due to the emphasis on Christ's meeting physical needs rather than on a larger, more comprehensive view of the kingdom of God. This concern is reflected in the remarks of Kenyan lecturer Peter Gichure at the Catholic University of East Africa, who expressed concern that "the emphasis on Jesus the healer can be another euphoria," opening the door for itinerant evangelists to exploit Africans who are "in very desperate situations" and cannot afford modern medical care.[49]

These are important concerns but they must be, at least, partially mitigated by two points. First, both popular and highly developed African Christologies that portray Christ as Healer and Life-Giver *do* tend to include, as noted above, a much more comprehensive view of healing than a mere physical healing of the body. To insist that this is only about physical healing is to caricature the actual usage and development of this image by most African Christians. Indeed, as Jean-Marc Ela has said, Jesus' healings are not expressions of a mere miracle worker, but "one who roots salvation in the web of history ... demonstrating that salvation is available in 'bodily' form."[50]

Second, the image of Christ as Healer and Life-Giver is as incapable of capturing a comprehensive view of the kingdom of God as is any other single image. It is impossible to come up with one Christological image that fully exhausts the glory of Christ. In short, this objection could be made against *any* Christological image. However, this should serve as an ongoing reminder of the importance of utilizing multiple images of Christ in our Christological catechesis with new believers.

2. Older church criteria. The notion of Christ as Healer and Life-Giver does come across as quite alien to the kinds of Christological statements made about Christ by the older, ecumenical formulations. The reason it does, as noted earlier, is that African theologians approach Christology from a different starting point and that they are gazing at the beauty of Christ from a different perspective. A Christology "from above," like the Chalcedonian formula, which focuses on the person of Christ, is not going to emphasize Christ's healing ministry among the sick. Because of the Chalcedonian precedent, all of the Christological work by subsequent Western theologians has tended to approach Christology from the upper side. Louis Berkhof, for example, in his renowned *Systematic Theology*, never mentions Christ as a healer in over 250

49. Ibid., 77.

50. Ibid., 78.

pages that he devotes to the person and work of Christ and its application in the lives of believers. A survey of all the major systematic theologies used in Western seminaries would reveal that this is not unusual.

Even when Christ is heralded as a healer, as he is in the second volume of Thomas Oden's systematic theology, it is not applied to believers today in a way that resonates with African presuppositions. Oden's application of Christ's healing ministry today is found in a section beneath the heading, "Can Miracles be Defined *a Priori* as Impossible?" Oden makes the point that advances in quantum physics make it more acceptable to understand modern-day miracles without also having to believe in the suspension of natural laws.[51] Oden's point is an important one. However, he is clearly seeking to convince skeptical, rationalistic Westerners that miracles really *can* happen, a point hardly necessary for a supernaturalist African.

Thus, even an image as straightforward as Jesus as Healer and Life-Giver can be articulated and comprehended in different ways. For the purposes of this chapter, we must concede that the image of Christ as Healer and Life-Giver is highly inadequate as a Christology focused on the *person* of Christ. However, it is a powerful Christological image that fully resonates with the *work* of Christ. This is not to say that the African image has any fundamental conflict with Chalcedon, merely that it is a very different image based on an entirely different perspective, but both are needed in the larger Christological puzzle.

3. Traditional African worldview. It is primarily on the basis of their traditional worldview that many African Christians have objected to the image of Christ as Healer and Life-Giver. The rather remarkable spectrum of African responses to this image is largely due to the different connotations various groups attach to the traditional healers who are central to many expressions of African Traditional Religion. In a survey conducted by Diane Stinton, approximately two-thirds of the Africans interviewed responded positively to the idea that Jesus was a Healer (*mganga*), whereas one third had a negative reaction to the image.[52] The negative reaction is due to the negative associations some Africans have with traditional healers. For these Africans, to associate Jesus with traditional healers may create a syncretistic association of Jesus with divination, manipulation, magic, and witchcraft. It is tantamount to associating the work of Jesus with the work of Satan.

By contrast, however, other African languages and cultures make important distinctions between traditional healers, witch doctors, herbalists, medicine men, and so forth. In their case, the traditional healers may carry none of the above negative associations. For them, this is a powerful way for Jesus to fulfill and to transcend the traditional role of the healer in African society. For these Africans, to discourage this application actually hurts the cause of Christ in Africa and further contributes to the spiritual amnesia that has been inflicted on that continent for centuries. It would seem, therefore, that the suitability of using the Christological image of Christ as Healer and Life-Giver as a dominant motif in Africa should be determined, at least in

51. Thomas C. Oden, *The Word of Life*, vol. 2 of *Systematic Theology* (Peabody, MA: Prince, 1989), 302.

52. Stinton, *Jesus of Africa*, 82–83.

part, by the associations a particular African language and culture attributes to the traditional healers.

4. Living experience of African Christians. African history and culture has been dramatically influenced by the legacies of slavery, colonialism, political corruption, disease, famine, and, more recently, the AIDS pandemic. There is little doubt that the image of Jesus as Healer and Life-Giver represents a wonderful expression of the good news of the gospel in the context of sub-Saharan Africa. Elizabeth Amoah and Mercy Oduyoye have observed that one of the features of the African Independent Churches, which constitute the fastest growing edge of African Christianity, is that "Christ, the great Healer, is seen as the center of the Christology of these charismatic churches."[53]

In conclusion, there are no major reasons why the Christological image of Jesus as Healer and Life-Giver should not be celebrated in Africa. It will not be an image that finds broad support in those parts of Africa with negative associations of traditional healers, but overall, many Africans will discover in this picture an expression of the good news of the gospel, and Jesus as Healer will be able to enter into Africa not as a stranger but as a friend, as one who speaks their language and knows their culture.

Jesus as Ancestor

African Traditional Religion cannot be spoken of in the singular if it conveys the notion that African religion embodies any singular, codified system of beliefs and practices. However, there are such profound similarities in the general structure of African religions and the religious outlook of many African peoples that most scholars speak of African Traditional Religion (hereafter, ATR) in the singular. Bolaji Idowu, for example, points out that "there is a common Africanness about the total culture and religious beliefs and practices of Africa."[54] Broadly speaking, therefore, ATR generally embraces a three-tiered religious system. At the highest tier is a Supreme Being, who oversees the entire cosmological system. For many Africans, this Supreme Being is a distant, vague, *deus otiosus*,[55] whereas other Africans have an articulate, more involved, conception of a Supreme Being.

In either case, the focus of the religious life in Africa is normally the second tier of power, which is inhabited by a pantheon of various divinities. This pantheon often includes nonhuman divinities as well as various divinized ancestors, whose earthly ancestry and descendants are known. This second tier is the focus of mediation between God and humanity. In ATR there is no fundamental contradiction in simultaneously embracing a Supreme Being as well as a pantheon of divinities, since

53. Elizabeth Amoah and Mercy Oduyoye, "The Christ for African Women," in *With Passion and Compassion: Third World Women Doing Theology*, ed. Virginia Fabella and Mercy Amba Oduyoye (Maryknoll, NY: Orbis, 1988), 39, as quoted in Stinton, *Jesus of Africa*, 73.

54. E. Bolaji Idowu, *African Traditional Religion* (Maryknoll, NY: Orbis, 1973), 103.

55. Latin for "hidden" or "neutral" God, used here in the sense of a high god who has withdrawn from the details of governing the world, but has delegated this task to various mediators such as ancestors and lower level functionary divinities.

African religion distinguishes between a "deity" and a "divinity," the latter having only derived powers. Bolaji Idowu captures the image well when he refers to the second tier as an expression of "diffused monotheism."[56] Thus, ATR can be simultaneously monotheistic and polydivinistic without contradiction.

The third level is the earthly tier, which is where various expressions of ritualized power take place to maintain harmony, balance, and order. This third tier embraces a wide range of religious functionaries including traditional healers, herbalists, chiefs, and priests. This section of the chapter will examine how African Christians have seen Christ as fulfilling the aspirations embodied by the belief in ancestors and how this has influenced their Christological reflection.

African writers regularly acknowledge the central place of ancestors and mediators in the African religious consciousness. Many African cultures believe that a person should never approach God (or even an important person) directly. Instead, this should be done through some kind of mediation. ATR provides various avenues for this kind of mediation, including, but not limited to, the ancestors. In fact, the ancestors function in a wide variety of roles in Africa, including serving as supernatural mediators, liturgical companions, guardians of a particular clan, or even, more simply, as models of good behavior. The Tanzanian scholar Charles Nyamiti defines an ancestor as "a relative of a person with whom he has a common parent, and of whom he is mediator to God, archetype of behavior, and with whom—thanks to his supernatural status acquired through death—he is entitled to have regular sacred communication."[57]

In order for any persons to be declared "ancestors," they should be widely regarded as having lived a virtuous life that upheld the moral fabric of the clan, they should have left descendants who remember them, and they should have "died well" (i.e., they lived to an old age and did not die an unnatural or untimely death).[58] Once they are declared ancestors, some remain as "family" or "clan" ancestors and are venerated only by the particular families who are their descendants. Other ancestors become "glorified" and are venerated by an entire people, even by different clans who have no direct blood relation or ancestral connection with that ancestor.[59] Ancestors of all types are often referred to as the "living-dead" because even though they have physically died, they "remain united in affection and in mutual obligations with the 'living-living.'"[60]

An "Ascending Christology"

In reflecting deeply on Jesus Christ within the African setting, many African laypeople and theologians began to see the image of ancestor as a bridge rather than a barrier to the expansion of the gospel in their continent. There are several nonnegotiable aspects of Christ's work and person that Africans felt the ancestor image could

56. E. Bolaji Idowu, *Olodumare God in Yoruba Belief* (London: Longmans, Green & Co., Ltd., 1962), 204. Idowu was speaking, in particular, about the second tier among the Yoruba, but his point can be applied to many expressions of ATR.

57. Charles Nyamiti, *Christ as Our Ancestor: Christology from an African Perspective* (Gweru, Zimbabwe: Mambo, 1984), 35.

58. Thomas Lawson, *Religions of Africa* (New York: Harper & Row, 1984), 63.

59. Ibid.

60. Bediako, *Christianity in Africa*, 94.

uniquely help explain, including the relation of Christ's humanity and deity, Christ's role as the sole and final mediator between God and humanity, and the risen, exalted Lord's role as head of the church, the redeemed community.

While this chapter has pointed out that African Christians do not use the person of Christ as the *starting* point in their Christology, it would be a mistake to conclude that their emphasis on the work of Christ is carried out untethered from the person of Christ. As noted earlier, African theologians generally hold in high esteem the ecumenical councils and the Christological formulations that emerged from them. Nevertheless, even African Christological expressions concerning the person of Christ start out "from below" and arrive at an understanding of his person through the lens of his work. This is known as an "ascending Christology," whereas the traditional, ecumenical Christological formulations are known as "descending Christologies."[61]

An ascending Christology starts with Jesus as a man in real history and gradually demonstrates that the works he accomplished could only be possible if he was more than a man. Indeed, deep reflection on his works demonstrates that he is the very Son of God, in a unique relationship with God the Father, fully sharing in his divine prerogatives and dignity. African theologians argue that this approach is essentially the path for Christological reflection that is modeled in the Gospels: the disciples of Jesus meet him as a man in history, gradually accept his messiahship and, eventually, as eyewitnesses of the resurrection, come to recognize his full dignity as the second person of the Trinity.

Applying this "ascending Christology" to African views of ancestorship, we can say that Jesus enters into Africa as a man, fully sharing in the suffering and pain that is central to African humanity. As the second Adam, Jesus fully assumes our humanity and, for the African, becomes the "proto"-Ancestor by becoming the head of the whole family of humanity, thus fulfilling and transcending the traditional role of the ancestor. Moreover, an examination of the life and teachings of Jesus clearly demonstrate that he is the archetype of virtuous behavior and serves in a mediating role between God and humanity. His death on the cross appeared, at first, as a tragic interruption to his work, giving him an untimely and ignominious death. However, his resurrection demonstrated that he continues as the Living One, overturning even death itself. The Gospels declare that he, in fact, "died well" since through his death he bore the sin of the world and "disarmed the principalities and powers ... triumphing over them by the cross" (Col. 2:15). Through his death and resurrection he is recognized as having had supernatural status. He is, in fact, not only the "firstborn" of the living, but "the firstborn over all creation" (Col. 1:15) as the Lord and Head of all the faithful. Just as Jesus declared that the God of Abraham, Isaac, and Jacob "is not the God of the dead, but of the living, for to him all are alive" (Luke 20:38), so Jesus' victory over death and his ascension into "the realm of spirit-power" allows him to be designated as "Supreme Ancestor."[62]

61. Nyamiti, *Christ as Our Ancestor*, 35.

62. Bediako, *Christianity in Africa*, 217.

In conclusion, the image or model of Jesus as ancestor clearly reflects an ascending Christology, which begins with Christ's humanity and culminates in his resurrection and exaltation. John Pobee says of the humanity of Jesus,

> On account of his humanity, Christ's Ancestorship is linked with Adam. This fact renders Christ a member of our race and gives his Ancestorship a transcendental connotation in virtue of which it transcends all family, clanic [sic], tribal or racial limitations.[63]

Furthermore, through his resurrection "Jesus is not only first-born of the living as elder brother, but also first-born of the living-dead as Ancestor."[64] His full deity and relationship with the Father entitles him to our worship, and he, as the Head of a new community, has promised his ongoing guidance and participation in the life of the community through his Spirit, thus fulfilling all of the key elements of a Glorified Ancestor.

Evaluation of Christ as Ancestor

This Ancestor Christology will now be evaluated according to our fourfold criteria.

1. Biblical criteria. Unlike the image of Healer and Life-Giver, the term *ancestor* is never explicitly applied to Christ in biblical writings. This single fact alone is sufficient for some to reject it as an appropriate Christological image. While I think this does reduce its potential as a universal image that the whole global church can embrace, it does not necessarily render it useless for Africans and other cultures with a strong emphasis on ancestors if it can be given sufficient theological grounding.

There are three major theological anchors used by Africans who employ ancestor imagery in their Christology. First, John's use of *logos* (λόγος) in the Fourth Gospel provides a precedent for utilizing a nonbiblical word and applying it to Jesus Christ. John's contemporaries would have understood *logos* as a philosophical term referring to a rational capacity or "generative principle" that is present in all of nature. In the prologue to his Gospel, John ingeniously uses the philosophical term *logos* as his starting point, but connects it with the divine, spoken word that in Genesis brings the whole created order into being. We must recognize that, in the Hellenistic setting, because the term *logos* referred to an impersonal, all-pervading force, its semantic starting point was actually closer to a Hindu worldview than to orthodox Christianity. Yet, John roots the term in biblical revelation when he declares, "the *logos* became flesh and dwelt among us" (cf. John 1:14).

Citing John's use of *logos* as a precedent, African scholars have asked whether a nonbiblical term like *ancestors* can be redirected toward Christian ends and rooted in biblical revelation. African scholar Kwame Bediako has frequently heard Ghanians praying to *Nana Yesu* (Ancestor Jesus). Bediako explores whether or not *Nana Yesu* is a modern equivalent of the apostle John's reference to *logos*. He asks, "Can the reality

63. See Nyamiti, *Christ as Our Ancestor*, 27.

64. John R. Levison and Priscilla Pope-Levison, "Emergent Christologies in Latin America, Asia and Africa," *The Covenant Quarterly* 52 (May 1994): 41.

and actuality of Jesus as intended in the Christian affirmation inhabit the Akan world of Nana in the same way that it could inhabit the Greek world of *logos*?"[65]

In other words, was the apostle John inspired to use the *logos* concept not only to communicate the reality of Jesus to the Greek world, but also to model an interpretive method that can, by extension, be applied to other languages and cultures as the church spreads around the world? If so, John's use of the *logos* is not only a sign of the theological translatability of the gospel among Greeks in his own time, but it is actually helping to train Christians today to be more effective communicators of the gospel within their own linguistic and cultural milieus. In short, many Africans find in John's *logos* an important precedent calling African Christians to "spoil the Egyptians" by taking the concept of ancestor and applying it to Jesus Christ.

A second theological connection between ancestors and Christ is the biblical role of Jesus Christ as mediator. First Timothy 2:5 declares that "there is one God and one mediator between God and men, the man Christ Jesus." This verse clearly invokes Christ's role as mediator, which is the central role of the ancestors. Indeed, the controlling idea of all ancestor veneration in Africa is that of exalted mediators between heaven and earth.[66]

Thomas Torrance, in *The Mediation of Christ*, demonstrates that this is the most important Christological image in the New Testament because only a proper doctrine of Christ as Mediator solves the "Christology from below" versus the "Christology from above" dilemma. Torrance argues that Christological vulnerabilities occurred with an either-or approach because "each approach ended up denying itself and passing over into the opposite, so that there was no solution to the problem created by their dualistic thinking of Christ."[67] Torrance goes on to say that "it was only as they allowed Jesus Christ in his whole undivided reality to disclose himself to them as the Mediator, that they were able to formulate a doctrine of Christ which did justice to the whole frame of the Gospel."[68]

A third important theological connection is the biblical relationship between the life and death of the Christian community. The Apostles' Creed declares that we believe in the "communion of the saints." However, traditional Christology has tended to focus on Christ "without consideration of his mystical relationship to his members."[69] Traditional Western Christology, argues Charles Nyamiti, "paid almost exclusive attention to the Head, but not to the whole of Christ, Head and members—with the result that one does not duly investigate the theological implications which Christ's mystical union with his members have on his resurrection."[70]

Indeed, all the biblical metaphors of Christology imply this connection. There can be no kingship without subjects of a kingdom; there can be no shepherd without sheep; there can be no head without a body. The African connectedness between their communities and their ancestral head gives them a strong sense of the continuity

65. Kwame Bediako, "The Doctrine of Christ and the Significance of Vernacular Terminology," *International Bulletin of Missionary Research* 22, no. 3 (July 1998): 110.

66. Raymond Moloney, "African Christology," *Theological Studies* 48 (1987): 510.

67. Thomas Torrance, *The Mediation of Christ* (Grand Rapids: Eerdmans, 1983), 63.

68. Ibid.

69. Nyamiti, *Christ as Our Ancestor*, 48.

70. Ibid.

beyond earthly life. When Christ enters Africa, Bediako argues, "the ancestors are cut off as a means of blessing and we lay our power-lines differently."[71] Thus, one of the values of Ancestor Christology is that it clarifies the place of the natural ancestors. "By making room among the 'living dead' for the Lord, the judge of both the living and the dead, it becomes more evident how they relate to Him, and He to them."[72]

2. Older church criteria. Ancestor Christology arrives at the doctrine of the person of Christ as fully God and fully man through a rather particularized lens. Because the starting point of African Christology is "from below," it may be less vulnerable to the docetic tendencies more characteristic of the descending Christologies. However, an ascending Christology such as "Ancestor Christ" is likely to be vulnerable to Arian tendencies, since the basic natural paradigm of the ancestors is that they were not eternally preexistent ancestors, but *became* ancestors through their virtuous life and the dedication of their descendants.

We did explore how respect for the traditional formulas as well as the centrality of mediation in the ancestor image may mitigate this vulnerability somewhat. Nevertheless, it seems that an Ancestor Christology, particularly if articulated in isolation from the older Christologies that set forth with unmistakable clarity the precise nature of the person of Christ, could be problematic. This may explain why the negative responses to the ancestor image by African Christians themselves range between 44 percent and 63 percent, depending on the region of Africa and the pre-Christian associations with the term *ancestor*.[73]

The difficulty in evaluating how *ancestor* is understood and responded to by the older churches is further nuanced by the keen observation of Kwame Bediako that the associations Africans attach to this English word are very different from the associations of the vernacular equivalents. For example, Bediako says that "while hardly anyone will pray in *English* to 'Ancestor Jesus' or 'Chief Jesus' many will readily pray in *Akan* to '*Nana Yesu*' (Ancestor Jesus)."[74] The reason that the English word "ancestor" can never really serve as an exact equivalent of the Akan word *Nana* is because the former is a generic term whereas *Nana* "is both a title and a personal name." Thus, for a Ghanaian to speak of Christ as *Nana* carries with it a personalized description of his unique *person* rather than a generic category such as the term *ancestor*, which may strike the hearer as too vague and impersonal.

Modern-day English speakers should not forget that this same challenge occurred when the ecumenical formulations that emerged from Constantinople and Chalcedon were translated into English. The original formulation declared that God is one in *ousia*, but has three distinctions known as *hypostases*. The English restatement of the councils might best be summed up by the Westminster Confession, which declared,

> In the unity of the Godhead there be three persons, of one substance [*homoousios*], power and eternity; God the Father, God the Son, and God the Holy

71. Bediako, *Christianity in Africa*, 217.
72. Ibid.
73. Stinton, *Jesus of Africa*, 123.
74. Bediako, "The Doctrine of Christ and the Significance of Vernacular Terminology," 110.

> Spirit. The Father is of none, neither begotten nor proceeding; the Son is eternally begotten of the Father; the Holy Ghost eternally proceeding from the Father and the Son.[75]

The three most important words found in this brief statement are *person*, *substance*, and *begotten*. Yet, all three of the corresponding Greek terms are difficult to translate into English. The word *person* is often thought of as "individual," which it cannot mean in the orthodox statement. The word *begotten* will conjure up in the mind of most English speakers some vague association with something mysteriously sexual, which the original statement would not. Finally, the word *substance* conveys in English the idea of something solid and material, which is not what was meant by the Greek word *ousia*.[76]

In a similar way, it is difficult to fully evaluate the image of Ancestor Jesus, since the connotations within the local idioms may be quite different than the English counterpart. The solution, it seems, is to learn a lesson from those unnamed believers who began to "speak to Greeks also, telling them the good news about the Lord Jesus" (Acts 11:20). They realized that the title *messiah* would not be comprehended as good news for a pagan Greek. Instead, they utilized the title *kyrios*, which, although richly used in the biblical tradition, would certainly be associated by pagans with, for example, *kyrios Serapis* or *kyrios Adonis*, not the Lord of biblical revelation.[77] Andrew Walls points out that surely some of the brethren must have "recoiled at the syncretistic possibilities." However, Walls goes on to say that even this "daring act of metaphysical translation" succeeded because they were prepared to give the new concept "explanation, qualification, supplementation, and definition as the identity of Jesus was explored in terms of Hellenistic language and thought."[78]

If we take this word of advice, then the term *ancestor* can be fully utilized in a way consistent with the earlier formulations as long as the term is accompanied by careful explanation, qualification, and supplementation such that the true identity of Jesus is manifested. Some of the obvious areas where further "explanation and qualification" would be necessary are that the ancestors have a human origin as part of the creation, whereas Jesus does not. The ancestors were sinners, Jesus was not. The ancestors are actually dead and have only achieved a symbolic and ritual victory over death, whereas Jesus is alive and truly conquered death. Clearly, if the term is to be retained and applied to Jesus, it requires significant qualifications and explanations in order to serve the church well.

75. Westminster Confession 2.3. For a full text of the Confession, see Robert L. Dabney, *The Westminster Confession and Creeds* (Dallas: Presbyterian Heritage, 1983). It should be noted that prior to the Cappadocian Fathers, even the terms *ousia* and *hypostasis* were sometimes used interchangeably.

76. This same phenomenon can be traced in the translation of Chalcedonian Christology into African languages. For example, the term *homoousious* translates in Yoruba as "of the same character with the Father," meaning the same reputation or ethical behavior rather than a reference to ontology. See Onaiyekan, "Christological Trends in Contemporary African Theology," 362.

77. *Kyrios Serapis* was the Greco-Egyptian deity of the sun. He eventually was regarded as lord of healing and fertility and his worship was prominent throughout the Mediterranean world.

78. Andrew F. Walls, "Old Athens and New Jerusalem: Some Signposts for Christian Scholarship in the Early History of Mission Studies," *International Bulletin of Missionary Research* 21, no. 4 (October 1997): 148.

3. *Traditional African worldview.* Raymond Moloney has suggested that all African Christologies can be divided into the two general categories: Christologies of liberation and Christologies of inculturation.[79] The two Christological models examined in this chapter (Christ as Healer/Life-Giver and Christ as Ancestor) belong to each of the two categories, respectively. The reason Christ as Ancestor is clearly an example of an inculturation Christology is that its very emergence among so many different African thinkers, independent of one another, testifies to how central the theme is in the traditional African worldview.

There are four major points of contact between Christ and the traditional African worldview concerning ancestors that must be taken into consideration. First, Jesus serves as the mediator between God and humankind. Second, Jesus is the founder and head of the redeemed community. Third, as the risen Lord, Jesus has an ongoing role to guide and direct the life of the community. Fourth, Jesus gives identity to and transmits life to his community.[80] Thus, for Christ to truly inhabit the African religious consciousness it seems vital that his person and work be explicitly demonstrated to be fulfilling and completing the key functions that the ancestors have traditionally occupied in African society, lest Christ enter Africa as a stranger.

Even John Mbiti has acknowledged the "deadness and rottenness" in traditional African religiosity that must be purged by the Christian faith.[81] Clearly, the only way to avoid syncretism is if the "natural ancestors" are transcended by the "spiritual ancestors," and the solidarity that was once shared by the tribes through the ancestor must now be shared by all believers everywhere through the headship of Christ alone. The "power lines" of the "natural" ancestors should be replaced by the new "spiritual" ancestors, which include Abraham, Moses, David, and, indeed, the entire "cloud of witnesses" (Heb. 12:1) who have gone before us, giving us what Andrew Walls calls "an Adoptive Past."[82] Mbiti believes that "the African field is ripe for this contact to be established, and for the transposition of tribal solidarity into Christ's solidarity."[83]

4. *Living experience of African Christians.* Another fascinating difference between Christ as Healer/Life-Giver and Christ as Ancestor is that the former is focused almost exclusively on the *work* of Christ whereas the latter, as explored above, starts "from below" with an indigenous concept, but moves in an ascending fashion ending up with more of a focus on his *person*. The result is that the image of Christ as Ancestor may not seem, on the surface, to have an overwhelming relevance in addressing African issues such as malnutrition, AIDS, political instability, discrimination, and so forth. However, after deeper reflection, it is clear that the ancestor imagery may, in fact, resonate deeply with the living experience of African Christians in several areas.

79. Moloney, "African Christology," 506.

80. Stinton, *Jesus of Africa*, 127–29.

81. John S. Mbiti, "Christianity and Traditional Religions in Africa," *International Review of Mission* 59, no. 236 (October 1970): 437.

82. Walls, "Africa and Christian Identity," 218. It should be noted that these new adoptive ancestors do not function in a mediatory role.

83. Mbiti, "Some African Concepts of Christology," 61.

First, proclaiming Christ as the second Adam who came into the world as the firstborn over all creation and was heralded by African Christians as the proto-Ancestor of the human race (since it was through him that the Father created the world) fills a cultural and religious void that otherwise might continue to be filled by the traditional religion. It sends a strong message that God in Jesus Christ desires a deep and intimate involvement with Africans that no longer requires them to look to their traditional religion to fill this void, as it can be found directly in the good news of the gospel.

In the early 1990s I conducted field research among Muslims in Nigeria to determine how ATR influenced the practice of Islam in West Africa.[84] Although my research focus was Islam, I found that African Muslims and Christians alike were profoundly shaped and influenced by the traditional religious and cultural worldview. This is because, as John Pobee has observed, words do not merely enable us to communicate, they actually assume "the weight of a culture."[85] To dismiss the term *ancestor* too hastily may also serve, inadvertently, to dismiss all of the African cultural elements that also rest on the word. In contrast, a more proactive, robust engagement with this worldview may gradually help to desacralize it, eventually enabling it to function as a *preparatio evangelica* to that which it can only serve as a shadow and vague anticipation of what was to come. Christ as Ancestor is one who is "fleshed out" in terms Africans can understand.

Second, since Christ as Ancestor transcends the particularities of any specific tribal identity, this image can help to unify African Christians. Many African countries, even those with extremely high percentages of Christian affiliation, have been beset by tribal conflict, ethnic tensions, and even genocide.[86] The African kinship system creates a powerful sense of solidarity and belonging among those who share the same ethnicity and a corresponding suspicion of outsiders. But if Christ is received by African Christians as the Head of the whole body of Christ, which encompasses peoples from all tribes and languages, such a development could create the basis for a new kind of African solidarity.[87]

If the nations of Africa are to be discipled in obedience to the Great Commission, it is essential that the issue of African identity be directly addressed. What does it mean to be an African belonging to a particular ethnic group? How is that identity affected by the fact that I am now an African *Christian*? What are the *ethical* ramifications for my African brothers and sisters now that we are together in Christ and share him as our common Elder Brother? This may be one of the most important contributions of African Christianity to the stability of African societies in the twenty-first century.

This survey of Christ as Ancestor reveals that it is an image that has great potential for good in Africa as well as for serious Christological error. Three serious objections

84. Timothy C. Tennent, "Islam and African Traditional Religion: A Study of Religious Interaction in Modern Nigeria," (master's thesis, Princeton Theological Seminary, 1991).

85. Quoted by Bediako, *Christianity in Africa*, 72.

86. The most obvious example in recent years has been the genocidal conflict in Rwanda between the Hutu and Tutsi.

87. This could be developed theologically in ways similar to how the apostle Paul helped first-century followers of Christ transcend their Jewish or Gentile ethnic identity and find a common identity in Christ, using a first Adam–second Adam motif.

to the African use of ancestor imagery should be noted. First, the image is so particularized for the African context that it may hamper the church's ability to bring out the true global universality of Jesus Christ. This is why, when interviewed, even many African Christians prefer to utilize only biblical images that are explicitly used of Christ in the Scriptures.[88] Second, building Christology on the foundation of African ancestor veneration creates a vulnerability to Arianism that may rob Christ of his full deity and eternal preexistence with the Father. Third, the ancestor image, as is the case with several other prominent African Christological images, including Christ as Chief and Christ as Liberator, tends to produce a *theologia gloriae*, leaving little conceptual space for a *theologia crucis*.[89] Ancestors, like chiefs, are distant and absent from most of the daily struggles of Africans and are carefully kept separate from all pain and suffering. However, the actual suffering and passion of Jesus Christ is central to any mature and fully biblical Christology.

In response to these criticisms, it has been pointed out that even an image as particularized as "Ancestor Jesus" can still resonate with classical, received orthodoxy as long as it is accompanied by appropriate clarifications and explanations. Bénézet Bujo has sought to quell these concerns by using the term "proto-Ancestor," which allows Jesus to fill the category while yet transcending any elements that do not resonate with biblical Christology. Others have suggested such terms as "Superior Ancestor" or "Ancestor with a Difference."[90] I think such an approach would satisfy the concerns noted above, particularly as this image is expressed through vernacular, rather than English, language discourse.

CONCLUSION

This chapter has examined Christological formulation in the African context. Even this limited study, focusing on only two of the six major Christological images, has demonstrated the challenges peculiar to all contextual Christologies. They emerge out of a certain set of cultural particularities that have often been neglected by mainstream theological discourse. The static categories of "upper side" Christology need to be balanced by some of the existential realities facing Christians in the Majority World church. Authentic African Christian reflection may help to deliver the West from the docetic tendencies that have often characterized its Christological discourse.[91]

These Christological images may also help to restore the biblical integration of the person and the work of Christ by shining light on the "underside" of the Christological puzzle. In today's global context where the majority of Christians live outside the West, far from the citadels of power, far from access to well-developed healthcare, and far from the comforts of affluence, we can no longer afford to take refuge in an

88. Stinton, *Jesus of Africa*, 123–26, 130–35.

89. John Pobee, *Toward an African Theology* (Nashville: Abingdon, 1979), 97.

90. Stinton, *Jesus of Africa*, 137.

91. A survey of the major heretical challenges to orthodoxy demonstrates that the tendency was to downplay the humanity of Christ (Gnosticism, Docetism, Monophysitism, Monotheletisim, etc.), although there were major challenges that downplayed his deity as well (Arianism, Adoptionism, etc.). However, the humanity of Christ was essentially assumed in the conversations, so the major Christological battles focused on the deity of Christ.

overly spiritualized Christology or an overly compartmentalized understanding of the salvation being wrought by him.

However, even beyond how African Christology may help us in the West, it is refreshing to see the African church "posing questions and problems from its own context of faith in Christ for which it received no preparation from Christianity in the West."[92] Undoubtedly, the Africans' struggle to produce Christologies that are faithful to the biblical text and yet responsive to the particular cultural, theological, and contextual challenges they face will be no less long or difficult than it was for the church in the West.

BIBLIOGRAPHY

Akinade, Akintunde. "Who Do You Say that I Am?—An Assessment of Some Christological Constructs in Africa." *Africa Journal of Theology* 9, no. 1 (April 1995): 181–200.

Bediako, Kwame. *Christianity in Africa—The Renewal of a Non-Western Religion*. Maryknoll, NY: Orbis, 1995.

_____. "The Doctrine of Christ and the Significance of Vernacular Terminology." *International Bulletin of Missionary Research* 22, no. 3 (July 1998): 110–11.

_____. *Jesus and the Gospel in Africa*. Maryknoll, NY: Orbis, 2004.

Bosch, David J. *Transforming Mission: Paradigm Shifts in Theology of Mission*. Maryknoll, NY: Orbis, 1996.

"Common Christological Declaration between the Catholic Church and the Assyrian Church of the East" (November 11, 1994). *Information Service* 88, no. 1 (1995): 1–6.

Cox, Harvey. *Fire from Heaven*. Reading, MA: Addison-Wesley, 1995.

Cullmann, Oscar. *The Christology of the New Testament*. Philadelphia: Westminster, 1959.

Dabney, Robert L. *The Westminster Confession and Creeds*. Dallas: Presbyterian Heritage, 1983.

Dulles, Avery. *Models of the Church*. Garden City, NY: Doubleday, 1974.

Erickson, Millard. *The Word Became Flesh: A Contemporary Incarnational Christology*. Grand Rapids: Baker, 1991.

Hiebert, Paul G. *Anthropological Reflections on Missiological Issues*. Grand Rapids: Baker, 1994.

Hurtado, Larry. *Lord Jesus Christ*. Grand Rapids: Eerdmans, 2003.

Idowu, E. Bolaji. *African Traditional Religion*. Maryknoll, NY: Orbis, 1973.

_____. *Olodumare God in Yoruba Belief*. London: Longmans, Green & Co., Ltd., 1962.

Idowu, Bolaji. *Towards an Indigenous Church*. London: Oxford University Press, 1965.

Jenkins, Philip. *The Next Christendom: The Coming of Global Christianity*. London: Oxford University Press, 2002.

Lawson, Thomas. *Religions of Africa*. New York: Harper & Row, 1984.

Levison, John R., and Priscilla Pope-Levison. "Emergent Christologies in Latin America, Asia and Africa." *The Covenant Quarterly* 52 (May 1994): 29–47.

92. Stinton, *Jesus of Africa*, 142.

Mbiti, John S. "Christianity and Traditional Religions in Africa." Pages 144–58 in *Crucial Issues in Missions Tomorrow*. Edited by Donald McGavran. Chicago: Moody Press, 1972 (first published in *International Review of Mission* 59, no. 236 [October 1970]: 430–40).

_____. "Some African Concepts of Christology." Pages 51–62 in *Christ and the Younger Churches*. Edited by Georg F. Vicedom. London: SPCK, 1972.

_____. "Theological Impotence and the Universality of the Church." Pages 6–18 in *Mission Trends, no. 3: Third World Theologies*. Edited by Gerald H. Anderson and Thomas F. Stransky. New York: Paulist; Grand Rapids: Eerdmans, 1976.

Minear, Paul. *Images of the Church in the New Testament*. Philadelphia: Westminster, 1960.

Moloney, Raymond. "African Christology." *Theological Studies* 48 (1987): 505–15.

Nyamiti, Charles. "African Christologies Today." Pages 3–23 in *Faces of Jesus in Africa*. Edited by Robert J. Schreiter. Maryknoll, NY: Orbis, 2005.

_____. *Christ as Our Ancestor: Christology from an African Perspective*. Gweru, Zimbabwe: Mambo, 1984.

Oden, Thomas C. *The Word of Life*. Vol. 2, *Systematic Theology*. Peabody, MA: Prince, 1989.

Onaiyekan, John. "Christological Trends in Contemporary African Theology." Pages 355–68 in *Constructive Christian Theology in the Worldwide Church*. Edited by William R. Barr. Grand Rapids: Eerdmans, 1997.

Pannenberg, Wolfhart. *Jesus: God and Man*. 2nd ed. Translated by Lewis Wilkins and Duane Priebe. Philadelphia: Westminster, 1968, 1977.

Pelikan, Jaroslav. *Jesus through the Centuries: His Place in the History of Culture*. New Haven, CT: Yale University Press, 1985.

Pobee, John S. "In Search of Christology in Africa: Some Considerations for Today." Pages 9–20 in *Exploring Afro-Christology*. Edited by John S. Pobee. New York: Peter Lang, 1992.

_____. "Jesus Christ—the Life of the World: An African Perspective." *Ministerial Formation* 21 (January 1983): 5.

_____. *Toward an African Theology*. Nashville: Abingdon, 1979.

Sanon, Anselme T. "Jesus, Master of Initiation." Pages 85–102 in *Faces of Jesus in Africa*. Edited by Robert J. Schreiter. Maryknoll, NY: Orbis, 2005.

Schaff, Philip, and Henry Wace, eds. *Nicene and Post-Nicene Fathers*. Vol. 14, *The Seven Ecumenical Councils*. 2nd series. Peabody, MA: Hendrickson, 1999.

Schreiter, Robert J., ed. *Faces of Jesus in Africa*. Maryknoll, NY: Orbis, 2005.

_____. "Jesus Christ in Africa Today." Pages vii–xiii in *Faces of Jesus in Africa*. Edited by Robert J. Schreiter. Maryknoll, NY: Orbis, 2005.

Shorter, Aylward. "Folk Christianity and Functional Christology." *Afer* 24 (1982): 133–37.

Stinton, Diane. "Africa, East and West." Pages 105–36 in *An Introduction to Third World Theologies*. Edited by John Parratt. Cambridge: Cambridge University Press, 2004.

_____. *Jesus of Africa: Voices of Contemporary African Christology*. Maryknoll, NY: Orbis, 2004.

Taylor, John V. *The Primal Vision: Christian Presence and African Religion*. London: SCM, 1963.

Tennent, Timothy C. "The Challenge of Churchless Christianity." *International Bulletin of Missionary Research* 29, no. 4 (October 2005): 171–77.

_____. "Islam and African Traditional Religion: A Study of Religious Interaction in Modern Nigeria." Master's thesis, Princeton Theological Seminary, 1991.

Torrance, Thomas. *The Mediation of Christ*. Grand Rapids: Eerdmans, 1983.

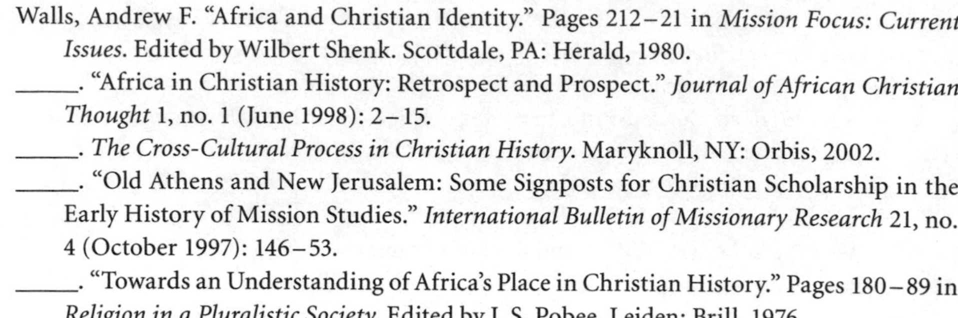

Walls, Andrew F. "Africa and Christian Identity." Pages 212–21 in *Mission Focus: Current Issues*. Edited by Wilbert Shenk. Scottdale, PA: Herald, 1980.

_____. "Africa in Christian History: Retrospect and Prospect." *Journal of African Christian Thought* 1, no. 1 (June 1998): 2–15.

_____. *The Cross-Cultural Process in Christian History*. Maryknoll, NY: Orbis, 2002.

_____. "Old Athens and New Jerusalem: Some Signposts for Christian Scholarship in the Early History of Mission Studies." *International Bulletin of Missionary Research* 21, no. 4 (October 1997): 146–53.

_____. "Towards an Understanding of Africa's Place in Christian History." Pages 180–89 in *Religion in a Pluralistic Society*. Edited by J. S. Pobee. Leiden: Brill, 1976.

Chapter 6

SOTERIOLOGY

IS "SALVATION BY GRACE THROUGH FAITH" UNIQUE TO CHRISTIANITY?

The well-known tension in Christian theology between the role of divine sovereignty and human responsibility in salvation has corresponding debates within the major non-Christian religions. For example, two important branches of Vaishnava Hinduism are the Vadagalais and the Tengalais.[1] The Tengalais teach that salvation comes through a total surrender to the sovereignty of Lord Vishnu and a full and complete trust in his bestowal of unmerited grace. Being saved and surrendering to God is like a young kitten totally dependent on its mother. We have all observed how a mother cat will pick up her kitten with her mouth and carry it by the scruff of the neck as it hangs helplessly and in complete trust. The Tengalais say that the baby kitten is the perfect picture of grace. Just as the kitten must totally surrender to the will of its mother, so the devotee must totally surrender (*prapatti*) to the will of Lord Vishnu.

In contrast, the Vadagalais teach that salvation depends on some exercise of our human will and our participation with God in his sovereign act of grace. Rather than a kitten, they use the analogy of the baby monkey. A baby monkey must actively cling to its mother as the mother moves around for food or shelter or seeks safety. The baby monkey is, for the Vadagalais, the picture of our participation with God in his sovereign work.

Many readers may be surprised to realize that while we sit around and debate the merits of "Calvinism" versus "Arminianism," there are Hindus in India debating the theological lessons represented by the "baby kitten" versus the "baby monkey"! Both sides of the Hindu version of this debate are devotees of Lord Vishnu and demonstrate this by painting a U-shaped white line on their forehead. These sacred marks are known as *pundrams* and are a normal way of publicly portraying which sect of Hinduism a person follows. However, in order to distinguish themselves from the Vadagalais, the Tengalais extend a short line at the bottom of the "U," making it more like a "Y" and

1. The Vadagalais are found in south India, mostly in Andra Pradesh and in the northern part of Tamil Nadu. The Tengalais are mostly found in the southern part of Tamil Nadu. There are a number of other doctrinal distinctions between the two groups that are beyond the scope of this chapter to explore.

bringing the painted line down to the bridge of the nose. This explains the well-known joke in India that the only thing that separates grace from works is a half inch of paint.

While it is easy to draw superficial parallels between Christian doctrines and those in other religions, the more fundamental question remains: Is the doctrine of salvation by grace through faith unique to Christianity, or not? This chapter seeks to explore this question, since fundamental to Christian theology is the conviction that the Christian understanding of salvation, particularly its emphasis on grace, is dramatically different from anything else found in the other major world religions.

For example, many of us have heard the oft-repeated statement that the difference between Christianity and all the other religions in the world is that the other religions are about men and women seeking after God, whereas Christianity is about God seeking after us. Furthermore, many of us have been left with the general impression that Christianity alone offers a doctrine of divine grace, whereas other religions only offer some version of works-righteousness—earning one's salvation through various forms of human effort. This chapter explores whether these generalizations are true, thereby enabling us to think about the place of the Christian doctrine of salvation within the larger global discourse.

In the past, reflection on these questions mainly took place among missionaries and religious studies specialists. However, in today's global context, Christian life and witness must be hammered out on the anvil of Majority World cultures where other religions predominate. These questions are now important for every Christian leader to think about. Pre-Christian ideas about God's holiness or lack of it, or previously held views about grace and merit transference, often accompany new believers when they come to faith in Jesus Christ. In this book's introduction I pointed out that the church is experiencing dramatic growth in regions of the world traditionally associated with Hinduism and Buddhism. As these new frontiers of church growth emerge, we no longer have the luxury of learning about the great doctrines of the Christian faith in isolation from these new contexts.

We must move beyond simple caricatures and wrestle with the actual realities of non-Christian teachings. Increasingly, we will come in contact with believers who have a background in another religious tradition. Therefore, we must have a more informed sense of how the new ideas of the gospel may or may not relate to previously cherished or unconsciously held views that formed their pre-Christian religious worldview. Different bridges to the gospel may surprisingly emerge, along with new barriers or difficulties we have not yet widely contemplated or prepared for. Certainly new clarifications and distinctions will become necessary. This is the exciting challenge of being a part of global Christianity today. What a privilege it is to witness the theological translatability of such familiar biblical themes as salvation, grace, and faith as they traverse into these unfamiliar, but vast, new domains.

SHINRAN SHONIN, JAPAN'S "MARTIN LUTHER"

Although there are numerous strands of "salvation by grace through faith" teachings in non-Christian religions, nowhere is the doctrine so clearly stated and, at least on the surface, so remarkably parallel to Protestant Christianity than in the popular

Jodo Shin Shu (True Pure Land) stream of Mahayana Buddhism, which first emerged in Japan in the thirteenth century AD through the Buddhist reformer Shinran Shonin (1173–1262). Karl Barth, in his *Church Dogmatics*, once described the *Jodo Shin Shu* teaching of Shinran as "the most adequate and comprehensive and illuminating heathen parallel to Christianity."[2] Barth was so struck by the parallels with Reformed Christianity that he called it "Japanese Protestantism."

Indeed, as far back as 1549, when the famous Jesuit missionary Francis Xavier first visited Japan and met the followers of Shinran, he was astounded because he thought that even Japan "had been penetrated by the Lutheran heresy"![3] The amazing parallels between the life of Shinran and the life of Martin Luther, which we will explore later, make the connection between the two movements even more fascinating. Therefore, this chapter will highlight the True Pure Land (also called *Shin* Buddhism, meaning "true" Buddhism), which is one of the most prominent and popular sects of Buddhism.

However, this movement must be understood within the larger historical development of Buddhism. We will begin with a brief overview of Buddhism and how this particular branch is situated within the larger universe of Buddhism. The latter part of the chapter will explore the meaning of "salvation by grace through faith" in the writings of Shinran as well as in the writings of Martin Luther (who will serve as a representative writer for Protestant theology, just as Shinran will serve as a representative writer of the True Pure Land tradition, since both are considered the "founding fathers" of their respective traditions).

Brief Historical Review of Buddhism and the Emergence of Mahayana

Buddha's Enlightenment

The Buddhist religion traces its origin to a dissent movement started by Siddhartha Gautama in the sixth century BC. Gautama (563–483 BC) was born into a life of wealth and privilege in a region located on the border of modern-day Nepal and Northeast India. After being shielded from suffering and pain for many years in the opulence of his surroundings, Gautama went on a chariot ride outside of the security of the palace walls and encountered the realities of old age, sickness, and death for the first time. Gautama was so moved by these inescapable realities that he forsook the wealth and privilege of his father's house, exchanged his clothes with a beggar, and at age twenty-nine went out into the world in search of the cause of human suffering and the path to liberation.

After several years of trying various meditative techniques and experimenting with extreme asceticism, Gautama remained in inner turmoil. He realized the futility of both his earlier life of extreme indulgence and his current state of extreme asceticism; neither helped him to break the cycle of birth, suffering, death, and rebirth. Gautama decided to take the "middle way," which would later become the central

2. Karl Barth, *Church Dogmatics*, vol. 1, part 2 of *The Doctrine of the Word of God*, ed. and trans. G. W. Bromiley and T. F. Torrance (Edinburgh: T. & T. Clark. 1956), 340.

3. Fritz Buri, "The Concept of Grace in Paul, Shinran, and Luther," *Eastern Buddhist* 9, no. 2 (2004): 30.

paradigm for the entire Buddhist religion. He took enough food to strengthen his body and then began to meditate under what would become known as the Bodhi tree (tree of enlightenment). According to Buddhist tradition, on the forty-ninth day of his meditation, Gautama received enlightenment and thereafter became known as the Buddha, meaning the "Enlightened One." Over the next forty-five years the Buddha traveled across India spreading his teaching before he died at the age of eighty.

Core Buddhist Dharma

Traditionally, the Buddha's teaching is known as the *dharma*. It established a philosophical and pragmatic "middle way" between various extremes and opened up the possibility that anyone, regardless of caste or background, could experience enlightenment. The Buddha began by teaching the Four Noble Truths, which serve as a prescription of the human predicament, followed by the "cure." The Four Noble Truths affirm that all of life is characterized by suffering and that we are trapped by our cravings and desires into an endless cycle of suffering and rebirth, known as the wheel of *samsara*. However, the Buddha claimed to have seen a pathway that breaks out of this cycle, leading to a state of enlightenment known as *nirvana*. This process is known in Buddhism as the Noble Eightfold Path, so called because it describes eight areas in a person's life that must be brought under complete control in order to extinguish all desires. To accomplish this goal and, ultimately, to break the tendencies toward desire and cravings, one must become a Buddhist monk and submit to rigorous training in the areas of wisdom, morality, and concentration.[4]

In addition to the Four Noble Truths and the Eightfold Path are two additional doctrines central to Buddhist thought that brought it into such sharp conflict with Hinduism that Buddhism emerged as a separate religion. The first is the doctrine of "no-self" (*anatman*). This doctrine denies that there is any substantive reality to the self. This is in stark contrast to Hinduism, which affirms that the soul, or *atman*, is the ground of all being and is, in fact, identical with the ultimate reality of the universe. The second distinctive Buddhist doctrine is known as "dependent arising" (*pratitya-samutpāda*), which affirms that everything is dependent on something else and that there is no first cause in the universe. This is why Buddhism denies the ontological existence of any God.[5] Today, this classic form of monastic Buddhism is represented by the school of Therevada, which means "Way of the Elders."

The Emergence of Mahayana Buddhism

Around the time of Christ, a vast corpus of new texts began to emerge that claimed to be from the Buddha himself. These new texts were critical of the monastic emphasis in Therevada Buddhism, claiming that it was too self-focused and that it had effectively made enlightenment possible for only a tiny minority. They claimed that the Buddha had secretly taught that there would someday be another, more accessible,

4. This is known as the "Threefold Training" in *prajna* (teaching or wisdom), *sila* (morality), and *samadhi* (concentration).

5. The fact that Buddhism is nontheistic may discourage you from reading further, but, as will be explored later, Buddhism develops a *functional* theism, while still denying any ultimate first causes.

path to liberation open to the laity. The fact that these texts were not known until more than five hundred years after the Buddha's death was explained by saying that people were only now able to understand this deeper dimension of the Buddha's dharma.[6] This dissent movement eventually became known as the Mahayana, which means the "Great Vehicle," and the Therevada were characterized as the Hinayana or the "Little Vehicle."

This new movement taught that many of the great Buddhist saints had come to the point of nirvana, had refused their liberation, and out of compassion, delayed nirvana in order to assist others to enlightenment. These saints are known in Mahayana Buddhism as *bodhisattvas*, which means "enlightened beings." For a Christian seeking to understand Buddhism the emergence of the bodhisattva ideal is an important step forward in the development of Eastern ideas of ethics and vicarious suffering, both central to Christian theology. For Mahayana Buddhists, the cosmos is filled with countless bodhisattvas and buddhas who, out of compassion, dwell in transcendent realms and who are ready to assist us on our spiritual pilgrimage toward enlightenment.[7] Enlightenment can now be achieved by a layperson and within this lifetime or, at least, within a few lifetimes.

The Mahayana justify this major innovation in Buddhist teaching by asserting that the early core instruction of the Buddha represents only the more elementary aspects of his full teaching. It only highlighted the long and arduous Eightfold Path, which through one's own efforts would take thousands of lifetimes to complete and could take place only within the confines of the monastic life. However, the Mahayana believed that the Buddhist community had finally matured to the point where the more advanced dimensions of the Buddha's teaching could now be taught. Through the compassion and vicarious efforts of the bodhisattvas, enlightenment was now possible for the laity. Therevada is sometimes known as "monastic Buddhism" whereas Mahayana is referred to as "messianic Buddhism," because of the proliferation and central role of these transcendent, salvific beings.

Over time, various streams or schools of thought within Mahayana Buddhism emerged that emphasized the benefits of some celestial bodhisattva or the insights of a particular sacred text, known as a *sūtra*. Some Mahayanist groups, such as Zen Buddhism, emphasized the importance of meditation in achieving enlightenment. Some of the meditative groups within Mahayana focus on a particular text such as the *Heart Sūtra*[8] or the *Lotus Sūtra*,[9] because they represent the distilled insight of a revered bodhisattva.

---

6. The original teachings, as transmitted by Therevada, were known as Turning the Wheel of Dharma. This new movement claimed that the Buddha turned the Wheel of Dharma a second time. Later, Varjanyana Buddhism, as exemplified by Tibetan Buddhism, claimed that the Buddha turned the Wheel of Dharma a third time. See, Carl Olson, *The Different Paths of Buddhism* (New Brunswick, NJ: Rutgers Univ. Press, 2005).

7. In Tibetan Buddhism these enlightened beings actually dwell in historical form and are called lamas. The Dalai Lama, for example, is believed to be an earthly incarnation of Avalokiteśvara. In the Mahayana tradition, the transcendent bodhisattvas can sometimes project themselves into a historical person in order to extend a particular teaching into the world. This chapter assumes a "three-vehicle" structure of Buddhism: Therevada (monastic), Mahayana (messianic), and Vajranyana (Tibetan).

8. The *Heart Sūtra* was composed between AD 300–500.

9. The *Lotus Sūtra* was composed in stages between the second century BC and the second century AD. The *Lotus Sūtra* is the principal text for several Buddhist groups, including the Tendai, the Nichiren, and the modern Soka Gakkai movement.

Other Mahayana groups focus on invoking or repeating the name of a particular bodhisattva in order to achieve enlightenment. For example, the bodhisattva Mañjuśrī is believed to have traveled to all the transcendent realms and now embodies the distilled wisdom of the cosmos. Many believe that by repeating his name or by thinking about him, you can reduce the number of your births into the cycle of suffering by thousands of lifetimes.[10] Our focus is on the emergence of a particular invocational stream within Mahayana Buddhism known as Pure Land Buddhism (*Jodo Shu*). The phrase "pure land" refers to the transcendental realm of bliss where the bodhisattva of this branch of Buddhism is believed to dwell. It is from this school of Mahayana that Shinran later developed a separate offshoot known as The *True* Pure Land (*Jodo Shin Shu*). We will now examine the emergence of Pure Land Buddhism in more detail as the basis for understanding its later development under Shinran.

PURE LAND BUDDHISM

Today, Mahayana Buddhism comprises about 80 percent of all Buddhists in the world, and Pure Land Buddhism is its most dominant stream. It is the most popular form of Buddhism in China and Japan.[11] This makes Pure Land the closest thing one can find to "representative" Buddhism, despite all of the diversity in the religion.

Pure Land is a form of invocational Buddhism that originated through a famous teacher named Hōnen (1133–1212), although most of the distinctive features that characterize this movement preceded him and were taught by earlier teachers such as T'an-luan (476–542), Shan-tao (613–681), and Genshin (942–1017). In fact, there are seven teachers considered the patriarchs of Pure Land, each contributing a major insight. Hōnen is the seventh patriarch, and his particular genius was his ability to synthesize all the various teachings, insights, and practices into a single school of thought that captured the popular imaginations of Buddhists in Japan, India, China, and throughout the Far East.[12]

At a young age Hōnen was ordained and studied in the famous Tendai monastery on Mount Hiei in Japan, which, at its height, had over 30,000 monks. There on Mount Hiei, Hōnen learned the *nembutsu* practice, which refers to the remembrance, the invocation of, or taking refuge in the name of a particular bodhisattva.[13] This practice seems to

10. In addition to these popular meditative and invocational strands within Mahayana, there are also various rationalistic and political streams that go beyond our scope in this chapter.

11. Paul Williams, *Mahayana Buddhism: The Doctrinal Foundations* (London and New York: Routledge, 1989), 251. See also Daisetz Teitaro Suzuki, "Development of the Pure Land Doctrine in Buddhism," *The Eastern Buddhist* 3, no. 4 (January–March 1925), 285. The dominance of Pure Land is also demonstrated by the extensive way that Pure Land practices have been incorporated into other schools and branches of Buddhism. Pure Land Buddhism originated in India, developed considerably in China, and was then transmitted to Japan in the Heian period. Because of our interest in Shinan, this chapter will focus on the Japanese development of Pure Land Buddhism.

12. One of the most important works of Hōnen that firmly established Pure Land Buddhism as a separate school is his *Senchaku Hongan Nembutsu Shū* (*The Choice of the Nembutsu of the Original Vow*), published in 1198. Others trace it back further to Hōnen's famous lecture on *nembutsu* at Ōhara in 1186. The seven Patriarchs are: Nagarjuna (second to third century), Vasubandu (fourth century), T'an-luan (476–542), Tao-ch'o (562–645), Shan-tao (613–681), Genshin (942–1017), and Hōnen (1133–1212). There are some modern Pure Land sects who recognize eight patriarchs, claiming an earlier founder in Aśvaghosha, the author of *Awakening of Faith in the Mahayana*.

13. The original meaning of *nembutsu* means "to remember" or "to contemplate." The vocalization of the *nembutsu* is an important, but later, development.

be another example of how Mahayana Buddhism took an idea within Therevada and extended or broadened it. Central to Therevada Buddhism is the notion of the Triple Refuge. Every monk is required, as part of his vows, to take refuge in the Buddha, the Dharma (the teaching), and the Sangha (the monastic community). Early on, Buddhist priests would invoke and praise the name of Buddha with the phrase *namo Buddhā-nām*, "Hail, Enlightened One!"[14] It was, therefore, easy for the idea to develop within Mahayana of invoking the name of a revered bodhisattva. This doctrine is so prominent within Pure Land that sometimes it is called the Nembutsu School of Buddhism.[15]

One of the most revered bodhisattvas in the Mahayana pantheon is Amida, a shortened form for Amitābha Buddha, meaning Buddha of Infinite Light, as well as Amitāyus Buddha, meaning Buddha of Infinite Life. According to a major Pure Land text, the *Larger Sukhāvati-yvūha Sūtra* (hereafter called simply the *Larger Sūtra*), Amida Buddha once dwelled on earth as a monk named Dharmākara. After extended meditations he decided that should he ever become enlightened he would, in the true manner of the compassionate bodhisattva ideal, delay nirvana in order to help save others.

In fact, Dharmākara was filled with such compassion for the lost that he made forty-eight vows, each with the attached condition, "If this vow is not fulfilled, then may I not become a fully enlightened Buddha." After an incalculable number of lifetimes and devotion to all kinds of virtues and meritorious practices, it is thought that Dharmākara did finally become fully enlightened and now dwells as Amida Buddha in a transcendent realm known as the Pure Land. This transcendent realm, they maintain, embodies all of the best features of all the other transcendent realms. Furthermore, it is believed that if anyone ever reaches the Pure Land, it is no longer possible to retrogress back to an inferior realm. This is known as the stage of nonretrogression.[16] Since Dharmākara has been exalted as Amida Buddha and now dwells in the Pure Land, then, Hōnen reasoned, all of his forty-eight vows must have been honored, since each vow was made with the condition that if it was not honored, he would not become fully enlightened. Therefore, the forty-eight vows are of particular importance in the emergence of Pure Land.

While this chapter will make reference to several of the vows, by far the most important is the eighteenth, known as the Primal or Original Vow. According to the *Larger Sūtra*, which records all of them, the eighteenth is as follows:

> If, when I attain buddhahood, the sentient beings of the ten quarters, with sincere mind entrusting themselves, aspiring to be born in my land, and saying my name even but ten times, should not be born there, may I not attain the supreme enlightenment.[17]

Hōnen taught that this vow meant that anyone who invokes the name of Amida ten times with sincerity will be guaranteed rebirth in the Pure Land. He also taught that we now live in such a degenerate period (Age of Mappō) that even if we devoted

14. Alan A. Andrews, "Nembutsu in the Chinese Pure Land Tradition," *The Eastern Buddhist* 3, no. 2 (October 1970): 22.

15. Daisetz Teitaro Suzuki, *Collected Writings on Shin Buddhism* (Kyoto, Japan: Shinshu Otaniha, 1973), 4.

16. Attaining a stage of "nonretrogression" is an important theme that appears in the writings of many Buddhist teachers.

17. Donald S. Lopez Jr., ed., *Buddhist Scriptures* (London: Penguin, 2004), 384.

tens of thousands of lifetimes to Buddhist practice, enlightenment would still elude us. Thus, Hōnen reasoned, since the "Path of the Sages" (*Shōdo* path) is no longer a viable option, the only other possibility is to invoke the assistance of Amida Buddha (*Jōdo* path). In this, Hōnen is following the teaching of Genshin, one of the patriarchs of Pure Land, who once described the practice of the nembutsu as "the eye-and-foot for those who live in this defiled world of this degenerated age."[18]

However, the distinctive element in Hōnen's teaching is that practicing the nembutsu to Amida was superior to all other Buddhist practices. Prior to Hōnen, the practice of nembutsu was generally regarded as one of many methods of helping someone to concentrate or to supplement other meditative or ritual practices. Under Hōnen's teaching, Pure Land insisted that no other practice was necessary for enlightenment, and the nembutsu to Amida trumped all other Buddhist practices. Indeed, the seventeenth vow of Amida taught that his name would be heard throughout the universe:

> If immeasurable and innumerable blessed Buddhas in immeasurable Buddha countries do not glorify my name, after I have obtained enlightenment; if they do not preach my fame and proclaim my praise, and utter it together, then may I not obtain the supreme enlightenment.

Clearly, the universalization of the adoration of Amida into the entire world was seen by Hōnen as the fulfillment of yet another one of Amida's forty-eight vows. Thus, Hōnen represents a strong evangelistic strand within Buddhism. It was also under Hōnen that Pure Land began to view the relationship between the devotee and Amida in more dualistic terms, unlike earlier teachers who believed that "the buddha and human beings are identical in substance, without any difference."[19]

However, one of the practical difficulties that Hōnen and his predecessors faced was determining when a person had invoked or fondly remembered the name of Amida ten times, because the eighteenth vow said that it must be done sincerely. How do you know for certain that you have vocalized the nembutsu with sincerity? To solve this difficulty, Hōnen advocated the continuous repetition of the nembutsu: *namu amida butsu*—Hail to Amida Buddha! Thus, it is not unusual for a follower of Pure Land to recite the nembutsu over ten thousand times in a single day.[20] For Hōnen no other religious practices were necessary.

In fact, just a few days before he died, Hōnen was asked to summarize his life work in a final testament. This famous Pure Land text is known as the *One Page Testament*. In it Hōnen summarizes the essence of his teaching:

> The method of final salvation that I have propounded ... is nothing but the mere repetition of the "*namu Amida Butsu*" without a doubt of his mercy, whereby one

18. Quotation from Genshin's *Ōjo-yōshū*, written in 985, as cited in Shizutoshi Sugihira, "The Nembutsu in Shin Buddhism," *Eastern Buddhist* 7, nos. 3–4 (July 1939): 342.

19. Yoshiro Tamura, *Japanese Buddhism: A Cultural History*, trans. Jeffery Hunter (Tokyo: Kosei, 2000), 82.

20. In my own experience I have seen devotees place the Amida *nembutsu* inside a prayer wheel and pay someone to turn the wheel hundreds of thousands of times, hoping to be permitted into The Pure Land with Amida.

> may be born into the Land of Perfect Bliss.... Thus without pedantic airs, one should fervently practice the repetition of the name of Amida, and that alone.[21]

It would be Shinran, one of Hōnen's most brilliant disciples, who fully developed Pure Land and, in the process, became known as one of the most remarkable thinkers in the history of Buddhism. Indeed, Shinran and his True Pure Land teaching, commonly called Shin Buddhism, has become the dominant strand of invocational Buddhism and will be the focal point in answering the question: Is "salvation by grace through faith" unique to Christianity?

Shinran and the Rise of True Pure Land Buddhism

Shinran Shonin lived during one of the most remarkable transitions in Japanese history: from the Heian age (794–1185) to the Kamakura period (1185–1333). A breakdown of the peace that had characterized the Heian age, a weak central government, and increased social turmoil stimulated the rise of some of the most remarkable Buddhist reformers and thinkers, such as Hōnen (1143–1212), Shinran (1173–1262), Dōgen (1200–1253), and Nichiren (1222–1282), all of whom lived on the seam between these two major periods of Japanese history.

At eight years old, Shinran was sent to Mount Hiei, where he became a Buddhist priest and learned all of the traditional disciplines of Buddhist practice. After twenty years at Mount Hiei, Shinran became disillusioned with traditional Buddhism and entered a period of inner turmoil and dissatisfaction with his spiritual condition, despite his mastery of Buddhist philosophy and the advanced techniques that were supposed to lead to enlightenment. In response to some mystical experience, perhaps a vision,[22] he left Mount Hiei and the formal priesthood in 1201 and moved to the capital, Kyoto. There he met Hōnen and for the next six years lived in Hōnen's hermitage.

During this time he became deeply influenced by the teaching of Pure Land with its emphasis on the nembutsu and trusting in Amida Buddha for salvation. It was during his first year with Hōnen that Shinron, in his own words, "abandoned the difficult practices and took refuge in the Original Vow."[23] Shinran became a devoted disciple of Hōnen and, despite his own later innovations to Pure Land, never wavered in his devotion to and admiration of his master.

In 1207 Hōnen and all of his disciples, including Shinran, were exiled from the capital. Shinran was banished to the northern Japanese seacoast city of Echigo, where he remained until he was pardoned in 1211. Shinran stopped wearing the saffron robe and shaving his head and lived among the common, unlearned people. This was a formative period for him because he was living in a kind of ecclesiastical no-man's land. He was no longer a priest, but his entire life had been spent in rigorous Buddhist training, so he could hardly fit in as a layperson. It was after his pardon that Shinran

21. William Theodore de Bary, ed., *The Buddhist Tradition in India, China and Japan* (New York: Vintage, 1972), 331.

22. Most of the accounts indicate that Shinran had a vision or revelation from the bodhisattva Avalokiteśvara while meditating in the Chōjōji Temple in Kyoto.

23. As quoted in Alfred Bloom, *Shinran's Gospel of Pure Grace* (Tucson: Univ. of Arizona Press, 1965), xi.

married a woman named Eshinni, raised a family, and "claimed for himself the status of 'neither priest nor layman.'"[24] He realized the challenges ordinary people felt in trying to live as Buddhists in the midst of all the normal challenges of life.

More important, Shinran became increasingly aware of his own wickedness. Alfred Bloom sums up this period in Shinran's life well when he says, "It is in this world that passion-ridden beings are encountered, where Shinran encountered himself, and became aware of the ineradicable sinfulness and desperate character of sentient existence."[25] Gradually, Shinran realized that the strong emphasis on the nembutsu had itself become another means of earning merit and justifying one's entrance into the Pure Land. Why else would their most exemplary devotees invoke the nembutsu ten thousand times or more each day?

Around 1224 Shinran wrote his famous *Kyōgyōshinshō* (*The True Teaching, Practice, Faith and Attainment [of the Pure Land Way]*), in which he brings together many famous Pure Land texts from previous masters and comments on them.[26] This work continued to expand over the years and was regularly revised until it reached its current, final form around 1247. His approach is a classic style of teaching in the East. According to this method, it is important to demonstrate one's loyalty and continuity with past teachers even if, in the process of your commentary, new teaching is being transmitted. Thus, even though the bulk of the anthology consists of quotations of sacred texts written by others as well as biographies of the Pure Land patriarchs, it is precisely in Shinran's careful selection, arrangement, and insightful commentary that his creative genius is revealed.

The *Kyōgyōshinshō* was written for a scholarly audience and established Shinran's own interpretation of Pure Land within the larger scholarly apparatus of Mahayana Buddhism in general and Pure Land in particular. Shinran also devoted his energies to several popular works that, while following the same commentary format, were written at a level that allowed his teachings to be communicated to ordinary laypeople. This is particularly evident in his *Notes on "Essentials of Faith Alone,"* where he comments on a famous text by Seikaku (1166–1235), one of his Pure Land predecessors.[27] We will now summarize the distinctive elements of Shinran's teaching, which eventually gives rise to a separate school of Pure Land Buddhism.

Four Key Elements in the Teaching of Shinran

There are four distinctive elements in Shinran's teaching that, taken collectively, serve as the basis for the emergence of the True Pure Land.

Turning through the Three Vows to Embrace "Other Power"

First, Shinran revisits and develops a Pure Land theme known as "Other Power" (*tariki*). "Other Power" refers to the power of Amida who, through the Primal Vow, is

24. Tamura, *Japanese Buddhism: A Cultural History*, 97.

25. Bloom, *Shinran's Gospel of Pure Grace*, 27.

26. A good English translation of Shinran's *Kyōgyōshinshō* can be found by Yoshifumi Ueda, ed., *The True Teaching, Practice and Realization of the Pure Land Way*, 3 vols. (Kyoto, Japan: Hongwanji International Center, 1978).

27. A good English translation of both the original *Essentials of Faith Alone* by Seikaku as well as Shinran's *Notes on "Essentials of Faith Alone"* can be found in Yoshifumi Ueda, ed., *Notes on "Essentials of Faith Alone"* (Kyoto, Japan: Hongwanji International Center, 1979).

able to bring salvation to the world. Hōnen, Shinran's master, had taught that all human effort, even religious activity, amounted to what he called "self-power" (*jiriki*). "Self-power" included not only the mainstream monastic rigors of Therevada, but also the meditative schools of Mahayana that emphasized discipline, austerities, and strenuous technique in order to accrue the necessary merit toward enlightenment. In contrast, Pure Land focuses on "Other Power," which depended on Amida by reciting the nembutsu.

In the broader Mahayana understanding of the Amida texts, including the forty-eight vows, there seems to be evidence of the importance of both self-power and Other Power in achieving enlightenment.[28] The genius of Shinran is in his development of the ultimate significance of Other Power as the end goal of a more comprehensive theory of religious growth.[29] The stages of spiritual growth that Shinran advocates clearly mirror his own spiritual development. Progressing through the various stages of spiritual growth is known as the "Process of Turning through the Three Vows" because each of the three stages is tied specifically to three of Amida's vows, namely, 19, 20, and 18 (in that order).[30]

Shinran argued that all religious and spiritual development must begin with a simple desire to be enlightened. This desire is reflected in a whole range of human attempts and efforts to earn one's salvation. This is what Shinran had first experienced during his early years on Mount Hiei. The nineteenth vow of Amida is as follows:

> If, after my obtaining Buddhahood, all beings in the ten quarters awakening their thoughts to enlightenment and practicing all deeds of merit should cherish the desire in sincerity to be born in my country and if I should not, surrounded by a large company, appear before them at the time of their death, may I not attain the Highest Enlightenment.

The emphasis on "practicing all deeds of merit" was, for Shinran, an elementary stage of "self-power" which, in his view, would ultimately create a sense of futility and longing for the enlightenment that can only come through Amida, that is, through "Other Power." The next stage in Shinran's notion of religious development is found in the twentieth vow, which declares:

> If, after obtaining Buddhahood, all beings in the ten quarters hearing my name should cherish the thought of my country and planting all the roots of merit turn in sincerity over to being born in my country, and if they should fail in obtaining the result of it, may I not attain the Highest Enlightenment.

28. Pure Land resonates with the "baby monkey" analogy, whereas True Pure Land holds to the "baby kitten" analogy. For example, E. B. Cowell comments on the *Larger Sukhāvati-vyūha Sūtra*, which is the text containing the Amida's forty-eight vows, as follows: The *Larger Sukhāvati-vyūha* lays great stress on prayer and faith in Amitabha, but it never neglects "the stock of merit." See E. B. Cowell, ed., *Buddhist Mahayana Texts* (New York: Dover, 1969), ix. This is a paperback reproduction of Max Müller's well-known publication of *The Sacred Books of the East*, vol. 49 of *Buddhist Mahayana Texts*, part II, *The Larger Sukhāvati-vyūha Sūtra* (New York: Dover, 1962).

29. Sugihira, "The Nembutsu in Shin Buddhism," 356. This is part of the teaching of the three vows, the three sutras, the three beings, and the three rebirths.

30. Bloom, *Shinran's Gospel of Pure Grace*, 33. For the full text of all the 48 vows see, Max Müller, ed., *The Sacred Books of the East*, 12–22.

The emphasis here, according to Shinran, is the movement from "self-power" (vow 19) to "Other Power" (vow 20). Rather than seeking merit, this vow seems to indicate that all merit seeking must eventually lead to cherishing the "thought of his country" (Pure Land) and sincerely desiring to be born there. For Shinran, this could only mean a commitment to the nembutsu and the Original Vow. However, he saw the twentieth vow as a kind of halfway house between "self-power" and "Other Power." On the one hand, all of the traditional paths toward merit accumulation have been abandoned, but, on the other hand, the *nembutsu* itself remained a Pure Land practice that people could cling to as a merit.

In Shinran's view, this is precisely what had happened in the Pure Land he had observed in his day. Alan Bloom refers to Shinran's interpretation of the twentieth vow as the "half self–half 'Other Power' way."[31] If the twentieth vow represents Shinran's years studying on Mount Hiei, then the nineteenth vow represents Shinran's time under the tutelage of Hōnen, when he became a devotee of Pure Land. For Shinran, this second stage cannot give final enlightenment, but is able to bring a person to the point of nonretrogression, where he or she will not be reborn into lower realms.

The third and final phase of the spiritual journey is found in the eighteenth vow, which is, of course, the Primal Vow for all Pure Land Buddhists. The Primal Vow represents the pinnacle of the spiritual journey. Its placement before the nineteenth and twentieth vow is meant first to demonstrate the goal of the journey and then to set forth the various stages of the journey, culminating in the Original or Primal Vow. However, as will become evident when all four features of Shinran's thought are discussed, Shinran interpreted the Primal Vow not as a way to *accumulate* merit, but as a way to *receive* the merit of Amida. The eighteenth vow represents the triumph of "Other Power" in the thought of Shinran.

Single Repetition of the Nembutsu

The second key innovation in the thought of Shinran was his new understanding of the endless repetitions of the nembutsu that had become so common in his day. Shinran saw two major problems with the way it was being practiced. First, encouraging a Pure Land devotee to vocalize the nembutsu thousands of times each day seemed to foster a lack of trust in Amida's vow, which clearly stated that one would be reborn in the Pure Land after thinking favorably upon Amida only ten times. Hōnen had emphasized the particular importance of reciting the nembutsu just prior to one's death, or one might not be reborn into the Pure Land.[32] This teaching naturally created anxiety, since no one knows the precise time of their own death.

Second, the preoccupation with the nembutsu, which filled every waking hour, had turned the recitation into another way of storing up merit. This, in his view, was an abandonment of the Amida texts and the Primal Vow, which he understood as the great, unmerited gift of Amida. Instead, the "Other Power" of Amida had been turned into the "self-power" of the devotee. That which was intended to produce "faith" had ended up becoming just another "work."

31. Bloom, *Shinran's Gospel of Pure Grace*, 34.

32. Tamura, *Japanese Buddhism: A Cultural History*, 97.

Shinran came to recognize that an important distinction must be made between the first vocalization and all subsequent vocalizations of the nembutsu. The very first one was salvific because of the efficacy of Amida's vow. All subsequent vocalizations were to be done out of sheer gratitude to Amida and to help promote the universalization of his name and honor throughout the world. The growth in the number of repetitions of the nembutsu originally occurred because of an inner doubt about whether a person had called upon Amida with sincerity. However, this is why Shinran emphasizes the other vows of Amida in one's overall spiritual journey. The first two stages of the journey established a person's sincerity because, by that stage, they have abandoned all hope in saving themselves. By focusing on the single repetition of the nembutsu, he "took the other-power doctrine to its logical extreme: *one moment of faith*, he maintained, was enough to guarantee rebirth in the Pure Land."[33]

Hard Way–Easy Way–Only Way

A theme central to all Mahayanist thought is that their multifaceted movement represents a "large vehicle" that can bring many to enlightenment, whereas Therevada is characterized as a Hinayana, or "little vehicle" for only a few. This "large vehicle" has often been characterized as the "easy way" versus the "difficult way." The great Buddhist saint and philosopher Nāgārjuna, who is credited to be the actual founder of Mahayana Buddhism, wrote the following in his *Commentary on the Ten Bodhisattva Stages*:

> In practicing the Buddha-way there is a path of difficult practice and a path of easy practice. The path of difficult practice is like going overland on foot; the easy path is like receiving a favorable wind upon the sealanes.[34]

The original notion of Mahayana being an easy way should not be understood as a qualitatively *better* way. Indeed, most Mahayanists deeply respect the monastic tradition and admire their diligence and sacrifices for the sake of enlightenment. It is the accumulated diligence of their merit-producing austerities and meditations that has populated the Mahayana universe with bodhisattvas who are now available to "put wind in your sails." The *large* vehicle imagery is better understood as more of an expedient concession to the realities of being a layperson who lives in this dark age when the "way of the Sages" is no longer possible. But the *easy* path of Mahayana always remained subservient to the *holy* path of the sages.[35]

The third innovation in Shinran's thinking emerged because of his deep, and growing, awareness of the depth of his own depravity. This, in turn, led Shinran to openly challenge the traditional understanding of the relationship between the Buddhist Vehicles. In his *Notes on "Essentials of Faith Alone"* Shinran refers to the world

33. Ibid., 98 (emphasis mine).

34. Nāgārjuna, *Commentary on the Ten Bodhisattva Stages*, as quoted by Seikaku in *The Essentials of Faith Alone*, which is also included in the same volume with Shinran's notes on Seikaku's text. See Ueda, *Notes on "Essentials of Faith Alone,"* 60.

35. One of the major features of Buddhism is the doctrine of expedient means that allows for the reconciliation of the tens of thousands of contradictory Buddhists texts to be reconciled by placing them on a hierarchy of "greater" (advanced) and "lesser" (elementary) texts.

as "the defiled world of the corrupt dharma." He insists that no one on earth has a "true and sincere heart" and that everywhere one can find countless examples of the "heart and tongue at odds."[36] Shinran believed that human depravity was so great and the age had become so evil that no amount of religious activity could possibly be sufficient to save someone. In fact, Shinran believed it was no longer possible, on our own, to even know whether an act was good or evil. We are so deeply lost in the middle of the forest of depravity we do not even know which way to go to start walking out. Shinran said:

> I know nothing of what is good or evil. For if I could know thoroughly, as is known in the mind of Amida, that an act was good, then I would know the meaning of "good." If I could know thoroughly, as Amida knows, that an act was evil, then I would know "evil." But for a foolish being full of blind passions in this fleeting world—a burning house—all matters without exception are lies and gibberish, totally without truth and sincerity. The *nembutsu* alone is true and real.[37]

Paradoxically, precisely because human nature is so inclined towards self-delusion and self-justification, Shinran believed that the so-called easy path of the Pure Land was actually the most difficult way because "men are always tempted to strive for their own salvation rather than simply relying on the Buddha (Amida)."[38] In fact, Shinran even asserted that wicked men are more likely to be saved than so-called "good" people, "since the former throw themselves entirely on the mercy of the Buddha, while the latter might be tempted to think that their chances of salvation were improved by their own meritorious conduct."[39]

Therefore, for Shinran, the traditional Buddhist disciplines, as well as any mixture of various disciplines alongside the nembutsu, are inferior to the sole trust in Amida alone for salvation. Anything else involves some form of self-power, whereas, for Shinran, the only hope for salvation is putting complete trust in Amida Buddha and the Primal Vow. Vows of celibacy mean nothing, worshiping Buddhas means nothing, becoming a monk means nothing, performing austerities means nothing, because only trusting in Amida will bring salvation.

Denial of the Merit Acquisition Principle

The fourth and final theme in Shinran's teaching is found in his creative recasting of the Buddhist understanding of the transference of merit. In classical Buddhism the

36. All quotations from Shinran's *Notes on "Essentials of Faith Alone,"* 49.

37. Shinran's postscript to the *Tannishō* as quoted in Roger Jackson and John Makransky, eds., *Buddhist Theology: Critical Reflections by Contemporary Buddhist Scholars* (Surrey, UK: Curzon, 2000), 358. The burning house is an important image in Buddhism, for it represents impermanence and thirst, two central images in Buddhism. See Takeuchi Yoshinori, "The Meaning of 'Other-Power' in the Buddhist Way of Salvation," *The Eastern Buddhist* 15, no. 2 (1982): 19.

38. Bloom, *Shinran's Gospel of Pure Grace*, 37.

39. See de Bary, *The Buddhist Tradition in India, China and Japan*, 332. One of the most frequently cited sayings of Shinran is: "If even a 'good' man can be reborn into the Pure Land, how much more so a wicked man!" See idem, 340–41.

whole purpose of the vows, austerities, and recitations was to accrue merit so that one might ensure a better rebirth and, eventually, attain nirvana. Although Mahayana introduces a concept of grace through the vicarious assistance of a bodhisattva, it was never fully "unmerited" grace, since there was some human effort required to receive this assistance. For example, a devotee may perform certain deeds exclusively on behalf of a particular deity, or focus on the study of a particular sacred text such as the *Lotus Sūtra*, or, as in Pure Land, practice a constant vocalization of the nembutsu.

Shinran steadfastly insisted that it was impossible, even after ten thousand lifetimes of effort, for a human to accrue one ounce of merit. For Shinran, grace means unmerited grace, or it is no grace at all. All merit must be unconditional and vicariously transferred to us in full *via* Amida himself, who is the very source of salvation for all who believe. Alfred Bloom says, "It is safe to say, perhaps, that the essential difference between Shinran and other Buddhist thinkers, of his time or any other time, hinges on the denial of the merit acquisition principle."[40]

Shinran's insistence on the total depravity of man meant, of course, that it included him as well.[41] In one of his poems, Shinran described himself as being "false and untrue without the least purity of mind."[42] Later, in a theological work, he paused to declare that he had "drowned in the broad sea of lust."[43] So Shinran had to go the final step and argue that he could not even take credit for his desire to be saved or his desire to dwell in the Pure Land. Even that is the gift of Amida. No one can utter the Primal Vow even one time, or place their faith in Amida, apart from the grace and prior initiative of Amida. It is Amida alone who transfers his merit to us. We do not "cash in" our accumulated merit for some greater benefit. Shinran, like the baby kitten, saw himself as helpless before Amida. His vocalization of the nembutsu and his desire for the Pure Land was a gift from Amida who, out of compassion, carried him through the Primal Vow. This radical grace is summed up well in a passage in which Amida declares, "For the sake of all beings I will open forth the treasure-store, and give away universally its treasure of virtues."[44]

The language that Shinran's followers use to describe this total abandonment of human effort and the reception of Amida's unmerited grace is close to the language Christians use for a radical conversion. Shinran refers to it as *eshin*, which, as a verb, means to "turn about." A contemporary follower of Shinran defines the controlling idea behind eshin as "the radical conversion experience brought about by the working of Other Power, whereby the center of one's being, the mind of self-power is overturned and abandoned. Man, thus, gives himself up completely to the working of Amida's Primal Vow."[45] Shinran himself taught in his *Kyōgyōshinshō* that this conversion could happen "in the space of one moment" when one finally crosses over into

40. Bloom, *Shinran's Gospel of Pure Grace*, viii.

41. As will be explored later in the chapter, total depravity did not apply to Amida in his earthly state because he lived in a different age when the attainment of righteousness was still possible.

42. Bloom, *Shinran's Gospel of Pure Grace*, 29.

43. Ibid.

44. Ueda, ed., *The True Teaching, Practice and Realization of the Pure Land Way*, 1:72. This is volume 1 of Shinran's *Kyōgyōshinshō*.

45. Ueda, ed., *Notes on "Essentials of Faith Alone,"* 107–8. See, definition of "Turn-About" (*eshin*).

Other Power in an experience he called "leaping crosswise."[46] Remarkably, this radical shift from self-power to the Other Power of Amida is also referred to in Pure Land literature as a "spiritual rebirth."[47]

From this brief survey it is clear that Shinran developed the Pure Land of his teacher Hōnen in several important ways. Shinran's keen sense of human depravity led him to put a far greater emphasis on both the exclusivity of "Other Power" and the single utterance of the nembutsu than his teacher. Shinran gathered quite a few disciples and, toward the end of his life, he was particularly productive in writing and spreading his views. However, Shinran always maintained a deep affection for Hōnen and insisted that everything he taught was entirely consistent with what his master taught. When Shinran used the term *Jodo Shin Shu* (*True* Pure Land), he did not intend it to become the name of a separate school of thought, but as a way to communicate that he was transmitting the *true* essence of the teaching of Hōnen. Nevertheless, after Shinran's death the term was increasingly used by his followers to distinguish themselves as a separate school of Pure Land such that today Shin (i.e., True) Pure Land is the largest school of Japanese Buddhism.[48]

LUTHER AND SHINRAN: CONVERGENCE AND DISCONTINUITY

With this background, we are now prepared to explore in more detail the points of convergence and discontinuity between Christian and Buddhist thought regarding the doctrine of salvation by grace. We will begin by exploring the similarities in the life and thought of Shinran and Luther. Then we will examine some of the most important differences in how salvation by grace through faith is understood by Protestant Christians and by True Pure Land Buddhists.

Convergence in Their Personal Lives

Quite apart from the specific content of their theological writings, the parallels between the personal lives of Luther and Shinran are remarkable. Both were born approximately 1,500 years after the birth of their respective religions. Both studied for the priesthood and were recognized as brilliant thinkers. Both became deeply conscious of their own sinfulness and depravity to the point of utter despair as they realized the insufficiency of any amount of human effort in achieving salvation. Both became increasingly disturbed by abuses and distortions in the official religious practice and teaching of their day, which, in their view, had lost touch with a proper doctrine of grace and, instead, placed too much emphasis on the accumulation of self-justifying merit.

Both left the priesthood, got married, and had six children. Both were committed to teaching and extensive writing and correspondence, which helped to gather followers and, ultimately, to stimulate a new movement of reform. Neither Luther

46. *Kyōgyōshinshō*, as found in Ueda, ed., *The True Teaching, Practice and Realization of the Pure Land Way*, 2:73–74.

47. See, for example, Sugihira, "The Nembutsu in Shin Buddhism," 349.

48. Ueda, ed., *Notes on "Essentials of Faith Alone,"* 103.

nor Shinran intended to start a separate religious movement. Both believed that their teaching was actually a recapturing of past orthodoxy and orthopraxis, rather than some novel departure advocating new doctrines.

General, Structural Convergence in Their Thought

The expression "salvation by grace through faith" is generally understood as a summary statement of the central theological contribution (or restoration) of the Reformation. The theological legacy of Luther, as well as the Reformation in general, has often been summarized by the four famous phrases: *sola gratia* (by grace alone), *sola fide* (by faith alone), *sola Scriptura* (by Scripture alone), and *solo Christo* (by Christ alone).[49] A study of Shinran reveals a strikingly similar structure in the general framework of his thought.

First, *sola gratia*. Shinran believed that salvation was possible only by being set free from our bondage to self-power and enabled to receive unmerited grace. Shinran would have been just as opposed to the sale of indulgences as Luther would have been opposed to the vain, endless repetition of the nembutsu. In fact, both would have condemned these practices on the same grounds, namely, because they undermined the doctrine of grace.

Second, *sola fide*. One of the key terms used by Shinran for the concept of "faith" is *shinjin*, which literally means "true (sincere) heart or mind." Frequently it is translated as "faith" in English writings. However, it is interesting to note a few of the reasons some True Pure Land Buddhist writers have been reluctant to translate shinjin as "faith." To begin with, the widespread circulation of Christian evangelistic materials has left some Buddhists with the impression that when Christians refer to faith, they are speaking of an independent operation of the human will. This is, of course, a caricature of the Christian view, but it is not hard to see how someone reading the material could come away with this impression, since the background details of election, regeneration, prevenient grace, and so forth are rarely explained in popular, evangelistic literature that calls people to exercise faith.

Another reason for the misunderstanding is that in the broader Therevada and non-Pure Land schools of Mahayana, the faith or trust one puts in the Buddha or a bodhisattva is, in fact, widely understood as an operation of the human will; therefore deeply held Buddhist ideas about faith are unknowingly superimposed onto the Christian ideas about faith. However, Shinran, like Luther, had come to see that, because of human depravity, such an exercise of the will was not possible.[50] Shinran understood shinjin "not as a decision or a commitment, but as the manifestation of Amida's working."[51]

49. See Jaroslav Pelikan, ed., *Luther's Works*, vol. 26, *Lectures on Galatians*, chapters 1–4 (Saint Louis: Concordia, 1963), 137–38, 160, 208. See Eric Gritsch, ed., *Luther's Works*, vol. 39, *Church and Ministry* (Philadelphia: Fortress, 1970), 167, 276. See also Timothy George, *Theology of the Reformers* (Nashville: Broadman, 1988).

50. Later in the chapter we will explore how the source of this depravity is conceptualized very differently by Shinran and by Luther. The point here is simply that just as Luther believed that it was "not possible not to sin," so Shinran believed that it was not possible for anyone to attain enlightenment through good works since, in this age, everyone is ensnared by the "five defilements."

51. Ueda, ed., *Notes on "Essentials of Faith Alone,"* 7.

Thus, on the surface level, shinjin is "entrusting oneself to Amida by virtue of the Primal Vow." However, on a deeper level, shinjin is actually *receiving* "the true and real mind and heart of Amida."[52] Without the gift of shinjin from Amida Buddha, all learning and initiation rights are in vain.[53] Thus, leaving aside for the moment the vast difference in the object of faith between Buddhism and Christianity, there is a striking similarity between the two in Shinran's general understanding of faith and how faith is engendered in the lives of believers.

Third, *sola Scriptura*. Shinran, as noted above, had no confidence in his own insights or abilities. He considered himself a "foolish being" (*bombu*) whose only hope was to cast himself on the Primal Vow and let it carry him to Amida and the Pure Land. Shinran once said,

> Whether the *nembutsu* brings rebirth into the Pure Land or leads one to Hell, I myself have no way of knowing. But even if I had been misled by Hōnen and went to Hell for saying the *nembutsu*, I would have no regrets. If I were capable of attaining Buddhahood on my own through the practice of some discipline, and yet went down to Hell for saying the *nembutsu*, then I might regret having been misled. But since I am incapable of practicing such disciplines, there can be no doubt that I would be doomed to Hell anyway.[54]

Once Shinran has abandoned all hope in self-power, he casts himself on the only sure link between himself and Amida, namely, the truth of the *Larger Sūtra*, which contains the text of Amida's forty-eight vows.[55] For Shinran, only the Primal Vow can be trusted. Shinran himself said, "I throw aside those practices not included in Amida's Vow … and now only throw myself upon the Original Vow of Amida."[56]

Fourth, *solo Christo*. As demonstrated earlier, one of the key developments in Shinran's thought is the reversal of the direction of merit. Traditional Buddhism is deeply entrenched in the whole idea of merit acquisition. Mahayana Buddhism made certain bold provisions for grace, but it is still not completely unmerited grace since it is set within the larger framework of merit acquisition. However, Shinran reversed the whole direction: "All transfer of merit comes from Amida Buddha to man … to stress the fact that Amida Buddha is the ultimate ground of salvation."[57] It is Amida alone who causes shinjin to engender faith in the lives of his devotees. It is Amida alone who, according to Shinran, has provided salvation for all through the efficacy of his forty-eight vows, especially the Primal Vow. Amida occupies the central place in the Pure Land. For Shinran, without Amida there is no hope, no basis for faith, and no final salvation. Shinran emphatically declares that he has been

52. Ibid., 8.

53. Clark Chilson, "Born-Again Buddhists: Twentieth Century Initiation Rites of Secretive Shinshu Societies in Central Japan," *Studies in Central and East Asian Religions* 11 (1999): 19.

54. From Shinran's *Tannishō*, as quoted in de Bary, *The Buddhist Tradition in India, China and Japan*, 340. *Tannishō* means "Collection Inspired by Concern over Heresy."

55. There are actually three major texts that are revered in Pure Land Buddhism: The Larger and Smaller *Sukhāvatī-vyūha* and the *Sūtra of the Meditations on Amitāyus.*

56. See de Bary, *The Buddhist Tradition in India, China and Japan*, 330.

57. Bloom, *Shinran's Gospel of Pure Grace*, 49.

"saved by Amida."[58] Amida is as central to Shinran's faith as Jesus Christ is central to Luther's faith.

Shinran died over two hundred years before Luther was even born. Nevertheless, Shinran could have easily adapted the basic structure of the Reformation's insights as his own. He and his True Pure Land Buddhists could have declared: *sola gratia*, *sola fide*, *sola Scriptura* (Primal Vow text), and *solo Amida*. Furthermore, Shinran would have been just as comfortable declaring that we are "saved by grace through faith" as any Protestant. However, despite the remarkable similarities, the final section of this chapter will explore several of the crucial differences in the understanding of this doctrine in Christianity and in True Pure Land Buddhism.

Discontinuity between Shinran and Luther

In recent years, we have witnessed a growing interest in the field of comparative religions. What once was a rather private, scholarly discussion in academic journals and among missionaries has now spilled out into the church and the public square. This change has been stimulated by a number of factors, including globalization, growing ethnic and religious diversity in the West, and an increased realization of the importance religious affiliation plays in modern political and social alignments around the world. Dozens of new books have been published in comparative religions and, since 9/11, interest in interreligious dialogue has been on the rise, particularly with Islam. In general, I find this trend encouraging because it is essential that Christians become more knowledgeable about and actively engaged in real world contexts.

There are, however, two aspects of this development that I find troubling. First, I am troubled when I encounter people who are put on a stage and given a microphone, or who pick up a pen in order to "represent" Christianity, but who are prepared to sacrifice the very doctrines that historically define the Christian faith.[59] For example, to deny the bodily resurrection of Jesus Christ as the decisive event in defining Christian identity is to cease being a Christian in any historical, traditional, or biblical sense of the word. Yet, it is not unusual to find people who actually stand outside the boundaries of historic Christianity speak on behalf of and are viewed as representing the Christian faith.

The second troubling aspect is that the popularization of interreligious dialogue and the growing interest in comparative religion has been accompanied by an equally dramatic rise in the superficiality of the analysis and the theological shallowness—even naïveté—of the discussions. Part of this is due to the relative ignorance of Western Christians about the actual faith and practice of the major non-Christian religions. It is still not unusual even for seminary students in the West to graduate without a single course in non-Christian religions. You are still more likely to graduate from a typical seminary having read Bultmann than having read the Qurʾan.

58. Sugihira, "The Nembutsu in Shin Buddhism," 355.

59. See, for example, John Hick, ed., *The Myth of God Incarnate* (Philadelphia: Westminster, 1977).

The superficiality is also fueled by the fact that we are now awash with simple comparisons that reduce comparative religions to a single foldout piece of paper. These world religion guides typically compare and contrast how different religions understand God, sin, salvation, eternal life, and so forth. However, these comparisons are sometimes flatly in error, at other times misleading, and, at best, representative of only one strand of a complex religious tradition. This chapter has sought to delve more deeply into the particular beliefs and perspective of True Pure Land Buddhists.

We have demonstrated some striking similarities between Christianity and True Pure Land. However, we must now take the next step and examine these traditions even more closely and discover how these two streams of thought, both of which can claim that salvation is by grace through faith, actually remain very different from each other. This will be shown by examining four major differences between the teachings of Shinran and the teachings of Protestant Christianity as they pertain to this doctrine.

The Source of the Human Predicament: Doctrine of Sin versus Age of Mappō

Any sustained discussion about salvation must, it seems, include some discussion about what we are being saved *from*. What is the source of the human predicament? These are vital questions to raise in any serious comparative evaluation between Pure Land Buddhism and Protestant views of salvation.

Buddhists in general, including Shinran, do not affirm a doctrine of sin in any Christian meaning of that word. In other words, Buddhists neither affirm the presence of an inherent sinful nature nor teach that our evil thoughts and deeds rebel against a holy, objective, personal God. Instead, Shinran taught that evil exists because of the particular *time* we live in. Shinran, following Buddhism in general, believed that at the time when the Buddha first taught, the dharma the human race was living in was a kind of golden age, known as the *shōbō* period, when the dharma could be understood and obeyed. We are currently living in a degenerate period known as the Age of *Mappō*.[60] In this period, the practice of true dharma is impossible. Shinran said, "In the age of the Latter Days of the *Dharma*, no matter how many sentient beings practice the Way, no one will attain enlightenment. The present age is the age of decadent *dharma*, the evil age of the five defilements."[61]

In Shinran's view, people who lived in an earlier time were able to save themselves, whereas now people are trapped by the increased weight of bad karma. Paul Ingram sums up the difference well when he writes, "*Mappō* is not the *condition* of man, but it is the *cause* of man's spiritual condition." Mappō is an external force of impersonal karma, whereas sin is rebellion against God. Jesus Christ was sent to "take away the sin of the world" (John 1:29). In Buddhism, there are no sins to be taken away. The language of evil and sin is used by Buddhists to refer to the weight of karma, not

60. The golden age of *shōbō* lasts 500 years, followed by *zōpō*, which lasts for one thousand, and the current age of *mappō*, which lasts for ten thousand years.

61. Shinran, *Kyōgyōshinshō*, SSZ, 2.168, as quoted by Paul Ingram, "Shinron Shonin and Martin Luther: A Soteriological Comparison," *Journal of the American Academy of Religion* 39, no. 4 (December 1971): 432. The five defilements are as follows: (1) impurity of living, (2) impurity of false teaching, (3) impurity of evil passions, (4) impurity of mind and body, and (5) shortening of the human life span.

rebellion against a holy God. For Shinran, evil is any "thought or action that creates negative karma."[62] Therefore, there can be no forgiveness, because there is nothing to forgive; there is no wronged party, no Judge who holds his creation accountable. Shinran's hopelessness before Amida is not because of any sense of judicial guilt, but simply because of his inability to escape the weight of karma and the inevitable cycle of rebirth. For Shinran, Amida's "Other Power" is nothing more than "a helping hand out of the quagmire from one who has just crawled out himself."[63]

The Nature of Amida and the Nature of God in Jesus Christ

The entire Christian gospel is predicated on the existence of God, who is the eternal, sovereign, personal Creator of the universe and all that is in it. The opening words of the Apostles' Creed affirm this when it declares, "I believe in God the Father Almighty, maker of heaven and earth." On the surface, the focus on Amida and the language of devotion attached to him come across as theistic. However, Amida is an expression of functional, subjective theism, not actual objective theism. He is neither a god nor a creator.

We must not forget that the doctrine of dependent arising (*pratitya samutpāda*) is central to the Buddha's dharma and is foundational even for all the Pure Land schools. This is the doctrine that rejects all first causes, including God. Even though Amida may serve as a kind of functional or devotional deity, he is, by Buddhists' own testimony, nothing more than "a metaphysical reality, a product of religious consciousness."[64] Amida is portrayed as a savior, but never as a god.

Amida has a vague historical origin in the incalculable number of lifetimes that began with Dharmākara. Dharmākara became Amida only after many lifetimes of meritorious practice. In short, Dharmākara is a *man* who became exalted as a savior. In Christianity, the Son of God is the eternal, second person of the Triune God, who became incarnate as the God-Man. In Jesus Christ, God himself has stepped into real history and into the world he had created as the redeeming Savior. Karl Barth sums it up well when he points out that despite striking similarities between Christianity and True Pure Land as religions of grace, in the end, "only one thing is really decisive for the distinction of truth and error ... that one thing is the name of Jesus Christ."[65]

Grace in Shin Buddhism and in Christianity

It is the doctrine of grace in Shinran's teaching that has attracted so much attention by Christians, leading many to agree with Karl Barth's assessment that Shinran's True Pure Land could "take its place with the purest form of Christianity as a religion of grace."[66] Barth states this as a way to make the larger point that even if Shin Buddhism

---

62. Gerhard Schepers, "Shinran's View of the Human Predicament and the Christian Concept of Sin," *Japanese Religions* 15, no. 2 (July 1988): 5.

63. Colin Noble, "Portraying Christian Grace: A Response to the Doctrine of Grace in Shin Buddhism," *Asia Journal of Theology* 11, no. 1 (April 1997): 63.

64. This is how Amida is described in D. T. Suzuki's commentary on the *Kyōgyōshinshō* as quoted by Buri, "The Concept of Grace in Paul, Shinran, and Luther," 28.

65. Barth, *Church Dogmatics*, vol. 1, part 2, 343. Barth goes on to say that "the truth of the Christian religion is in fact enclosed in the one name of Jesus Christ, and nothing else."

66. Ibid.

were to be found to have a pure doctrine of grace, it should still be considered a false religion because of the absence of Jesus Christ.

Nevertheless, it seems that Shinran's doctrine of grace is where the True Pure Land path comes the closest to Reformed Christianity, particularly in Shinran's strong affirmation of human depravity and his understanding of grace as an unmerited gift. However, once it is clear that Buddhism has neither a doctrine of God, nor a concept of sin, nor a savior who has any objective basis for bestowing grace, then despite the structural and linguistic similarities, the conception of grace must likewise be dramatically different. Many implications could be explored, but this analysis will focus, in particular, on the way grace is applied to the believer through the transfer of Amida's merit.

In True Pure Land Buddhism, grace comes as an undeserved transfer of merit from the compassionate Amida to the karma-laden devotee who has vocalized the nembutsu. According to Shinran, in his *Notes on "Essentials of Faith Alone,"* a "single utterance" of the nembutsu results in the extinguishing of "tenfold eight-billion *kalpas* of evil karma."[67] A single kalpa is ten million years, so "tenfold eight-billion kalpas" is such an enormous length of time, covering an even more staggering weight of karma, that it is interpreted as a creative way of saying that all karma has been satisfied, effectively making a person identical in nature with Amida himself.

In the broader Mahayana teaching about bodhisattvas, it is generally understood that the reason a particular bodhisattva has prepared a "buddha-land" for his followers is so that when the devotee arrives, they enter into a realm which is like the golden age of shōbō. There the devotees are able to sit at the feet of the bodhisattva and learn to practice the dharma without the hindrance of karma, and thus they are able to quickly become enlightened.

Shinran goes beyond mainstream Mahayana thought by equating the Pure Land with enlightenment itself. To enter the Pure Land is to instantly realize one's own Buddha nature.[68] Shinran in his *Kyōgyōshinshō* writes, "Masters of the Mahayana and Hinayana and people burdened with karmic evil, whether heavy or light, should all in the same way take refuge in the great treasure ocean of the selected Vow and attain Buddhahood through the *nembutsu*."[69] The logic is as follows: karma-laden people can do nothing to save themselves; Amida gives the gift of shinjin (faith), which enables the devotees to vocalize the nembutsu; the nembutsu takes away all karma, allowing each person to instantly realize their true Buddha nature, which is within; they are now free to enter the Pure Land.

In Protestant theology, there is no doctrine of a *material* merit transference between Christ and the believer. When a believer is justified, it is a *declarative, judicial* act whereby God declares "on the basis of the righteousness of Jesus Christ, that all the claims of the law are satisfied."[70] As a judicial act, "it is not something wrought in man

67. Ueda, *Notes on "Essentials of Faith Alone,"* 52.

68. Bloom, *Shinran's Gospel of Pure Grace*, 66.

69. Shinran, *Kyōgyōshinshō*, 1.69. See Ueda, *The True Teaching, Practice and Realization of the Pure Land Way*, 1:136. Later in the *Kyōgyōshinshō* (3.37), Shinran states that "when we reach the Buddha-land of happiness, we unfailingly disclose Buddha-nature" (see ibid., 3:437).

70. Louis Berkhof, *Systematic Theology* (Grand Rapids: Eerdmans, 1941), 513.

but something declared of man. It does not *make* upright or righteous, but *declares* righteous."[71] When Protestant theologians say that we have had the righteousness of Christ imputed[72] to us, it means "reckoned" to us or "credited" to our account (Rom. 4:3). This restores us to God's favor even though we are not yet righteous in ourselves. The forensic declaration of our righteousness must then be followed by sanctification, the process through which the alien righteousness of Christ is gradually assimilated and appropriated into the actual life experience of the believer through the ministry of the Holy Spirit.

This is why Martin Luther declared that even after our justification we remain sinners. Luther asks about a new believer:

> Now can we say that he is perfectly righteous? No. But he is at the same time both a sinner and righteous (*simul iustus et peccator*), a sinner in fact, but righteous by virtue of the reckoning and the certain promise of God that he will redeem him from sin in order, in the end, to make him perfectly whole and sound.[73]

However, even after regeneration, justification, a lifetime of sanctification, and our final glorification and full union with Christ, we never become identical with the essence of Christ as the followers of Pure Land envision, who affirm the ultimate identity of Amida and his followers into a cosmic unity whereby all distinctions between Amida and those saved by him are obliterated.

Christian Faith and Pure Land Shinjin

Even first-time readers of Shinran are often moved by his genuine sincerity as well as his capacity for self-reflection. Shinran's early attempts to master Buddhist practice and his later abandonment of all such hope rings with the same authenticity as Luther's own earnest approach to the monastic vows and daily confession and his later sense of despair as his personal spiritual journey unfolds. Furthermore, the sheer joy of Shinran's discovery of the nembutsu is described in ways similar to Luther's own joy in discovering that the righteousness of God comes as God's gift, not as something we can ever earn.

Years ago, I learned that a critical analysis of the truth claims of another religion does not require that I prove the insincerity of the leading proponents of these religions. We do not need to doubt the sincerity of Shinran's promotion of the nembutsu any more than we doubt the sincerity of Muhammad's call for the Arabs to forsake idolatry. It is, unfortunately, quite possible to be simultaneously sincere and wrong.

71. Henry Theissen, *Lectures in Systematic Theology* (Grand Rapids: Eerdmans, 1979), 271.

72. This is in contrast to the Roman Catholic view, which insists that at justification we are "infused" with righteousness, that is, "righteousness that God actually puts into us and that changes us internally and in terms of our actual moral character" (Wayne Grudem, *Systematic Theology* [Grand Rapids: Zondervan, 1994], 728). It is beyond the scope of this work to explore how the "new perspective" understands Luther. This chapter is responding to historic Protestant interpretations of Luther.

73. Martin Luther, *Lecture on Romans*, trans. Wilhelm Pauck (Library of Christian Classics 15; Philadelphia: Westminster, 1961), 127.

This is precisely what seems to be the case with Shinran. Even if we grant that he had some sort of dramatic conversion (eshin) and "turn about" that left him with a whole new sense of shinjin or a "true and sincere heart," it does not change the fact that the object of Shinran's faith is someone other than the Lord Jesus Christ. Shinran's faith is in the words of a human being who through the accumulation of merit created his own paradise named the Pure Land and made a vow that can "take away the karma of the world" and allow others to be reborn into this Land. Yet, we have no certainty if Dharmākara ever actually lived, or any evidence that he now dwells exalted and enlightened in the Pure Land.

Indeed, Christians do not accept the idea that there was a golden age when salvation was possible through human effort. Adam was created in fellowship with God and, prior to the fall, did not need to be saved. However, once Adam sinned against God, the entire human race became fallen and instantly moved from *posse non peccare* (able not to sin) to *non posse non peccare* (not able not to sin).

In contrast, Buddhists believe in a five-hundred-year period where the dharma was practiced in purity. However, upon what basis can we trust that the meritorious lives of Dharmākara accrued sufficient merit to bring liberation to the entire world? The Christian view is that the universality of sin renders the entire human race ineligible to bring salvation. It was only possible through the incarnation of God into the world as Jesus Christ. In the final analysis, the whole Pure Land soteriological structure is built on the *autosoteria* (self-salvation) of a man, whereas the whole Christian soteriological structure is built on Jesus Christ. In this light, it seems that Karl Barth's analysis is quite right: Jesus Christ really is the decisive and determinative factor that declares Christianity to be true and Pure Land to be in error.

CONCLUSION

This survey of Shinran's True Pure Land has demonstrated that a doctrine of "salvation by grace through faith" does, indeed, exist in Buddhism, although not in the Christian understanding of the phrase. Similar studies could demonstrate this motif in Bhakti Hinduism and even in certain Sufi sects of Islam. There is a remarkable sense in which the helplessness of the human condition and the desperate cry for grace continue to push their way to the surface of world religions—even those like Hinduism, Buddhism, and Islam, where a doctrine of grace is not central to the original soteriological structure of the religion.

There are some instances where a case can be made that a doctrine of grace and a conception of salvation by faith is the result of a prior exposure to Christianity. However, most of the examples of grace in non-Christian religions are more likely examples of God's providence in general revelation through which he provides regular and overwhelming empirical evidence for the depravity of the human race and the corresponding inward concurrence that we are unable to save ourselves without some outside or heavenly assistance. Regardless of the source, we should learn to expect doctrines of grace rather than be surprised by them. Certainly this chapter should provide sufficient information to dispel the often-repeated myth that only in Christianity do we find a doctrine of grace and all other religions know only about a doctrine of works and the hope of the accumulation of merit within some larger scheme of autosoterism.

Nevertheless, even allowing for doctrines of grace in other religions, it is still unusual to meet a doctrine of uncompromised, unmerited grace as forcefully set forth and as central to a thinker's whole theological program as that which is found in the writings of Shinran. Here we meet many of the larger structural features that, in a broad sense, mirror the Christian understanding of human depravity, sincere faith, and unmerited grace. It is clear why Karl Barth refers to True Pure Land as "Japanese Protestantism" and a "religion of grace."[74]

Yet, once we begin to probe beneath the surface and look beyond the identity in language and sentiment, the differences become more obvious. Many will concur with Jannie du Preez who, after a reflection on grace in True Pure Land and in Protestant Christianity, remarked that "at a deeper level ... it becomes crystal clear that a difference of such magnitude exists between the two religions that injustice is done to both when an attempt is made to interpret one in terms of the other. As David Bosch has said, 'we are dealing with different worlds.'"[75]

However, are we really left with nothing more to say once we have declared that this massive gulf exists and that "we are dealing with different worlds"? If, indeed, the absence of Jesus Christ and the decisive acts of redemption wrought by him are the determinative factors that separate truth from error, do we have anything else to say except, "True Pure Land is in error"? After hearing the verdict of "not true," do we cast True Pure Land into the same bin with various forms of witchcraft that affirm salvation through ritual, sadistic torture? What about the providence of God in providing *preparatio evangelica* before we come to Jesus Christ? Could we not accept the final error of True Pure Land, but still acknowledge it as an example of the truth that, even within Buddhism, God "has not left himself without testimony" (Acts 14:17)? Would not the great church father Justin Martyr remind us that while only in the Christian gospel do we meet the "whole *logos*, which is Christ," God in his providence has "implanted" the "seed of reason [*logos spermatikos*] ... in every race of men"?[76]

If God is truly active in all races of people, one of the more striking examples of it could very well be in the "providential disposition" whereby True Pure Land may serve as a guide or a bridge to the saving knowledge of Jesus Christ.[77] The prescription of the human need has been already provided by Shinran. Granted, Shinran's solution has placed unwarranted faith in Amida who, as we noted above, is only a "metaphysical reality, a product of religious consciousness."[78] But, from the gospel's perspective, Amida is also a dim shadow, seen by the flickering light of Pure Land, which, in God's

74. Barth, *Church Dogmatics*, vol. 1, part 2, 342–43.

75. Jannie Du Preez, "A Buddhist Form of Salvation by Grace Alone?" *Missionalia* 21, no. 2 (August 1993): 183. This quotation of David Bosch occurs in his *Theology of Religions* [study guide] (Pretoria: Univ. of South Africa Press, 1977), 181.

76. Justin Martyr, *Second Apology* 8 (see Alexander Roberts and James Donaldson, eds., *Ante-Nicene Fathers* [Peabody, MA: Hendrickson, 1999], 1:178).

77. Karl Barth employs the phrase "providential disposition" in the context of God providing what he calls an "illuminating parallel to Christianity, a religious development in the Far East" that "is parallel not to Roman or Greek Catholicism, but to Reformed Christianity" (Barth, *Church Dogmatics*, vol. 1, part 2, 340).

78. See footnote 64.

grace, may point to the true reality, our Lord Jesus Christ, who alone can truly bear the titles falsely attributed to Amida as Lord of "infinite light" (Amitābha) and "infinite life" (Amitāyus). All other lesser lights must ultimately point to Christ's infinite light and life.

BIBLIOGRAPHY

Andrews, Alan A. "Nembutsu in the Chinese Pure Land Tradition." *The Eastern Buddhist* 3, no. 2 (October 1970): 20–45.

Barth, Karl. *Church Dogmatics.* Vol. 1, part 2, *The Doctrine of the Word of God.* Translated and edited by G. W. Bromiley and T. F. Torrance. Edinburgh: T. & T. Clark, 1956.

Berkhof, Louis. *Systematic Theology.* Grand Rapids: Eerdmans, 1941.

Bloom, Alfred. *Shinran's Gospel of Pure Grace.* Tucson: University of Arizona Press, 1965.

Bosch, David. *Theology of Religions* (study guide). Pretoria: University of South Africa Press, 1977.

Buri, Fritz. "The Concept of Grace in Paul, Shinran, and Luther." *Eastern Buddhist* 9, no. 2 (2004): 21–42.

Chilson, Clark. "Born-Again Buddhists: Twentieth Century Initiation Rites of Secretive Shinshu Societies in Central Japan." *Studies in Central and East Asian Religions* 11 (1999): 18–35.

Cowell, E. B. ed. *Buddhist Mahayana Texts.* New York: Dover, 1969.

De Bary, William Theodore, ed. *The Buddhist Tradition in India, China and Japan.* New York: Vintage, 1972.

Du Preez, Jannie. "A Buddhist Form of Salvation by Grace Alone?" *Missionalia* 21, no 2 (August 1993): 176–85.

Grudem, Wayne. *Systematic Theology.* Grand Rapids: Zondervan, 1994.

Hick, John, ed. *The Myth of God Incarnate.* Philadelphia: Westminster, 1977.

Ingram, Paul. "Shinron Shonin and Martin Luther: A Soteriological Comparison." *Journal of the American Academy of Religion* 39, no. 4 (December 1971): 430–47.

Jackson, Roger, and John Makransky, eds. *Buddhist Theology: Critical Reflections by Contemporary Buddhist Scholars.* Surrey, UK: Curzon, 2000.

Lohse, Bernhard. *Martin Luther: An Introduction to His Life and Work.* Philadelphia: Fortress, 1986.

Lopez, Donald S. Jr., ed. *Buddhist Scriptures.* London: Penguin, 2004.

Luther, Martin. *Lectures on Romans.* In Library of Christian Classics 15. Translated by Wilhelm Pauck. Philadelphia: Westminster, 1961.

Martyr, Justin. *Second Apology.* Alexander Roberts and James Donaldson, eds. *Ante-Nicene Fathers.* Vol. 1. Peabody, MA: Hendrickson, 1999.

Müller, Max, ed. *The Sacred Books of the East.* Vol. 49, *Buddhist Mahayana Texts*, Part II, *The Larger Sukhāvati-yvūha Sūtra.* New York: Dover, 1962.

Noble, Colin. "Portraying Christian Grace: A Response to the Doctrine of Grace in Shin Buddhism." *Asia Journal of Theology* 11, no. 1 (April 1997): 54–71.

Olson, Carl. *The Different Paths of Buddhism.* New Brunswick, NJ: Rutgers University Press, 2005.

Schepers, Gerhard. "Shinran's View of the Human Predicament and the Christian Concept of Sin." *Japanese Religions* 15, no. 2 (July 1988): 1–17.

Shinran. *The Kyōgyōshinshō: The Collection of Passages Expounding the True Teaching, Living, Faith, and Realizing of the Pure Land.* Kyoto, Japan: Shinshu Otaniha, 1973.

Sugihira, Shizutoshi. "The Nembutsu in Shin Buddhism," *The Eastern Buddhist* 7, nos. 3–4 (July 1939): 342–62.

Suzuki, Daisetz Teitaro. *Collected Writings on Shin Buddhism.* Kyoto, Japan: Shinshu Otaniha, 1973.

_____. "Development of the Pure Land Doctrine in Buddhism." *The Eastern Buddhist* 3, no. 4 (January–March 1925): 285–326.

Tamura, Yoshiro. *Japanese Buddhism: A Cultural History.* Translated by Jeffrey Hunter. Tokyo: Kosei, 2000.

Theissen, Henry. *Lectures in Systematic Theology.* Grand Rapids: Eerdmans, 1979.

Ueda, Yoshifumi, ed. *Notes on "Essentials of Faith Alone": A Translation of Shinran's Yuishin-shō-mon'i.* Kyoto, Japan: Hongwanji International Center, 1979.

_____. *The True Teaching, Practice and Realization of the Pure Land Way.* 3 vols. Kyoto, Japan: Hongwanji International Center, 1978.

Uene, Kametani, and Ohori Michihata. *Buddhist Priests Choose Christ.* Translated by Satsuki Wakabayashi and John Terry. Wilmington, DE: Dawn, 1989.

Williams, Paul. *Mahāyāna Buddhism: The Doctrinal Foundations.* London and New York: Routledge, 1989.

Yoshinori, Takeuchi. "The Meaning of 'Other-Power' in the Buddhist Way of Salvation." *The Eastern Buddhist* 15, no. 2 (1982): 10–27.

Chapter 7

PNEUMATOLOGY

THE HOLY SPIRIT IN LATIN AMERICAN PENTECOSTALISM

On April 18, 1906, San Francisco was rocked by a massive earthquake that destroyed much of the city and killed thousands of people, making it the largest natural disaster in the history of the United States. The next day, on April 19, a group of poor, racially mixed Christians gathered in an old, dilapidated warehouse building on 312 Azusa Street in Los Angeles to pray and to ask God for the meaning of the earthquake. The leader of the meeting was William J. Seymour, a one-eyed black preacher from Louisiana who had come to Los Angeles only a few months earlier. Seymour (1870–1922) taught that the earthquake was the beginning of the great tribulation. Yet he believed that God was pouring out his Spirit in these last days to provide a window of opportunity for repentance before the return of Christ. God was restoring the first-century apostolic church, proclaimed Seymour, including a fresh visitation of Pentecost whereby believers could be baptized in the Holy Spirit, speak in unknown tongues, be empowered for witness, and live a holy life.

Seymour had first learned this message from the former Methodist preacher and now healing evangelist from Kansas, Charles Parham (1873–1929). Seymour fervently believed that the time of God's visitation had come to Los Angeles. It all began on Easter Sunday, April 15, 1905, when Jenny Evans Moore spoke in tongues at the conclusion of the service at the Azusa Street Mission. News about this spread throughout Los Angeles. A few days later, the front page of the *Los Angeles Daily Times* contained the extended headline: "Weird Babble of Tongues, New Sect of Fanatics Breaking Loose, Wild Scene Last Night on Azusa Street, Gurgle of Wordless Talk by a Sister."[1] This was the first public announcement that something dramatic was happening on Azusa Street.

1. "Weird Babble of Tongues," *Los Angeles Daily Times* (April 18, 1906), 1.

The revival lasted from April 1906 through the early months of 1909 and drew tens of thousands of people from all over the world, who came to witness the outpouring of the Holy Spirit during one of the three daily services. Over the three-year period the Azusa Street Mission could hardly contain the crowds as thousands found redemption in Jesus Christ and experienced what was known as a "second Pentecost." It is not surprising that when Seymour began to publish a newspaper to help spread his teachings in September 1906, his lead article in the inaugural edition was entitled, "Pentecost Has Come!" However, the movement was not yet called "Pentecostalism." In those early days it was known simply as "The Apostolic Faith," which also became the name for the newspaper Seymour published.[2] Few realized just how profoundly the global church would be affected by this and similar revivals that were simultaneously and independently breaking out around the world.

The year 2006 marked the centennil anniversary of the beginning of the Azusa street revivals, widely credited as the cradle of Pentecostalism in North America.[3] Similar revivals, independent of the Azusa Street meetings, included the famous Welsh revival that lasted from September 1904 to June 1905 and witnessed over ten thousand people coming to Christ. A few years later, revivals broke out in Korea, several of which occurred in what is today North Korea, including Wonsan and Pyongyang. These Korean revivals became known as the "Korean Pentecost."[4]

The evangelistic and missionary fervor that burst forth from these revivals, in turn, helped to spark new waves of Pentecostalism around the world. For example, Welsh missionaries working in India, fresh from the revivals in Wales, witnessed dramatic Pentecostal revivals in the Kashi Hills of Northeast India. In 1906, another revival broke out near Pune, India, at the Mukti Mission of the famous Brahmin convert to Christianity, Pandita Ramabai. Similar revival movements occurred in China as well as several countries of Africa, including the Ivory Coast, Ghana, and Nigeria.

Pentecostal scholar Allan Anderson points out that the Azusa Street revival "turned a fairly localized and insignificant new Christian sect into an international movement that sent workers to more than twenty-five nations in only two years."[5] In the first one hundred years of Pentecostalism the movement has grown from a few scattered revival meetings to a major global force of a half a billion adherents, second in size only to Roman Catholicism.[6] What began as a small flame among an assortment of poor janitors, horse drivers, factory laborers, hotel waiters, washers, and maids has become a whole new branch of Christianity. If one also considers the impact

2. Seymour printed 5,000 copies of the inaugural edition of *The Apostolic Faith* and sent them without charge to the leaders of the churches. By 1907 its distribution reached 40,000. The paper was published on an occasional basis from September 1906 to May 1908. For a collection of several of the sermons and writings of William Seymour see Larry Martin, *The Words That Changed the World: Azusa Street Sermons* (Joplin, MO: Christian Life, 1999).

3. For more on the historic connection between the Azusa Street Mission and the emergence of Pentecostalism in Latin America, see Douglas Petersen, "The Azusa Street Mission and Latin American Pentecostalism," *International Bulletin of Missionary Research* 30, no. 2 (April 2006): 66–67.

4. Allan Anderson, *An Introduction to Pentecostalism* (Cambridge: Cambridge Univ. Press, 2004), 37.

5. Allan Anderson, "To All Points of the Compass: The Azusa Street Revival and Global Pentecostalism," *Enrichment Journal*, online journal of the General Council of the Assemblies of God (http://enrichmentjournal.ag.org/200602/200602_164_AllPoints.cfm)(accessed July 19, 2006).

6. Edith Blumhofer, "Revisiting Azusa Street: A Centennial Retrospect," *International Bulletin of Missionary Research* 30, no. 2 (April 2006): 59.

of Pentecostal theology as reflected in the Charismatic and neo-Charismatic movements that have deeply influenced both Protestant and Roman Catholic churches, then the number swells to nearly 600 million Christians around the world who are Pentecostal in belief, in practice, or by denominational affiliation.[7] If Pentecostalism is, as the title of Harvey Cox's landmark book declares, a "fire from heaven," then it is a fire that has spread around the whole world.[8] We ignore to our own detriment the vital role Pentecostalism is playing in shaping theological discourse and practice throughout the world.

WHAT IS MEANT BY "PENTECOSTALISM"?

Pentecostalism is a diverse movement that defies easy categorization or generalizations.[9] More than a half billion adherents firmly planted on every inhabited continent, comprising thousands of denominations, is difficult to summarize except in the broadest of strokes. A common problem that plagues most attempts to define and characterize Pentecostalism is that the emphasis is often placed on the *distinctiveness* of Pentecostal faith and experience rather than on the broad *agreement* between Pentecostals and evangelicals. Therefore, it should be made clear from the outset that the overwhelming majority of Pentecostal groups are solidly within the boundaries of historic Christian orthodoxy.[10]

Pentecostals fully affirm the authority of the Bible. They affirm the centrality of Christ's work on the cross for salvation and the historic reality of the resurrection of Jesus Christ. They affirm the importance of repentance, conversion, and living a holy life. They eagerly anticipate the glorious return of Jesus Christ at the end of the age. Indeed, most Pentecostals, although typically noncreedal, are able to affirm every

7. David B. Barrett, George T. Kurian, and Todd M. Johnson, *World Christian Encyclopedia*, 2nd ed. (New York: Oxford Univ. Press, 2001), 4. Barrett, Kurian, and Johnson cite 523,777,994 in 2000, but with more than an 8 percent growth rate until 2025, the growth of Pentecostals and Charismatics will swell to 811,551,594. In this context, "classical" Pentecostalism refers to the emergence of new denominations and Christian movements defined in some way by Pentecostal theology. Charismatic and neo-Charismatic refers to various waves of renewal that have occurred within—and stayed within—the older, established churches.

8. Harvey Cox, *Fire from Heaven: The Rise of Pentecostal Spirituality and the Reshaping of Religion in the Twenty-First Century* (Reading, MA: Addison Wesley, 1995).

9. David Barrett and Todd Johnson identify twelve broad forms of Pentecostalism in the world, six under the broader heading "Classical Pentecostals" and six under the broad heading, "Indigenous Charismatic." Latin American Pentecostalism reflects this same diversity with churches planted by Pentecostal immigrants who have relocated to Latin America, churches started through missionary labors from classical Pentecostals from outside Latin America, indigenous Pentecostal churches, and neo-Pentecostal/Charismatic churches as a result of revivals within their own congregations.

10. The most important exception would be the "Oneness" Pentecostals, who deny the Trinity. The largest group within this category would be the United Pentecostal Church International (UPCI) with approximately 500,000 in the USA and 500,000 in other parts of the world. Their denial of the Trinity is based on a modalistic view of the Trinity, not because they deny the deity of Christ. While I do not want to diminish the significance of this heresy, it is worth noting that Jaroslav Pelikan makes the helpful comment that "throughout Christian history men have been frequently condemned for denying the deity of Christ, but rarely for denying the distinction between the Father and the Son. To deny the former has generally seemed unchristian; to deny the latter only unintelligent." See Jaroslav Pelikan, *The Christian Tradition: A History of the Development of Doctrine*; vol. 1: *The Emergence of the Catholic Tradition, (100–600)* (Chicago: Univ. of Chicago Press, 1971), 182. For a full treatment of Oneness Pentecostal views, see Gregory A. Boyd, *Oneness Pentecostals and the Trinity* (Grand Rapids: Baker, 1992). Pentecostal scholar Walter Hollenweger concedes that the strong emphasis in the West on defining pneumatology through Christology in the wake of the *filioque* controversy has hindered a full development of the person of the Holy Spirit in Pentecostal circles. See Walter Hollenweger, *Pentecostalism: Origins and Developments Worldwide* (Peabody, MA: Hendrickson, 1997), 218–19.

phrase of the Apostles' or Nicene Creed. Indeed, most Pentecostals do not claim to bring any new teachings at all, but rather a *restoration* of biblical and apostolic faith. In short, Pentecostals are our brothers and sisters in Christ, from whom we have much to learn.

Another problem with defining Pentecostalism in precise doctrinal terms is that the global movement is broader than the theology of "classical" Pentecostal denominations, which tend to dominate North American Pentecostalism. Even the basic generalization that "all Pentecostals speak in tongues" is difficult to apply, since the debate about tongue-speaking being the "initial evidence" of the baptism in the Holy Spirit is not a crucial part of the larger, global Pentecostal discourse. A final issue is that Pentecostalism has so deeply influenced mainline Protestant and evangelical Christianity in Latin America that it is nearly impossible to speak of beliefs or practices that are distinctive of Pentecostals to the exclusion of all other groups. Likewise, mainline Protestantism and evangelicalism have exerted considerable influence on Pentecostals.[11]

Keeping this qualification in mind, certain broad statements can nevertheless be fruitfully made to help characterize how the word "Pentecostal" is being used in this study. First, Pentecostals believe in a postconversion (or postregeneration) experience known as "the baptism in (or with) the Holy Spirit." Pentecostals derive their name from the account in Acts 2, which records that on the day of Pentecost the Holy Spirit descended on the church in the form of "tongues of fire" and empowered those gathered for bold witness (Acts 2:2–4). Pentecostals believe that the empowerment of the Holy Spirit must be appropriated into the life of each believer, and while this experience might occur on the same day as a person's conversion, it should not be considered as coming automatically along with one's justification and faith in Jesus Christ. Thus, baptism of the Holy Spirit is a central theme that unites all Pentecostals, even if differences exist regarding the precise nature of this baptism, the methods of appropriation, and the evidences that are highlighted to verify that one has received the Holy Spirit.

Second, Pentecostals believe that the full range of gifts and miraculous manifestations of the Spirit present in the New Testament are available for believers today. Pentecostals reject any notion that these gifts were either limited to the first century or passed away with the apostles. This view is, perhaps, summed up best by one of the early pioneers of Pentecostalism, the itinerant evangelist Aimee Semple McPherson, who once asked, "Is Jesus Christ the Great I Am? or is He the Great I Was?"[12] Pentecostals believe that the full range of Jesus' miraculous ministry as well as the apostolic "signs and wonders" are available to believers today through the power of the Holy Spirit.

11. Some writers go so far as to argue that the terms *evangelical*, *Protestant*, and *Pentecostal* can and should be used interchangeably when examining Latin America, especially since Roman Catholics refer to all of them collectively as *evangélicos*. See, for example, Karl-Wilhelm Westmeier, *Protestant Pentecostalism in Latin America* (London: Associated Univ. Presses, 1999), 1; David Stoll, *Is Latin America Turning Protestant?* (Los Angeles: Univ. of California Press, 1990), 4. Some Pentecostal groups, for example, have adopted mainline Protestant liturgies.

12. Aimee Semple McPherson, from her *Divine Healing Sermons*, as quoted in Cecil Robeck Jr., "Pentecostals and Apostolic Faith: Implications for Ecumenism," *Pneuma: The Journal of the Society for Pentecostal Studies* 8 (Fall 1986): 64.

Third, Pentecostals are known for less formalized and expressive forms of worship, including lifting hands, dancing, shouting, and clapping.

Finally, Pentecostals are marked by a special urgency to evangelize the world because they believe that we are living in the last days before the return of Jesus Christ.

None of these defining features of Pentecostalism should be understood as isolated doctrinal positions that are regularly confessed in some formal or creedal way. Rather, these four features form part of the shared experience of being a Pentecostal.

PENTECOSTALISM IN LATIN AMERICA

Reasons for Focusing on Latin America

This chapter will focus on how the rise of global Pentecostalism has influenced theological formulation and practice around the world, particularly as it relates to the doctrine of the Holy Spirit. Although Pentecostalism is a global phenomenon with adherents in nearly every country in the world, we will focus primarily on Pentecostalism in Latin America.

There are several important reasons for this. First, after only seventy-five years in Central and South America, Pentecostals make up "three-quarters of all Latin American Protestants."[13] This is important to recognize because the vast majority of what is called "Protestant," "independent," or "indigenous" growth in Latin America is made up of Pentecostals. As early as 1962 *Time* magazine declared Pentecostalism to be the "fastest growing church in the Western Hemisphere."[14] Reflecting on the growth of Latin American Protestantism, which is growing three times faster than population, David Stoll predicts that "by 2010 evangelicals will be a third of the population" of Latin America.[15] Even Roman Catholic journalist Penny Lernoux observed that "every hour four hundred Latin Americans convert" to Protestantism. The vibrant life of this new branch of Christianity in Latin America is almost without parallel and exceeds the growth rate of Protestantism in Central Europe during the time of the Reformation.[16] This transformation deserves our attention.

Second, Latin American Pentecostalism provides an excellent place to examine the breakup of the Christendom arrangement that has dominated the Latin American religious and political landscape since the sixteenth century. For centuries evangelism in Latin America meant a process of general acculturation whereby people were Christianized and incorporated into "a monocultural Christendom in which they were subject to Christian authorities, both ecclesiastical and civil."[17] The once secure Roman Catholic hegemony over Latin America is passing away, particularly

---

13. Everett A. Wilson, "Latin American Pentecostals—Their Potential for Ecumenical Dialogue," *Pneuma: The Journal of the Society for Pentecostal Studies* 9, no. 1 (Spring 1987): 86.

14. "Fastest-Growing Church in the Hemisphere," *Time* (November 2, 1962), 56.

15. David Stoll, "A Protestant Reformation in Latin America?" *The Christian Century* 107, no. 1 (January 3–10, 1990): 45.

16. Russell Watson, "Latin America: John Paul Goes to War," *Newsweek* (February 12, 1996), 39. See also C. Peter Wagner, "The Greatest Church Growth Is beyond Our Shores," *Christianity Today* (May 18, 1984), 27–28. Wagner estimates that the growth rate of Protestantism (mostly Pentecostal) is three times the rate of population. It is estimated that about 8,000 are being baptized every day with over 100 million on the continent. See also David Stoll, *Is Latin America Turning Protestant?* xiv.

17. John F. Gorski, "How the Catholic Church in Latin America Became Missionary," *International Bulletin of Missionary Research* 27, no. 2 (April 2003): 60.

in countries like Brazil, Chile, and Guatemala.[18] Several countries in Latin America already have more Pentecostal pastors than Roman Catholic priests.[19] By 2010 the evangelicals (who are mostly Pentecostals) will outnumber the Roman Catholics in some countries.[20]

However, Latin America is not merely the story of the rise of Pentecostalism and the decline of Roman Catholicism, or the intrusion of Pentecostals onto Roman Catholic territory. As with the European Reformation, this new reformation has helped to stimulate vitality in the Roman Catholic Church, resulting in a renewed emphasis on evangelism and mission. As Roman Catholic missiologist John Gorski has noted, "evangelization in the specific sense of announcing the Gospel to enable a personal encounter with the living Christ, leading to conversion and discipleship, became a conscious concern of the Catholic Church only within the past half century."[21] The point is, the Reformation has finally arrived in Latin America! Just as the sixteenth-century Protestant Reformation in Europe challenged and helped to foster the emergence of a new branch of Christianity as well as bringing reformation to the established church of its day, so today the Pentecostals in Latin America are seeing the emergence of new Christian movements and the renewal of Roman Catholicism, as well as theological discussions that mirror many of the broad contours of the Protestant Reformation in Europe.

But this is not merely a repeat of the European Reformation or a delayed extension of it. The Latin American struggle has its own unique features and identity, particularly in the emphasis on the Holy Spirit, which was not a prominent feature of the European Reformation. Latin American Pentecostalism is also influenced by modern forces of globalization. The single, all-embracing system of religious life in the region has been replaced by a new religious marketplace and the democratization of religious choice. This "Third Force"[22] of Christianity is bringing "*la renovación*" to Christians throughout the region and, in the process, transforming the religious landscape.

Third, the theological discourse of Latin American Pentecostals represents several important challenges to traditional evangelical discourse concerning the work of the Holy Spirit in the world and in the lives of believers, which is of particular importance to the theme of this study. Latin Americans have long insisted that traditional European and North American theologies of the Spirit were too static and disconnected from

18. Stoll, "A Protestant Reformation in Latin America?" 46. Stoll provides a chart showing 1985 percentages of evangelicals in Brazil (15.95%), Chile (21.57%), and Guatemala (18.92%). He then extrapolates to predict the potential evangelical population in 2010.

19. Stoll, *Is Latin America Turning Protestant?* 6. In Brazil, for example, Stoll points out that there are 13,000 Roman Catholic priests and 17,000 ordained Protestant pastors and 13,000 non-ordained ones.

20. Anderson, *An Introduction to Pentecostalism*, 63.

21. Gorski, "How the Catholic Church in Latin America Became Missionary," 60.

22. The expression "Third Force" was coined by Henry P. Van Dusen in 1958 to describe the new wave of missionary activity coming out of Pentecostal Christianity. See Henry P. Van Dusen, "The Third Force in Christendom," *Life* (June 9, 1958), 113–24. The first wave was Roman Catholicism, the second wave was Protestantism. It is interesting to note that Eastern Orthodoxy is omitted, despite their vigorous and inspiring missionary work in the nineteenth century. Furthermore, according to Walter Hollenweger (*Pentecostalism: Origins and Developments Worldwide*, 154), the Charismatic movement has also swept through portions of the Eastern Orthodox Church. Todd Johnson documents 3,300,000 Eastern Orthodox Christians who would identify themselves as part of the Charismatic renewal and an additional 628,000 who are part of the Neo-Charismatic renewal ("Three Waves of Christian Renewal: A 100-Year Snapshot," *International Bulletin of Missionary Research* 30, no. 2 [April 2006]: 76).

the suffering and economic hardships of the peoples of Latin America. Furthermore, Pentecostals have felt that many of the mainstream North American theologies were overly preoccupied with theoretical issues within theological discourse and have lost the evangelistic urgency needed to evangelize the world.

It has taken a long time for North American historians and theologians to take seriously either the global Pentecostal movement or any critique it might offer to their theology. As late as 1968 William McLoughlin contributed a chapter to *Religion in America* entitled, "Is There a Third Force in Christendom?" where he dismissed the Pentecostal movement as a passing "effluvia." He predicted that "the pietistic upthrust by fringe-sect dissenters and come-outers does not in itself constitute the creation of a significant new religious movement in Christendom." He went on to say that Pentecostalism does "not constitute a dynamic new force capable of replacing or seriously threatening the old order."[23]

What McLoughlin failed to realize is that the very thing he predicted would not happen had, in fact, *already happened*! By 1968 the global shift, while yet unrecognized, had already occurred and Christendom as McLoughlin knew it was being dismantled. The shift happened swiftly and dramatically because at the same time that Pentecostals around the world were in the process of rediscovering the vibrancy of historic Christian faith, the mainline churches were largely abandoning it, losing members by the millions and thereby accelerating their move to the sidelines of American religious life.[24] As Andrew Walls has noted, "one has to go back many centuries to find such a huge recession in one part of the world paralleled by such a huge simultaneous accession in another."[25]

It is our turn to humbly admit that we have much to learn from this dramatic and global work of God in our time. It is my hope that the questions we consider in this chapter will help us learn and grow from the experiences of our Pentecostal brothers and sisters around the world, especially in Latin America.

Three Key Questions to Consider

This chapter is focused on pneumatology and how Latin American Pentecostals are contributing to the global discourse about the person and work of the Holy Spirit in the twenty-first century. We will consider three major themes. First, how might the rise of Pentecostalism influence the broad contours of how the person and work of the Holy Spirit is discussed and developed in North American theology? Second, what can we learn from Latin American Pentecostals about the role of the Holy Spirit (strategically as well as practically) in evangelism and missions? Finally, could Latin American Pentecostals provide us with a potential new basis for ecumenical dialogue and cooperation? Have Pentecostals simultaneously discovered not only the *sola Scriptura*

23. William G. McLoughlin and Robert Bellah, eds., *Religion in America* (Boston: Houghton Mifflin, 1968), 47.

24. Donald McGavran has pointed out that "theological liberalism shows the highest negative correlation with growth" (see Peter Wagner, *Church Growth and the Whole Gospel* [San Francisco: Harper & Row, 1981], 196).

25. Andrew F. Walls, "Eusebius Tries Again: Reconceiving the Study of Christian History," *International Bulletin of Missionary Research* 24, no. 3 (July 2000): 105.

principle of the Reformation, but also a deeper pre-Protestant recognition of what one observer has called a "common spiritual center" that unifies Christians?[26]

These themes will help us not only to grow in our appreciation of Pentecostalism in Latin America, but will hopefully help in shaping and expanding our own understanding of the person and work of the Holy Spirit in the twenty-first century. But before we address the first question, it will be helpful to briefly survey the development of pneumatology in the Western world.

Historical Development of Pneumatology

Doctrine of the Holy Spirit in the West/North Atlantic

Jaroslav Pelikan, in his masterful survey of the development of Christian doctrine, points out that the doctrine of the Trinity represents the apex of doctrinal development in the early church. He writes, "In this dogma the church vindicated the monotheism that had been at issue in its conflicts with Judaism." Jesus Christ, the Redeemer, did "not belong to some lower order of divine reality, but was God himself."[27] Jesus shares fully in the essence of the Father (*homoousios*, not *homoiousios*). Likewise, the Holy Spirit shares fully in the divine essence, since the Scriptures give him both the titles and the prerogatives of deity. The church affirmed one God (one *ousia*), in three eternal personal distinctions (three *hypostases*).

However, the relative paucity of biblical references to the deity of the Holy Spirit as compared with the deity of Jesus Christ meant that it took quite some time for a full orbed Trinitarian theology to develop. In fact, for some time there was a fairly strong Spirit-Christology that did not acknowledge the Holy Spirit as a third person of the Trinity, and even as late as 380 Gregory of Nazianzus conceded that "of the wise men among ourselves, some have conceived of him (the Holy Spirit) as an activity, some as a creature, some as God; and some have been uncertain what to call him ... and therefore they neither worship him nor treat him with dishonor, but take up a neutral position."[28]

This ambiguity and neutrality is reflected in the Apostles' Creed (which is probably based on the earlier second-century Roman Creed) and the original Nicene Creed of AD 325, which simply states, "We believe in the Holy Spirit," without further commentary. In 381, a second ecumenical council met in Constantinople. The further deliberations on the Holy Spirit led the council to amplify and to clarify the faith of the Nicene Creed so that it unequivocally declared the deity of the Holy Spirit.[29] The Niceno-Constantinopolitan Creed declares, "We believe in the Holy Spirit, the Lord and Giver of Life, who proceedeth from the Father, who with the Father and the Son together is worshipped and glorified, who spoke by the prophets."[30]

---

26. Westmeier, *Protestant Pentecostalism in Latin America*, 19.

27. Pelikan, *The Emergence of the Catholic Tradition*, 172–73.

28. Ibid., 213.

29. The first ecumenical council (Nicea, AD 325) was preoccupied with responding to various challenges to the deity of Jesus Christ and therefore was not in a position to consider the deity of the Holy Spirit. The deity of the Father, Son, and Holy Spirit, which was affirmed in AD 381, implies the Trinity, although the full doctrine of the Trinity was not officially reaffirmed until the fifth ecumenical council in Constantinople in 553.

30. Philip Schaff and Henry Wace, eds., *Nicene and Post-Nicene Fathers*; vol. 14, *The Seven Ecumenical Councils* (Peabody, MA: Hendrickson, 1999), 163. It should be noted that the phrase

Even though the deity of the Holy Spirit was resolved by 381, discussions about the exact nature and relations of the Trinity continued for almost a century.[31] All of this had a profound, cumulative effect on theological discourse in the Western tradition concerning the Holy Spirit. Because the ecumenical discussions about the Holy Spirit were focused primarily on his deity and his relationship within the Trinity, there was a serious neglect of a full development of his work. Indeed, William Menzies points out that "the ancient church from the second century through the ninth century was almost totally preoccupied with questions pertaining to the identity of Jesus Christ, so that what was said of the Holy Spirit was largely an appendage to theology, and was limited largely to ontology, the Being of God within his inter-trinitarian relationships."[32] That remained largely unchanged during medieval scholarship.

The Reformation's emphasis on the authority of Scripture, ecclesiology, and Christology are clearly reflected in the post-Reformation attempt to systematize the theological deposit of the Reformers. However, this meant that, as was the case during the patristic period, a full development of the doctrine of the Holy Spirit was delayed and several vital aspects of his person and work were neglected in post-Reformation Protestant theology in the West. Over time, several major theological traditions developed that either denied completely or extremely limited the active role of the Holy Spirit in performing miracles, divine healing, demonic deliverance, prophecy, tongue-speaking, and other elements that later became central features of the Pentecostal doctrine of the Holy Spirit. For example, this tendency is evident in many expressions of Reformed theology as well as in the later nineteenth-century emergence of dispensationalism, although the precise lines of their argumentation against the exercise of the gifts of the Holy Spirit today are different from one another.

Space does not permit an analysis and evaluation of each of the systems of thought and how they argue the cessationist perspective. Indeed, there are many different forms and degrees of cessationism. Some would go so far as to deny all subjective forms of guidance, such as people claiming that the Lord was leading them to do something or that the Holy Spirit had helped them in understanding a particular passage of Scripture. Others are, practically speaking, partial cessationists, opposing the exercise of certain gifts, such as prophecy and tongue-speaking, but they are functionally continuationists when it comes to praying for the sick or believing that the Holy Spirit can directly speak to someone.

There are also different ideas as to the original purpose of these supernatural gifts. For example, some argue that the apostolic miracles served to grant authority to the ministers in the church, whereas others claim they were given only to attest to his Word.

"and the Son" (*filioque*) was not inserted after the phrase "who proceedeth from the Father" until the year 447 at the Synod of Toledo in Spain. The Eastern Church does not accept the addition of this phrase.

31. Acknowledgment of the deity of the Holy Spirit must not be confused with a full affirmation of the Trinity. The Trinity was officially reaffirmed in the fifth ecumenical council in Constantinople in 553. As late as 380 Gregory of Nazianzus conceded that "to be only slightly in error (about the Holy Spirit) was to be orthodox." See Pelikan, *The Emergence of the Catholic Tradition*, 213.

32. William W. Menzies, "The Holy Spirit in Christian Theology," in *Perspectives on Evangelical Theology*, ed. Kenneth Kantzer and Stanley Gundry (Grand Rapids: Baker, 1979), 67. The most important example of this was the ongoing controversy related to the *filioque* clause.

There are also different ideas as to exactly when and why these gifts stopped. For example, some argue that the gifts ceased after the canon of Scripture was completed, while others say it was when the last apostle died. Still others insist that the gifts died out gradually over the first four centuries until the official persecution ceased and Christianity was granted full legal status in the Roman empire. Some argue that while the gifts are not a normal part of the life of the church, they might still be manifested by God in extraordinary situations. But regardless of which of these schemes were followed, the point is that theological reflection in the West gradually became dominated by a range of theological systems that denied that the exercise of the supernatural gifts of the Holy Spirit was a normative, much less essential, part of the church's ongoing life and witness in the world.

B. B. Warfield, the great nineteenth-century Princeton theologian, is one of the most influential writers representing the cessationist viewpoint. In his book *Counterfeit Miracles*, Warfield argued that the diffusion of miraculous gifts by the Holy Spirit was confined to the apostolic church and "they necessarily passed away with it." He insisted that "the theologians of the post-Reformation era, a very clear-headed body of men, taught with great distinctiveness that the charismata ceased with the Apostolic age."[33] This Princeton theological tradition[34] influenced a large part of Reformed theology and subsequent systematic theologies in the West.

A typical example can be found in Louis Berkhof's *Systematic Theology*, a classic text in Reformed theology still in use today. Berkhof devotes significant attention in part 1 ("Doctrine of God") to defending the deity, personality, and prerogatives of the Holy Spirit within the larger setting of his defense of the doctrine of the Trinity. Later, in part 4 ("Doctrine of the Application of the Work of Redemption"), Berkhof discusses the work of the Holy Spirit in applying the work of Christ into our lives (e.g., regeneration) and in personal holiness (e.g., sanctification). In part 5 ("Doctrine of the Church") Berkhof is silent about the role of the Holy Spirit in empowering the church for witness and mission.

In summary, Berkhof's treatment of pneumatology is adequate in its treatment of the Spirit's place in the Trinity and his role in soteriology, but he is silent about all the key features of Pentecostalism, including the baptism of the Holy Spirit, divine

33. B. B. Warfield, *Counterfeit Miracles* (New York: Charles Scribner's Sons, 1918), 6. Warfield's view is that the miracles ceased with the last person on whom the apostles' conferred the working of miracles through the imposition of their hands, explaining the gradual decline of miracles (23). It should be noted that Warfield specifically uses A. J. Gordon's *The Ministry of Healing, or Miracles of Cure in All Ages* as the best book representing his opponent's position (see 159–60). Gordon taught, for example, that "it is still the duty and privilege of believers to receive the Holy Spirit by a conscious, definite act of appropriating faith, just as they received Jesus Christ.... To say that in receiving Christ we necessarily received in the same act the gift of the Spirit, seems to confound what the Scriptures make distinct. For it is as sinners that we accept Christ for our justification, but it is as sons that we accept the Spirit for our sanctification ... logically and chronologically the gift of the Spirit is subsequent to repentance" (*The Ministry of the Spirit* [Philadelphia: American Baptist Publication Society, 1894], 76–77). A century earlier, Jonathan Edwards taught that the gifts of prophecy, tongues, and revelations would cease and "vanish away" when the church reached maturity. Edwards did not accept the supernatural gifts as valid for today and he explicitly states that he did not expect, or desire, a restoration of these miraculous gifts in the latter days prior to the inauguration of the millennium (see C. C. Goen, ed., *Works of Jonathan Edwards*; vol. 4, *The Distinguishing Marks* [New Haven, CT: Yale Univ. Press, 1972], 280–81).

34. The Princeton theology refers to the period when great theologians such as Archibald Alexander, Charles Hodge, A. A. Hodge, and B. B. Warfield taught at Princeton Theological Seminary.

healing, speaking in tongues, the role of the Holy Spirit in the mission of the church, and so forth. In fact, it is not unusual to find Western systematic theologies that do not develop the person and work of the Holy Spirit as a separate category of study, but develop their theology of the Holy Spirit as subsets under the doctrine of God and the doctrine of soteriology.[35]

In recent years, the growth and impact of Pentecostalism has begun to positively influence how systematic theologies, even from a Reformed perspective, are being written in the West. The most dramatic example is Wayne Grudem's 1,300-page *Systematic Theology*. Grudem devotes an entire chapter to "Baptism in and Filling with the Holy Spirit." He plainly says that it is the growth of global Pentecostalism that motivated him to write a chapter on this theme:

> Systematic theology books have not traditionally included a chapter on baptism in the Holy Spirit or filling with the Holy Spirit as a part of the study of the "order of salvation." ... But with the spread of Pentecostalism that began in 1901, the widespread influence of the charismatic movement in the 1960's and 1970's, and the remarkable growth of the Pentecostal and charismatic churches worldwide from 1970 to the present, the question of a "baptism in the Holy Spirit" distinct from regeneration has come into increasing prominence.[36]

Grudem goes on to carefully set forth the Pentecostal understanding of the doctrine of the baptism of the Holy Spirit and to critique it from a Reformed perspective. In the end, Grudem does not accept the Pentecostal view, but he is to be commended for taking it seriously and engaging with Pentecostals in a thoughtful way. Similar positive trends can be demonstrated among the ranks of dispensationalists, as seen, for example, in the recent publication edited by Dallas Theological Seminary professor Daniel Wallace, entitled *Who's Afraid of the Holy Spirit?*[37] All of these are positive testimonies to how global Pentecostalism is already beginning to change theological discourse about the Holy Spirit in the West.

Historical Roots of Pentecostalism

Pentecostal theology is, of course, highly critical of all forms of cessationist theology. But there are several reasons why Pentecostals were slow to work out their own systematic theology that reflected a fuller understanding of the person and work of God the Spirit. First, the earliest Pentecostals tended to have little formal education and were therefore unfamiliar with sophisticated theological argumentation. They simply could not articulate their theology in a way that would capture the attention of and demand a response from traditional theologians from the North. This problem was exacerbated by many cruel caricatures from their critics, who dismissed the whole movement as being a group of fanatics focused solely on glossolalia, a characterization that sometimes continues to the present day.

35. See, for example, Henry C. Thiessen, *Lectures in Systematic Theology*, rev. ed. (Grand Rapids: Eerdmans, 1979).

36. Wayne Grudem, *Systematic Theology: An Introduction to Biblical Doctrine* (Grand Rapids: Zondervan, 1994), 763–64.

37. Daniel Wallace and M. James Sawyer, eds., *Who's Afraid of the Holy Spirit?* (Dallas: Biblical Studies, 2005).

Second, as with any dynamic new movement, Pentecostals were so busy preaching the gospel, baptizing new believers, and planting churches that they did not have the time to devote to sustained theological reflection. The saying "missions at sunrise, missiology at sunset" captures the point well. In the early "sunrise" of a new movement, there is little time for formal theological or missiological reflection. Only as the movement matures and reaches a critical mass can certain leaders look back and reflect on what has been happening and why. Pentecostals have now reached this point, and they have begun to articulate not only solid biblical arguments for their theological positions, but also to present formal critiques of the North American pneumatological tradition.[38]

Third, some Pentecostals themselves have resisted setting forth a theological defense of their pneumatology out of a sense of triumphalism because, they argued, one of the signs of a true movement of God is that it does not need a defense or require any explanation. Pentecostalism is seen as a sovereign intervention by God himself to restore apostolic faith. The church's role is to submit to what God is doing, not provide any systematic defense.

Before we examine some of the central Pentecostal critiques of North American pneumatology, it is important to recognize that, despite claims to the contrary, the Pentecostal movement did not, in fact, arise in a theological or experiential vacuum. This is not to diminish the initiative of God in raising up the Pentecostal movement, but to underscore that God has worked in similar ways in the past. Pentecostalism has three main roots in long-standing theological traditions in the West.

Methodist Roots of Pentecostalism

The most important link between Pentecostalism and historic expressions of Protestantism is through Methodism. Donald Dayton, in *Theological Roots of Pentecostalism*, devotes an entire chapter to the Methodist roots of Pentecostalism. Likewise, Pentecostal scholar Vincent Synan, in *The Holiness-Pentecostal Movement in the United States*, says that "the historical and doctrinal lineage of American Pentecostalism is to be found in the Wesleyan tradition."[39]

Methodism, founded by John Wesley, was itself an eighteenth-century protest movement to revitalize the church of its day. Because Methodism arose two centuries after the Reformation, Wesley was able to observe the long-term fruit of the weak pneumatology of the Reformation. Therefore, Methodism represented, among other things, a pneumatological corrective to the theology of the magisterial Reformers, who

38. See Gordon Fee, *God's Empowering Presence: The Holy Spirit in the Letters of Paul* (Peabody, MA: Hendrickson, 1994); Amos Yong, *Beyond the Impasse: Towards a Pneumatological Theology of Religions* (Grand Rapids: Baker, 2003), are just two of many examples of Pentecostal scholars who exhibit outstanding scholarship at the highest level. As noted above, the Western *filioque* controversy made it difficult for Pentecostal scholars to have a theological framework to develop a proper doctrine of the person of the Holy Spirit. Thus Pentecostal theology often reflects this weakness by producing more of a pneumapraxis than a pneumatology (see Hollenweger, *Pentecostalism: Origins and Development: Worldwide*, 218).

39. Vincent Synan, *Holiness-Pentecostal Movement in the United States* (Grand Rapids: Eerdmans, 1971), as quoted in David Martin, *Tongues of Fire* (Cambridge, MA: Basil Blackwell, 1990), 28. See also Hollenweger, *Pentecostalism: Origins and Development: Worldwide*, 144–52.

had inadvertently created a functional subordinationism in their doctrine of the Holy Spirit.[40] Early Methodist revivals, like those among Pentecostals, took place mainly among poor, uneducated people, and Wesley was not inclined to produce systematic theological defenses of the movement, insisting that it was part of God's sovereign providence to return the church to its true apostolic, "primitive" roots.

Nevertheless, Wesley advocated several positions crucial to Pentecostal pneumatology today. He emphasized the Spirit's role in the sanctification of believers and accepted the idea of a "second" crisis experience subsequent to justification, a key feature in later Pentecostal pneumatology. He referred to this experience in various ways, including "perfect love," "eradication of inbred sin," and "entire sanctification," all of which influenced the theology of the Holiness tradition.[41] Wesley insisted that the reason the supernatural gifts of the Spirit were not active in the churches of his day was because of spiritual deadness, not God's plan. While he was more interested in the fruit of the Spirit than the gifts of the Spirit, Wesley was still derided as an "enthusiast" by his critics because of the emotional and exuberant nature of the early Methodist meetings.

Keswick Reformed Roots of Pentecostalism

Pentecostalism also has roots in a range of nineteenth-century revival movements that influenced Christians in the Reformed tradition. For example, in 1859 Reformed writer W. E. Boardman published a widely distributed book entitled *The Higher Christian Life*, which reflected a robust pneumatology. However, the most important of these movements that had a direct influence on Pentecostalism was that strand of the Holiness movement known as the Keswick movement. The name derives from a series of meetings that originally took place in Keswick, England, in 1873. The teachings that emanated from these meetings were brought over to North America and propagated through Bible schools, Christian conferences, and revivals, eventually forging a distinctive pneumatology.

The Keswick movement broadly agreed with the Wesleyan idea of a work of grace, subsequent to one's justification, that emphasized the Holy Spirit. However, what made Keswick teaching unique was that it opposed two aspects of the Wesleyan-Holiness conception of sanctification and the subsequent experience of the Holy Spirit in the life of the believer.

First, Keswick teaching, like the rest of the Holiness movement, was dissatisfied with Luther's doctrine of *simul iustus et peccator* (see ch. 6). That view seemed to accept sin as the inevitable and ongoing experience of the believer. Keswick thinkers were inspired by the earlier German Pietists, who shared their concerns about the neglected emphasis on sanctification and affirmed that "in the grace of Christ one might 'overcome' sin

40. Some might argue that they did not "create" this problem, but they simply built on the inevitable subordination of the Holy Spirit to Christology in the wake of the *filioque* controversy.

41. It should be noted that Wesley's doctrine of "entire sanctification" does not imply that believers are without sin. Also, Wesley himself did not use the phrase "baptism in the Holy Spirit," but it was used by John Fletcher, the theologian of Methodism, who applied the phrase to Wesley's doctrine of sanctification in his multivolume work, *Checks to Antinomianism*.

and the world."[42] However, they could not accept Wesley's notion of a subsequent experience of entire sanctification. What emerged was a position that emphasized a subsequent experience with the Holy Spirit, but still acknowledged the presence of sin and held that sanctification was a process that continues throughout the life of a believer.

Second, the Keswick teaching had a different understanding of the purpose of the "second blessing" or "baptism of the Holy Spirit." The Wesleyan-Holiness view was focused on holiness and the eradication of sin. The Keswick teaching emphasized that the Holy Spirit empowered the believer for witness, service, and evangelism. The former was focused on the inner life of the believer, whereas the latter was more focused on our external witness. Overall, the Keswick movement tended to try as much as possible to reconcile itself with a Reformed view of Christian theology. For example, they found support for their pneumatology in Puritan writers such as John Owen and Richard Baxter.[43]

Roman Catholic Spirituality

Latin American Pentecostalism arose almost exclusively from people whose entire background was rooted in Roman Catholicism. Protestant presence in Latin America was (and is) widely believed to have financial backing from the United States government in order to help to destabilize the region and further its interests.[44] At the conference of Latin American bishops help in Santo Domingo in 1992, Pope John Paul II called the Protestants "ravenous wolves," warning the bishops of the danger of this "invasion of the sects."[45] The Pope went on to add that Protestants were "pseudo-spiritual movements" that would cause "division and discord in our communities." It is not unusual to see a sign in the window or on the door of a home that says, "We practice the Roman Catholic religion, evangelicals are not welcome here."

Yet there were many natural affinities between Roman Catholics and Pentecostals, especially in the area of spirituality and mysticism. As Cecil Robeck has pointed out, "monastic spirituality is not all that different from Pentecostal spirituality."[46] The focus on personal piety, the long hours spent in worship, prayer, and meditation, and the emphasis on miracles and healing in Catholicism all helped to provide a contextual bridge for the emergence of Pentecostalism in Latin America that was not *by necessity* tied to North American Protestantism.

Walter Hollenweger devotes an entire chapter to exploring the oft-neglected pre-Reformation roots of Pentecostalism in Roman Catholic spirituality. Indeed, Hollenweger argues that "there is a greater relationship between Catholics and Pen-

42. Donald W. Dayton, *Theological Roots of Pentecostalism* (Grand Rapids: Francis Asbury, 1987), 37.

43. See William Menzies, "The Non-Wesleyan Origins of the Pentecostal Movement," in *Aspects of Pentecostal-Charismatic Origins*, ed. Vinson Synan (Plainfield, NJ: Logos International, 1975), 67–79. John Owen, for example, is the first major writer to articulate a view of progressive sanctification (in *The Holy Spirit: His Gifts and Power* [Grand Rapids: Kregel, 1954, reprint], 278–99).

44. Stoll, *Is Latin America Turning Protestant?* xiv–xv.

45. Hannah W. Stewart-Gambino and Everett Wilson, "Latin American Pentecostals: Old Stereotypes and New Challenges," in *Power, Politics and Pentecostals in Latin America*, ed. Edward L. Cleary and Hannah W. Stewart-Gambino (Boulder, CO: Westview, 1997), 228.

46. Cecil M. Robeck Jr., "The Nature of Pentecostal Spirituality," *Pneuma* 14 (1992): 105.

tecostals than between Catholicism and historic Protestant churches."[47] The bond between Pentecostals and Roman Catholics was deepened further with the emergence of the neo-Pentecostal movement, better known as the Charismatic movement, among Roman Catholics. Beginning in 1967, laymen on the faculty of Dusquesne University in Pittsburgh began to receive the "baptism of the Holy Spirit." The movement spread to Notre Dame and then around the country and the world as tens of thousands of Roman Catholics embraced the general parameters of Pentecostal pneumatology. This renewal was particularly popular among Roman Catholic Hispanics, which also helped to foster a climate of acceptance for the Pentecostal message among Roman Catholics in Latin America, especially among those who held a distrust of North American Protestantism.

PENTECOSTALISM'S INFLUENCE ON TRADITIONAL WESTERN/ NORTH ATLANTIC PNEUMATOLOGY

We are now able to provide some reflection on the first key question noted above, namely, how the rise of Pentecostalism and the witness of Pentecostals concerning the Holy Spirit might influence the broad contours of North American theology concerning the person and work of the Holy Spirit.

The preceding overview of the influences on Pentecostalism underscores the diversity in the various ways pneumatology is understood by Christian groups in North America. Therefore, it is nearly impossible to make sweeping assessments or critiques since Pentecostalism not only has derived its life from, but also continues to contribute its energy back into, the mainstream of American religious life. Nevertheless, Reformed and dispensationalist theologies continue to dominant North American theological discourse, and cessationism, partial cessationism, and functional cessationism are common. Pentecostal theology is only now beginning to be taken seriously. In 1941, when Harold J. Ockenga supported the entrance of Pentecostals into what would become the National Association of Evangelicals (NAE), he met stiff resistance.[48] However, Ockenga argued passionately that the Pentecostals were "evangelical, Bible-believing, Christ honoring, Spirit-filled brethren, who manifest in character and in life the truths expressed in the statement of faith of the NAE."[49]

It is still not uncommon for missionary candidates to be rejected by certain mission boards when on the application form they affirm the ongoing exercise of supernatural

47. Hollenweger, *Pentecostalism: Origins and Developments Worldwide*, 153.

48. See Harold Ockenga, "The 'Pentecostal' Bogey," *United Evangelical Action* 6, no. 1 (February 15, 1947): 12–13. In November of 1947 Ockenga addressed the opening convocation of Fuller Theological Seminary and provided even greater clarity as to his theological rationale. Ockenga saw the Western world as in a fundamental conflict between what he called "Reformation supernaturalism, with a theocentric outlook" and "Renaissance secularism" with a naturalistic outlook. Ockenga prophetically understood that the outcome of this conflict would unleash the forces that would determine the future of Western civilization. Ockenga was also critical of the fundamentalists of his day, whom he saw as unconcerned with social and cultural issues and who could not, therefore, help in the struggle with secularism. Since Pentecostalism was so thoroughly supernaturalistic and understood the gospel more holistically (since they emerged in the context of urban poverty and marginalization), it was strategic to include them. See Harold Ockenga, "God Our Only Hope," *United Evangelical Action* 6, no. 18 (November 1, 1947): 12–13. R. L. Decker, president of the NAE in 1947, also explains why both Pentecostals and Baptists should be part of the NAE (see "What the NAE Is and How It Operates," *United Evangelical Action* 6, no. 18 (November 1, 1947): 7.

49. Ockenga, "The 'Pentecostal' Bogey," 12–13.

gifts in the contemporary life of the church. This problem is further exacerbated by the erosion of orthodox Christianity among Methodist and Holiness churches, where we would expect to find a more robust pneumatology, but instead we find many of these churches paralyzed by spiritual fatigue and fighting for their very survival. Thus, despite the eighteenth- and nineteenth-century correctives to a deficient pneumatology in North American and European theologies, the Pentecostals represent the most vibrant sector of Christianity to offer constructive contributions to Western/North Atlantic pneumatology.

The most important contribution may be found in the expanded Pentecostal understanding of the work of the Holy Spirit. Traditional Western theologies were written by scholars who received their education in respected universities that were deeply influenced by Enlightenment assumptions. The Enlightenment worldview creates a high wall separating the experiential world of the senses—governed by reason and subject to scientific enquiry—from the unseen world beyond the wall; such a world either does not exist (naturalism) or, if it does, we can know little about it (deism). The result has been essentially a two-tiered universe that separates the world of science from the world of religion.

Biblical evangelicalism has challenged this worldview by insisting that God has supernaturally broken through this wall in the incarnation and that knowledge of the unseen world has been provided by the certainty of divine revelation. Evangelicals argued that through prayer we can have sustained communication and fellowship with God. The problem with this approach is that the basic two-tiered universe of the Enlightenment worldview remains intact. It has merely been modified so that Christians punch a few holes in the wall to provide a framework whereby God can come into the empirical world through the incarnation and revelation and we, in turn, can have access to the unseen world through prayer. The basic separation is left unchallenged.

However, much of the world finds this mechanistic, rationalistic worldview of the Enlightenment unintelligible. For most people there is no real wall of separation, and the border that separates this world from the unseen world is more of an open frontier than a high wall with a few approved border crossings. The whole of creation is animated by spirits and various dynamic unseen forces, including demons and angels. Frequently, spiritual explanations are more common than naturalistic ones because their overall worldview is more spiritualistic and relational than naturalistic and mechanical.

This perspective was brought home to me in a personal way when I was teaching in India shortly after the tragic murder of Graham Staines and his two children in Orissa, India, on January 22, 1999. In a story that made international headlines for many weeks, a dedicated missionary who had spent his entire life working with poor lepers in India was surrounded by Hindu fanatics while he slept in his car. The car was set on fire and Graham Staines along with two of his sons, nine-year-old Timothy and seven-year-old Philip, perished in the attack. A few months later (October 18 and 29, 1999) two massive cyclones hit the coast of Orissa, leaving thousands dead and millions injured or homeless. Everywhere I went, in conversations with Hindus or in the print media, I found that Indians were convinced that this cyclone was the Christian

God's judgment on Orissa for murdering the missionaries. In the entire aftermath of that storm I never heard a single person give a naturalistic explanation for the cyclones, even though such storms are fairly common in India.

I had a similar experience after a major earthquake erupted in Gujarat, India, on January 26, 2001, after some notorious cases of state-sponsored persecution against Christians. In traveling to rural villages in North India and listening to people explain why someone is ill, I often observe how spiritual explanations are likely to trump naturalistic ones, just the opposite of what one finds in the West.

In the past, when missionaries arrived with their modified Enlightenment worldview and their restricted, truncated pneumatology, they did not know what to say when someone claimed that a drought was caused by God's judgment, or when concerned parents came and asked the missionary to cast out the demon tormenting their daughter, or when someone claimed they had received a vision to preach the gospel in a particular new region. Sadly, the missionary had no training or categories to respond to this worldview. They had inhabited a Christianized version of a two-tiered universe, whereas they were working among people who lived in what Paul Hiebert insightfully calls the world of the "excluded middle."[50] The only category the missionaries had was a term like "superstition," which they frequently resorted to in order to explain these "spiritualized" explanations of what surely had its basis, they reasoned, in naturalistic explanations. These missionaries were evangelical in their theology, but when it came to applied pneumatology in real life contexts, they were functional deists. This is why Lesslie Newbigin argued that Western missionaries were one of the greatest forces of secularization in history.[51]

Pentecostalism, by contrast, emerged among uneducated peoples whose worldview was the least influenced by the truncated enlightenment worldview. Their personal experience with the Holy Spirit gives them reason to believe that the same Holy Spirit who acted supernaturally in the lives and witness of the apostles is active today in similar ways. The result of this conviction has been the emergence of a Pentecostal pneumatology that generously provides an *expectation* of God the Holy Spirit's ongoing personal intervention in the world through miraculous healings, prophetic guidance to the church, demonic deliverance of evil, empowered witness to the world, and so forth.

The work of the Holy Spirit is to bring the "not yet" of the kingdom into the "already" of our fallen world. All the future realities of the kingdom are now fully available to all believers through the person and work of the Holy Spirit. Doctrines of cessationism or partial cessationism are, in the final analysis, detrimental concessions to an Enlightenment worldview that has unduly influenced the church with its naturalistic presuppositions. Sustained contact with Pentecostals will serve to invigorate our doctrinal articulation of the *work* of the Holy Spirit as well as the *praxis* of traditional Western pneumatology; in turn, Pentecostals will greatly benefit from the sustained theological reflection in the North American church on the *person* of the Holy Spirit.

50. Paul G. Hiebert, *Anthropological Reflections on Missiological Issues* (Grand Rapids: Baker, 1994), 189–201.

51. Lesslie Newbigin, *Honest Religion for Secular Man* (Philadelphia: Westminster, 1966), as cited in Hiebert, *Anthropological Reflections on Missiological Issues*, 197.

EVANGELISM AND MISSIONS IN LATIN AMERICAN PENTECOSTALISM

The second key question this chapter addresses is what we can learn from Latin American Pentecostals about the role of the Holy Spirit in evangelism and missions. The answer to that issue falls into two distinct parts: the death of Christendom in Latin America that gave new life to evangelism, and a distinctive pneumatology that has mobilized and empowered all believers for witness and mission in the world. Both of these will now be explored.

Death of Christendom — Birth of Evangelism

In 1493, just one year after Columbus's famous voyage to the New World, Pope Alexander VI issued the *Padroado*, which gave Spain exclusive rights to evangelize and colonize the new world in the West, and Portugal the exclusive right to evangelize and colonize the Eastern world. After some adjustments, the imaginary line that was finally drawn to separate the rights of Spain and Portugal was drawn at 360 leagues west of Cape Verde. Under this division of the world most of the coastline of Brazil fell to Portugal, and the rest of America and West Indies to Spain. The result was that through Spanish, Portuguese, and later French colonization, Latin America became an extension of European-Roman Catholic Christendom.

Such "Christendom" necessitated an intimate relationship between the church and civil society, exemplified best by the medieval synthesis of the two swords: emperor and pope. Because Christendom does not coexist with either the concept of religious choice (i.e., pluralism) or the need to convince someone of the truth of the faith (i.e., persuasion), the very nature of evangelism is dramatically transformed. Christian adherence comes through territory and birth rather than through repentance and personal conversion.[52]

The colonization of Latin America continued for centuries, and European hegemony (politically and religiously) remained unchallenged until 1815, when the stirrings of independence began with the overthrow of the French in Haiti. By 1914 almost all of Latin America was independent and under republican forms of government, although political instability and military dictatorships often prevailed.[53] However, even under independence Roman Catholicism remained the established religion either explicitly enshrined in the new constitutions or implicitly upheld through social and cultural conventions. Thus, the basic underlying assumptions of Christendom remained unchallenged.

All of this changed in the twentieth century. In fact, by 1960 Latin America finally entered what Pablo Richard calls an "open period," in which the cultural, economic,

52. René Padilla ("The Future of Christianity in Latin America: Missiological Perspectives and Challenges," *International Bulletin of Missionary Research* 23, no. 3 [July 1999], 105–12) borrows this terminology from Arend T. van Leeuwen's categories but applies them to Latin America (see *Christianity in World History: The Meaning of the Faiths of East and West* [London: Edinburgh House, 1964]). It is vital that theological students become acquainted with the way Christendom worked in the Middle Ages since this is one of the key sources of conflict today between Islam and the West. Islam is committed (via *Sharia*) to establish the Islamic equivalent of a Christendom that marries the two swords of Islam.

53. In 1914, French Guiana and a few islands in the West Indies remained under French sovereignty. See, Kenneth Scott Latourette, *A History of Christianity* (Peabody, MA: Prince, 2000), 2:1284.

and religious structures of what he calls "old Christendom" began to be dismantled. Richard argues that for the first time in the history of the Christianization of Latin America, the Christian faith has become a popular, grassroots movement.[54] René Padilla agrees, pointing out that during the twentieth century Latin America was dramatically transformed from an "ontocratic" society to a "technocratic" one.[55] An ontocratic society is one that is highly religious, closed, inward directed, and traditional. A technocratic society is one that is open and outward directed, may or may not be religious, and is open to change. The dramatic rise of Protestantism as a grassroots movement eventually achieved sufficient critical mass to challenge the religious monopoly held for centuries by the Roman Catholic Church. The result, for better or for worse, was a religious marketplace that made the hegemonic power of any one religious group impossible. This situation, in turn, sparked the need for active evangelism.

One of the great ironies of history is that only with the death of Christendom can there be a proper birth of evangelism. Christendom had always been effective in producing great numbers of nominal Christians, but it is hopeless when it comes to biblical evangelism. So with the "medieval period" finally fading away, the sunrise of evangelism was made possible—and the Pentecostals proved to be highly successful at it. In fact, if global church growth can be used as a rough barometer, Pentecostals are arguably the most effective evangelists in the entire history of Christianity. Part of the reason for this is that Pentecostalism represents the antithesis of the old Christendom model: it is nonhierarchical, with a popular, grassroots organization; it stands on the periphery, not at the center, of the political and business elite, which seem to be perpetually mired in corruption; and it puts a strong emphasis on the call to repentance and the need for personal conversion.

The Pentecostals also made the Roman Catholics better evangelists, as is clearly seen in the growing Roman Catholic work and witness in the impoverished, base communities of the region.[56] That is the other irony of the rise of Pentecostalism: it not only produced a whole new branch of Christianity, but it also helped to create the climate that forced the Protestants and Roman Catholics to be better Christians as well.[57] This should be an important (although counterintuitive) reminder that evangelism and church growth is not likely to be stimulated through the Christianization

54. Pablo Richard, *Death of Christendoms, Birth of the Church* (Maryknoll, NY: Orbis, 1987), 65. Richard distinguishes between "old" Christendom and "new" Christendom because he fears that once the Protestants rise in sufficient numbers, they might seek to impose a "new" *Protestant* Christendom on Latin America. However, once pluralism and persuasion have been introduced into a culture, it is difficult to retreat to a point that disallows both.

55. Padilla, "The Future of Christianity in Latin America," 105.

56. A "base community" refers to a small group of people who are in relationship one with another and connected to a particular community. As the Word is shared, they can discuss the text together for the purpose of effective action (which may be pastoral action, not necessarily political action). In contrast, large impersonal meetings implicitly encourage people to sit passively and only listen to the gospel. Base communities have been called "gospel creators" rather than "gospel consumers." Pentecostals have been strategic in working closely with these base communities. Jesuit theologian John A. Coleman points out that for Pentecostals, base communities are "not tied explicitly to liberation theology" but "like small Pentecostal units, they provide small-scale welfare, networks of support, and indigenous leadership" (see "Will Latin America Become Protestant?" *Commonweal* 118, no. 2 (January 1991): 61.

57. Samuel Escobar has provided compelling evidence that Catholic missiologists have taken many lessons from evangelicals in Latin America (see "Conflict of Interpretations of Popular Protestantism," in *New Face of the Church in Latin America*, ed. Guillermo Cook [Maryknoll, NY: Orbis, 1994], 112–34).

of the citadels of power. Christianity, it seems, flows more vibrantly from the bottom up than from the top down.

Distinctive Pneumatology

The effective evangelism exhibited by Pentecostals can also be attributed to their distinctive pneumatology, which was not encumbered by the truncated pneumatology that was so prevalent in North American theologies. The Holy Spirit is not only a full person of the Godhead, a part of the Trinity; he not only inspired the Holy Scriptures and regenerates us; but he also empowers us for effective evangelism. Pentecostals were convinced that the Holy Spirit confirms the preaching of the gospel and the declaration of the resurrection of Jesus through giving signs and wonders, just as he did to those unlearned fishermen and tax collectors who were his first apostles. Pentecostals understand that if someone is demon-possessed, then having the demon cast out in the name of Jesus is still part of the good news and the practical extension of Christ's triumphant victory over the principalities and powers (Eph. 6:12; Col. 2:14–15). In other words, if the Holy Spirit is alive and real, then he must have the power and means to extend his dynamic life in real and concrete ways into the lives of those who are suffering. If God raised the dead in the first century, why can't he do it in the twenty-first century?

This robust pneumatology provided the theological basis for an effective Pentecostal missiology. For example, a common Pentecostal belief is that you never witness or evangelize alone, because you are always accompanied by God the Evangelist, who speaks and works through you by the power of the Holy Spirit. This view of the Holy Spirit as being actually present and prepared to manifest his power in practical ways gave the Pentecostals the theological basis to mobilize the entire laity for witness, including the very newest Christians.[58] With God the Evangelist present, the success of their efforts did not depend on foreign financial backing, nice buildings, detailed planning, or highly trained professionals with seminary degrees.

Orlando Costas notes that mission practice that comes from the North arises out of "carefully thought out, written reflection," whereas in the South it appears as an "oral, popular reflection which is done 'on the road,' prompted by a significant event or a specific issue."[59] The laity understands the struggles and issues that are at the heart of the Latin American experience, and they relate the gospel to these concerns. Despite stereotypes to the contrary, Everett Wilson observes that Pentecostals are neither passive nor otherworldly. "They are in the movement because they have found solutions to practical problems."[60]

Pentecostals have had their most dynamic growth in the poorest regions of Latin America, far removed from modern health care. This has opened the door for an extensive ministry of praying for the sick.[61] As with the Gerasene man whom Christ

58. This can be observed in Pentecostalism worldwide. In China, for example, there are several house-church networks that will not permit someone to be baptized until they have led at least one person to Christ. The praxis of evangelism becomes part of the initial catechesis into the faith.

59. Orlando Costas, *Theology of the Crossroads* (Amsterdam: Editions Rodopi, 1976), 19.

60. Wilson, "Latin American Pentecostals: Their Potential for Ecumenical Dialogue," 87.

61. See Daniel Chiquete, "Healing, Salvation and Mission: The Ministry of Healing in Latin American Pentecostalism," *International Review of Mission* 93, nos. 370–371 (July–October

delivered in the New Testament (Mark 5:1–20), when anyone experiences healing and comes to faith in Christ, they are immediately asked to publicly testify to their faith. In Pentecostalism, anyone who knows enough to receive Christ knows enough to lead someone else to Christ. Thus, the laity was unleashed for evangelism and witness, and Pentecostalism became known among the masses as a "Protestantism of the people."[62] It is difficult to overestimate the significance of this shift. One observer put it well that "what is happening is a revolution in the Copernican sense of the term, a complete reversal. A switch is being made from a church resting on the point of a pyramid, in the person of bishop or priest, to a church resting on its base."[63]

Indeed, the Roman Catholic structure is hierarchical and relied heavily on foreign funds and foreign trained professionals. Even mainline Protestant mission work in Latin America depended on paid professionals who were, by comparison to those they were seeking to reach, highly educated. Roland Allen's words still ring true today: "It is almost universally taken for granted that missionary work is the work of a paid professional class, and that the utmost that can be expected of those who do not belong to this class is to support those who do."[64] These professionals generally arrived from North America, fueling further local distrust and the nagging suspicion that Protestant missionaries were just the "spearhead of American imperialism." This is a big part of why mainstream Protestant efforts were unable to "crack the Christendom nut."

From the perspective of evangelism the emergence of this elite, professional class of missionaries, whether Protestant or Roman Catholic, inadvertently caused a twofold tragedy. First, it rendered the vast majority of indigenous Christians passive and inactive, effectively sidelining them from the joyful overflow of evangelism. Second, those who were rendered passive were actually the most strategic group to mobilize, since they alone could communicate as cultural insiders. They were closer to the traditional folk spirituality than their foreign counterparts and they instinctively knew how to connect that with the dynamic sense of the supernatural that was inherent in Pentecostal preaching.[65]

The unleashing of the laity also meant that churches could be quickly established, since they were not reliant on the construction of church buildings or in need of foreign funds to support an expensive foreign missionary. Pentecostals found out that God the Evangelist seemed to be just as pleased to be present in a little house church or a store front church as he was in the big cathedrals whose spires seemed to pierce the

---

2004): 474–85. Chiquete makes a compelling case that this is the reason why speaking in tongues is emphasized more in North American Pentecostalism and divine healing is emphasized more in Latin American Pentecostalism.

62. Gamaliel Lugo Morales, "Moving Forward with the Latin American Pentecostal Movement," *International Review of Missions* 87, no. 347 (October 1998): 505–6.

63. "A New People: Emergence of the Laity"; see http://www.dominicans.org/~ecleary/crisis/crisis05.pdf.

64. Roland Allen, *The Spontaneous Expansion of the Church* (London: World Dominion, 1956), 136, 140. He also observed that "those converts who are most eager to propagate the faith of Christ, are frequently the men who have received the least education at our hands" (123).

65. For more on the ability of Pentecostalism to take advantage of pre-Christian folk religiosity, see Michael Bergunder, "The Pentecostal Movement and Basic Ecclesial Communities in Latin America: Sociological Theories and Theological Debates," *International Review of Missions* 91, no. 361 (April 2002): 169–70, 175.

sky.[66] The multiplication of churches rather than of individual Christians is one of the most important reasons Pentecostalism spread so rapidly and so effectively. They were not just preaching individual salvation; they were planting the church, communities of redeemed people, who could live out the reality of the kingdom in the context of their larger communities with whom they have a functional connection.

Pneumatology also influenced Pentecostals' understanding of missions and the global witness of the gospel. Nineteenth-century missiology, exemplified by William Carey's groundbreaking book, *An Enquiry*,[67] focused on the importance of *obeying* the text of the Great Commission. The subsequent missions literature of the nineteenth century is filled with motivating calls to *obey* this final command of our Lord.

There is, of course, nothing inherently wrong with this. Nevertheless, it should be noted that while the Great Commission is never *less* than the command of Scripture, it is certainly *more* than the command of Scripture. Remarkably, Matthew 28:18–20 (or any of the other commissioning texts that conclude the public ministry of Christ) is never cited a single time in Acts as the motivation for their witness.[68] Instead, the Great Commission was not so much a text to be obeyed as the living Christ who went before them and the Holy Spirit who bore witness to Christ through them. The Holy Spirit was continuing to extend the presence and power of the resurrected Christ through the witness of the church.

It was precisely this connection by Pentecostals between their Christology and their pneumatology that has made them such a vibrant force in global missions. For Pentecostals, "the commission is no longer merely an outward command, an ethical demand. It is now personified by the missionary Spirit's indwelling presence."[69] It is not merely that God gave us a missionary command; God is, by nature, a missionary God! This does not diminish the importance of the text and its commands, nor does it diminish the importance of the text in formulating strategy and reflecting on biblical principles of missiology. The point is merely that ultimately Jesus embodies the Great Commission—and we are, in the final analysis, confronted not by a command but by Jesus himself.[70]

THE ROLE OF PENTECOSTALISM IN ECUMENISM

Meaning of the Term "Ecumenical"

The third and final key theme this chapter addresses concerns the role of Latin American Pentecostals in providing a potential new basis for ecumenism. This may

66. In my own missionary experience some of the most powerful moments of worship and a sense of the presence of God have been in small house churches or thatched roof "prayer sheds" filled with new believers fervently praising God for who he is and thanking him for his mercy in saving them.

67. This is arguably the most influential missionary tract ever written. See William Carey, *An Enquiry into the Obligations of Christians to Use Means for the Conversion of the Heathens*, new facsimile edition of 1792 original (London: Carey Kingsgate, 1961).

68. For a complete exposition of this, see Harry Boer, *Pentecost and Missions* (Grand Rapids: Eerdmans, 1961). Boer makes a convincing case that the universal scope of the "command" of the Great Commission was not fully recognized and appreciated in isolation from Pentecost (28–47).

69. Paul A. Pommerville, *The Third Force in Missions* (Peabody, MA: Hendrickson, 1985), 75.

70. Expanding our view of missions beyond obeying a command also liberates us from the church-centered, anthropocentric view that pervades much of missions today. Seeing God as the embodiment of missions recognizes the role of the Father (John 6:44) in preparing people to receive the gospel before we arrive (*preparatio evangelica*), Christ's role as the risen Lord standing in our midst as we proclaim the gospel in specific cultural contexts, and the Holy Spirit's role in confirming the Word and helping

come as a shock to some readers because for many Pentecostals the very word *ecumenical* is evil, a synonym for the failed legacy of Protestant and Roman Catholic liberalism. However, the word is used in a variety of ways. It is derived from the Greek word *oikoumenē*, signifying the entire inhabited world. In early biblical usage the word implies the global scope of the Christian mission. However, over time and with usage, the term has developed three other meanings.

First, the term is frequently used to denote the common creedal confessions, such as the Nicene Creed, that unite all branches of Christianity. It is common to hear someone speak, for example, of the "ecumenical" councils, referring to the seven church councils that represented both branches of Christianity (East and West). Unfortunately, Pentecostals have not been particularly interested in articulating their theological continuity with the ecumenical councils, even though in practice they are in broad conformity with them.

Second, the term *ecumenical* is also used to refer to interreligious dialogue between Christian and non-Christian religious groups as well as to the need for greater cooperation among other Christian groups. This is the usage that provokes a negative reaction in some Pentecostals who understand it to be advocating, at best, a gigantic, structural merger of the church around the world, and, at worst, the complete blurring of every distinctive doctrine of Christianity in the face of challenges from other religions. In Latin America in particular the word is often understood to be associated with communism or with Protestant churches that have "sold out" to Roman Catholicism.[71]

This should not be taken to mean that Pentecostals have not participated in these formal ecumenical bodies. Earlier in the chapter I pointed out how difficult it was for evangelicals to accept Pentecostals into the National Association of Evangelicals (NAE). Nevertheless, the Pentecostal Holiness Church, the Open Bible Standard Churches, the Church of God, and the Assembly of God, among others, have become full members of the NAE. In 1961 the first Pentecostal churches joined the World Council of Churches.[72] Latin American Pentecostals have also become full participants in the Latin American Council of Churches. Despite all of this, there is still a general negative reaction among Pentecostals to phrases like "an ecumenical gathering" or "an ecumenical dialogue," especially when it stresses the work and ministry of the Holy Spirit outside the church.

Finally, the term has come full circle to refer to the emergence of global Christianity of which we (despite our various denominations) are all participants. The global church is so large and diverse that it is virtually impossible to comprehend all the differences. Yet, there are certain great "ecumenical" truths—most notably Christ

new believers to assimilate the faith long after the missionary agent may have departed. With this framework we have a Trinitarian, God-centered mission that reflects him as the subject of missions rather than the church as the subject focused on the aggrandizement of its institutional life. In short, missions should never be reduced to mere tasks that the church does out in the world; rather, missions is Christ's resurrected life calling the world through us to enter the community of his kingdom.

71. Morales, "Moving Forward with the Latin American Pentecostal Movement," 509.

72. Ibid., 511.

himself, who is the Truth—that unite all Christians in every age, affirmations that have been held *semper ubique ab omnibus.*

This is more than the unity expressed by a creed or packaged neatly in conceptual theological language. Rather, it refers to a deeper spiritual unity that acknowledges our catholicity because we are all members of the body of Christ and share a common union with Jesus Christ and a burden to bear witness to him in authentic ways throughout the whole world. It has more to do with a shared sense of belonging to Christ and a common commitment to global witness than anything about the specifics of ecclesiastical structures or even precise doctrinal formulations. This usage of the word is implied when we hear statements such as "Lausanne is an ecumenical gathering."[73]

This broad semantic range of the term *ecumenical* explains why Pentecostalism can be considered antiecumenical in one sense and yet proecumenical in another. When this chapter claims that the Pentecostals are ecumenical, it is using the term according to this last usage. In other words, Pentecostalism, despite its diversity and dizzying array of denominations, has managed to form an ecumenical basis for cooperation with many other groups who may not share their exact theology, but who share in the Pentecostal experience, even if their background is Roman Catholic or mainline Protestant.

Pentecostal Contributions to Ecumenism

I will never forget being invited to my first Full Gospel Business Men's Fellowship meeting[74] in the fall of 1977. I arrived and was shocked to discover Pentecostals and Roman Catholics worshiping and praying together. These were two groups I assumed were about as far apart as any two Christian groups could get, but I could not deny the genuine Christian fellowship and joy these men shared together. This was a new experience for me. I understood the *theological* basis for ecumenism, but I had never properly understood, for good or for ill, the power of an *experiential* basis for ecumenism. Because Pentecostals deride the term *ecumenical* and, quite frankly, because they have exhibited as much sectarianism and engaged in as many theological squabbles as any other Christian group, it is easy to miss three remarkable ways Pentecostalism has actually contributed positively to global ecumenism.

Beyond Denominational Sectarianism

First, Pentecostals were among the first to understand the global implications of transcending the traditional denominational divides that have characterized Protestant identity for centuries. Because Pentecostalism did not have its origin in a single church tradition or geographic region, it was birthed in diversity. Modern-day Pentecostalism can be traced to classical Pentecostal denominations as well as to indigenous revivals erupting on five different continents. A second wave of Pentecostalism has swept through mainline Protestant, Roman Catholic, and Eastern Orthodox

73. Lausanne is shorthand for the Lausanne Congress for World Evangelization, a global organization with a membership of hundreds of different groups, all committed to the evangelization of the world.

74. Full Gospel Business Men's Fellowship International is a fellowship of Charismatic and Pentecostal men around the world.

churches. This diverse background forced Pentecostals to embrace unity in spiritual terms rather than in structural or doctrinal terms.

This is why the term *Pentecostal* is frequently used both as an adjective and a noun in a way which is not generally found with terms such as *Lutheran* or *Methodist*. One can consider themselves to be a Pentecostal Roman Catholic or a Pentecostal Methodist without fear of contradiction. In fact, one of the most dynamic Pentecostal movements in Chile emerged within the Methodist Church under the leadership of an American Methodist missionary named Willis Hoover.[75] This spiritual basis for unity means that a Pentecostal can "have true ecumenism or genuine *koinōnia* with all Christians who have a personal relationship with God."[76] Discovering this "common spiritual center" is, according to Westmeier, the reason that Pentecostalism has been able to work across denominational lines, particularly in Latin America.[77]

Because Pentecostals saw themselves as reviving the apostolic faith rather than breaking off from or emerging out of any existing movements, it allowed them, even if naïvely, to provide a basis for ecumenism around their common commitment to the biblical witness in Scripture and their shared experience of the Holy Spirit. The Pentecostals learned the principle of *sola Scriptura* from the Reformation, but then used it as a basis for celebrating a supernatural, apostolic faith, an emphasis they felt was largely lost in North American Protestantism.

Ecumenism through Theopraxis

Second, Pentecostals have found a basis for ecumenical unity not only in their common experience with God, but also in their commitment to focus outward on evangelism and missions rather than inward on either defending themselves against their critics or expending a lot of energy on defining their own identity. In the formative stages of the emergence of Pentecostalism, the movement held a distrust of academic scholarship, which they called a "tragedy, whose fruit is empty churches ... the result of our 'theologizing to death.'"[78] Although this anti-intellectualism among Pentecostals has changed significantly in recent years, it is still true that Pentecostals are more interested in theopraxis than in theology in the formal sense.

Pentecostals still provide an important check against the tendency for theology to lose its missiological focus and become too rationalistic and theoretical. Our tendency toward a cerebral-oriented scholasticism must come to appreciate and benefit from the counterbalance of the Pentecostal orientation towards a heart-oriented praxis. God used the seventeenth-century movement of Pietism to balance out the tendency towards an overly cerebral scholasticism in post-Reformation Protestant theology in Europe. Pietism became unconsciously ecumenical as it quietly spread its influence

75. See Willis C. Hoover, *History of the Pentecostal Revival in Chile* (Santiago, Chile: Imprenta Eben-Ezer, 2000).

76. Robeck, "Pentecostals and the Apostolic Faith," 65.

77. Westmeier, *Protestant Pentecostalism in Latin America*, 19. This is also celebrated in Matthew Marostica's chapter entitled "The Defeat of Denominational Culture in the Argentine Evangelical Movement," in *Latin American Religion in Motion*, ed. Christian Smith and Joshua Prokopy (New York and London: Routledge, 1999), 148–72.

78. Hollenweger, *Pentecostalism: Origins and Developments Worldwide*, 194.

through most of European Protestantism. There is hardly a Protestant movement in the world that has not in some way been influenced by Pietism.

Today, God is using the Pentecostals in the same way. Indeed, one of the neglected stories of global Pentecostalism is not so much how they have grown as distinct, identifiable Pentecostal groups, but how deeply they have influenced so much of the faith and practice of non-Pentecostals around the world. It is the Pentecostal sense of the immediacy of God's presence and power that has struck a responsive chord in Christians everywhere. It is also a wonderful reminder of how crucial it is that the *noetic* principle in theology (reflection, reason, propositional statements, etc.) must always be balanced by the *ontic* principle (immediacy of God's presence, personal experience with God, etc.).[79] If either of these tendencies is allowed to run unchecked, the church falls into error.

Beyond the Homogenous Unit Principle in Mission Strategy

Finally, Pentecostals have provided an important counterbalance to the strong emphasis on reaching unreached people groups on the basis of Donald McGavran's Homogenous Unit Principle, which has dominated both the church-growth movement and evangelical missions since 1974.[80] According to McGavran, a homogenous unit refers to "a section of society in which all the members have some characteristic in common."[81] The Homogenous Unit Principle focuses on identifying particular peoples who share a common cultural, linguistic, and social identity and stimulating a "people-movement" within this particular ethnic group.

The whole basis for the Homogenous Unit Principle is the proven sociological fact that people prefer to not cross social and ethnic barriers when becoming a Christian. Furthermore, people prefer to worship with people who are culturally like themselves.[82] This is the principle that drives the church-growth movement to focus, for example, on young, middle-class unchurched professionals in building megachurches. This is the same principle used by mission organizations when they, for example, target a particular caste group in India to evangelize. Over the last thirty years, the focus on people groups has become the "holy grail" of evangelical missions, and undoubtedly there are tens of millions of new Christians in the world today because of the effective application of this principle.

But the Pentecostals, by and large, have been reluctant to embrace this principle in their evangelism and mission work. The Azusa Street Mission was, from the start, a multiracial event that transcended the normal social and ethnic barriers. Pentecostalism and neo-Pentecostalism demonstrated over and over again the power of the Pentecostal message to penetrate high church Anglicans as well as poor, uneducated laborers and then bring them together in a way that confounds the dynamics of proven sociological expectations.

---

79. Pommerville, *The Third Force in Missions*, 68.

80. The year 1974 is the year Ralph Winter delivered his now famous paper at the first Lausanne Congress on World Evangelization, entitled "The Highest Priority: Cross-Cultural Evangelism." This date marks the shift in mission practice from a focus on "places" to a focus on "peoples."

81. Donald McGavran, *Understanding Church Growth*, rev. ed. (Grand Rapids: Eerdmans, 1990), 69.

82. This is the basis for the well-known saying that 11:00 a.m. is the most segregated hour in America.

Pentecostals have modeled on a global scale what happened to Peter and Cornelius in Acts 10, which I alluded to in the preface. The two men were completely separated, both theologically and culturally. One was an uncircumcised Gentile, the other a law-abiding Jew. In short, they were certainly not part of the same "homogenous unit." They were not even able to share table fellowship, and certainly it was thought that they could not stand in the presence of God together. However, once the Holy Spirit came on the whole household (Acts 10:44), everything was changed. Peter and Cornelius had a new basis for unity through the power of the Holy Spirit, who sovereignly yoked them to one another and to Christ.

We normally read Acts 10 as the story of Cornelius's conversion, but a more reflective reading reveals that both men went away transformed. Cornelius was now a full member of the body of Christ and Peter now had his own truncated view of God enlarged and transformed. He now understood that God was a missionary God with a heart for the whole world. The Pentecostals may make evangelicals uncomfortable with their comparative disinterest in formal theology, but they also have the capacity to transform our understanding of God in many positive ways.

CONCLUSION

This chapter has focused on several ways in which Latin American Pentecostalism in particular and global Pentecostalism in general can help strengthen North American discourse concerning pneumatology. As this study has demonstrated, I am interested not only in how our doctrine of the Holy Spirit is formally shaped and articulated in our systematic theologies, but also in the many integrative ways the doctrine can be applied to real life contexts that could have a profound effect on how we talk about mission practice and global ecumenism.

There are, of course, glaring inconsistencies and theological problems within Pentecostalism. The so-called "prosperity gospel," which weds an American consumer culture with outlandish interpretations of certain biblical texts, is well known. Moreover, several prominent Pentecostal figures have brought embarrassment and shame not only to Pentecostalism but to the broader cause of Christ in the world. If, in this study, I have neglected the "mote" in the Pentecostal eye, it is only because I am so painfully aware of the "beam" in my own eye. In other words, I maintain that despite the incongruities, Pentecostalism remains the most important corrective to the blind spots in our pneumatological theory and practice on the planet today.

By God's grace, we may very well represent the most important corrective to the blind spots in their pneumatology. However, that discussion will have to wait for another day. The point is, we have much to learn from one another. As Samuel Escobar has wisely stated, evangelical Protestantism emphasized the "continuity in truth by the Word," whereas Pentecostalism has emphasized the "continuity in life by the Spirit."[83] To be effective, the twenty-first century church desperately needs the dynamic union of both.

83. Samuel Escobar, "A Missiological Approach to Latin American Protestantism," *International Review of Mission* 87, no. 345 (April 1998): 172.

BIBLIOGRAPHY

Allen, Roland. *The Spontaneous Expansion of the Church*. London: World Dominion, 1956.

Anderson, Allan. *An Introduction to Pentecostalism*. Cambridge: Cambridge University Press, 2004.

_____. "To All Points of the Compass: The Azusa Street Revival and Global Pentecostalism." *Enrichment Journal*, 2006. http://enrichmentjournal.ag.org/200602/200602_164_AllPoints.cfm (June 19, 2006).

Barrett, David B., George T. Kurian, and Todd M. Johnson. *World Christian Encyclopedia*. 2nd ed. New York: Oxford University Press, 2001.

Bergunder, Michael. "The Pentecostal Movement and Basic Ecclesial Communities in Latin America: Sociological Theories and Theological Debates." *International Review of Mission* 91, no. 361 (April 2002): 163–86.

Blumhofer, Edith. "Revisiting Azusa Street: A Centennial Retrospect." *International Bulletin of Missionary Research* 30, no. 2 (April 2006): 59–64.

Boer, Harry. *Pentecost and Missions*. Grand Rapids: Eerdmans, 1961.

Boyd, Gregory A. *Oneness Pentecostals and the Trinity*. Grand Rapids: Baker, 1992.

Carey, William. *An Enquiry into the Obligations of Christians to Use Means for the Conversion of the Heathen*. London: Carey Kingsgate, 1961 (facsimile edition of 1792 original).

Chiquete, Daniel. "Healing, Salvation and Mission: The Ministry of Healing in Latin American Pentecostalism." *International Review of Missions* 93, nos. 370–71 (July–October 2004): 474–85.

Coleman, John A. "Will Latin America Become Protestant?" *Commonweal* 118, no. 2 (January 1991): 59–63.

Costas, Orlando. *Theology of the Crossroads*. Amsterdam: Editions Rodopi, 1976.

Cox, Harvey. *Fire from Heaven: The Rise of Pentecostal Spirituality and the Reshaping of Religion in the Twenty-First Century*. Reading, MA: Addison Wesley, 1995.

Dayton, Donald W. *Theological Roots of Pentecostalism*. Grand Rapids: Francis Asbury, 1987.

Decker, R. L. "What the NAE Is and How It Operates." *United Evangelical Action* 6, no. 18 (November 1, 1947): 7–8.

Escobar, Samuel. "A Missiological Approach to Latin American Protestantism." *International Review of Mission* 87, no. 345 (April 1998): 161–73.

_____. "Conflict of Interpretations of Popular Protestantism." Pages 112–34 in *New Face of the Church in Latin America*. Edited by Guillermo Cook. Maryknoll, NY: Orbis, 1994.

"Fastest Growing Church in the Hemisphere." *Time* (November 2, 1962), 56.

Fee, Gordon. *God's Empowering Presence: The Holy Spirit in the Letters of Paul*. Peabody: MA: Hendrickson, 1994.

Goen, C. C., ed. *Works of Jonathan Edwards*. Vol. 4, *The Distinguishing Marks*. New Haven, CT: Yale University Press, 1972.

Gordon, A. J. *The Ministry of Healing: Miracles of Cure in All Ages*. Harrisburg, PA: Christian Publications, 1961.

_____. *The Ministry of the Spirit*. Philadelphia: American Baptist Publication Society, 1894.

Gorski, John F. "How the Catholic Church in Latin America Became Missionary." *International Bulletin of Missionary Research* 27, no. 2 (April 2003): 59–64.

Grudem, Wayne. *Systematic Theology: An Introduction to Biblical Doctrine.* Grand Rapids: Zondervan, 1994.

Hiebert, Paul G. *Anthropological Reflections on Missiological Issues.* Grand Rapids: Baker, 1994.

Hollenweger, Walter. *Pentecostalism: Origins and Developments Worldwide.* Peabody, MA: Hendrickson, 1997.

Hoover, Willis C. *History of the Pentecostal Revival in Chile.* Santiago, Chile: Imprenta Eben-Ezer, 2000.

Johnson, Todd M. "Three Waves of Christian Renewal: A 100-Year Snapshot." *International Bulletin of Missionary Research* 30, no. 2 (April 2006): 75–76.

Latourette, Kenneth Scott. *A History of Christianity.* Peabody, MA: Prince, 2000.

Marostica, Matthew. "The Defeat of Denominational Culture in the Argentine Evangelical Movement." Pages 148–72 in *Latin American Religion in Motion.* Edited by Christian Smith and Joshua Prokopy. New York: Routledge, 1999.

Martin, David. *Tongues of Fire.* Cambridge, MA: Basil Blackwell, 1990.

Martin, Larry. *The Words That Changed the World: Azusa Street Sermons.* Joplin, MO: Christian Life, 1999.

McGavran, Donald. *Understanding Church Growth.* Rev. ed. Grand Rapids: Eerdmans, 1990.

McLoughlin, William G., and Robert Bellah, eds. *Religion in America.* Boston: Houghton Mifflin, 1968.

Menzies, William W. "The Holy Spirit in Christian Theology." Pages 67–79 in *Perspectives on Evangelical Theology.* Edited by Kenneth Kantzer and Stanley Gundry. Grand Rapids: Baker, 1979.

_____. "The Non-Wesleyan Origins of the Pentecostal Movement." Pages 81–98 in *Aspects of Pentecostal-Charismatic Origins.* Edited by Vinson Synan. Plainfield, NJ: Logos International, 1975.

Morales, Gamaliel Lugo. "Moving Forward with the Latin American Pentecostal Movement." *International Review of Mission* 87, no. 347 (October 1998): 504–12.

"A New People: Emergence of the Laity" (http://www.dominicans.org/~ecleary/crisis/crisis05.pdf (July 23, 2006).

Newbigin, Lesslie. *Honest Religion for Secular Man.* Philadelphia: Westminster, 1966.

Ockenga, Harold. "God Our Only Hope." *United Evangelical Action* 6, no. 18 (November 1, 1947): 12–13.

_____. "The 'Pentecostal' Bogey." *United Evangelical Action* 6, no. 1 (February 15, 1947): 12–13.

Owen, John. *The Holy Spirit: His Gifts and Power: Exposition of the Spirit's Name, Nature, Personality, Dispensation, Operations and Effects.* Reprint. Grand Rapids: Kregel, 1954.

Padilla, C. René. "The Future of Christianity in Latin America: Missiological Perspectives and Challenges." *International Bulletin of Missionary Research* 23, no. 3 (July 1999): 105–12.

Pelikan, Jaroslav. *The Christian Tradition: A History of the Development of Doctrine.* Vol. 1, *The Emergence of the Catholic Tradition (100–600).* Chicago: University of Chicago Press, 1971.

Petersen, Douglas. "The Azusa Street Mission and Latin American Pentecostalism." *International Bulletin of Missionary Research* 30, no. 2 (April 2006): 66–67.

Pommerville, Paul A. *The Third Force in Missions.* Peabody, MA: Hendrickson, 1985.

Richard, Pablo. *Death of Christendoms, Birth of the Church.* Maryknoll, NY: Orbis, 1987.

Robeck, Cecil M. Jr. "The Nature of Pentecostal Spirituality." *Pneuma: The Journal of the Society for Pentecostal Studies* 14 (1992): 104–6.

_____. "Pentecostals and the Apostolic Faith: Implications for Ecumenism." *Pneuma: The Journal of the Society for Pentecostal Studies* 9 (1987): 61–84.

Schaff, Philip, and Henry Wace, eds. *Nicene and Post-Nicene Fathers.* Vol. 14, *The Seven Ecumenical Councils.* Peabody, MA: Hendrickson, 1999.

Stewart-Gambino, Hannah W., and Everett Wilson. "Latin American Pentecostals: Old Stereotypes and New Challenges." Pages 227–46 in *Power, Politics and Pentecostals in Latin America.* Edited by Edward L. Cleary and Hannah W. Stewart-Gambino. Boulder, CO: Westview, 1997.

Stoll, David. "A Protestant Reformation in Latin America?" *The Christian Century* 107, no. 1 (January 3–10, 1990): 44–48.

_____. *Is Latin America Turning Protestant?* Los Angeles: University of California Press, 1990.

Synan, Vincent. *Holiness-Pentecostal Movement in the United States.* Grand Rapids: Eerdmans, 1971.

Thiessen, Henry C. *Lectures in Systematic Theology.* Rev. ed. Grand Rapids: Eerdmans, 1979.

Van Dusen, Henry P. "The Third Force in Christendom." *Life* (June 9, 1958): 113–24.

Van Leeuwen, Arend T. *Christianity in World History: The Meaning of the Faiths of East and West.* London: Edinburgh House, 1964.

Wagner, C. Peter. *Church Growth and the Whole Gospel.* San Francisco: Harper & Row, 1981.

_____. "The Greatest Church Growth Is beyond Our Shores." *Christianity Today* (May 18, 1984), 27–28.

Wallace, Daniel, and M. James Sawyer, eds. *Who's Afraid of the Holy Spirit?* Dallas: Biblical Studies, 2005.

Walls, Andrew F. "Eusebius Tries Again: Reconceiving the Study of Christian History." *International Bulletin of Missionary Research* 24, no. 3 (July 2000): 105–8, 110–11.

Warfield, B. B. *Counterfeit Miracles.* New York: Charles Scribner's Sons, 1918.

Watson, Russell. "Latin America: John Paul Goes to War." *Newsweek* (February 12, 1996), 39.

"Weird Babble of Tongues." *Los Angeles Daily Times* (April 18, 1906).

Westmeier, Karl-Wilhelm. *Protestant Pentecostalism in Latin America.* London: Associated University Presses, 1999.

Wilson, Everett A. "Latin American Pentecostals—Their Potential for Ecumenical Dialogue." *Pneuma: The Journal of the Society for Pentecostal Studies* 9, no. 1 (Spring 1987): 85–90.

Yong, Amos. *Beyond the Impasse: Towards a Pneumatological Theology of Religions.* Grand Rapids: Baker, 2003.

Chapter 8

ECCLESIOLOGY

FOLLOWERS OF JESUS IN ISLAMIC MOSQUES

One of the recurring themes in this book is that a truly vibrant theology cannot exist in some hermetically sealed vacuum, blissfully ignorant of the real and difficult cultural and contextual challenges of our world. Thus, one of the most important ways the global missionary movement serves the church is by bringing many new and sometimes exceedingly difficult and controversial issues to the table, demanding the attention of theologians who might not be aware of these developments.

Nowhere is this more evident than in the area of ecclesiology. Indeed, as noted in chapter 1, the church is experiencing unprecedented growth outside the West, far away from the traditional centers of theological reflection. In these new contexts that the church is increasingly calling home, the very terms *Christian* and *church* have strong connotations of Western culture or foreignness. For many, these words call to mind British imperialism or colonialism—or worse. In short, for many the phrase "Christian church" carries negative, cultural connotations whereas "Jesus" may not.

This reality has caused many to rethink the nature of the church as it has been known in the Christian West. Reexamining the doctrine of ecclesiology is a welcome and important development, since the doctrine has often become unnecessarily tethered to Western expressions of the church that may be inappropriate for the growing church in the Majority World. This chapter focuses on the emerging and growing phenomenon known as "churchless Christianity."

CHURCHLESS CHRISTIANITY

India

Herbert Hoefer, in his book *Churchless Christianity*, has compiled data from devoted followers of Christ living in rural Tamil Nadu and in urban Chennai who have not joined a visible Christian church and, indeed, remain within the Hindu community. He does not call them Christians, but *Jesu bhakta* (i.e., devotees of Jesus;

bhakti means "devotion"). Hoefer's research suggests that there are more nonbaptized followers of Jesus in Madras than there are formal, visible Christians in the traditional sense.[1]

The *bhakti* movement allows for Hindus to focus their worship on a particular god, so it is not scandalizing for someone in their community to choose to worship Jesus—even exclusively Jesus. These *Jesu bhakta* follow an *ishta devata* theology within Hinduism. The practice of *ishta devata* allows a person to worship a particular, chosen deity without necessarily denying that other gods exist. They are, therefore, allowed to focus their worship exclusively on Jesus and yet maintain their cultural and social particularities as Hindus.[2] If asked, they continue to call themselves Hindus. They will not identify themselves as Christian, and many do not attend any church.[3] This unwillingness to identify with the church or with baptism is not due to any shame about following Christ, but to strong cultural associations surrounding the terms.

During a two-year period from 2001 to 2003 I surveyed the perceptions that North Indian Hindus have regarding the church and Christianity.[4] I found that many Hindus do, indeed, have distorted and unfortunate notions about the church or organized Christianity. They infer, for example, that Christians are disrespectful because they keep their shoes on in the presence of God. They look on Christians as culturally foreign because they sit on pews rather than on the floor or use Western musical forms rather than the indigenous *bhajans*.[5] They simply do not understand why Christian women will no longer wear bangles or participate in popular cultural festivals. Many Hindus think that to become a Christian means using Western style eating utensils, eating beef, and drinking alcohol. In short, even if a Hindu is drawn to Christ, they may find membership in the church or the term *Christian* repugnant.[6] This raises the vital issue: Can someone say "yes" to Jesus and "no" to the visible church?

Muslim Background Believers and the Western Church

Distorted views of the terms *church* and *Christianity* are not limited to India, nor is the presence of nonbaptized followers of Jesus who do not identify with the visible church limited to Hinduism. These tendencies have also been observed throughout

1. Herbert Hoefer, *Churchless Christianity* (Pasadena, CA: William Carey Library, 2001), 96. Hoefer cites at least 156,000 "nonbaptized believers in Christ" (30,000 high caste, i.e., Brahmin; 70,000 middle castes, i.e., Kshatriya and Vaisya; 56,000 scheduled castes, i.e., Sudra and Dalit). See his Appendices II–V, pp. 277–352.

2. *Ishta devata* literally means a "chosen [or favorite] deity." See *Harper Collins Dictionary of Religion*, ed. Jonathan Smith (San Francisco: HarperCollins, 1995), 494.

3. Some will make pilgrimage to a large church on an occasional basis in the same way that Hindus make periodic pilgrimages to great temples in India.

4. This research has been published in a question-and-answer format in English and in Hindi under the title, *Your Questions–Our Answers* (Dehra Dun, Uttaranchal: Bharat Susamachar Samiti, 2003).

5. A *bhajan* is a devotional song or hymn, often associated with a particular form or style.

6. Similar stories can be told within a Buddhist context. For example, a Thai Buddhist follower of Jesus named Chai refused to call himself a Christian because, for him, it meant "foreigner." Instead, he began referring to himself as a "Child of God" and a "new Buddhist." See Frank Decker, "When 'Christian' Does Not Translate," *Mission Frontiers* 27, no. 5 (September–October 2005): 8.

the Muslim world. Robby Butler tells the story of a Kuwaiti Muslim who was asked what he knew about Christians and Christianity. He replied that a Christian is someone who promotes immorality, pornography, and sexually oriented television programs like *Sex in the City*, *Desperate Housewives*, and so on. Butler goes on to comment that "for a Muslim to say that he has become a Christian is to communicate that he has launched into a secret life of immorality."[7] In short, Butler argues that becoming a Christian is perceived by Muslims to be entering a prayerless, apostate community.[8] Yet, despite these perceptions, Muslims generally hold positive views of Jesus Christ. The Qurʾan teaches that Christ had a miraculous birth, was a miracle worker, and was a prophet without sin.[9]

These positive views of Christ alongside such embarrassing perceptions regarding terms like *Christian*, *church*, and *Christianity* within the Muslim community have also spawned a range of churchless, but Christ-loving movements. For example, Rafique Uddin and David Cashin have observed many Muslim followers of Jesus (*Isa*) who do not separate from the mosque or unite with a visible church.[10] *Mission Frontiers* highlighted a missionary couple named Alejandro and Bertha Ortiz, who have nurtured several of these "Jesus mosques" in the African country of Benin. They claim that in another Muslim nation there are over 100,000 Muslims who worship Jesus as *Isa* in Islamic mosques.[11]

This marked association of the Christian message with Western culture has led to more vigorous attempts to appropriately contextualize the Christian message for Muslims and Hindus. There has been a sincere and necessary effort to be more self-critical about our comparative failure to penetrate the gospel into Islamic contexts. We have gradually come to see that many Muslims who seem resistant to the gospel are not rejecting the gospel per se, but Westernized forms, distortions, and misunderstandings of Christianity that Muslims find repugnant. This realization has given rise to vigorous attempts to envision and implement more contextually appropriate methods for communicating Christ to Muslims without unnecessary foreign baggage.

CASE STUDY IN MAJORITY WORLD ECCLESIOLOGY

The following study on ecclesiology will focus on these Muslim followers of Jesus who continue attending the Islamic mosque and retain their identity as Muslims. How do these followers of Jesus relate to the rest of the global church? Can someone

7. Robby Butler, "Unlocking Islam," *Mission Frontiers* 13, no. 1 (January–March 1991): 24.

8. Ibid.

9. See Surah 19:15–22; Surah 3:49–50. Christ is given at least fourteen major titles in the Qurʾan, including Messiah, Servant of God, Prophet, Messenger, the Word, a Sign, etc. For a full exploration of Qurʾanic teachings concerning Christ see chapter 7 of my book, *Christianity at the Religious Roundtable: Evangelicalism in Conversation with Hinduism, Buddhism and Islam* (Grand Rapids: Baker, 2002).

10. Rafique Uddin, "Contextualized Worship and Witness," in *Muslims and Christians on the Emmaus Road*, ed. J. Dudley Woodberry (Monrovia: MARC, 1989), 269–72; David Cashin as reported to Barry Yeoman, "The Stealth Crusade," *Mother Jones* 48 (May–June 2002), 48.

11. Erich Bridges, "Of 'Jesus Mosques' and Muslim Christians," *Mission Frontiers* 19, nos. 7–10 (July–October 1997): 19. See also the anonymous article "A Different Kind of Mosque," *Mission Frontiers* 19, nos. 7–10 (July–October 1997): 20–21.

say "yes" to Jesus and "no" to the church? Are the biblical and theological arguments made in support of this movement valid?

C–1 to C–6 Spectrum

The best-known summary of the spectrum of Muslim background believers (known as MBBs) found in the Islamic world was published by John Travis in 1988 and has become the standard reference point for discussing contextualization in the Islamic context.[12] The spectrum is known as the C–1 to C–6 Spectrum. Significantly, the "C" stands for Christ-centered communities.[13] The various numbers reflect differences based on three main areas: the language of worship, the cultural and/or religious forms used in both the MBBs' public life and worship, and their self-identity as Muslims or Christians.

C–1 refers to a "traditional church using outsider language," that is, a language other than that used by the Muslim population. This would be a church that, for example, worships in English, uses pews, and follows a Western liturgy. It can also refer to MBBs who have joined one of the many ancient churches in the Islamic world that predate the rise of Islam, use Latin or Greek, and follow an ancient liturgical rite. These believers all call themselves Christians.

C–2 refers to a "traditional church using insider language," that is, a church that worships in the language of the Muslim population, such as Arabic or Turkish, but otherwise is the same as a C–1 church. Travis argues that the majority of churches in the Islamic world are either C–1 or C–2, but only a fraction of MBBs have united with churches of either type.[14]

C–3 refers to "contextualized Christ-centered communities using insider language and religiously neutral cultural forms." These churches not only adopt the language of the surrounding Islamic community, but they also embrace nonreligious cultural forms such as folk music, dress, and artwork. Nevertheless, a C–3 church intentionally seeks to filter out any religious forms that were specifically associated with Islam, such as keeping the fast of Ramadan or praying with raised hands, and so forth. Although members of C–3 churches continue to call themselves Christians, the majority of the membership is made up of MBBs.

C–4 refers to "contextualized Christ-centered communities using insider language and biblically permissible cultural and Islamic forms." These churches are like C–3, except that Islamic cultural and religious forms are adopted as long as they are not explicitly forbidden in Scripture. For example, Islamic terms for God (*Allah*), prayer (*salat*), and the Gospels (*injil*) are accepted in a C–4 context. Likewise, a C–4

12. John Travis, "The C1 to C6 Spectrum," *Evangelical Missions Quarterly* 34, no. 4 (1998): 407–8. John Travis is a pseudonym. See also Phil Parshall, "Danger! New Directions in Contextualization," *Evangelical Missions Quarterly* 34, no. 4 (1998): 404–6, 409–10; Mark Williams, "Aspects of High-Spectrum Contextualization in Ministries to Muslims," *Journal of Asian Mission* 5, no. 1 (2003): 75–91.

13. In the introductory article Phil Parshall refers to the "C" as referring to "Cross-Cultural Church-Planting Spectrums." However, it is important in my later analysis of this spectrum to note that John Travis in both the text of his explanation as well as the article heading indicates that the "C" stands for "Christ-centered communities." This is confirmed in the numerous citations of the Travis scale throughout the literature.

14. Travis, "The C1 to C6 Spectrum," 407.

church embraces outward practices normally associated as symbols of Islamic faithfulness, such as avoiding pork, abstaining from alcohol, removing shoes when coming to worship, or fasting during Ramadan. C–4 believers normally do not identify themselves with the term *Christian* but would refer to themselves as "followers of *Isa al-Masih*" (Jesus the Messiah), as members of the *Isaya Umma* (Community of Jesus), or other similar expressions.[15] Despite the intentional contextualization, these followers of *Isa* are not regarded by those in the Islamic community as Muslims.

C–5 refers to "Christ-centered communities of 'Messianic Muslims' who have accepted Jesus as Lord and Savior." These followers of *Isa* remain legally and socially within Islam, referring to themselves as Muslims, and are, in fact, regarded by the Muslim community as Muslims. Features of Islamic theology that are clearly incompatible with biblical faith are rejected or cleverly reinterpreted if possible. Approximately half of these C–5 believers continue to attend the mosque, even if they also attend small gatherings of other C–5 believers.[16] Sometimes these gatherings are referred to in missionary writings as "Jesus mosques."[17] Furthermore, the presence of these Christ-loving Muslims who remain fully embedded in the Islamic community are often referred to as being part of an "insider movement."[18] These insider movements have generated considerable discussion in missiological circles in recent years, and articles have even begun to appear in nonmission journals and popular magazines.[19]

C–6 refers to "small Christ-centered communities of secret/underground believers." This category encompasses believers who are living under the threat of extremely hostile persecution and retaliation from the government or from their family or community if they were to reveal that they were followers of Jesus. Therefore, they worship Christ secretly. If discovered, C–6 believers would almost certainly face "a life of suffering, imprisonment, or martyrdom." The C–6 category should be understood as an exceptional circumstance that is one of the tragic challenges to Christian faith in many parts of the world where public confession of Christ is tantamount to imprisonment or martyrdom. Any and all C–6 believers should be the subject of our prayers, not our analysis,[20] so it will not be a part of this discussion, especially since all parties in the contextualization debate are in total agreement that C–6 is a regrettable state and we look for the day when open and free dialogue about religious affiliation in the Islamic world will make C–6 a thing of the past.[21]

15. *Isa* is the Arabic word for Jesus. *Umma* is the Arabic word for community.

16. Parshall, "Danger! New Directions in Contextualization," 406.

17. See, for example, Bridges, "Of 'Jesus Mosques' and Muslim Christians," 19.

18. See, for example, *Mission Frontiers* 27, no. 5 (September–October 2005), which devoted the entire issue to insider movements. Also, the 2005 Conference of the International Society for Frontier Missiology was dedicated to the theme "Insider Movements: Doing Church Where There is No Church."

19. See, for example, Decker, "When 'Christian' Does Not Translate," 8, or Yeoman, "The Stealth Crusade."

20. The church has, of course, faced this situation before. How the church responds to brothers and sisters who risk martyrdom or remain secret believers in times of intense persecution has always had important pastoral as well as theological implications.

21. It should also be noted that C–6 should not be viewed as a continued "extension" along the contextualization scale, since if allowed to express their faith these believers could, quite possibly, choose to worship anywhere along the C–1 to C–5 spectrum.

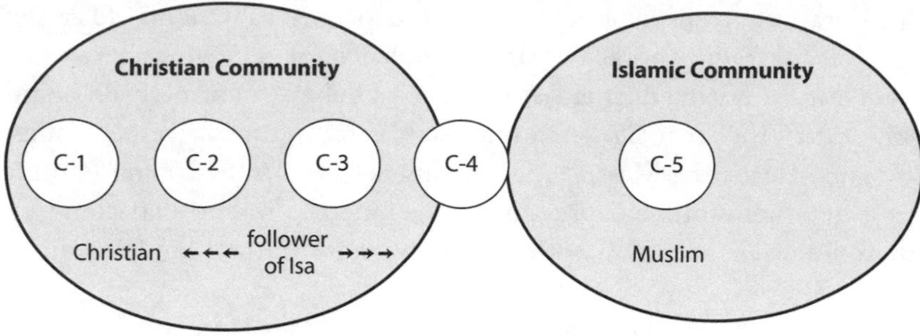

Figure D

Figure D will help to visually place C–1 through C–5 in relation to Christianity and Islam.

Use of the Word "Contextualization"

Before I offer an evaluation of the C–1 to C–5 spectrum, I need to clarify how the term *contextualization* is being used in this discussion. The C–1 to C–5 spectrum is often spoken of as moving from "low" contextualization at the C–1 end of the scale to "high" contextualization at the C–5 end of the scale.[22] This use of the word is rather broad, referring to various ways groups have rejected, accommodated, or embraced the particularities of a local context. In this general usage one could have "good" contextualization and "bad" contextualization.

However, the word *contextualization* is also used more narrowly to refer to the *goal* of a process whereby the universal good news of Jesus Christ is authentically experienced in the particularities of a local context.[23] Thus, what is called "low" contextualization may, in fact, not be contextualization at all but an expression of ethnocentric *extractionism*.[24] Further, what is called "high" contextualization may not be contextualization at all but an expression of *syncretism*. In this definition of the word, contextualization is the positive goal.

In the evaluation that follows, therefore, we will be discussing various models of contextualization while simultaneously searching to discover whether all, or some, or none of these models properly capture contextualization in the Islamic context. Phil Parshall seeks to accommodate the various uses of the term by creating a chart that allows for a "range" of appropriate contextualization to be found, but he also acknowledges a point where it potentially crosses over into syncretism (see Figure E).

The advantage of the chart is that it demonstrates that even though contextualization is the goal, there may be different points along a spectrum whereby in a particular

22. Williams, "Aspects of High-Spectrum Contextualization," 75–91.

23. For a fuller treatment of the meaning and uses of the term *contextualization*, see "Contextualization" in *Evangelical Dictionary of World Missions*, ed. A. Scott Moreau (Grand Rapids: Baker, 2000), 225–27.

24. *Extractionism* is a term used in missiology for the practice of excessive separation from one's cultural context.

Figure E

context the goal of contextualization is achieved. For example, MBBs from an urban, secular subculture in Iran might achieve legitimate contextualization at a point quite different from, say, an ultraorthodox Wahhabi from Saudi Arabia.[25] The shortcoming of Parshall's chart is that it fails to show that just as "high" spectrum contextualization risks the possibility of syncretism, so "low" spectrum contextualization risks the possibility of extractionism. Parshall does note in his article that all must be "constantly cross-referenced and subordinated to biblical truth," but he does not show on the chart what would happen if a particular example of "low" spectrum contextualization were proved unbiblical. Thus, the following chart will, I think, better help us to conceptualize a framework for evaluating the C–1 to C–6 spectrum (see Figure F).

Evaluation of C–1 to C–4

Generally speaking, C–1 and C–2 churches are considered to be overly biased toward foreign cultural and religious forms of Christianity. These churches, while serving the longstanding historic Christians in the region, have not been successful at reaching Muslims with the gospel. It would be naïve to expect these churches to make any significant breakthroughs among Muslims.[26] The reason is that these churches are, by definition, extractionistic in their attitude towards Islamic cultural forms.

By contrast, C–3 and C–4 churches are clearly more effectively positioned to reach Muslims in culturally appropriate ways such that the gospel of Jesus Christ is not overly tainted by foreign associations. Indeed, both C–3 and C–4 church-planting strategies enjoy wide support throughout the missionary community and are regarded

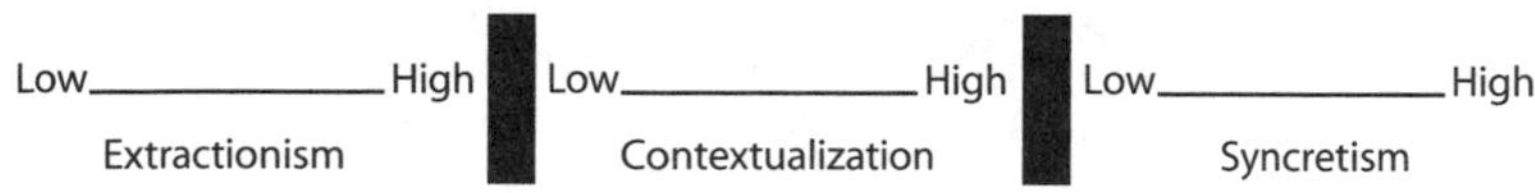

Figure F

25. Joshua Massey has offered an M–1 to M–9 spectrum showing the attitudes of various Muslims towards Islam, ranging from nominal Muslims to Ultra-Orthodox. See his "God's Amazing Diversity in Drawing Muslims to Christ," *International Journal of Frontier Missions* 17, no. 1 (Spring 2000): 12.

26. Joshua Massey argues that there is a number of Iranian MBBs who are so disillusioned with Islam that they strongly object to any cultural or religious forms associated with their past and actually prefer C–1 or C–2 churches. However, rather than simply present C–1 to C–6 as all equally legitimate options as Massey does, we should recognize the vital catechesis needed to help these "disillusioned Muslims" to reject the religion of Islam, but not to reject their cultural and ethnic heritage. After all, extractionism occurs when *either* the missionary insists that new believers leave their culture or when new believers on their own accord leave their culture because they think it is inherently evil and cannot sustain Christian faith. See Joshua Massey, "His Ways Are Not Our Ways," *Evangelical Missions Quarterly* 35, no. 2 (April 1999): 196.

as contextually sensitive as well as biblically sound. In my view, most C–3 and C–4 churches fall within the acceptable parameter of contextualization as depicted in the chart above.

There are some who find it troubling that C–4 followers do not use the term *Christian* and wonder if this movement is actually the beginning of creeping syncretism and, therefore, should be avoided. However, several points about C–4 usually allay these concerns. First, avoidance of the term *Christian* by C–4 MBBs should not be construed as a denial of their Christian identity, since they continue to identify themselves publicly as followers of Jesus.

Second, although MBBs find the term *Christian* offensive, published case studies about MBBs demonstrate that they acknowledge the common faith they share with all those who follow Jesus, even those who may follow Jesus in less contextually sensitive ways. Their unwillingness to call themselves Christians, therefore, is not meant to distance themselves from either Jesus Christ or others who follow Jesus Christ, but is simply an acknowledgment that the word carries connotations that are offensive in their context and actually obscure, rather than illuminate, their identity as a follower of Jesus.[27]

Finally, we should remember that the label *Christian* was not used for the followers of Jesus until the emergence of the first predominately Gentile church in Antioch (Acts 11:26). In fact, it was probably originally a term given by opponents of the church, since it appears only twice in Acts and both times it is a title given to believers by others.[28] There is not a single instance of the apostle Paul using the Greek word *Christianos* to describe the followers of Christ. The earliest believers preferred to identify themselves as belonging to "the Way" (Acts 9:2; 19:23; 24:14).[29] Thus, there is simply no scriptural mandate that insists that those who follow Jesus must be called by a particular communal name.

Evaluation of C–5

Our case study in ecclesiology focuses on C–5. Thus, a more detailed analysis and evaluation will follow. A survey of the published literature concerning C–5 ministries in the Islamic world reveals two things of interest. First, most of the argumentation in favor of C–5 is decidedly ad hoc and is developed as a reaction against criticism that has been posed, rather than given as an independent case that biblically, theologically, historically, and contextually sets forth the necessary arguments. There is currently no single source where a reader can find a complete case for C–5 that sets forth all of the evidence found in the literature.[30]

27. Even in the West, the legacy of "Christendom" has given rise to millions who call themselves "Christian" but who still need to hear and respond to the good news of Jesus Christ. Thus, we must look beyond the outward descriptor in these situations.

28. Acts 11:26; 26:28; the opponents also referred to them as a "sect" or "sect of the Nazarene." This also seems to be the context of the use of the word "Christian" in 1 Peter 4:16.

29. Christians among the Hausa in Islamic-dominated Northern Nigeria refer to themselves as "*Masu Bi*" (lit., "those who believe").

30. This is frequently true of missionary writings driven by field-based realities that often do not afford the time or "luxury" of in-depth writing. Typically, missiological reflection on an issue arises about ten years after the field missionaries first start encountering the problem.

Second, when one closely examines the extensive arguments in favor of C–5, it becomes clear that the vast majority of them are actually brilliant defenses of C–4 ministries and do not really get to the heart of what is required if one is to properly defend C–5 practice. For example, all of the evidence regarding the problems with using the term *Christian* or the effective use of Islamic cultural and religious forms has already, by definition, been accepted by C–4 practitioners. Sometimes, even the case studies provided as empirical evidence to support C–5 are actually case studies of C–4 ministries.[31]

The crucial difference that separates C–4 and C–5 is that of *identity*. All of the major proponents of C–5 agree on this point. For example, Joshua Massey, one of the leading advocates of C–5 practice, writes, "Who could have predicted 20 years ago that God would raise up still another group of missionaries who believe that God wants to take them beyond C4? C4 surely paved the way for C5, *whose major difference is one of identity*."[32]

There are, of course, two sides to the question of identity: how *others* (in this case, Muslims) identify you, and how you identify yourself (i.e., your *self*-identity). Admittedly, there is considerable contextual ambiguity about how Muslims may identify followers of Jesus in the Muslim world. A C–1 Christian, for example, may be identified as an idolatrous fornicator. We have only limited control over how people from other religious communities identify us. The point is, all of the "foreign-type Christians" (C–1 and C–2), the "contextually sensitive Christians" (C–3), and the "followers of *Isa*" (C–4) are identified by Muslims as *not* part of their own Islamic community. I am intentionally stating this in the negative because such an identification does not necessarily imply the positive corollary that Muslims will always identify C–4 practitioners as being part of *some* kind of Christian community.

For example, if a Muslim has been exposed only to C–1 type Christianity and has never actually met MBBs from a C–4 context, it is likely that even though he recognizes that they are not a part of his religious community, he has no ready category in which to place them. That, of course, is one of the strategic advantages of C–4, according to the advocates of C–4 ministries.

But the crucial issue at stake is *self*-identity. C–5 believers are fully embedded in the cultural and religious life of Islam. That is why their presence in the mosque is referred to as an "insider movement," because they really *are* insiders. It is even inaccurate to refer to them (as they often are) as MBBs, because, for them, Islam is not in their *background*; rather, it remains as their primary *identity*. Therefore, they should be called simply Muslim believers (MBs), not Muslim background believers (MBBs).

In other words, the real "bottom-line" question before us is whether a solid case can be made for encouraging a C–5 "Muslim" to continue to identify himself or

31. A classic example of this is found in John Travis's case study about a MBB who "faithfully attends a weekly C4/C5 fellowship and may soon be appointed one of its first elders." Clearly, attending a distinct fellowship that appoints elders is illustrative of an MBB in a C–4, not a C–5 context.

32. Massey, "His Ways Are Not Our Ways," 191, emphasis mine. This is also clear in the original publication of Travis's scale, where he notes that C–5 believers "are viewed as Muslims by the Muslim community and refer to themselves as Muslims who follow *Isa* the Messiah" ("The C1 to C6 Spectrum," 408).

herself as a Muslim, fully part and parcel of the religious and cultural life of Islam, even after such a person has accepted Jesus Christ as Lord and Savior.

The Key Arguments for C–5 Evaluated

All of the evidence offered in missiological literature that actually focuses on C–5 (not just C–4 argumentation embedded in C–5 literature) falls into three general categories. First, *biblical and exegetical* arguments are offered to provide scriptural support for C–5. Second, several *theological* considerations are vital to the very nature of what it means to even be called a follower of Jesus Christ. Indeed, there are important theological implications inherent in the issue of identity that are directly and indirectly present in the C–5 literature. Finally, important *ethical* issues are often addressed in the C–5 writings. I will explore each of these categories to determine whether the growing interest in developing C–5 strategies should be encouraged.[33]

Biblical/Exegetical Arguments

The biblical texts most frequently cited in support of C–5 strategy are Acts 15:19; 1 Corinthians 7:20; 1 Corinthians 9:19–22; and 2 Kings 5:18–19. In addition to these specific texts, supporters of C–5 frequently make reference to the role Judaizers played in opposing the first-century gospel as recorded in various texts of the New Testament.[34] As noted above, while several of these texts do seem to provide compelling support for C–4, the question before us is whether or not they provide support for C–5 and the issue of one's identity as a Muslim in continuity with the religious and cultural context of Islam.

Acts 15 and the Jerusalem Council. The Jerusalem Council is a relevant text for consideration since it involves the first formal church discussion regarding the relationship between two distinct cultural communities, Jewish and Gentile, who, quite surprisingly, were finding a new identity in Jesus Christ. Many of the Jewish leaders harbored deep suspicions and even prejudice against Gentiles and found it scandalizing that they might now be welcomed by God as full and equal participants in the people of God on their own cultural terms. The Jerusalem Council was called to discuss this problem, which is best summarized by the opening verse that captures the heart of the complaint against these new Gentile believers: "Unless you are circumcised, according to the custom taught by Moses, you cannot be saved" (Acts 15:1).

Before examining the decision of the Jerusalem Council, it is crucial to understand that long before the advent of the New Testament, there was already in place an

---

33. I am quite intentional about using the word "should." There is no doubt that, *descriptively* speaking, there will probably always be Muslims who follow Christ in the mosque. The concern of this chapter is whether or not this should be advocated *prescriptively* as a part of an overall mission strategy, as is common in the literature.

34. I am intentionally omitting the extensive biblical case given by Joshua Massey that cites repeated examples throughout the Bible where God does things that are "unexpected" and that go against our conventional expectations. While it is true that "God's ways are not our ways" and that God may, indeed, be doing a sovereign work through C–5 that will surprise us, it could as easily be a movement that ultimately proves fruitless. The point is, it is a classic case of an argument from silence and cannot be offered as proper evidence. Such a line of reasoning could have been used, for example, to support the new, emergent Arianism of the fourth century.

accepted method through which a Gentile could become a full (if not always equal) participant with a Jew in God's redemptive plan. The Old Testament contains many verses that reveal God's heart for the Gentiles.[35] In response to this, there developed an accepted protocol for how a Gentile could be accepted in Israel. A Gentile could become a Jewish *proselyte* by separating from his own culture, becoming circumcised, accepting all of the dietary restrictions of Judaism, and fully accepting the covenantal obligations of the Torah. As Andrew Walls has noted, "to become a proselyte involves the sacrifice of national and social affiliations. It involves a form of naturalization, incorporation into another milieu."[36]

Since this was the established procedure, it should not surprise us that these Judean believers were angry when Paul and others were welcoming Gentiles who continued to live as full participants in their own culture, including following a diet unacceptable to Jews and even remaining uncircumcised. The Jerusalem Council met to discuss whether any or all of these new practices, which had started in Antioch and were later replicated by Paul, should be accommodated or not.

The account of the Jerusalem Council opens with a statement almost identical to the one that opens the entire chapter. Acts 15:5 records that "some of the believers who belonged to the party of the Pharisees stood up and said, 'The Gentiles must be circumcised and required to obey the law of Moses.'" After a heated discussion, Peter, Paul, and Barnabas offered a series of testimonies that made it clear that God, through his giving of the Holy Spirit, was sovereignly accepting and saving the Gentiles (15:6–12) without their following the proselyte model and becoming dislocated from their own culture.

James (Jesus' brother and the leader of the church in Jerusalem) then adds further weight by quoting scriptural support from the prophet Amos. At this juncture James makes the crucial statement that is frequently cited in support of C–5: "It is my judgment, therefore, that we should not make it difficult for the Gentiles who are turning to God" (Acts 15:19). The application made by C–5 advocates is that asking Muslims to separate from their Muslim identity is creating an unnecessary and difficult barrier. Indeed, to insist that a Muslim become a Christian is to follow the old proselyte model. Instead, to allow a Muslim to stay fully connected and integrated with their existing Islamic identity is consistent with the new model posed by the Jerusalem Council.

It seems evident that Acts 15 does provide powerful and compelling support for C–4 strategy in the Muslim world since the Gentiles are not asked to sacrifice their social and national identity. However, in order for this text to be used as a basis for C–5, one must also demonstrate that the Gentiles are not asked to abandon their *religious* identity. In my view, this is a difficult task. James goes on to recommend a list of four things that the Gentiles should be asked to avoid: food polluted by idols,

35. For a good overview of this, see Walter C. Kaiser Jr., *Mission in the Old Testament: Israel as a Light to the Nations* (Grand Rapids: Baker, 2000).

36. Andrew F. Walls, "Old Athens and New Jerusalem: Some Signposts for Christian Scholarship in the Early History of Mission Studies," *International Bulletin of Missionary Research* 21, no. 4 (October 1997): 148.

sexual immorality, the meat of strangled animals, and blood. The council accepts these guidelines.

However, it is important to note that the council did not accept these four prohibitions as some kind of "add-ons" to the Gentiles' faith, so that they were saved by faith plus a short list of duties that served as a kind of Jewish-law-in-miniature. No! The Gentiles were being saved by grace through faith, without compromise or qualification. The prohibitions served to visibly separate the Gentiles from their former *religious* identity as pagans, since all four of these requirements are linked to common pagan practices of the time. This proposal, in turn, would enable the Jews and Gentiles to live out their common faith with a new identity, which, remarkably, is linked to neither the law (the Judean proposal) nor pagan religious practices (the Gentiles' experience) but to a new identity in Jesus Christ.

Thus, Acts 15 represents a generous compromise—the church will retain multiple cultures and lifestyles, but there will always be only one body of Christ. Thus, this passage does seem to provide compelling support for the proposal that Muslims be allowed to retain their cultural identity (C–4), but no support for the view that they be allowed to retain their *religious* identity (C–5). Those who say that Muslims cannot separate religion and culture are ignoring over thirty years of successful C–4 contextualization throughout the entire Islamic world that has proved that MBBs' new identity in Christ is so powerful that it does, in fact, provide a new religious identity without the need to sever their former cultural identity.

Some readers might raise the question if it is fair to equate *pagan* identity with *Islamic* identity since Islam is far closer to Judaism than either is to paganism.[37] Would the Jerusalem Council have insisted that Muslims forsake their *monotheistic* religious identity the way they insisted that the Gentiles forsake their *pagan* religious identity? I think the answer becomes clear by posing two hypothetical scenarios—one from the "Jewish" side of the question (i.e., those who want to compare Islam to Judaism rather than paganism), and the other from the "Gentile" side of the question (i.e., those who longed for the Jewish believers to embrace them with as little dislocation as possible).

Scenario #1. If, hypothetically speaking, Jews had accepted Jesus Christ as the true fulfillment of their own prophetic expectations in sufficient numbers so that faith in the deity and dignity, the person, and the work of Christ became fully identified with Jewish *religious identity*, there would be no reason whatsoever for them to abandon their religious identity with the synagogue and temple.[38] Indeed, the earliest Christians continued to worship in the temple for some time. They were there in the hope that their fellow Jews would see Christ as the proper fulfillment of their own scriptural texts, as he truly was. After all, they had found Jesus *within* Jewish religious identity.

---

37. It is beyond the scope of this chapter to explore the role of pagan practices in folk Islam around the world, which further complicates the C–5 case; thus, in the spirit of charity, we will focus on Islam at its best.

38. It is difficult to fully imagine how the wide acceptance of Jesus would have changed the legal and ritual practices of faithful Judaism. However, this is only hypothetical because there is not a single known example in the ancient world where an entire synagogue community turned to Jesus Christ. There are reports of mosques that have completely turned over to become worshipers of *Isa*, but it is unclear how that has affected their overall identity as Muslims.

However, once they realized that the mainstream Jewish community was not going to accept the view that Jesus was the Lord and the Messiah of their own scriptural, prophetic expectations, it became clear that they had to form a *new* religious identity, namely, the church, which would properly celebrate their identity in Jesus Christ.

How does this apply to our discussion concerning the religious identity of C–5 Muslim believers? It should be noted at the outset that it is difficult to fully compare the situation of Jews (who have the "Old" Testament) hearing the gospel with Muslims (who have the Qur'an) hearing the gospel because of the more profound continuity between Judaism and Christianity. Nevertheless, continuing with our hypothetical scenario, if the vast majority of Muslims were to miraculously recognize the true deity and dignity, the person, and the work of Jesus Christ, such that the mosque became a place where Jesus was truly worshiped, then there would be no reason for a Muslim believer to seek a new religious identity, because the very religious identity of Islam would have changed. But since this did not occur, there must inevitably be a separation at the level of religious identity, which is precisely what happened with the early Jewish believers.

It should be noted that encouraging a new and separate religious identity (contra C–5) does not mean that there are not points of *continuity* between one's former identity and their new identity. Indeed, the transference of religious identity does not necessitate a complete disruption or dislocation with the prior religious identity. The point is simply that the unique person of Jesus creates a new identity.

Scenario #2. The second hypothetical scenario seeks to discover if some minimalist list of prohibitions could be agreed upon that would allow a Muslim to retain his or her religious identity with Islam, *along with some qualifications* such that they could retain their status as a Muslim. The challenge is that the prohibitions would have to be strong enough to allow a Muslim follower of Jesus to be faithful to Christ and the gospel even within his Islamic religious identity, yet generous enough to allow him to maintain his religious identity without falling into a life of constant lying and deception. In this imaginary scenario, which I will call the Cairo Council, Gentile followers of Jesus (who are now the insiders!) meet and after a heated discussion decide not to make life too difficult for these new believers within Islam, but to set forth the following three mandates, which are then sent to key leading Muslim followers of Jesus in the Arab world:

1. During the daily *salat*, refrain from saying the *Shahadah* unless you omit the second phrase, "and Muhammad is the Prophet of Allah," and instead insert, "and *Isa* is the Eternal Word of Allah" or "and *Isa* is the Sovereign Lord."[39]
2. Acknowledge that only the Bible is the Word of God and that the Qur'an, while containing beautiful Arabic and important insights into Arab culture, has no authority over the Bible.[40]

39. Surah 4:171 extends the honorific title "Word" (of Allah) to Jesus, providing a contextual bridge to John 1:1.

40. It is true that the Qur'an is not nearly as offensive to Christian doctrine as is sometimes supposed. However, the only way MBBs have successfully been able to retain the Qur'an (or some portions of it) is if the Bible is used as the hermeneutic to constantly redirect, reinterpret, and clarify various texts in the Qur'an. For more on this see chapter 7 of my *Christianity at the Religious Roundtable*, 169–94.

3. When you are reciting the ninety-nine beautiful names of Allah with a *shubha*, add the following three: (a) God and Father of our Lord Jesus Christ, (b) Holy Spirit, and (c) Blessed Trinity (or Tri-unity).[41]

It should be noted that there are several at the Cairo Conference who insist that a fourth be added, namely, the "Risen One." But, after much discussion the council thinks that Christ's resurrection is sufficiently implied in the titles "Lord Jesus Christ" and "Blessed Trinity" (or Tri-unity) and so it is not necessary to add a fourth. The point is, the Cairo Conference really works hard to be as generous as possible with these new Muslim believers. The question is this: Can a "Muslim" disciple of Jesus Christ, as espoused by the C–5 strategists, maintain his or her *religious* identity with Islam even if the only adjustments they make are the above three minimalist prohibitions?

The answer is most certainly not. These three strike at the heart of Islamic *religious* identity, namely, the prophethood of Muhammad, the sacred perfection and superiority of the Qur'an, and a rejection of Allah's Triune nature. The moment any Muslim discovers that someone claiming to be a Muslim has these particular beliefs in these three areas, they will automatically see that particular "Muslim" as someone with a religious identity in discontinuity with their own identity. Furthermore, the Muslim believer (MB) who is seeking to maintain his self-identity as a Muslim must also sense the profound ethical burden of living a life of integrity while knowing that his central core confession is in profound discontinuity with the core confession of Islam. Thus, while I find Acts 15 a compelling defense for C–4, I am less convinced that it provides a sufficient basis for justifying C–5.

1 Corinthians 7:20. The apostle Paul declares in 1 Corinthians 7:20 that "each one should remain in the situation which he was in when God called him." The context of the verse has to do with Paul's heightened eschatological sense that the coming of Jesus has thrust us into the climax of the ages. In Jesus Christ, the age to come is breaking into the present evil age, calling us to decisive action. The in-breaking of the kingdom is so powerful and the gospel is such good news that Paul did not want the Corinthians to waste their time being preoccupied with their earthly status. You can sense the urgency in the text: If you are unmarried, don't seek to get married (v. 27)! If you are a slave, don't be troubled about it (v. 21)! If you are uncircumcised, then don't get circumcised (v. 18)! The question before us is whether this text can, by extension, be construed to mean, "If you are a Muslim, don't worry about becoming a non-Muslim!" In other words, can the text be applied to one's religious identity?

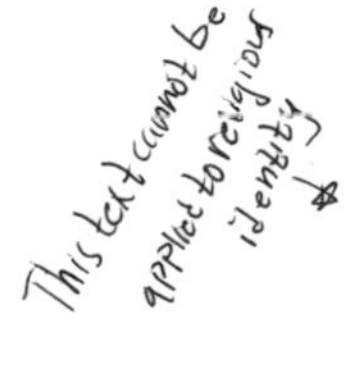

Two of the three examples Paul gives, slavery and marriage, clearly relate to *social* status and cannot reasonably be held to apply to a *religious* context. The reference to cir-

41. A *shubha* is a set of rosary-like prayer beads that are commonly used by Muslims to recite the ninety-nine beautiful names of Allah. Since most Muslims use a *shubha* with only thirty-three beads, which they will cycle through three times, it is also practical to only add "three" names to the ninety-nine. It means, practically speaking, adding only one extra bead. Although it should be noted that even when Islam and Christianity agree on a certain attribute of God, such as "power" (*al-muqtadir*, one of the ninety-nine names), there may be striking differences on how it is understood. For example, Christians sees God's greatest power over Satan exhibited in the weakness and vulnerability of the cross; Muslims would not understand God's power in such terms. Thus, all of the ninety-nine names require adjustments as they are conformed to the biblical witness.

cumcision is more interesting. For a Jew, the act of circumcision carried strong social, cultural, *and* religious connotations. Being circumcised was clearly a part of Jewish *religious* identity. So could Paul be saying that Gentile believers should not worry about changing their religious identity? If so, then this text could be interpreted as saying, in effect, "The time is so urgent, if you are a follower of Jesus in the mosque, don't worry about leaving the mosque—stay there, because time is short and the kingdom is at hand!"

However, since the whole purpose of this urgency is to help more and more people to recognize the true identity of Jesus Christ, it is unlikely that such an application can be made from this text since the mosque is a place where the deity of Jesus is denied. The well-known text in Hebrews 10:25, "let us not give up meeting together," is apparently a reference to Jewish Christians who were starting to neglect their attendance at the Christian assemblies and, instead, were attending only the Jewish synagogue worship. The writer of Hebrews does not encourage those early Christians to "stay in the synagogue"; rather, he emphasizes the priority of their new Christian identity, even though they were ethnic Jews.

Paul in 1 Corinthians 7:20 is most likely referring to Gentile believers who were wondering if they should follow the old "proselyte model" discussed earlier and be circumcised to gain full acceptance into the kingdom. Their problem was actually just the opposite of what is posed by C–5 advocates. These Gentiles who were showing interest in becoming circumcised are more like those cultural reactionaries who want to completely leave their cultural background and unite with a C–1 or C–2 church! Paul tells them that such a drastic change is not necessary. Once again, this text provides possible support for C–4, but given the context, it is unlikely that it can be cited with confidence to support C–5 strategy.

1 Corinthians 9:19–22. This second text from 1 Corinthians is often cited in support of C–5 ministries. Here Paul boldly declares his willingness to submit to and enter into the context of those whom he is seeking to reach:

> I make myself a slave to everyone, to win as many as possible. To the Jews I became like a Jew, to win the Jews. To those under the law I became like one under the law (though I myself am not under the law), so as to win those under the law. To those not having the law I became like one not having the law (though I am not free from God's law but am under Christ's law), so as to win those not having the law.... I have become all things to all men so that by all possible means I might save some.

I think missiologists are in broad agreement that this text provides support for those who are engaged in incarnational, rather than extractionistic, ministries. The first job of missionaries is to enter into the experience and life-view of those they are seeking to reach; the incarnation of our Lord is the greatest example of this. This text does appear to provide further support for C–4 ministries. Indeed, we must fully enter the sociopolitical and cultural world of those we are seeking to reach for Christ. But does this text also teach that we should take on the *religious* identity of Jews or Gentiles—and, by extension, that of Muslims in reaching them for Jesus Christ?

It seems inconceivable to me that this could be presented as a reliable exegesis of this text. The very fact that Paul could become *like* a Jew in one context and *like* a Gentile in another clearly demonstrates that he is not becoming self-identified as a Jew or Gentile in the way that would be required if one wanted to quote this text in support of C–5. Indeed, through the use of the two qualifiers, Paul clearly shows in the text that he is *not* fully identifying with them in this way. When he is with a Jew, he lives as a law keeper, but then he qualifies the statement by reminding the readers that in his actual identity in Christ, he is not under the law. Likewise, when he is with a Gentile, he lives like one without the law, but then he qualifies that as well by reminding them that our identity with Christ does not give us a license for antinomianism, a message the Corinthians certainly needed to remember!

In recent years this text has become even less relevant to the discussion, since both of the leading advocates of C–5 contextualization, John Travis and Joshua Massey, have restricted C–5 to those who were brought up in Islam and later became followers of Christ, rather than using it as a prescriptive missionary strategy for outsiders seeking to win Muslims for Christ. In other words, even the leading advocates of C–5 are not encouraging outsiders to "become Muslims" in order to reach Muslims. For example, in "Messianic Muslim Followers of Jesus," John Travis says, "I personally cannot endorse Christians claiming to be Muslims for outreach."[42] We must keep this vital point in mind as more and more mission organizations and large churches are discussing how C–5 may or may not be utilized in the development of mission strategy and policy decisions.

2 Kings 5:18–19. The final text to be considered in this survey of the key passages quoted by supporters of C–5 is found in the Old Testament. The passage is about a request made to the prophet Elisha by the mighty soldier Naaman as he is about to return home to Aram. Naaman says, "But may the LORD forgive your servant for this one thing: When my master enters the temple of Rimmon to bow down and he is leaning on my arm and I bow there also—when I bow down in the temple of Rimmon, may the LORD forgive your servant for this." In reply, Elisha declares, "Go in peace." Because Elisha does not sharply rebuke Naaman, this passage has been seized as an example of God's grace for Muslims who continue to perform ritual prayers (*salat*) in the mosque but in their heart are actually worshiping Jesus, thus providing legitimacy for C–5.

It is difficult to fully evaluate the application of this passage to a C–5 situation because of several contextual ambiguities in the text. We do not know, for example, precisely *why* Naaman's master would be leaning on his arm as they enter the temple. Is it because of the frailty of the master, who physically could not bow down before Rimmon without the assistance of his trusted commander? If so, then it is out of pure compassion for his master that he is assisting him in the temple of Rimmon. Thus, we could perhaps make a case for a MBB who does not normally attend the mosque

42. John Travis, "Messianic Muslim Followers of Jesus," *International Journal of Frontier Missions* 17, no. 1 (Spring 2000): 55. See Parshall, "Danger! New Directions in Contextualization," 409, as well as John Travis, "Two Responses," *Evangelical Missions Quarterly* 34 (1998): 411–15. Travis agrees with Parshall's concerns about "outsiders" becoming Muslims (413). See also Massey, "God's Amazing Diversity," 5.

being forgiven if he, as an act of honoring his father, helps his ailing and feeble father into the mosque every Friday. We have already noted in chapter 4 the importance of honor in the ancient world.

Another possibility is that Naaman raises this issue before Elisha because he fears for his life if he does not accompany his master and bow down beside him in the temple. Would his master have him executed if he did not bow? If so, this text could actually provide some encouragement for a C–6 believer who remains silent about his faith because of a real threat of torture, imprisonment, or martyrdom.

The point is, the ambiguities in the text do not allow for a substantial exegetical contribution to this discussion. The one thing we *do* know is that the context of the passage is about Naaman asking for *forgiveness* for doing something they both know is wrong. Clearly, the prophet is not *blessing* Naaman or promoting any strategy of Naaman as a follower of Rimmon who actually worships Yahweh in order to draw other worshipers of Rimmon to the true knowledge of Yahweh. It seems clear that Naaman sees his bowing as a barrier to his effective witness rather than as a stepping-stone to a more effective witness.

We will conclude this biblical section by reflecting on the frequent parallels that are drawn between the first-century Judaizers who opposed Paul and the twenty-first century Christians who oppose the C–5 advocates. The Judaizers were Pharisees who believed in Christ but maintained that no non-Jew could be saved without being circumcised and observing the law of Moses. In short, the Christian faith was seen to be a subset of Judaism, lacking the cultural translatability that proved so decisive in the gospel's powerful penetration of the Hellenistic world. In our current discussion, the Judaizers become symbolic of those who are skeptical and defensive about Muslims finding Christ on their *own* cultural terms rather than first converting to some "foreign" religion known as "Christianity."

Many of the writers promoting C–5 "contextualization" make use of this comparison, but none quite as extensively as Joshua Massey, who adopts it as a major part of his important article, "God's Amazing Diversity." Massey writes, "C5 practitioners insist that even as Paul argued tirelessly with Judaizers that Gentiles did not have to convert to Judaism to follow Jesus, Muslims do not have to convert to 'Christianity' to follow Jesus."[43] Massey goes on to set up a kind of dialogue between a C–5 opponent (the Judaizer) and a C–5 practitioner (Joshua Massey). The C–5 opponent argues, "How could anyone who identifies himself as any kind of Muslim be a genuine follower of Jesus? To call oneself 'Muslim' means they adhere to certain Islamic beliefs that flatly contradict Scripture!"[44] Massey's reply is as follows:

> That sounds like the same argument Judaizers used against Paul since Gentiles were well known by all Jews to be unclean, uncircumcised, and mostly sexually immoral idolaters—all violating clear biblical teachings. "How is it possible,"

43. Massey, "God's Amazing Diversity," 8. Even Ralph Winter invokes the Judaizer parallel in his editorial introducing the cover story, "Can We Trust Insider Movements?" See *Mission Frontiers* 27, no. 5 (September–October 2005): 4.

44. Massey, "God's Amazing Diversity," 8.

> Judaizers must have asked Paul, "to be both Gentile and a follower of Jesus? The two terms are mutually exclusive!"[45]

The argument in a nutshell is that Gentiles did not have to convert to Judaism to follow Jesus; therefore, Muslims should not have to convert to "Christianity" to follow Jesus. In response, we must begin by remembering that the choice is not a binary one between C–5 Muslims who are culturally and religiously identified with Islam and some shockingly extractionistic C–1 church plopped down into the middle of an Islamic country with wooden pews, an English liturgy, tall steeples, and stained-glass windows. C–4 practitioners already agree that a Muslim does not have to convert to "Christianity" (read, *Western* forms of Christianity) to follow Jesus. As noted earlier, the most striking feature of pro-C–5 literature is that the vast majority of what is argued actually reinforces the good missiology of C–4 and remains largely silent about the identity question, which is the central difference between C–4 and C–5.

In other words, it *would* be Judaistic to pressure a new believer in the Muslim world to adopt all of our cultural accoutrements. But this does not provide much help in resolving the issue of Islamic *religious* identity, because from Paul's perspective the issue was not about "staying in" Judaism or "staying in" paganism, but about the recognition that both Jew and Gentile must together identify themselves as sinners in need of grace and together find their new identity in Jesus Christ. The Judaizers were wrong, not so much because they saw the paganism in the Gentile world but because they failed to see the wickedness in their own. The only hope is to find a new identity together as the redeemed people of God, made up of both Jew and Gentile.

In conclusion, this survey demonstrates that the key texts and the commentaries/expositions about these texts in C–5 literature fall into two general categories: (1) texts and commentary that actually support C–4 and are not germane to the C–5 discussion; (2) a widespread use of proof-texting whereby a predetermined conclusion has already been reached and texts are then found to provide some kind of vague support for the idea.

I have tried to remedy this deficiency by focusing squarely on the key issue of one's self-identity and then honestly engaging with the most-cited texts to determine if their original meaning can be used to support more aggressive methods of contextualization. My conclusion is that several of these texts *do* seem to provide strong support for C–4, but I remain unconvinced that they have provided any substantial support to the proponents of C–5. However, there are several important theological and ethical matters that have not yet been addressed, and it is to them that we now turn.

Theological Arguments

Until recently, no published research has appeared on the theology of Muslim believers (MBs) who follow Jesus (*Isa*) and yet retain their identity as Muslims.[46]

45. Ibid.

46. This is mainly due to important security issues, as well as the limited access outsiders have to these insider movements.

However, in 1998 well-known author and missionary Phil Parshall published a study performed by twenty-five teams who interviewed seventy-two key leaders from sixty-six villages who are all C–5 believers and are believed to represent 4,500 C–5 believers.[47] Several encouraging things were revealed in the survey. For example, many of these leaders (76 percent) were quietly meeting with other C–5 believers for worship, Bible study, and fellowship. A surprising 97 percent said that "Jesus is the only Savior," indicating that the exclusivist tendencies that typify much of Islamic theology has been transferred over and applied to Jesus Christ by these Muslim believers. Another encouraging sign is that there did seem to be a growing recognition of the limitations of Muhammad as compared with Jesus Christ. For example, 97 percent said that "they are not saved because of Muhammad's prayers."[48]

Despite this good news, there was also some disturbing information. For example, 96 percent still believed that the Qur'an was one of four holy books from heaven, along with the Torah (Law), the Zabur (Prophets), and the Injil (Gospel); 66 percent even said that the Qur'an was the greatest of the four; and a full 45 percent do not even affirm that God is Father, Son, and Holy Spirit (i.e., the Trinity).[49] These details are particularly disturbing since the figures represent the *leadership* of the movement, which one should assume has the highest level of knowledge about the Christian faith.

Parshall is concerned enough about these findings to question whether Muslim believers in Christ who retain their Islamic identity can reasonably be expected to flourish as the church of Jesus Christ.[50] Joshua Massey, among others, downplays these theological problems by insisting that this is just another example of imposing what he calls "Greco-Roman Gentile categories of orthodoxy."[51] Instead, he argues that we should focus on their personal faith experience with Jesus. He argues that

47. For an examination of the results of this survey, see Parshall, "Danger! New Directions in Contextualization," 404–10. All of the findings mentioned in this section of the chapter are from this study.

48. Although the Qur'an does not teach the efficacy of Muhammad's prayers, the *Hadith* does. Therefore, it is a widely held belief among some groups of Muslims.

49. Parshall, "Danger! New Directions in Contextualization," 406. It gives me little comfort to hear someone quote statistics on the declining faith in mainstream, liberal Protestants where the content of faith may be even less than some of these C–5 MBBs. These liberal Protestants are living in disobedience to their own tradition, which, despite their defiance and unbelief, fully affirms the historic creeds of the faith.

50. Ibid.

51. Joshua Massey, "Misunderstanding C–5: His Ways Are Not Our Orthodoxy," *Evangelical Missions Quarterly* 40, no. 3 (July 2004): 297. In the full-text online version of this article, Massey clearly distances himself from historic Christian views of Christology. Massey, for example, does not affirm the eternal preexistence of Christ. For him, Christ is preexistent only "in the mind, plan and intentions of God, before the foundations of the earth." He is supportive of those theologians who, in his words, "describe the incarnation not as the human birth of an eternally pre-existent Son within the Godhead, but as the self-revelation of God in Christ" (p. 4, online version: http://bgc.gospelcom.net/emis/pdfs/Misunderstanding_C5.pdf). Like the Arians of old, Massey affirms that Jesus is "far greater than any prophet, judge or former 'representative of God,'" but Massey does not believe that Jesus shares the same essence with the Father. He provides a detailed survey of most of the major biblical texts related to Christology and consistently demonstrates that he favors an Arian, rather than Chalcedonian, explanation. Indeed, Massey regards Chalcedonian Christology as an expression of Greek arrogance rather than a careful study of the biblical evidence concerning Christ. However, the precision of the Chalcedonian formula was necessary to defend against the Arians, who denied Christ's true and full deity, and the Apollinarians, who denied his true and full humanity. Massey has forgotten that the Arians were good at quoting Scripture, but, in the long run, the church did not accept their position as the best answer for *all* of the biblical data. It was necessary to use the most precise words available to them to respond to various proposals, such as Monophysitism, Nestorianism, and Arianism. See Jaroslav Pelikan, *The Christian Tradition: A History of the Development of Doctrine*, vol. 1, *The Emergence of the Catholic Tradition (100–600)* (Chicago: Univ. of Chicago Press, 1975), 249.

C–5 advocates should be "more concerned about true Christ-centeredness than with conformity to Gentle Christian traditions and doctrinal codifications developed centuries after the apostolic era."[52]

Rick Brown agrees, stating that "there is no verse that says one must understand the divinity of Jesus to be saved." He continues:

> These doctrines about the deity of Jesus and his substitutionary punishment are wonderful parts of the Good News, and it is worthwhile discussing them with seekers, as Paul demonstrated in Romans. But the overwhelming biblical witness is that although these doctrines are important for the disciple to understand, an understanding of them is not required for salvation.[53]

Brown does not expressly set out to demean the importance of the core doctrines of the faith, although the tone of his writing may initially strike the reader in that manner. Rather, his purpose is to make a distinction between what may be important to know in the long run as opposed to what is absolutely necessary to know in order to be saved.

There are other mission organizations working among Muslims that disagree strongly with this position and insist on certain basic theological understandings that must accompany faith from the outset. Some, for example, insist on belief in the authority of the Bible and the Trinity. Others focus specifically on theological propositions related to the person of Christ, such as faith in the deity of Christ or his resurrection.[54] Who is right? This is obviously a crucial question for all evangelists and missionaries, but it seems particularly important for those contemplating a ministry among Muslims, where certain unorthodox views about Christ (that he is a prophet, not God) and the Bible (it has been distorted and is inferior to the Qur'an) are already present in the "DNA" of Islam.

An evaluation of this problem must begin by acknowledging that it is a long-standing issue in the church, which cannot be resolved easily. The issue is complex and fraught with several potential misunderstandings. Nevertheless, three crucial points of clarification must be made before any further light can be shed on it.

First, popular Protestant theology has tended to equate the doctrine of salvation with the doctrine of justification. Biblically, the doctrine of salvation does include justification, but it also includes the doctrines of sanctification and our final glorification.[55] This is why the Scripture speaks of salvation in all three tenses: you *were* saved (justification), you are *being* saved (sanctification), and you *will be* saved (glorification).[56]

A theological reductionism that equates salvation with justification is so common in popular Protestant writings that we often fail to recognize how this influences our discussions related to soteriology. For example, it often gives rise to a minimalistic

52. Massey, "Misunderstanding C–5: His Ways Are Not Our Orthodoxy," 300.

53. Rick Brown, "What Must One Believe about Jesus for Salvation," *International Journal of Frontier Missions* 17, no. 4 (Winter 2000): 14–15.

54. Ibid., 13.

55. Louis Berkhof, for example, states that "God does not impart the fullness of His salvation to the sinner in a single act." It is only by distinguishing between God's "judicial" acts and his "re-creative" acts that we can properly discuss the fullness of God's plan of salvation for us (*Systematic Theology* [Grand Rapids: Eerdmans, 1941], 416).

56. See, for example, Ephesians 2:5; 1 Corinthians 1:18; 3:15.

emphasis in Protestant discussions concerning salvation. We are often preoccupied with what is the absolute bottom-line minimum an individual has to know or believe in order to be *justified.* Of course, when the issue is framed in this way, it is evident that little is required. After all, how much theology did the thief on the cross know? What about the Philippian jailer or Lydia and her household? I think everyone can agree, as Dean Gilliland has correctly pointed out, that the Holy Spirit can still be active "in poorly informed, sometimes misguided believers."[57] So the issue is framed, at least in part, around what is actually meant by the word *salvation.*

Second, popular Protestant theology has also tended to emphasize the faith of the individual rather than the collective faith of the community of believers. We are much more comfortable speaking about the faith of *individuals* than we are about the faith of the *church.* When Jude says, "I had to write and urge you to contend for the faith that was once for all entrusted to the saints" (Jude 3), both of the words "you" and "saints" are in the plural. Paul, in his great chapter on the resurrection, declares, "this is what we preach, and this is what you believed" (1 Cor. 15:11). Paul saw his preaching in continuity with the apostolic preaching ("*we* preach"), and he declares this to the church ("*you* [plural] believed"). It is important to recognize this phraseology even though the very context of the passage reveals that there were *individuals* in the church who did not, at least on this point, believe along with the church.

So, once again, how the question is framed tends to produce a particular answer. If you ask, "What is the minimal core confession of the church regarding salvation?" then the bar is raised and we find the church far more articulate about the core of salvific faith. The Apostles' Creed and the Nicene Creed are examples of the early church's attempt to put down into a short list the most basic theological propositions that unite the *church* in a common faith. The church did this even though they also must surely have realized, as we do today, that there are many justified *individuals* who neither understand, nor fully believe, every single article of faith in these documents.

The gap between the faith of the historic church and the faith of many of the individuals in the church is why these truths are confessed week after week in the churches. It is essential that the faith of the church be reinforced on all those who claim to be followers of Christ. So a technical rewording of Rick Brown's article, "What Must One Believe about Jesus for Salvation?" is actually, "What must an *individual* believe about Jesus for *justification*?" for *that* is what his article addresses.

Third, this debate tends to slip into the modern trap of putting the "personal" and the "propositional" at odds with one another. For example, some want to emphasize that a personal relationship with Jesus Christ is all that matters; others want to make sure that certain historic propositions are affirmed. This latter group is accused of placing too much emphasis on defending the written words of Scripture and certain doctrinal formulations (rather than Jesus Christ). They are asked, "What is the value of confessing a mountain of creeds and doctrinal formulations if, at root, we do not have a personal relationship with Jesus Christ?"

57. Dean Gilliland, "Context Is Critical in 'Islampur' Case," *Evangelical Missions Quarterly* 34, no. 4 (October 1998): 417.

Those who emphasize the propositional truths respond by insisting that the only way we know anything about God that is distinctively and properly called *Christian* is because God has spoken to humanity in a free act of self-disclosure. In obedience to this revelation, God's servants have faithfully recorded these words in the Bible. Without the Bible, they argue, how can we distinguish between the personal faith of a Muslim and the personal faith of a Christian?

Thus, we are put in the unenviable position of being forced to choose between God revealing himself or God revealing truths about himself. A close examination of the articles related to C–5 reveals that this dichotomy is present in much of the discussion, although it is never acknowledged.

Hopefully the reader is now beginning to realize the importance of the relationship between soteriology and ecclesiology. On the one hand, the farther the doctrine of salvation is allowed to drift away from the church and closer to individualism, the more likely a group will downplay the particulars of specific doctrinal formulations, because the focus is on the individual's personal relationship with Christ. Also, it is far more likely that this group would tend to equate the doctrine of salvation with the doctrine of justification. On the other hand, the closer the doctrine of salvation is tethered to the life of the church through time (history) and space (around the world), then the more likely it is that a group will emphasize our common faith and the importance of even a brand-new believer realizing the faith he or she is being united with.

A new convert not only *has* faith, he or she is brought *into* a common faith. This group will have more of a long-term view of salvation, even if they still emphasize the importance of a particular point of conversion. They will also tend to emphasize that even if a particular MBB is the only Christian in a region or village, they should be made to understand from the outset their connection to other Christians or followers of Jesus who share a common faith. This understanding explains why parachurch organizations that focus on *evangelism* often have very different views on this issue compared to *church-planting* organizations. This is clearly seen, for example, in the article by David Garrison entitled "Church Planting Movements vs. Insider Movements," which points out the need to connect the evangelistic energy of parachurch sodalities with new dynamic models of church planting.[58]

In conclusion, an examination of the current evidence of the theological content of C–5 believers in Jesus as well as the general theological framework of the advocates of C–5 reveals the following. First, C–5 writings tend toward theological reductionism by tacitly embracing a narrow, minimalistic view of salvation. If these new believers are not encouraged to unite their fledgling faith with the faith of the church, then it is unlikely that these new believers will be able to properly reproduce the faith, which is the whole reason the C–5 strategy exists—namely, to reduce every possible barrier so that the gospel can more easily reproduce among Muslims.

Second, the theological framework and analysis present in C–5 writings has been overly influenced by Western individualism and the privatization of faith,

58. David Garrison, "Church Planting Movements vs. Insider Movements: Missiological Realities vs. Mythiological Speculations, *International Journal of Frontier Missions* 21, no. 4 (Winter 2004): 151–54.

which tends to keep the doctrines of soteriology and ecclesiology at arms length.[59] Joshua Massey concedes this point when he observes that "C5 nomenclature was quickly adopted by those whose theology of mission is more Christ-centered than church-centered."[60]

While Massey is correct in criticizing an ecclesiology that merely extends a Western, structural form of Christianity into the Muslim world, we must not forget that we cannot have a Christ-centered theology of mission that does not place the church at the center of Christ's redemptive plan. Rejecting this old "proselyte model" does not and should not necessitate a rejection of a proper ecclesiology. Indeed, as Lesslie Newbigin has pointed out, "true conversion involves both a new creation from above ... [and] also a relationship with the existing community of believers."[61] To encourage Muslim believers to retain their self-identity as Muslims reveals a view of the church that is clearly sub-Christian.[62]

Finally, the separation of the personal from the propositional in the Muslim world can only lead to a dangerous separation of the person of Christ from the church's proclamation about Christ. This separation fails to attend to the proper connection between our personal testimony (however thrilling and exciting) and the apostolic proclamation of the gospel. This is not just a hypothetical concern, as this dichotomy has already begun to emerge in such articles as "Proclaiming a 'Theologyless' Christ" by Herbert Hoefer, a leading proponent of "high spectrum" contextualization. Hoefer writes:

> Can we look upon the church as a house with many doors? It doesn't matter which door you use to enter. As you explore the house, you will come to the fullness of truth. The key to each door in the house is the acceptance of Jesus as Lord of one's life. How one explains that is a matter of freedom and creativity, in consultation with the others in the house.[63]

The unintended result of this view is that personal experience can be used to ignore the specifics of the apostolic proclamation. Or to put it in the popular terminology of postmodernism, the apostolic "metanarrative" takes a backseat to the personal narratives of those who come to Christ.[64] However, our personal faith in Christ must be brought into resonance with the apostolic proclamation *about* Christ.

59. For more on the relationship between "conversion" and "community" see Timothy Tennent, "The Challenge of Churchless Christianity: An Evangelical Assessment," *International Bulletin of Missionary Research* 29, no. 4 (October 2005): 171–77.

60. Massey, "Misunderstanding C-5: His Ways Are Not Our Orthodoxy," 300.

61. Lesslie Newbigin, *The Finality of Christ* (London: SCM, 1969), 107. Roland Allen prophetically warned the missionary community working with Muslims that if they did not advocate a strong ecclesiology, they would produce "mere isolated Churchless Christians" (*The Spontaneous Expansion of the Church* [London: World Dominion Press, 1956], 35).

62. There is an inherent contradiction in the fact that all of the "Cs" in the C–1 to C–6 scale stand for "Christ-centered community," and yet as long as the believer retains one's self-identity as a Muslim, he or she remain in an Allah-centered community.

63. Herbert Hoefer, "Proclaiming a 'Theologyless' Christ," *International Journal of Frontier Missions* 22, no. 3 (Fall 2005): 98.

64. See C. S. Lewis, *Mere Christianity* (New York: Macmillan, 1952), 135–36. Lewis makes the helpful analogy comparing a "map" of the shoreline with a person who has actually experienced the shoreline. Lewis points out that although the person who walks along the shore has a more immediate experience, it should not take away from us the importance of the map based on previous and accumulated knowledge. The apostolic tradition is an essential guide to our own individual experience.

Undoubtedly, millions of people come to Christ every year with a deficient theology. But it is central to the task of discipleship to help new believers conform their faith to the faith of the church. Pragmatism can never be allowed to trump the theological integrity of the gospel message. Cultural accommodations cannot be extended at the expense of theological compromise. This is not to raise questions about the justification of any of these new believers; rather, it is a commitment to make sure that from the beginning we are committed to raising up believers whose personal faith resonates with the "faith that was once for all entrusted to the saints" (Jude 3).

Ethical Arguments

The third and final area necessary to completing this analysis of C–5 is that of ethics. Several writers and field missionaries have raised questions about the ethics of the C–5 strategy. Is it ethical, they ask, to encourage followers of Jesus to remain embedded within Islamic community and retain their Muslim self-identity? In reply, it should be noted that all of the leading advocates of C–5 are in broad agreement that it is both unwise and unethical for a person with a non-Islamic background to enter into a Muslim community and pretend to be a Muslim. As I understand it, C–5 is about someone *retaining* one's identity, not taking on a Muslim identity. The real question is whether it is ethical for Muslim followers of Jesus Christ to retain their identity as Muslims even after they have become devoted followers of Jesus Christ.

Joshua Massey argues that the negative associations with "Christianity" are so strong that these new believers identify more with Islam than they do with Christianity. He points out that

> when C5 believers compare themselves to C1–C2 Christians they say, "I don't pray like a Christian, unwashed in a pew with my shoes on; I pray like a Muslim. I don't dress like a Christian, with Western pants and collared shirts; I dress like a Muslim. I don't talk like a Christian with all their strange terms to describe God and his prophets; I talk like a Muslim. I don't eat like a Christian ... eating *haram* meats.... I don't have a Christian name, like John, Tom or Paul; I have a Muslim name." Thus, C5 believers are being entirely honest when they identify themselves as "Muslim" followers of Jesus.[65]

In response, it is not entirely clear how this actually addresses the ethical point under consideration, since the C–4 contextualized witness would answer all of the above concerns. Massey's argument would be an excellent defense against C–1 or C–2 Christians who were insisting that MBBs identify with some noncontextualized expression of Christianity. The real point that must be defended is the ethics of retaining Muslim *religious* identity, not just Islamic *cultural* identity. We must not lose sight of the fact that what distinguishes C–5 from C–4 is the *religious* self-identity as a Muslim, not the cultural identification that is at the heart of C–4.

65. Massey, "God's Amazing Diversity in Drawing Muslims to Christ," 9. The term *haram* is defined by Massey as "meat not butchered in the 'kosher' way."

The retaining of one's *religious* identity within Islam after becoming a follower of Christ is, in my view, unethical. As Parshall has pointed out, "the mosque is pregnant with Islamic theology. There, Muhammad is affirmed as a prophet of God and the divinity of Christ is consistently denied." Parshall goes on to point out the sacramental nature of the ritual prayers (*salat*).[66] Lesslie Newbigin once wrote the following in response to a movement of churchless Christians in India, but which powerfully applies to the Muslim background believers as well:

> The acceptance of Jesus Christ as central and decisive creates some kind of solidarity among those who have this acceptance in common. If it did not do so, it would mean nothing. The question is, what is the nature of this solidarity? It has always been understood to include the practice of meeting together to celebrate with words, songs and formal actions the common faith in Jesus ... a man who is religiously, culturally and socially part of the Hindu community is a Hindu. [67]

In short, one's religious identity with Jesus Christ should create a necessary rupture with one's Islamic identity, or else our identity in Jesus Christ would mean nothing. It is unethical to pretend this discontinuity does not exist or to act as if it is merely a matter of cultural forms. Rather, it is more like a "fifth column" inside Islam, which, when discovered by Muslims, creates such a strong negative reaction that it inadvertently damages the credibility of Christians and feeds further distrust toward those who follow Christ. A more open witness in a straightforward, but contextually sensitive way seems to hold the greatest promise for effective and ethical Christian penetration into the Muslim world.

Reformation in Reverse?

This study has put forth a range of objections to the proponents of a C–5 "churchless" or "mosque-centered" ecclesiology. We have highlighted several biblical, exegetical, theological, and ethical problems that must be addressed if this new "mosque-centered" ecclesiology is to be embraced as a prescriptive strategy by Muslim followers of Jesus in the Islamic world. Nevertheless, no one can deny that, descriptively speaking, there are Muslims coming to Christ in some dramatic ways today. How should we respond to the genuine movement to Christ among these Muslims, many of whom have encountered Christ in dreams and visions?

I think the best approach is to see C–5 as a temporary, transitional bridge by which some Muslims are crossing over into explicit Christian faith, hopefully to one of a C–3 or C–4 character. On the one hand, a wide number of C–3 and C–4 church movements have long and distinguished track records showing that they are sustaining faith in the lives of MBBs without major cultural disruption and yet maintaining historic Christian orthodoxy. C–5, on the other hand, does not have a long track

66. Parshall, "Danger! New Directions in Contextualization," 409.

67. Leslie Newbigin, "Baptism, the Church and Koinonia," *Religion and Society* 19, no. 1 (March 1972): 78.

record and there is, as yet, no empirical evidence to confirm or to deny that it will emerge as an independent movement in its own right, or if it will serve as a temporary, transitional bridge to explicit Christian faith and identity.

Could this be an example of the "Reformation in reverse"?[68] In other words, our own Reformation history is the story of a people who saw themselves as Christians because they belonged to the formal, ecclesial "structure" of Christianity, that is, they were members of Christendom. The Reformation was, among other things, the gradual recognition over several hundred years by "Christians" that they were, in fact, not Christians at all and needed to become followers of Jesus Christ even though they were baptized Christians in the public, formal sense.

In the Islamic context we have been considering, could the exact opposite be taking place—a kind of Reformation in reverse? Could there be tens of thousands of people who belong to Islam in a public, formal sense who gradually, over many years, realize that they are no longer Muslims but Christians? Could we be seeing thousands of Muslim followers of Jesus who currently are wrongly trying to maintain their Islamic identity but who gradually come to see that their truest identity is with the people of God throughout space and time who also know, serve, and follow Jesus Christ as Lord?

In the New Testament, despite decades of hostility and suspicion, Jews and Gentiles found that in Jesus Christ the "dividing wall of hostility" had been destroyed (Eph. 2:14). There were not two bodies of Christ, one Jew and one Gentile, nor was there one "Western" and one "Eastern" Church. There was and is *one* body of Christ throughout the world, culturally diverse and yet one church of Jesus Christ, against whom the powers of hell itself cannot prevail.

BIBLIOGRAPHY

Berkhof, Louis. *Systematic Theology*. Grand Rapids: Eerdmans, 1941.

Bridges, Erich. "Of 'Jesus Mosques' and Muslim Christians." *Mission Frontiers* 19, nos. 7–10 (July–October 1997): 19.

Brown, Rick. "What Must One Believe about Jesus for Salvation." *International Journal of Frontier Missions* 17, no. 4 (Winter 2000): 13–21.

Butler, Robby. "Unlocking Islam." *Mission Frontiers* 13, no. 1 (January–March 1991): 24.

Decker, Frank. "When 'Christian' Does Not Translate." *Mission Frontiers* 27, no. 5 (September–October 2005): 8.

Dharmanand, Premraj [author's pseud.]. *Your Questions—Our Answers.* Dehra Dun, Uttaranchal: Bharat Susamachar Samiti, 2003.

"A Different Kind of Mosque." *Mission Frontiers* 19, nos. 7–10 (July–October 1997): 20–21.

68. I am indebted to Jonathan Bonk, director of the OMSC in New Haven, CT, for this insight.

Garrison, David. "Church Planting Movements vs. Insider Movements: Missiological Realities vs. Mythiological Speculations." *International Journal of Frontier Missions* 21, no. 4 (Winter 2004): 151–54.

Gilliland, Dean. "Context Is Critical in 'Islampur' Case." *Evangelical Missions Quarterly* 34, no. 4 (October 1998): 415–17.

Hoefer, Herbert. *Churchless Christianity.* Pasadena, CA: William Carey Library, 2001.

_____. "Proclaiming a 'Theologyless' Christ." *International Journal of Frontier Missions* 22, no. 3 (Fall 2005): 97–100.

Kaiser, Walter C. Jr. *Mission in the Old Testament: Israel as a Light to the Nations.* Grand Rapids: Baker, 2000.

Lewis, C. S. *Mere Christianity.* New York: Macmillan, 1952.

Martindale, Paul. "Reaching Muslims in America with the Gospel." DMin thesis, Gordon-Conwell Theological Seminary. 2006.

Massey, Joshua. "Misunderstanding C–5: His Ways Are Not Our Orthodoxy." *Evangelical Missions Quarterly* 40, no. 3 (July 2004): 296–304.

_____. "Misunderstanding C–5 and the Infinite Translatability of Christ: Why C–5 Has Been so Misunderstood by Its Critics." *Evangelical Missions Quarterly* 40, no. 1 (2004): 1–18. Unabridged online ed.: http://bgc.gospelcom.net/emis/pdfs/Misunderstanding_C5.pdf.

_____. "God's Amazing Diversity in Drawing Muslims to Christ." *International Journal of Frontier Missions* 17, no. 1 (Spring 2000): 5–14.

_____. "His Ways Are Not Our Ways." *Evangelical Missions Quarterly* 35, no. 2 (April 1999): 188–97.

Moreau, A. Scott, ed. *Evangelical Dictionary of World Missions.* Grand Rapids: Baker, 2000.

Newbigin, Lesslie. *The Finality of Christ.* London: SCM, 1969.

_____. "Baptism, the Church, and Koinonia," *Religion and Society* 19 (March 1972): 78.

Parshall, Phil. "Danger! New Directions in Contextualization." *Evangelical Missions Quarterly* 34, no. 4 (1998): 404–17.

Pelikan, Jaroslav. *The Christian Tradition: A History of the Development of Doctrine.* Vol. 1, *The Emergence of the Catholic Tradition (100–600).* Chicago: University of Chicago Press, 1971.

Smith, Jonathan, ed. *Harper Collins Dictionary of Religion.* San Francisco: HarperCollins, 1995.

Tennent, Timothy C. "The Challenge of Churchless Christianity: An Evangelical Assessment." *International Bulletin of Missionary Research* 29, no. 4 (October 2005): 171–77.

_____. *Christianity at the Religious Roundtable: Evangelicalism in Conversation with Hinduism, Buddhism and Islam.* Grand Rapids: Baker, 2002.

Travis, John. "Messianic Muslim Followers of Jesus." *International Journal of Frontier Missions* 17, no. 1 (Spring 2000): 53–59.

_____. "The C1 to C6 Spectrum." *Evangelical Missions Quarterly* 34 (1998): 407–8.

_____. "Two Responses." *Evangelical Missions Quarterly* 34 (1998): 411–17.

Uddin, Rafique. "Contextualized Worship and Witness." Pages 269–72 in *Muslims and Christians on the Emmaus Road.* Edited by J. Dudley Woodberry. Monrovia: MARC, 1989.

Walls, Andrew F. "Old Athens and New Jerusalem: Some Signposts for Christian Scholarship in the Early History of Mission Studies." *International Bulletin of Missionary Research* 21, no. 4 (October 1997): 146–50, 152–53.

Williams, Mark. "Aspects of High-Spectrum Contextualization in Ministries to Muslims." *Journal of Asian Mission* 5, no. 1 (2003): 75–91.

Winter, Ralph. "Can We Trust Insider Movements?" *Mission Frontiers* 27, no. 5 (September–October 2005): 4.

Yeoman, Barry. "The Stealth Crusade." *Mother Jones* 48 (May–June 2002): 42–49.

Chapter 9

ESCHATOLOGY

JONATHAN EDWARDS AND THE CHINESE BACK TO JERUSALEM MOVEMENT

A cartoon appeared some time ago in *Leadership Journal* about eschatology. It showed a man standing in front of a class teaching about the book of Revelation and the doctrine of the "last things." Behind him on the wall was an elaborate eschatological chart showing in great detail all the events that often accompany discussions about the end times. The cartoon shows a woman in the class standing up attempting to ask a question. The inscription at the bottom of the cartoon has the teacher saying, "No questions, please, I find they disrupt the flow of my answers."[1]

Indeed, there are few areas of Christian doctrine marked by so many vastly different views as those that emerge when the discussion turns to eschatology. Just a small sampling of some of the more popular questions underscore the many fissures in the church's eschatological firmament: Is the millennial reign of Christ spoken of in Revelation 20 a literal or symbolic period of time?[2] If there is a millennium, will Christ return before it or after it?[3] Does the phrase "the last days" refer to a specific period just prior to the return of Christ or is it a description of the entire history of the church?[4] Is the return of Christ a single, climactic event or does it occur in two stages, once "in the sky" *for* his saints and once "on the earth" *with* his saints?[5] Does the Bible teach a final, "secret" rapture of the church, as the popular *Left Behind* series claims?[6] If there is a rapture, does it occur before the tribulation, in the middle, or at the end

1. *The Best Cartoons from Leadership Journal*, vol. 1 (Nashville: Broadman & Holman, 1999), 116.

2. For a summary of different views about the millennium, see Darrell Bock, ed., *Three Views on the Millennium and Beyond* (Grand Rapids: Zondervan, 1999). Premillennialism is presented by Craig Blaising, postmillennialism by Kenneth Gentry Jr., and amillennialism by Robert Strimple.

3. See George Eldon Ladd, *The Blessed Hope: A Biblical Study of the Second Advent and the Rapture* (Grand Rapids: Eerdmans, 1980).

4. For a discussion on this, see George Eldon Ladd, *The Presence of the Future*, rev. ed. (Grand Rapids: Eerdmans, 1996).

5. For a summary of dispensational eschatology, see Charles Ryrie, *Dispensationalism* (Chicago: Moody Bible Institute, 1995).

6. This title of the multivolume, popular *Left Behind* series by Tim LaHaye and Jerry Jenkins refers to the belief that Christ's return occurs in two stages, beginning with a secret return whereby the church is raptured away just prior to the outpouring of God's wrath during the great tribulation. Those who are not raptured are "left behind."

of it?[7] Does God have a separate, eschatological program planned for ethnic Jews? How many judgments will there be at the end of time and who will be judged? Does the book of Revelation refer to events that have mostly been fulfilled, or does it refer primarily to events that still lie in our future, or, perhaps, was it written to provide ongoing help to the church throughout its history?[8] Clearly, the church has not reached any consensus concerning the nature and timing of the events associated with the last days.

Despite all of these differences, it is important to remember that there are many themes in eschatology where the church has found broad agreement. For example, historic Christianity has always affirmed the visible, bodily return of Christ, the resurrection of the dead, the final vindication of his church, the certainty of final judgment, God's absolute victory over evil, and the promise of everlasting life. Another area that is normally affirmed in common by most eschatological schemes is the belief that the end of time will be accompanied by widespread preaching of the gospel to all nations. This understanding is normally based on a wide range of texts (e.g., Isa. 49:6; 56:6–8; Acts 1:8; 15:14–18; Rom. 9:24–26; Eph. 2:11–20), but none more than Jesus' statement in Matthew 24:14: "And this gospel of the kingdom will be preached in the whole world as a testimony to all nations, and then the end will come."

Christians may disagree about the precise timing of this worldwide event, but most agree that it will occur.[9] This agreement explains the warm relationship that has often existed between missiology and eschatology. Many of the great missionary initiatives throughout history have been launched in obedience to this promise about the end times, in anticipation of Christ's glorious return, or, in some cases, even to hasten or speed up the day when he will return.[10]

This chapter will focus on how eschatology continues to shape the church's theology of world evangelization. Specifically, it will highlight how eschatology has influenced the popular "Back to Jerusalem" missionary initiative by various networks of house churches in China. Defying the stereotype that mission work is about the "West reaching the rest," there are thousands of Chinese Christians who are determined to complete the global circuit by bringing the gospel from China, across central Asia and North Africa, and back to Jerusalem, where Jesus first gave the Great Commission.

7. For a survey of different views regarding the rapture of the church, see Gleason Archer Jr., Paul Feinberg, Douglas Moo, and Richard Reiter, *Three Views on the Rapture: Pre-, Mid-, or Post-Tribulation* (Grand Rapids: Zondervan, 1996). See also Michael J. Svigel, "The Apocalypse of John and the Rapture of the Church: A Reevaluation," *Trinity Journal*, n.s. 22, no. 1 (Spring 2001): 23–74.

8. For a summary of different overall approaches to Revelation, see Steve Gregg, ed., *Revelation: Four Views: A Parallel Commentary* (Nashville: Nelson, 1997).

9. Those holding to a historist interpretation of Revelation understand the "last days" as including the entire history of the church and therefore the fulfillment of Matthew 24:14 may be a gradual process over many centuries of Christian witness in the face of tribulations, which Jesus describes as a normal part of the church's life in the world. In contrast, dispensationalists generally see the fulfillment of Matthew 24:14 as taking place after the return of Christ and the rapture of the church through the faithful witness of the 144,000 spoken of in Revelation 7.

10. A. B. Simpson, for example, the founder of the Christian and Missionary Alliance, taught that "world evangelization would not only make ready a people for the King's return, but could in fact speed his coming." Simpson once described missionary work as the "key to the bridal chamber and the lever that will hasten his return." See David F. Hartzfeld and Charles Nienkirchen, eds., *The Birth of a Vision: Essays on the Ministry and Thought of Albert B. Simpson* (Regina, SK [Canada]: His Dominion, 1986), 204. For an overview of the connection between eschatology and world evangelization in the twentieth century, see Todd M. Johnson, "The Crisis of Missions: The Historical Development of the Idea of the Evangelization of the World by the Year 1900," *International Journal of Frontier Missions* 5, nos. 1–4 (January–October 1988): 1–103.

However, in keeping with the objectives of this book to foster global, integrative, cross-cultural sensitivity in theologizing, this chapter will compare and contrast how eschatology and missions have come together in the Chinese Back to Jerusalem movement with the same themes in the writings of Jonathan Edwards, widely considered one of the greatest of all American theologians. Examining the Back to Jerusalem movement in China alongside the eschatology of Jonathan Edwards will serve to model one of the major objectives of this book, namely, to foster an integrative approach to global theology.

It is an important first step for Christians in the West to be aware of how the eschatology of Chinese Christians has influenced their understanding of global missions. It is vital, however, that we also take the next step and think about how this compares and contrasts with similar currents in our own history. The eschatology of Jonathan Edwards represents a striking departure from many in his generation and has several fascinating parallels with what is now taking place among Chinese Christians. This chapter will begin with a survey of how Jonathan Edwards' eschatology influenced his understanding of world evangelization, followed by a discussion of the Chinese Back to Jerusalem movement.

JONATHAN EDWARDS' ESCHATOLOGY

Moving beyond the Stereotype

The persistent, but distorted, stereotype of Jonathan Edwards is that of an angry revivalist preacher who terrified his congregations with vivid descriptions of God dangling helpless sinners by a spider's thread over the very flames of hell. This image, drawn from the famous sermon, "Sinners in the Hands of an Angry God," is not characteristic of Edwards, who was captivated by the power of God's grace and the beauty of his character.[11] In fact, one of the things that make the study of Edwards so compelling is that he had the capacity to continue to surprise his readers with interests, reflections, and views that were well ahead of his time and were certainly neither popular nor characteristic of his evangelical peers.

For example, few eighteenth-century evangelicals can remotely compare with Edwards' interest in non-Christian religions and his sustained reflections about the presence of *prisca theologia* (ancient theology) in these religions.[12] While never surrendering his absolute commitment to the uniqueness of Jesus Christ, Edwards took seriously the Deists' charge against the "scandal of particularity" that lay behind Calvinist soteriology.[13] It is intriguing in light of the theme of this chapter that Edwards also had a particular interest in China and Chinese culture. He "claims to find the Trinity in the *Dao-de-Jing*, expectations of a suffering messiah in one of the Confucian classics,

11. For a representative sampling of Edwards' sermons, see *The Works of Jonathan Edwards*; vol. 22, *Sermons and Discourses, 1739–1742*, ed. Harry Stout and Nathan Hatch (New Haven, CT: Yale Univ. Press, 2003).

12. See Gerald McDermott's excellent study, *Jonathan Edwards Confronts the Gods* (New York: Oxford Univ. Press, 2000).

13. The scandal of particularity refers to the tension between the Christian affirmation that the entire world must consciously repent and receive the good news of Jesus Christ in order to be saved, and yet only one-sixth of the world in Edwards' day had even been exposed to the Christian message. The Deists looked for hope in some universal revelation accessible to all.

and a supposed statement by Confucius that a saint would come from the West to banish sin and suffering."[14]

Edwards was also fascinated by eschatology and the book of Revelation. Like many of his Puritan forbearers, eschatological interests regularly surface in his writings.[15] However, with Edwards the fascination with Revelation reaches new heights. In fact, Revelation is the only book of the Bible to which Edwards devotes an entirely separate commentary. In contrast, it is the only book of the Bible for which John Calvin did not write a commentary.[16] It is Edwards' eschatological views and his application of them to global evangelism that will serve as the backdrop to our particular study in this chapter.[17]

Edwards' Eschatology in the Context of Post-Reformation Exegesis of Revelation

Many modern-day readers of Jonathan Edwards find his eschatological views to be rather odd and filled with negative assessments of Roman Catholicism.[18] However, it is important to read Edwards' eschatology within the context of his time. Edwards was much a man of his time in his general approach to eschatology.[19] The purpose of this brief overview is to demonstrate his perspective on the world and the role of the church in global evangelization rather than to examine the particulars of his exegesis of Revelation. It is difficult to read Edwards without coming away humbled by his avid attention to global events, as his copious notes and newspaper clippings reveal, which stands in contrast to the insular provincialism that often characterizes modern North American evangelicalism.

Edwards accepted the basic historicist hermeneutic in interpreting Revelation, which had been popular since the time of the Reformation. This interpretation argues that Revelation is a book that describes world history leading to the final climax of the ages and the end of the world. The interpreter must demonstrate how the fantastic

---

14. McDermott, *Jonathan Edwards Confronts the Gods*, 92. Some of Edwards' claims are based on misunderstandings of the original teachings in Chinese philosophy and religion. However, the important point is Edwards' openness to *preparatio evangelica* in China, including his belief that the Chinese knew about the need for regeneration and that "the Chinese possessed all the essential truths of the Reformed religion, but in 'mythological' form" (see ibid., 215).

15. Puritan leaders such as John Cotton (1585–1652), Roger Williams (1603–1684), Increase Mather (1639–1723), and Cotton Mather (1663–1728) showed a great fascination with eschatology, including the anti-Catholic interpretation of the text.

16. Stephen J. Stein, ed., "Editor's Introduction," *The Works of Jonathan Edwards*, vol. 5, *Apocalyptic Writings* (New Haven, CT: Yale Univ. Press, 1977), 5:3.

17. This chapter will not focus on how Edwards' eschatology influenced his social theory. For this, see Robert Westbrook, "Social Criticism and the Heavenly Vision of Jonathan Edwards," *Soundings* 59 (1976): 397–409.

18. I do not concur with Edwards' negative assessment of Roman Catholicism, but one cannot understand Edwards' eschatology without also understanding the hostility against Roman Catholicism that was so prominent in the Protestant writings of the day. The Westminster Confession of 1647 as well as the Congregationalist adaptation of it in the Savoy Declaration of 1658 (adopted in the Synod of Boston at 1680) identify the Pope as "that Antichrist, that man of sin and son of perdition." See Philip Schaff, ed., *The Creeds of Christendom* (Grand Rapids: Baker, 1993), 3:659, 723. The Westminster Confession is silent about the millennium, the tribulation, and the precise time of Christ's return.

19. For a good survey of how Edwards fits into the larger stream of eschatological thought of his day, see John F. Wilson, "History, Redemption, and the Millennium," in *Jonathan Edwards and the American Experience*, ed. Nathan Hatch and Harry Stout (New York: Oxford Univ. Press, 1988). While Edwards' general historicist approach was typical of his day, many of his contemporaries expressed skepticism concerning several of Edwards' specific interpretations, such as the identification of the two witnesses, the meaning of the various trumpets, etc.

and symbolic images found in Revelation apply to or correspond with actual historical events in human history. Not since the legalization of Christianity by Constantine through the Edict of Milan (AD 313) had the church undergone such a radical transformation as that which occurred during the Protestant Reformation.

Thus, it was common for post-Reformation sermons and commentaries on Revelation to identify the rise of the papacy in the Roman Catholic Church with the rise of the beast predicted in Revelation (or the Antichrist of the letters of John) and the Reformation with the beginning of the demise of the Antichrist.[20] In Edwards' unfinished magnus opus, *History of Redemption*, he equates the revelation of the "man of lawlessness" (2 Thess. 2:3) with the rise of the papacy: "It is prophesied that this man of sin should set himself up in the temple or visible church of God, pretending to be vested with divine power, as head of the church (vs. 4). And all this has exactly come to pass in the Church of Rome."[21] In fact, Edwards accepts without question that in Revelation, Babylon is a reference to Rome and the power of Roman Catholicism (which he calls the "anti-Christian church"), whereas Jerusalem refers to the true church that emerged at the Reformation.[22]

In eschatological calculations that emerged in post-Reformation exegesis, the rise of the papacy is linked to either the year 606, when the bishop of Rome was recognized as having authority over the whole church, or the year 756, when the pope acquired temporal power.[23] Based on the references in Revelation to 1,260 days (Rev. 11:3; 12:6) or 42 months (11:2), commentators of the day believed that the Antichrist (i.e., the pope) would only reign for 1,260 years.[24] In that time period the church entered a stage of apostasy, during which the pope was given authority to make war against the "saints of the Most High" (cf. Dan. 7:25).

Edwards accepted this basic interpretation but was less concerned about fixing a precise date from which to begin the 1,260 year domination of the papacy. For our purposes, it is important to note that Edwards argued that just as the rise of the papacy was a gradual one, so its demise and defeat would also occur gradually. Edwards in "An Humble Attempt" writes:

> I do not deny that the time when Mr. Lowman supposes the reign of the beast began, even the time when Pepin confirmed to the Pope his temporary

20. For the "beast," see Revelation 11:7; 13:1–18; 14:9, 11; 15:2; 16:2, 10, 13; 17:3–17; 19:19, 20; 20:4, 10. For the "Antichrist," see 1 John 2:18–19; 4:3; 2 John 1:7. John's use of the title "Antichrist" seems to refer to someone or something already present in the world. However, Protestant exegesis has often identified the Antichrist with titles that appear in Revelation, which are then applied to the end of time.

21. Jonathan Edwards, "A History of the Work of Redemption," in *The Works of Jonathan Edwards*, ed. Edward Hickman (Edinburgh: Banner of Truth Trust, 1974), 1:603 (ch. 13). Edwards was reluctant to accept the presidency of Princeton (College of New Jersey) because he wanted to complete this work. However, his untimely death occurred shortly after his inauguration as president because of a smallpox inoculation he was given.

22. In "Tractate on Revelation 16:12," Edwards writes, "I need not strive particularly to shew [sic], that the anti-Christian church is in this book of Revelation everywhere compared to Babylon, and called by the name Babylon the Great, as the true church is called Jerusalem; because to mention all the places would be very tedious, and because none can be ignorant of it" (see *The Works of Jonathan Edwards*, 5:299).

23. C. C. Goen, "Jonathan Edwards: A New Departure in Eschatology," *Church History* 28, no. 1 (March 1959): 29.

24. It is common in the historicist interpretation of Revelation to assume that "days" in apocalyptic writing correspond with "years" in human history. Also, 42 months is reconciled with 1,260 days on the assumption that a "month" is a thirty-day period. This is also conformed to the "times, times and a half a time" as three and a half years, based on 360-day years.

> dominions in Italy, was a time of the great increase and advancement of the power of Antichrist in the world, and a notable epoch ... [yet] as the power of Antichrist, and the corruption of the apostate church, rose not at once, but by several notable steps and degrees; so it will in like manner fall.[25]

Edwards accepted the general framework of a "creation eschatology," which understood the whole of human history as consisting of six thousand years, corresponding to the six days of creation, followed by the thousand-year millennial reign, corresponding to the seventh day of rest in the creation account.[26] Thus, while not committing himself to exact predictions, Edwards calculated that if you count ahead the 1,260 years from the time of the rise of the papacy, the date roughly corresponds with the year 2000 as the beginning of the millennium.[27] Edwards was, like several of his Puritan predecessors, *post*millennial, arguing for a golden age for the church on earth, followed by the return of Christ after the millennium.[28]

Edwards' Understanding of the Vials in the Premillennial Church

This study is particularly interested in how Edwards understood the time in which he lived and how his eschatology influenced his understanding of global missions. Edwards was determined to identify the seven bowls or vials of God's wrath that are poured out by seven angels in Revelation 16. He eventually became convinced, following contemporary scholars like Moses Lowman (1680–1752), that the fifth vial referred to the Reformation.

Revelation 16:10 says, "The fifth angel poured out his bowl on the throne of the beast, and his kingdom was plunged into darkness." According to Edwards, the fifth bowl represented God's judgment on Roman Catholicism and the unleashing of the Reformation.[29] Verse 12, describing the sixth vial, pictures the angel pouring out a bowl on the "great river Euphrates," causing its water to dry up and prepare for a massive invasion. After a lengthy explanation of his reasoning, Edwards concludes that the sixth vial symbolizes the depletion of the financial assets of the papacy. This vial will result in "drying the streams of the wealth of the new Babylon, the temporal supplies, revenues and vast incomes of the Romish Church, and riches of the popish domin-

25. Jonathan Edwards, "An Humble Attempt," in *The Works of Jonathan Edwards*, 5:407–8. Edwards is also fascinated with the possibility that God may "shorten the days," thus making precise calculations impossible. See ibid., 5:393–96. The reference to Mr. Lowman refers to the pastor and scholar Moses Lowman (1680–1752), whose commentary on Revelation influenced several of Edwards' views.

26. Edwards, "Notes on the Apocalypse," *The Works of Jonathan Edwards*, 5:129–30. Edwards says "the first 6000 years are 6 days of labor ... and the seventh day there shall be rest, putting a thousand years for a day, as the apostle Peter does" (2 Peter 3:4, 8).

27. The time frame falls between 1866 and 2016, but because of his "creation eschatology," Edwards was inclined to accept the year 2000 as the likely beginning of the millennium. For a fuller discussion of this by Edwards, "Notes on the Apocalypse," 5:129–36; also "An Humble Attempt," 5:410–11.

28. The Westminster Confession is silent about the millennium, so Edwards could fully affirm the Westminster Confession as postmillenialist, dispelling the common notion that postmillennialism is only identified with liberal theology. John Cotton (1585–1652) and John Owen (1616–1683) are also examples of Puritans with postmillennial views. See John Jefferson Davis, *Christ's Victorious Kingdom* (Grand Rapids: Baker, 1986), 16–22.

29. Prior to 1738 Edwards had identified the Reformation with the second vial, but he became convinced that the Reformation was actually the fifth vial after reading Moses Lowman. Edwards wrote, "Mr. Lowman has, I think, put it beyond all reasonable doubt, that the 5th vial was poured out in the time of the Reformation." See also Edwards' "Tractate on Revelation 16:12," where he praises Lowman's "excellent exposition of the Revelation" that showed "with great evidence that the fifth vial ... was poured out in the time of the Reformation" (5:298).

ions."[30] Since each vial is followed by revival in the church, Edwards eagerly looked for signs in the daily news of the wealth of Rome being dried up.[31] He was delighted, for example, to read in the *Boston Gazette* on September 20, 1748, about the capture of a Spanish ship laden with riches that had been headed for Roman Catholic Spain.[32]

Edwards was convinced that if the fifth vial had ushered in a revival as significant as the Reformation, the sixth must be attended by an even greater "outpouring of the Spirit," especially since this is the last vial before the final one, which ushers in the millennium.[33] So, when a major revival broke out in his Northampton church in 1733–34 bringing in hundreds of new believers, followed in 1739–1740 by the Great Awakening, Edwards was convinced that the sixth vial of Revelation 16:12 was being poured out.

It is important to recognize that Edwards saw these revivals as signs of the sixth vial and not of the actual millennium, which he understood as still in the distant future. The often-discussed phrase in Edwards' "Some Thoughts Concerning the Revival" (1742), where he speaks of "that glorious work of God" that "must be near," is often thought to refer to an imminent millennium. However, it is far more likely to be a reference to the pouring out of the sixth vial.[34] In short, Edwards was optimistic about a *pre*millennial rise of religious fervor and the expansion of global evangelism. This is in stark contrast to the popularly held notion that the millennial age would be inaugurated only after the most severe trials, calamities, and difficulties for the church.

Eschatology and Global Evangelism in Jonathan Edwards' Writings

The title of Edwards' 1747 work is usually known as "An Humble Attempt." However, knowing the full title provides a helpful insight into the overall thesis of the work: *An Humble Attempt to Promote Explicit Agreement and Visible Union of God's People in Extraordinary Prayer for the Revival of Religion and the Advancement of Christ's Kingdom on Earth, Pursuant to Scripture Promises and Prophesies Concerning the Last Time.* In this book, Edwards earnestly calls for the church to come together in "concerts of prayer" for the outpouring of revival. Edwards felt that the revivals of 1733–34 and 1739–40 were but the firstfruits of a major, premillennial, global movement to Christ. The tenor of the whole book is in eager anticipation of what Edwards calls the "church's latter-day glory."[35]

30. Edwards, "An Humble Attempt," 5:414. For his full argument, see 5:412–27.

31. Identifying the successive "bowls of wrath" with the decline of Roman Catholicism and the papacy accords with Edwards' notion of the gradual decline of Rome beginning with the Reformation and continuing through to the seventh bowl, which ushers in the millennium.

32. Brandon G. Withrow, "A Future of Hope: Jonathan Edwards and Millennial Expectations," *Trinity Journal* 22, n.s., no. 1 (Spring 2001): 95–96. The fact that this treasure was brought to the United States was, for Edwards, also a fulfillment of the promise of Isaiah 60:9.

33. Edwards, "An Humble Attempt," 5:426, says, "The fifth vial was attended with such revival, and reformation, that greatly weakened and diminished the throne or kingdom of the beast, and went far towards its ruin. It seems as though the sixth vial should be much more so; for 'tis the distinguishing note of this vial, that it is the preparatory vial, which more than any other vial prepares the way for Christ's coming to destroy the kingdom of Antichrist, and set up his own kingdom in the world." Note that Edwards is anticipating a premillennial revival, not (as Goen seems to argue in "Jonathan Edwards: A New Departure in Eschatology," 29) the actual arrival of the millennium.

34. For a fuller discussion concerning this phrase, see Gerald McDermott, *One Holy and Happy Society* (State College, PA: Pennsylvania State Univ. Press, 1992), 51. I find McDermott's argument compelling, which argues that "Edwards here referred not to the millennium but to a long period of intermittent revival that would lead up to the millennium."

35. Edwards, "An Humble Attempt," 5:313.

However, Edwards understood that the church faced major obstacles in extending the gospel around the world besides the challenges he saw in the papacy and the Roman Catholic Church. Edwards made an important distinction between the kingdom of the Antichrist (Roman Catholicism) and the kingdom of Satan. He believed that the kingdom of Satan was divided into three major parts, which he identifies with the three unclean spirits like frogs that come out of the mouths of the dragon, the beast, and the false prophet (Rev. 16:13–21). The three parts consist of a "false Christian kingdom," which, as we have seen, he identifies with Roman Catholicism; a "Mahometan kingdom," which refers to all the Muslim peoples in the world; and a "heathen kingdom," which refers to all the remaining unbelievers in the world. Edwards identifies these three kingdoms with the beast (the pope), the false prophet (Muhammad), and the dragon ("heathen" world) of Revelation 16.[36]

In "An Humble Attempt" Edwards saw the decline of Roman Catholicism, beginning with the Reformation (the fifth vial), as the start of a process that would eventually lead to the fall of Islam and the conversion of the Jews.[37] Edwards felt that the seeds of the collapse of Roman Catholicism had already been set in motion, but he felt that unified prayer by the church could help to usher in the final stages of Christian expansion leading up to the millennium. Edwards even set out a general time frame, which would begin with Protestants completing their ascendancy in what he calls "the popish world." This would be followed by a five-hundred-year period in which the church "subdues the greater part of the Mahometan world, and brings in the Jewish nation, in all their dispersions."[38]

Edwards' eschatological hopes were further confirmed by accounts he read in the newspapers about the conversion of Muslims to Christianity.[39] Finally, in the closing period, Edwards anticipated "the whole heathen world should be enlightened and converted to the Christian faith, throughout all parts of Africa, Asia, America, and Terra Australis, and be thoroughly settled in Christian faith and order."[40]

Edwards taught a similar progression of global evangelism during the premillennial period between the sixth and seventh vial in his *History of Redemption*.[41] After the kingdom of the Antichrist was overthrown, it would be followed by "Satan's Mahometan kingdom." Edwards explored the wide dissemination of Islam in the world and yet looked to the day when "this smoke, which has ascended out of the bottomless pit, shall be utterly scattered before the light of that glorious day, and the Mahometan empire shall fall." After the fall of Islam, Edwards anticipated the day when "Jewish infidelity shall be overthrown." Edwards looked forward to the day when the "veil that blinds

36. Edwards, "Notes on the Apocalypse," 5:173–74. Edwards refers to this trio as false Christianism, Mahometanism, and heathenism.

37. Edwards, "An Humble Attempt," 5:410.

38. Ibid., 5:411.

39. See, for example, Jonathan Edwards, "Events of an Hopeful Aspect on the State of Religion," *The Works of Jonathan Edwards*, 5:286, 292, 294–95.

40. Edwards, "An Humble Attempt," 5:411. Edwards does affirm that God has providentially chosen American Protestants to be lights in a world of darkness. New England was providentially settled as the "city on a hill." However, his millennial views concerning the global expansion of the gospel transcend any particular nation of the world, including America.

41. For the entire progression of Edwards' various stages of revivals, see Edwards, "A History of the Work of Redemption," 1:607–8 (part 7, sec. 3).

their eyes" would be removed (cf. 2 Cor. 3:16) and the "house of Israel" would be saved. Finally, he anticipated the day when the entirety of "Satan's heathenish kingdom" would be overthrown and all the nations of the world would be "visited with glorious light."[42]

Edwards became so concerned with the importance of the conversion of the Muslims in preparation for the millennium that he expanded his interpretation of the drying up of the Euphrates associated with the sixth vial or bowl to include "the destruction of the Turkish Empire, and so letting the true religion into those territories that lie on the eastern borders of the popish empire."[43]

This general optimism in Edwards' eschatology should not be taken to mean that he did not anticipate difficulties and painful setbacks for the church. In fact, his conception of the gradual overthrow of all those who stand against Christ allows for regular periods of advance and recession.[44] However, Edwards did believe that the greatest days of persecution were over.

This was largely based on his interpretation of the two slain witnesses (Rev. 11).[45] He understood them as representative of the tiny, faithful remnant who, prior to the Reformation, kept the light of the gospel shining. Edwards looked back on the days of the Hussites, the Waldensians, and similar groups as the darkest days of the church. The martyrdom of those early leaders is symbolized by the slaying of the two witnesses. After the two witnesses lay dead in the streets for two days, "a breath of life from God entered them, and they stood on their feet" (Rev. 11:11). Edwards identified this event with the Reformation.[46] In his view, never again could the Antichrist or Satan prevail against the church as in the days before the Reformation.

Nevertheless, Edwards' view of the gradual advance of the kingdom meant that he did anticipate major conflicts ahead. He saw increasing conflict and persecution as the millennium drew closer, a view that has been called an "afflictive model of progress."[47] In "An Humble Attempt" Edwards writes:

> 'Tis true, there is abundant evidence in Scripture, that there is yet remaining a mighty conflict between the church and her enemies, the most violent struggle of Satan and his adherents, in opposition to true religion, and the

42. Another similar progressive scheme is outlined in Edwards' "Notes on the Apocalypse." In this scheme he argues for the following progression: First, the "Turks in Europe shall be overthrown, and the true religion established in those parts of Europe." Second, "Antichrist shall be overthrown ... and perhaps religion shall begin to be gloriously propagated among the heathen." Third, "the Jews shall be called." Fourth, "this will be succeeded by a universal propagation of religion through the vast regions of the earth." The major difference in this scheme is that the collapse of Islam precedes that of the demise of Roman Catholicism. All four of these apocalyptic events are set forth by Edwards as occurring *prior* to the millennium.

43. Edwards, "Notes on the Apocalypse," 5:188. Edwards engages in a lengthy explanation of how the Muslims can be identified symbolically by the Euphrates River.

44. Edwards accepts the distinction between the current "church militant" and the millennial "church triumphant." "As long as any considerable part of the world remains under the dominion of Satan, Michael and his angels will be at war with the devil and his angels; and the church will be going forth, fighting against her enemies with the sword of the Spirit, the sword of Christ's mouth, which is the Word of God" ("Notes on the Apocalypse," 5:179).

45. For a full exposition of Edwards' views regarding the two witnesses of Revelation 11, see "An Humble Attempt," 5:378–94.

46. Edwards, "Notes on the Apocalypse," 5:211.

47. McDermott, *One Holy and Happy Society*, 56. Also, as will be explored later, Edwards accepted a harvest model of revival whereby spiritual ingatherings, like the agricultural harvests, occur at specific, condensed periods, followed by long period of labor and preparation where there is no visible fruit.

> most general commotion that ever was in the world, since the foundation of it to that time; and many particular Christians, and some parts of the church of Christ may suffer hard things in this conflict: but in the general, Satan and Antichrist shall not get the victory, nor greatly prevail; but on the contrary be entirely conquered, and utterly overthrown, in this great battle.[48]

In fact, even after the millennium was over, according to Edwards' postmillennialism, Satan would be released for a short time to deceive the nations once more before Christ triumphantly returned, slew all his enemies, and announced the final judgment.

Summary of Edwards' Eschatology in Relation to Global Evangelism

This brief overview of Jonathan Edwards' eschatology reveals four important features that are relevant to this study. First, Edwards anticipated a major global expansion of Christianity that would *precede* the ushering in of the millennium. It is important to note that Edwards' views regarding this special end-time dispensation of grace involved a shift in the accepted ecclesiology of his day. All of the magisterial Reformers held strong territorial (*landeskirchlich*) views of Christianity that were crucial to their whole understanding of the Christendom arrangement. These views, in turn, had an important impact on early Protestant missiology, because they did not provide a theological basis for entering a non-Christian realm that was not under the jurisdiction of a Christian ruler.

However, while Edwards generally accepted the received ecclesiology of his day, he believed that after the pouring out of the sixth vial and leading up to the millennium, God would, apart from the normal expectations of the Christendom model, sovereignly bring Muslims and idol worshipers to himself in response to the "concerts of prayer." Edwards' rationale was based on the fact that during the millennium Christ's kingship superseded all earthly rulers, transcending Christendom, where a Christian ruler could only, at best, be a dim reflection of Christ's kingship.[49]

In fact, in "An Humble Attempt" Edwards asserted that devotion to prayer would bring about a unity of the church that would transcend the traditional ecclesiastical divisions. But because he believed in the gradual transition to the millennium as exemplified by the period between the sixth and the seventh bowls, he anticipated a massive, global outpouring of God's Spirit, which would cause nations throughout the world to turn to Christ in preparation for his millennial reign. In "An Humble Attempt" Edwards often reminded his readers that there were many unfulfilled prophecies in the Old Testament that predicted the universal worship of God:

> It is evident from the Scripture, that there is yet remaining a great advancement of the interest of religion and the kingdom of Christ in this world, by an

48. Edwards, "An Humble Attempt," 5:394. Edwards was concerned that if one's eschatology was linked only to persecution and calamity, then the concerts of prayer would only be hastening the day when the church would be persecuted. Instead, Edwards did not deny persecution, but focused on latter-day revivals and the global expansion of the church.

49. John H. Gerstner, *The Rational Biblical Theology of Jonathan Edwards* (Orlando, FL: Berea, 1993), 3:370–73.

> abundant outpouring of the Spirit of God, far greater and more extensive than ever yet has been. 'Tis certain, that many things, which are spoken concerning a glorious time of the church's enlargement and prosperity in the latter days, have never yet been fulfilled. There has never yet been any propagation and prevailing of religion, in any wise, of that extant [sic] and universality, which the prophecies represent.[50]

Edwards did not simply see this as some distant millennial promise but as one that was on the verge of being fulfilled in his own day: "The Scriptures give us reason to think, that when once there comes to appear much of a spirit of prayer in the church of God for this mercy, then it will soon be accomplished."[51]

Second, Edwards understood this global advancement of the gospel as unfolding in various stages, with a particular emphasis on the culminating eschatological conversion of Muslims and Jews. Because, as noted above, distinguishing between the kingdom of Antichrist and the kingdom of Satan, Edwards saw the collapse of the Roman Catholic Church as just the beginning of the gradual collapse of Satan's kingdom, he anticipated a period lasting hundreds of years when the gospel would be brought to the Islamic world. He also anticipated the day when the Jews would return to their historic homeland and experience a great latter-day ingathering to the church of Jesus Christ. In commenting on the pouring out of the sixth vial, Edwards spoke of the day when "a door will be opened to the conversion of the Jews ... and other eastern nations. And that nothing might hinder the Israelites returning to their God and their land, which indeed would make way for the converting and enlightening of all the nations of Asia."[52]

Third, while Edwards understood that the darkest days of persecution and trial were behind the church, he nevertheless believed that the church would continue to face persecution and setbacks until the millennium. He took seriously the opposition that the church faces internally through heretical Christians who want to destroy the church as well as externally through Islam and the rest of the non-Christian world. Edwards even insisted that the rise of true religious devotion would be met with persecution. He wrote that the "church of Christ has never as yet been for any long time, free from persecution; especially when truth has prevailed, and true religion flourished."[53] However, Edwards understood the latter-day persecution against the backdrop of the even greater story of the church's advance against the kingdom of Satan.

Finally, Edwards was convinced of the vital importance of unified prayer in bringing about revival, not only in the church but also in the whole world. This conviction was, of course, the whole occasion for Edwards writing "An Humble Attempt," in which he called the church to "renewed and extraordinary earnestness in their prayers

50. Edwards, "An Humble Attempt," 5:329. See 5:410–11 for Edwards' emphasis on the gradual unfolding of Christ's rule and reign.

51. Ibid., 5:351.

52. Edwards, "Notes on the Apocalypse," 5:116, 140. See also "An Humble Attempt," 5:337.

53. Edwards, "An Humble Attempt," 5:336.

to him, for the fulfillment of the promised downfall of Antichrist, and that liberty and glory of his church that shall follow."[54] Edwards was not merely extending a general call for the church to pray. Rather, he was seeking to bring the churches in the colonies as well as Christians throughout Christendom into unity with an earlier proposal by Scottish ministers in October of 1744 to form "concerts of prayer."

These concerts of prayer were gatherings of Christians committed to unite in intercessory prayer every Saturday evening, Sabbath morning, and the first Tuesday of every quarter.[55] Edwards' eschatology did not encourage a sense of defeatism as the church experienced attacks on every side, nor did it encourage a sense of passivism while we wait for Christ to return. Rather, his strong emphasis on the extended period of renewal and evangelization, which, in his view, occurred between the pouring out of the sixth and the seventh vials, provided an important period for the church to be actively engaged in prayer and evangelism. Edwards already experienced the firstfruits of this in the revival that took place in his church in Northampton. He was now experiencing the revivals of the Great Awakening, and he anticipated the day when the Spirit of God would sweep the entire globe in fulfillment of Matthew 24:14.

We will now compare and contrast these themes found in the eschatology of Jonathan Edwards in the eighteenth century with the emergence of the Back to Jerusalem movement by Chinese Christians today.

BRIEF OVERVIEW OF THE HISTORY OF CHINESE CHRISTIANITY

Setting the Earliest Context of Christianity in China

Western students of church history are often exposed only to the steady, westward expansion of the gospel. The story we are most familiar with is the spread of the gospel from Jerusalem to Europe and, eventually, to the New World. However, at the same time, Nestorian Christians were moving eastward, bravely traversing the rugged terrain of central Asia and planting the church all along the 6,200 miles of the famous Silk Route, reaching China as early as AD 635. A large limestone stele was discovered in China that chronicles the early arrival of these Nestorian missionaries. The official title of the stele is the *Memorial of the Propagation in China of the Luminous Religion from Daqin*.[56] This early missionary trip along the Silk Route is important since it forms a central feature of the modern-day Back to Jerusalem movement.

Later Christian Penetration in China

When Marco Polo arrived in China in 1288, he recorded the presence of Nestorian Christians. However, because of the policies of isolation adopted by the Ming dynasty, it was many centuries before Christian missionaries were able to return to China.

54. Ibid., 5:359.

55. Ibid., 5:320.

56. Christianity is appropriately called *jing jiao*, the "luminous religion." The term "Daqin" is a Chinese reference to the Roman empire. The stele was discovered in 1623.

The Counter-Reformation in the Roman Catholic Church after the emergence of the Reformation sparked a major wave of global missions, spearheaded by the dedicated and highly educated Jesuits, who arrived in China in the sixteenth century. Legendary Jesuits such as the Spaniard Francis Xavier and the Italian Matteo Ricci were among the most famous Christian missionaries in the history of the church.[57] The Jesuits were soon followed by the Franciscans, the Dominicans, and the Augustinians, all of whom labored to help spread the gospel in China.

The nineteenth-century witnessed the arrival of Protestant missionaries. The remarkable cultural challenges and complex theological issues that were raised as the gospel spread among the Chinese could easily have provided enough rich and textured detail to make China the focus of every chapter in this book. The discussions in chapter 2 about Muslims and Christians debating the meaning of the word Allah resonate powerfully with the challenge missionaries faced in trying to find the best Chinese word for "God." Indeed, the debate about the relative usefulness of such terms as Tianzhu (Lord of Heaven), or Shandgi (Lord on High), or Shen (god, spirit) continues to challenge the Chinese church.

Famous Protestant translators such as Robert Morrison and James Legge were among the pioneers who first grappled with how to translate biblical concepts into the Chinese language. The tensions between the Christian gospel and human culture as discussed in several of our studies would be an excellent preparation to engage in the "gospel and culture" discussions that swirled around the Rites Controversy in China, one of the longest and most fractious internal debates in the history of the church.[58] The efforts that Protestant pioneer missionary Hudson Taylor made to accommodate to Chinese culture while remaining true to the gospel are legendary in Christian circles.

The association of Christianity with foreign domination and colonialism as discussed in the context of African Christianity is similar to the problems that the Chinese had with Christianity in the wake of the Opium Wars (1839–1843, 1856–1860). The growth of Pentecostalism as a percentage of Christianity in Chinese church growth is even greater than that in Latin America.

Finally, the personal sacrifice of Chinese Christians seeking to be faithful to Christ is humbling and can stand alongside any of the struggles endured by Christians anywhere else. The 1900 Boxer Rebellion alone produced thousands of Chinese Christian martyrs, as well as 230 martyrs among Western missionaries. In short, China is a land with a long and fascinating history of contact with Christianity. Space does not permit a development of the influence of Western Christian missionaries in China. Rather, in

57. For an excellent study of the Jesuit mission in China, see Andrew C. Ross, *A Vision Betrayed: The Jesuits in Japan and China, 1542–1742* (Edinburgh: Edinburgh Univ. Press, 1994).

58. The Jesuits believed that the Chinese Rites (e.g., ancestor veneration) were a part of Chinese social and cultural life and did not conflict with the Christian gospel. In contrast, the Dominicans insisted that participation in the Chinese Rites was syncretistic and should be condemned by the church. For a good overview of the challenges, see Paul A. Rule, "The Chinese Rites Controversy: A Long-Lasting Controversy in Sino-Western Cultural History," *Pacific Rim Report* 32 (February 2004): 1–8. This University of Southern California periodical is available at www.pacificrim.usfca.edu/research/pacrimreport/.

keeping with the primary focus of this study, we will highlight the growth and missionary efforts of indigenous Christianity in modern China.

Christianity in Modern China

October 1, 1949, marks the victory of the Communists in China under the leadership of Mao Zedong (Tse-tung) and the emergence of the People's Republic of China. In the first year of the Communist rule thousands of foreign missionaries were forced out of China. At that time there were approximately four million Christians in all China.[59] The new Communist leadership declared their unequivocal opposition to all theistic religions, insisting instead on the worship of the state, especially the personality cult of Mao Zedong, known simply as Chairman Mao.

In 1951 the Communist Party set up the Religious Affairs Bureau to oversee and supervise what it anticipated to be the final death throes of theistic religion in China. When the rapid demise of religion did not occur, the Chinese government opted for a policy of draconian control. The Protestant churches were controlled through an official government body that eventually became known as the Three-Self Patriotic Movement (TSPM).[60] The TSPM closed the majority of churches and forced all pastors in China to acknowledge that Christianity in China had largely been used as a force for imperialism and Western aggression against China. The TSPM claimed that the legacy of Protestant missions in China was a church divided hopelessly into a multitude of denominations.

The TSPM ostensibly sought to unite the church under a single "patriotic" banner. Any pastor who refused to sign a statement of patriotic loyalty to China, which included a denunciation of all expressions of Protestantism other than those registered by the TSPM and controlled by the Religious Affairs Bureau, would result in imprisonment, beating, and public shaming. The Roman Catholic Christians were likewise persecuted and controlled through a similar organization known as the Catholic Patriotic Association (CPA), which is also part of the Religious Affairs Bureau. However, since the Roman Catholic bishops were forced by the government to reject papal authority, they were excommunicated by Pope Pius XII in 1957.[61]

During the Cultural Revolution (1966–1976) Chairman Mao stepped up official hostility toward Christianity by promoting the destruction of church buildings, the confiscation of church property, and the disenfranchisement of all public expressions of faith. This was a part of his campaign against what he called the "Four Olds": old ideas, old culture, old customs, and old habits. The triumphalistic attitude of Communist leaders who maintained that Christianity would perish in China was reflected in

59. The estimated numbers are 3,274,740 Roman Catholics and 936,000 Protestants. See David Aikman, *Jesus in Beijing: How Christianity Is Transforming China and Changing the Global Balance of Power* (Washington, DC: Regnery, 2003), 52.

60. The best collection of primary source materials concerning the TSPM can be found in Wallace Merwin and Francis Jones, eds., *Documents of the Three-Self Movement: Source Materials for the Study of the Protestant Church in Communist China* (New York: National Council of Churches, 1963). For a historical overview of the rise of the TSPM, see Richard C. Bush Jr., *Religion in Communist China* (Nashville: Abingdon, 1970), 170–208.

61. Millions of Roman Catholics refused to join the CPA and opted instead to worship in underground churches. They continue to quietly confess loyalty to Rome and respect for papal authority. The Communist government also set up a third "patriotic" arm of religion under the RAB for Muslims, known as the Chinese Patriotic Islamic Association.

the headline of the *South China Morning Post* in August 1966, which proudly declared, CHRISTIANITY IN SHANGAI COMES TO AN END.[62] As it turned out, this was hardly the case.

Throughout these early decades of Communist rule in China, God raised up a number of prominent Chinese dissidents, such as Wang Mingdao (1900–1991), Allen Yuan (1914–2005), and Moses Xie (b. 1918), who remained faithful to the gospel and steadfastly refused to register with the TSPM. Each of these men spent at least two decades in prison and were repeatedly intimidated, beaten, and interrogated by Chinese authorities because of their faith in Jesus Christ. Other famous dissidents who spent decades in prison are Watchman Nee (1903–1972) and Samuel Lamb (b. 1925). These leaders also opposed the politicization of the church and wrote many Christian books, pamphlets, and hymns that helped to foster and nurture networks of unregistered house churches completely independent of the TSPM.[63]

At the time of the 1949 Communist revolution in China, there were less than one million Protestants in China. After the Cultural Revolution was over, the Religious Affairs Bureau again permitted properly registered churches to meet publicly. In 1980 the China Christian Council was formed as a service organization of the TSPM to facilitate social concerns, the printing of Bibles, and theological education.[64] Today, it is estimated that the TSPM churches "serve about 15 million Protestant believers," and the CPA claims to have "6 million registered Catholics."[65]

However, despite a few brief respites of openness, the hostility of the Chinese government to Christianity continues. The more significant, even dramatic growth of the Chinese church has occurred in the unregistered house churches in the country. Ironically, the government's forced separation of the Chinese church from outside associations has actually helped stimulate indigenous Christianity, which was not associated with or dependent on foreign funds, personnel, or initiatives. The result has been an explosion of the independent, unregistered churches in China, which appear to be impacting almost every segment of Chinese society. While estimates vary, there are probably over ninety million Christians in China today, making it one of the fastest growing churches in the world.[66] It is from these new Chinese Christians, mostly found in unregistered churches, that the Back to Jerusalem movement emerges.

---

62. As quoted in Tony Lambert, *The Resurrection of the Chinese Church* (Wheaton, IL: Harold Shaw, 1994), 9.

63. Watchman Nee founded a network of house churches known as the Little Flock. Nee published many books, including *The Normal Christian Life*, *The Spiritual Man*, and *Christ the Sum of All Spiritual Things*. Samuel Lamb is the pastor of a famous house church in Guangzhou, which is responsible for thousands of Chinese coming to Christ. Lamb also distributed his sermons through a cassette tape ministry and produced many pamphlets and hymns to spread the gospel. Because he managed to openly operate a nonregistered church and to receive foreign guests, he is credited for encouraging thousands of others to start house churches. For a survey of some of the major independent, house church movements, both before and after the rise of Communism, see Alan Hunter and Kim-Kwong Chan, *Protestantism in Contemporary China* (Cambridge: Cambridge Univ. Press, 1993), 119–23.

64. G. Thompson Brown, *Christianity in the People's Republic of China* (Atlanta: John Knox, 1986), 172.

65. Aikman, *Jesus in Beijing*, 7, 137. Bishop K. H. Ting, who retired in December 1996, served as the head of the TSPM and the China Christian Council (CCC) for many years. The TSPM and CCC now have separate leadership under Luo Guanzong and Cao Shengjie respectively.

66. David B. Barrett, George T. Kurian, and Todd M. Johnson, *World Christian Encyclopedia*, 2nd ed. (New York: Oxford Univ. Press, 2001), 191. David Aikman (*Jesus in Beijing*, 7) estimates 80 million.

BACK TO JERUSALEM MOVEMENT

Peter Wagner predicted that "by the year 2025 China will be sending out more foreign missionaries to other countries than any other nation."[67] This bold prediction was based on two realities: the dramatic growth of the Chinese church, and a growing conviction of tens of thousands of Chinese Christians that God has sovereignly called them to play a central role in global evangelization. This development is in rather surprising contrast to other parts of the world, where the missionary vision has lagged behind the initial phase of evangelism and church planting for generations.

The missionary vision gripping the Chinese church is also significant for our purposes in this study because it is part of a larger *eschatological* vision of Chinese Christians, which finds its fulfillment in the glorious return of Jesus Christ. Eschatology has always played an important role in missions, but the central emphasis is normally on obedience to the Great Commission or on the soteriological need of those apart from Christ. However, in China, eschatology is more central to the overall vision. A house church leader summed it up well when he said:

> We believe God has given us a solemn responsibility to take the fire from his altar and complete the Great Commission by establishing his kingdom in all of the remaining countries and people groups in Asia, the Middle East, and Islamic North Africa. When this happens, we believe that the Scripture says the Lord Jesus will return for his bride.[68]

This resulting missionary movement among Chinese Christians is known informally as the Back to Jerusalem Movement (BTJM). The origins of BTJM have been traced to a movement of God in 1942–1943 at the Northwest Bible Institute in Shaanxi Province.[69] Mark Ma, the vice principal of the Institute, and several students began to be burdened for the Muslim people groups located in the province of Xinjiang in Northwest China. Soon Ma and the other students began to sense that Xinjiang was not only a mission field, but also the training ground for a major missionary initiative back across the ancient Silk Route, directly into the heart of the Islamic countries of central Asia.

The Chinese province of Xinjiang borders the central Asian Islamic countries of Kazakhstan, Kyrgyzstan, Tajikistan, Afghanistan, and Pakistan. After prayer and fasting, Mark Ma received a direct call from God to "bring to completion the commission to preach the gospel to all the world."[70] Ma understood that the broad sweep of the missionary movement had moved from Jerusalem to Antioch to Western Europe to North America and eventually arrived in China at port cities like Shanghai, Macau, and Guangzhou on the eastern and southern coast of China. To complete the circuit, the Lord impressed on Ma and the others that the gospel should continue into Northwestern

---

67. See C. Peter Wagner, "Foreword" to Carl Lawrence and David Wang, *The Coming Influence of China* (Artesia, CA: Shannon, 2000), x.

68. Paul Hattaway, *Back to Jerusalem: Three Chinese House Church Leaders Share Their Vision to Complete the Great Commission* (Carlisle, UK: Piquant, 2003), 20.

69. Ibid., 23.

70. Ibid., 25.

China, across central Asia, and on to Jerusalem, from where the Great Commission was first given. A contemporary Chinese leader expressed this vision as follows:

> We believe that the farthest the gospel can travel from Jerusalem is to circle the entire globe and come all the way back to where it started—Jerusalem! When the fire of the gospel completes its circuit of the whole globe, the Lord Jesus will return! "*For the earth will be filled with the knowledge of the glory of the Lord, as the waters cover the sea*" (Hab. 2:14).[71]

These Chinese believers were probably aware that the gospel had also spread eastward and had, in fact, first arrived in China through Nestorian missionaries via central Asia across the Silk Route. But there are several observations that place this missionary vision in its proper context. First, the dominant thrust of the missionary movement in history was *primarily* a westward expanse, as the "center of gravity" map in chapter 1 clearly demonstrates. Second, the modern missionary movement to China, both Roman Catholic and Protestant, had arrived into Eastern and Southeastern China, not Western or Northwestern China. Finally, the churches planted by Nestorian missionaries along the Silk Route had all but disappeared after the rise of Islam in the seventh century.

The movement was originally called the Preach Everywhere Gospel Band (*Bian Chuan Fuyin Tuan*), but in May 1946 was formally organized as the Back to Jerusalem Evangelistic Band.[72] A few Chinese Christians began to capture the Back to Jerusalem vision, and gradually the movement targeted all of the Islamic countries in central Asia and North Africa, culminating in the Jews in Palestine itself. In fact, Mark Ma himself claims that the Lord spoke to him that the "hardest field of labor is my own people the Jews ... it is not that their hearts are especially hard, but I have kept for the Chinese church a portion of [the] inheritance."[73]

Several of these early pioneers began to make their way toward Xinjiang to start learning the language and culture of that part of China.[74] However, this coincided with the political upheaval in China culminating in the Communist rise to power in 1949. The Communists, as explored earlier, relentlessly opposed all missionary activity, forcibly imprisoned several of the pioneers, and forced the movement underground. Probably the most important of these early pioneers was a man named Simon Zhao, who survived over forty years of imprisonment in Xinjiang. Zhao was able to "keep alive the original Back to Jerusalem vision and impart it to the current leadership of China's house church networks."[75] The vision has now spread to a number of these networks, and the 1990s brought a dynamic rekindling of the Back to Jerusalem vision.

71. Ibid., 20.

72. Aikman, *Jesus in Beijing*, 196–97. Aikman argues that Ma decided on the name "Back to Jerusalem Evangelistic Band" as early as May 1942. The year 1946 represents the official adoption of the name and the acceptance of a formal mission statement by the group.

73. Hattaway, *Back to Jerusalem*, 26.

74. China has 56 different nationalities and several hundred minority groups, even though 92 percent of China are Han and an additional 3 percent have been assimilated into the Han.

75. Aikman, *Jesus in Beijing*, 200. Simon Zhao died in Henan province on December 7, 2001, at 83 years old.

In the fifty-year gap between the original vision of Mark Ma and the release of Simon Zhao from prison in Xinjiang, the Chinese church had dramatically changed in several important ways. First, the number of Chinese Christians had grown from a few million to over seventy million. There were now far more laborers to dedicate themselves to the Back to Jerusalem vision.

Second, the church's phenomenal growth had also contributed to a sense of confidence, sometimes bordering on triumphalism, about the divine, eschatological role the Chinese church has been called to fulfill.

Third, fifty years of Communist rule had uniquely prepared the Chinese to work in Islamic contexts. They had learned how to work, and even prosper, in a hostile environment. They had learned how to endure and maintain their witness in the face of persecution, beatings, and long imprisonments. As Brother Yun once commented, "there is little that any of the Muslim, Buddhist, or Hindu countries can do to us that we haven't already experienced in China."[76] They had also learned how to organize outreach apart from expensive and complicated administrative structures as is common in the West. It is certainly ironic that the atheistic communists were actually instrumental in creating an environment that has forged some of the most uniquely prepared missionaries in history.

What is becoming increasingly clear over the last fifteen years of the rekindled movement is that the BTJM is not a structured, defined, organized movement operating under a single bureaucratic umbrella. Instead, it is more of a vision statement that many Chinese Christians have identified with, and yet which provides no formal connection among its adherents. In this respect the BTJM is similar to the Lausanne movement, which has—through the Lausanne Covenant—captured a vision for cooperation and networking in completing the Great Commission, but without sharing a common ecclesiastical or administrative center.[77]

Even though there is no unified administrative structure, there have been a number of strategic gatherings of house church leaders to promote unity and to better coordinate efforts. Some of the most significant of these meetings occurred throughout 1996 and later in 2002. The 1996 meetings focused on prayer and developing a common confession of faith that would bring greater unity to the house church movement and further refine the vision of the BTJM. One of the leaders of these unity meetings, Peter Xu Yongze, made it clear that their purpose was not to unite in any formal, structural way, but to unify for the sake of the Back to Jerusalem vision. He said, "It needs to be understood that the reason we came together was not for the sake of unity in itself. It was unity for the sake of fulfilling the common vision God had given to us—the vision of taking the gospel back to Jerusalem, thus completing the Great Commission and hastening the return of our Lord!"[78]

---

76. Hattaway, *Back to Jerusalem*, 58. Chinese Christians are taught to expect to go to jail and to regard the prison as a receptive mission field.

77. See "Who 'Owns' Back to Jerusalem?" an article posted on www.backtojerusalem.com. This has at times fostered isolation and disunity among the unregistered, house church Christians. See Bob Whyte, "Some Reflections on Protestant Life in China," in *All under Heaven: Chinese Tradition and Christian Life in the People's Republic of China*, ed. Alan Hunter and Don Rimmington (Kampen, Netherlands: Kok, 1992), 63–64.

78. Hattaway, *Back to Jerusalem*, 66.

On November 26, 1998, several key house church leaders who were part of the unity meetings adopted a common Confession of Faith, the first of its kind to be adopted by several networks of house churches in China.[79] The confession and accompanying statements condemned various heresies,[80] sought to clarify why they have chosen not to register with the TSPM,[81] and set forth their commitment to remain within the doctrinal boundaries of historic Christian confessions. The confession affirms that the sixty-six books of the Bible are inspired and without error. It affirms the Trinity and all of the central features of Christ's incarnation, death, and resurrection, which have been proclaimed by Christians throughout history.

This confession explicitly rejects cessationism, reflecting the influence of the Pentecostal movement in the nonregistered churches in China.[82] The confession also has a strong statement on the church, affirming the priesthood of all believers and rejecting any reliance on political power to achieve its goals.[83] The church's role in missions is also given a prominent place. Missions is understood to be the responsibility of all Christians and includes not only training and sending out missionaries, but also "defending the truth by refuting heresies and bringing them to the correct path."[84] As for eschatology, the statement strongly affirms the return of Jesus Christ and the bodily resurrection of believers. It is clearly premillennial but refuses to endorse either a pretribulationist or posttribulationist view.[85]

Another strategic meeting, known as the Beijing Forum, met in the capital in 2002 and included several Western and Korean mission leaders. Dr. Luis Bush, the chairman of the AD 2000 and Beyond Movement, was present to help coordinate the emerging Chinese missionary thrust with the many international efforts to reach central Asia, the Islamic world, and Israel with the gospel.[86] Remarkably, the Beijing Forum even included some churches registered with the TSPM. Out of this meeting

---

79. The full text of the various statements, including the Confession of Faith, may be found in Appendix B of Aikman, *Jesus in Beijing* (295–303). This formal confession should not be understood as the most important evidence for the essential orthodoxy of the house church movement. William Dyrness has convincingly pointed out that the theology of the house church movement is best captured in their testimonies, their sacrificial love for one another, and the sincere piety evidenced in and through the lives of Chinese believers. See William Dyrness, *Invitation to Cross-Cultural Theology: Case Studies in Vernacular Theologies* (Grand Rapids: Zondervan, 1992), 42–63.

80. The statement condemns the popular Oriental Lightning movement, which believes that Jesus has returned as a thirty-five-year-old Chinese woman named Mrs. Deng. For more on this see, Matthew Forney Dengfeng, "Jesus Is Back, and She's Chinese," *Time* (Asia) 158, no. 18 (November 5, 2001): 42.

81. This is significant because even though this confession is technically an internal document, it directly explains why the house churches have refused to unite with the TSPM. Thus, it indirectly represents communication with the Chinese government from a group that has been officially kept underground.

82. The Confession states as follows, "We do not believe in the cessation of signs and miracles or the termination of the gifts of the Holy Spirit after the apostolic period. We do not forbid speaking in tongues and we do not impose on people to speak in tongues; nor do we insist that speaking in tongues is the evidence of being saved. We refute the view that the Holy Spirit is not a person in the Trinity, but only a kind of influence" (see Aikman, *Jesus in Beijing*, 300).

83. The statement says, "We are opposed to the expansion of the church by relying on political power, whether domestic or international" (ibid., 301).

84. Ibid.

85. The statement says, "As to the interpretation of whether Christ will come before or after the tribulation, we acknowledge that there are different views among different church groups and that we cannot absolutely endorse any view. The responsibility of Christians is to be alert and be prepared to welcome the Second Coming of Christ" (ibid., 302).

86. The AD 2000 and Beyond Movement serves to help coordinate global missionary efforts. Luis Bush is the one who coined the expression 10/40 window, which helped to draw attention on the location of the most unreached people groups in the world. Interestingly, the 10/40 window corresponds precisely with the same region that has burdened the Chinese Christians, the nations all around the Silk Route.

came the specific target for the BTJM to mobilize 100,000 Chinese missionaries for the task.[87] This would be a missionary force twice as large as any sent out by North America.

However, the Chinese church envisions most of these workers to be self-supporting, using their talents and vocations to relocate all along the ancient Silk Route.[88] It will help them to blend into the culture without suspicion and sidestep the financial and administrative challenges that often hamper mission organizations. In fact, one Chinese leader has called the frequent "grandiose strategies" of the West "elephant plans." He points out that elephants make a great deal of noise and are almost impossible to hide. In contrast, he sees the BTJM as a quiet, grassroots movement, pictured more as an "army of insects" or the slow, relentless, and yet quiet work of "termites."[89] Through these means, one leader exclaims, the house churches of China will "pull down the world's last remaining spiritual strongholds—the house of Buddha, the house of Muhammad, and the house of Hinduism—and to proclaim the glorious gospel to all nations before the Second Coming of our Lord Jesus Christ."[90]

Jonathan Edwards and the Back to Jerusalem Movement

In the first part of this study we examined four key features of Jonathan Edwards' eschatology as they relate to global missions. First, Edwards anticipated a massive, global advance of the gospel prior to the millennium. Second, he understood this latter-day revival as occurring in several defined stages, with specific focus on Muslims and Jews. Third, while Edwards was optimistic about the spread of the gospel, he was also realistic about the likelihood of persecution for all true believers. Finally, Edwards was deeply committed to prayer as central to the effectiveness of this period of evangelism and witness. Each of these areas will now be compared to the eschatological vision for missions as found in the BTJM.

Premillennial Global Advance

The eschatologies of both Edwards and the Chinese house church leaders share a strong sense of optimism about the expansion of the church during the period just prior to the millennium. Both strongly reject the notion that the inauguration of the millennium will be preceded by nothing but apostasy, despair, and calamity for the church. Edwards' eschatology linked this latter-day movement of God to the angel pouring out the sixth vial. He understood each of the vials as not only pronouncing judgment on some aspect of Satan's kingdom, but also stimulating a major revival and expansion of the church.

Like Edwards, the Chinese anticipate a major global revival and the expansion of the Christian faith to accompany the latter days. They do not link this global Christian advance to the vials of Revelation 16, nor do they anticipate any *necessary* collapse

87. "A Captivating Vision," *Christianity Today* 84, no. 4 (April 2004): 84.

88. This is similar to the initial Protestant phase of global missions, which was fueled by the Moravians, who sent out self-supporting, sometimes called "tentmaking," missionaries.

89. Hattaway, *Back to Jerusalem*, 91.

90. Ibid., 57.

of Roman Catholicism, as did Edwards. Instead, they understand this great ingathering to have two main reference points. First, it is a necessary part of our obedience to Jesus Christ and the fulfillment of the Great Commission. Second, it is particularly urgent as we prepare for the return of Christ.

For the Chinese, the most important portent that will mark the "end of the world" is not wars or natural disasters or the establishment of the nation of Israel; rather, the "final sign" will be the fulfillment of Matthew 24:14: "And this gospel of the kingdom will be preached in the whole world as a testimony to all nations, and then the end will come."[91] Because the Chinese are premillennial rather than postmillennial like Edwards, the promise of Christ's return plays a more central role among them than in Edwards. However, both Edwards and the Chinese are highly motivated by the role of eschatology in missions and both are equally enthusiastic about various global signs that will accompany the advent of the millennium.

From a Western perspective not informed by global realities, it is easy to become discouraged and pessimistic about the advance of the gospel because of the rapid decline of Christianity in the West.[92] However, from the Chinese perspective, it seems that everywhere one turns—in the city and in the country, among the educated as well as the peasants—people are coming to Christ and new churches are emerging. When Paul Hattaway was interviewing the leaders of the BTJM, he asked them if they were optimistic enough to expect as many as two hundred or even three hundred million believers in China over the next thirty years. After a long silence, one of the leaders said, "in thirty years *all* of China will know the Lord."[93] It is easy to dismiss the statement as an example of overly optimistic triumphalism, but it does underscore the confidence and energy of the Chinese church in contrast to the timidity and lethargy of the Western churches bound by the chains of consumerism and narcissistic self-focus.

Jonathan Edwards and the Chinese missionaries both share a remarkable optimism about the advance of the gospel around the world in the period prior to the millennium. The Chinese speak about missions as a "race towards the finish line" and, as we have seen throughout this study, clearly link missions with eschatology: "Success means nothing less than the fulfillment of the Great Commission and the return of our Lord Jesus Christ."[94] Or, as another leader put it, "Let's rush to the front line one more time for our King and Christ will come! We can have a holiday for 1,000 years when it is all finished!"[95]

After the revival at Northampton (1733–1734) and the emergence of the Great Awakening (1739–1740), Edwards' writings are filled with similar optimism. His "Events of an Hopeful Aspect on the State of Religion" chronicles dozens of newspaper clippings and letters that testify to his optimism concerning the "advance of religion

91. Ibid., 109.

92. Contrary to popular notions, European and European descent peoples are currently the most resistant to the gospel in the world. Todd Johnson and David Barrett lay out an extensive case for how to statistically measure responsiveness (see *World Christian Trends* [Pasadena, CA: William Carey Library, 2001], Part 26, "Georesponse," 773–78). In Part 11 (Listings) they list the ten most responsive and the most resistant (see secs. 137–38). Remarkably, the top ten most responsive people-groups in the world are all located in China and India. In contrast, all ten of the most resistant peoples are located in Europe (see p. 404).

93. Hattaway, *Back to Jerusalem*, 3.

94. Ibid., 70.

95. Ibid., 112.

and the kingdom of Christ."[96] In his Revelation commentary, Edwards specifically links the pouring out of the sixth vial with the establishment of the gospel among Muslims prior to the millennium.[97] Throughout his "Notes on the Apocalypse," "An Humble Attempt," and his "History of Redemption," Edwards repeatedly links his missiology with his eschatology, as do the Chinese. To both of them, the overall future of the church and the prospects for the gospel in the world are bright and promising as we eagerly await the advent of the millennium.

The Stronghold of Islam, Judaism, and the Rest

Another shared feature in the eschatology of Edwards and the BTJM is a deep awareness of the challenges posed by non-Christian religions in the fulfillment of the Great Commission. As explored earlier in his "History of Redemption," Edwards endorsed a progressive scheme through which different parts of Satan's kingdom would fall like dominos.[98] First would be "Satan's Mahometan kingdom," followed by the day when "Jewish infidelity shall be overthrown." Finally, the entirety of "Satan's heathenish kingdom" would be overthrown and all the nations of the world would be "visited with glorious light." This glorious light was, for Edwards, a reference to the universal, global preaching of the gospel, which encompassed every nation and would mark the advent of the millennium.[99]

The eschatology that undergirds the missiology of the BTJM is characterized by a reverse Silk Route approach whereby the Chinese envision bringing the gospel back along the various trade routes, straight through the heart of Islamic central Asia and, finally, to Jerusalem. Integral to the whole BTJM is a commitment to "tear down the world's last remaining spiritual strongholds" and to take the gospel "to the nations that lie between China and Jerusalem, the place where the fire of the gospel first started to spread."[100] Like Edwards, the Chinese see this as occurring in definite stages: first, the Islamic groups in Northwest China, then the Muslims of Central Asia, and finally the Jews in Israel itself. The early church began with a "first the Jews, then the Gentiles" approach. The Chinese anticipate a "first the Gentiles, then the Jews" ending.

One of the significant differences in Edwards' scheme as outlined in the "History of Redemption" and the Chinese Christians' view of the world is that Edwards did not anticipate that the dramatic spread of the gospel in Africa would *precede* any major movement to Christ among either Muslims or Jews. Nevertheless, Edwards did foresee the day when Africa would be "visited with glorious light, and delivered from all their

96. Edwards, "Events of an Hopeful Aspect on the State of Religion," *The Works of Jonathan Edwards*, 5:285–97, which is included by Stein as one of the seven sections of Edwards' "Notes on the Apocalypse" (cf. also 5:196).

97. Edwards, "Notes on the Apocalypse," 5:196–97. In "An Humble Attempt" (5:363–64), Edwards gives a sweeping overview of revivals around the world, demonstrating his optimism about the global expanse of the gospel after the pouring out of the sixth vial.

98. Similar schemes of the progressive collapse of Satan's kingdom are found in "An Humble Attempt" and "Notes on the Apocalypse." See footnotes 39, 42, and 43, above.

99. Edwards' postmillennialism makes it unlikely that this refers to the return of Christ. See "Notes on the Apocalypse," 5:177–78. See T. M. Moore, ed., *Praying Together for Revival* (Phillipsburg, NJ: Presbyterian & Reformed, 2004), 34–38, which brings together various statements about prayer and revival in the writings of Jonathan Edwards.

100. Hattaway, *Back to Jerusalem*, 57, 63.

darkness, and shall become a civil, Christian, understanding, and holy people."[101] Edwards would have been delighted to know that in the early decades of the twenty-first century it is anticipated that Africa will have more Christians than any other continent.

The Chinese fully expect that the Africans will preach the gospel and plant churches all across sub-Saharan Africa. In the earliest days of the birth of the Chinese mission-sending vision, as noted earlier, it was known by the name Preach Everywhere Gospel Band (*Bian Chuan Fuyin Tuan*). However, as the movement has matured and became more focused, it has become clearly focused on reaching Muslims, followed by reaching Jews. This is an overall scheme that Edwards would have understood and, largely, embraced. His biggest surprise would be that the Chinese are leading the charge rather than the Americans.

Persecution of God's People in the Latter Days

One of the often neglected aspects of Edwards' eschatology is his expectation of persecution. This anticipation of persecution is largely because Edwards interpreted the slaying of the two witnesses in Revelation 11 as occurring *prior* to the Reformation and their subsequent resuscitation as the Reformation itself.

However, two important observations must be made. First, it is true that Edwards believed that the most dangerous days of persecution were behind the church, if by dangerous one means the threat of the church's extinction rather than a reference to the severity of any particular persecution. Edwards was greatly encouraged by the spread of the Reformation to so many different countries and anticipated further growth of Christianity around the world. He reasoned that the sheer geographic dispersion of Christians in the world made it nearly impossible for the light of the gospel to be extinguished in any single, localized persecution, however severe. For Edwards, this state of affairs was in real contrast to those perilous days prior to the Reformation when the faithful few were being relentlessly persecuted and the gospel did not have any secure foothold outside of Western Europe. The light of the gospel nearly perished from the earth, as symbolized by the two witnesses being killed by the beast (Rev. 11:7).[102] Edwards said that now only a major global calamity could threaten the life of the church.

Second, Edwards nevertheless did anticipate violent, and even increasing, attacks on the faithful as the time came for the pouring out of the seventh vial and the ushering in of the millennium. In fact, it is precisely because of the church's geographic spread that Edwards anticipated a corresponding reaction by those arrayed against the church. He wrote, "For the greatest persecutions of Antichrist have been since

101. Edwards, "A History of the Work of Redemption," 1:608.

102. The battle between the beast and the two witnesses represents, for Edwards, the struggle between the papacy and the Waldenses, Albigenses, and the Bohemians, all of whom the Reformers looked back on as faithful, but persecuted, precursors of the Reformation. Edwards believed that the crusade of Pope Innocent III against the Albigenses in the early thirteenth century is the most likely specific reference to the battle referred to in Revelation 11:7 (see "An Humble Attempt," 5:390–91). He understood the significance of there being only "two" witnesses in Revelation 11 with the small number of true believers in the world prior to the Reformation (see "Notes on the Apocalypse," 5:207–8).

the beginning of the Reformation, since the gospel has ceased to be confined, and has been preached to all nations and kindreds and tongues."[103] With the gospel on the ascendancy and the millennium approaching, persecution would increase, for "the church of Christ has never as yet been for any long time, free from persecution; especially when truth has prevailed, and true religion flourished."[104]

The birth and the later rebirth of the BTJM is inextricably linked to the persecution and suffering of Simon Zhao, who was part of the original vision and, after forty-five years in prison, was able to rekindle the vision in a new generation of house church leaders. All of the pioneers of the BTJM have spent considerable time in prison, many for decades. The hymnology that has come out of the BTJM reflects a suffering church, as reflected in this hymn written by Simon Zhao in prison:

> I want to experience the same pain and suffering of Jesus on the cross;
> the spear in his side, the pain in his heart;
> I'd rather feel the pain of shackles on my feet,
> than ride through Egypt in Pharaoh's chariot.[105]

Many of the Chinese Back to Jerusalem hymns draw heavily on images of persecution and suffering as the Chinese preach the gospel all the way to Jerusalem. Their eyes are lifted up to the harvest, but they speak of their eyes being "filled with tears" and blood being "splattered across our chests"; nevertheless, they remain determined to take up their "heavy crosses" and "march on toward Jerusalem."[106] The Chinese expect thousands of martyrs, and they call on the "house church warriors to write their testimonies with their own blood."[107]

Peter Xu Yongze, one of the leaders of the BTJM, explains the reason for this expectation: "The devil, who has kept Muslim, Buddhist and Hindu nations captive for thousands of years, will not surrender without a strong and bloody fight."[108] Brother Yun, one of the house church leaders, expects that of the 100,000 missionaries sent out from China, 10,000 will be martyrs in the first decade.[109] In fact, unlike Western ministerial training, part of the training of Chinese missionaries includes instruction on how to be an effective witness in prison.

The Chinese connection between suffering, missions, and eschatological fulfillment resonates with Sun-Hee Kwak's conclusion in his *Eschatology and Christian Mission* when he says, "In realizing the missiological significance of suffering in an eschatological sense, we find a source of strength to overcome our suffering and to proclaim the gospel to the world."[110]

---

103. Edwards, "Notes on the Apocalypse," 5:162.
104. Edwards, "An Humble Attempt," 5:336.
105. Hattaway, *Back to Jerusalem*, 46.
106. Ibid., 54, for a full text of the hymn.
107. Ibid., 58.
108. Ibid., 70. Note that there is also the unheralded persecution that occurs not from the government, but from within Chinese families. As many as 70 percent of Chinese Christians are women and, according to one estimate, 40 percent of them are persecuted by their husbands and other family members because of their faith in Christ. See Paul Estabrooks, *Great Bible Women of China* (Santa Ana, CA: Open Doors, 1997), 45. For an excellent portrayal of life inside the persecuted house church movement in China, see C. Hope Flinchbaugh, *Daughter of China* (Minneapolis: Bethany, 2002).
109. "A Captivating Vision," 86.
110. Sun-Hee Kwak, *Eschatology and Christian Mission* (Seoul, Korea: Data World, 2000), 348.

The Role of Prayer in Stimulating Missions and Preparing for the Millennium

A prominent feature in Jonathan Edwards' theology is that there are particular seasons of harvest or ingathering when God accelerates the pace of those who are entering the kingdom as well as those who are being brought into a "state of wrath."[111] Edwards drew heavily on agricultural imagery in which, after a long time of work and toil, there was a compressed period of harvest when the fruit was brought in.

Likewise, Edwards believed that there were certain junctures in history where we are able to discern that the time for a spiritual ingathering or harvest has come. Such times "mark milestones in sacred history, and propel it along."[112] For Edwards, the period following the pouring out of the sixth vial was an important harvest time in preparation for the coming millennium, ushered in with the pouring out of the seventh vial. These "seasons of ingathering" could be greatly assisted by prayer, since Edwards fully affirmed that God accomplishes his sovereign purposes through the human instrumentality of the church, especially through preaching and prayer.

Edwards wrote "An Humble Attempt" for the sole purpose of organizing concerts of prayer dedicated to intercessory prayer, asking God to bring about the great spiritual harvest as seen in the revivals and global preaching that accompany the last days and precede the millennium. The central text that undergirds this treatise on prayer is Zechariah 8:20–22, which calls God's people to "entreat the LORD and seek the LORD Almighty."

In Edwards' sermon on this text, "Prayer for the Coming of Christ's Kingdom," he demonstrates the connection between prayer and the coming of Christ's kingdom: "'Tis a very suitable thing and well-pleasing to God, for many people in different parts of the world, by express agreement to unite in extraordinary, speedy, fervent and constant prayer for the promised advancement of God's church and kingdom in the world."[113] For Edwards, devoted, concerted prayer was one of the distinguishing marks of a true revival and the necessary posture to assure the demise of Satan's kingdom and the extension of the gospel into the world.

China is experiencing a harvest of ingathering that in sheer numbers far surpasses anything Edwards saw during the Great Awakening. One of the distinguishing marks of a true revival is a deep burden for those without Christ and an increased fervency in prayer.[114] The Chinese house church and the BTJM are both characterized by prayer. In fact, Carl Lawrence and David Wang argue that "the distinguishing feature of the present day church growth in China is the disciplined prayer life of every believer."[115]

---

111. Jonathan Edwards, "Seasons of Ingathering," in *Works of Jonathan Edwards*, 22:482.

112. Ibid., 22:477 (the editor's introduction to "Seasons of Ingathering").

113. Jonathan Edwards, "Prayer for the Coming of Christ's Kingdom," as quoted by Stein, "Editor's Introduction," *Works of Jonathan Edwards*, 5:83. See also Edwards, "An Humble Attempt," 5:350–51. In his "Some Thoughts Concerning the Revival," Edwards advocates the organization of "praying companies or societies" who will devote themselves to prayer for revival and spiritual renewal (see *The Works of Jonathan Edwards*, ed. C. C. Goen (New Haven, CT: Yale Univ. Press, 1972), 4:519.

114. See William Cooper, preface to Jonathan Edwards' "The Distinguishing Marks," *The Works of Jonathan Edwards*, 4:217–25.

115. Lawrence and Wang, *The Coming Influence of China*, 38.

As with Edwards, the Chinese place great emphasis on the role of prayer and fasting. They pray for the progress of the gospel in China, the tearing down of the spiritual strongholds of Islam, and, remarkably, that Bible schools and seminaries in the West will remain faithful to the Word of God.[116]

The Chinese have discovered the powerful connection between devoted prayer and the eschatological fulfillment of Matthew 24:14. As a senior pastor in Gwangwashi commented, "We need to pray for more people, that this church will reach out to the city. We want to pray that everyone in Beijing knows Jesus and that Jesus will be known in the whole country and that China will be a country from which the gospel is spreading to the rest of the world."[117] As the Chinese retrace the steps of those early Nestorian pioneers and make their way back to Jerusalem directly through the heart of Islamic people groups, many of whom are hostile to the Christian gospel, they do so knowing that these spiritual strongholds will not crumble unless the church around the world is praying and interceding for them and with them.

CONCLUSION

This chapter has explored the vital link between eschatology and global missions in the thinking of Jonathan Edwards and the Back to Jerusalem Movement in China. For Edwards, eschatology was not primarily speculation about future events, but a way of understanding and interpreting the inbreaking of God's work in his own time. Even reading the daily newspaper was, for Edwards, an opportunity to reflect on his eschatology. Likewise, for the Chinese, eschatology represents a powerful critique against the entire structure of Communist China in which they live. David Aikman keenly observed that one of the key differences between the state approved registered churches and the independent house churches in China is that "it is unlikely that a worshipper in a three-self church would ever hear a sermon on the Second Coming of Christ."[118] The reason is that eschatology demands a *telos* to human history that subsumes all of human social and political history under the larger redemptive work of God in the world.

This is why the Chinese government once arrested Samuel Lamb for preaching an eschatological sermon.[119] This is why Jonathan Edwards understood revival and global evangelism not as a mere shift in the sociological demographics of contemporary religion, but as a development within the larger context of eschatology and God's sovereign unfolding purposes in the world. Both Edwards and the Chinese witnessed a remarkable increase in the number of people coming to Jesus Christ, without the help of paid staff, trained experts, financial resources, or sophisticated programs. We have much to learn from their perspective and experience. They understand profoundly that whenever God's people experience a "season of ingathering," it gives us the courage and faith to anticipate that great day when "the earth will be filled with the knowledge of the glory of the LORD, as the waters cover the sea" (Hab. 2:14).

---

116. Ibid.
117. Aikman, *Jesus in Beijing*, 138.
118. Ibid., 136–37.
119. Ibid., 61.

BIBLIOGRAPHY

Aikman, David. *Jesus in Beijing: How Christianity is Transforming China and Changing the Global Balance of Power.* Washington, DC: Regnery, 2003.

Archer, Gleason, Jr., Paul Feinberg, Douglas Moo, and Richard Reiter. *Three Views on the Rapture: Pre-, Mid-, or Post-Tribulation.* Grand Rapids: Zondervan, 1996.

Barrett, David B., George T. Kurian, and Todd M. Johnson. *World Christian Encyclopedia.* 2nd ed. New York: Oxford University Press, 2001.

Barrett, David B., and Todd M. Johnson, eds. *World Christian Trends, AD 30–AD 2200: Interpreting the Annual Christian Megacensus.* Pasadena, CA: William Carey Library, 2001.

The Best Cartoons from Leadership Journal. Vol. 1. Nashville: Broadman & Holman, 1999.

Bock, Darrell, ed. *Three Views on the Millennium and Beyond.* Grand Rapids: Zondervan, 1999.

Brown, G. Thompson. *Christianity in the People's Republic of China.* Atlanta: John Knox, 1986.

Bush, Richard C., Jr. *Religion in Communist China.* Nashville: Abingdon, 1970.

Cumming, Bruce. "The Chinese Rites Controversy: A Long-Lasting Controversy in Sino-Western Cultural History." *Pacific Rim Report* 32 (February 2004). www.pacificrim.usfca.edu/research/pacrimreport (June 19, 2006).

Davis, John Jefferson. *Christ's Victorious Kingdom.* Grand Rapids: Baker, 1986.

Dengfeng, Matthew Forney. "Jesus Is Back, and She's Chinese." *Time* (Asia) 158, no. 18 (November 5, 2001).

Edwards, Jonathan. *The Works of Jonathan Edwards.* Edited by John E. Smith et al. 22 volumes. New Haven, CT: Yale University Press, 1959–.

Estabrooks, Paul. *Great Bible Women of China.* Santa Ana, CA: Open Doors, 1997.

Flinchbaugh, C. Hope. *Daughter of China.* Minneapolis: Bethany, 2002.

Gerstner, John H. *The Rational Biblical Theology of Jonathan Edwards.* Vol. 3. Orlando, FL: Berea, 1993.

Goen, C. C. "Jonathan Edwards: A New Departure in Eschatology." *Church History* 28, no. 1 (March 1959): 25–40.

Gregg, Steve, ed. *Revelation: Four Views: A Parallel Commentary.* Nashville: Nelson, 1997.

Hartzfeld, David F., and Charles Nienkirchen, eds. *The Birth of a Vision: Essays on the Ministry and Thought of Albert B. Simpson.* Regina, SK (Canada): His Dominion, 1986.

Hattaway, Paul. *Back to Jerusalem: Three Chinese House Church Leaders Share Their Vision to Complete the Great Commission.* Carlisle, UK: Piquant, 2003.

Hickman, Edward, ed. *The Works of Jonathan Edwards.* 2 vols. Edinburgh: Banner of Truth Trust, 1974.

Hunter, Alan, and Kim-Kwong Chan. *Protestantism in Contemporary China.* Cambridge: Cambridge University Press, 1993.

Johnson, Todd M. "The Crisis of Missions: The Historical Development of the Idea of the Evangelization of the World by the Year 1900," *International Journal of Frontier Missions* 5, nos. 1–4 (January–October 1988): 1–103.

Kwak, Sun-Hee. *Eschatology and Christian Mission.* Seoul, Korea: Data World, 2000.

Ladd, George Eldon. *The Blessed Hope: A Biblical Study of the Second Advent and the Rapture.* Grand Rapids: Eerdmans, 1980.

_____. *The Presence of the Future.* Rev. ed. Grand Rapids: Eerdmans, 1996.

LaHaye, Tim, and Jerry B. Jenkins. *Left Behind.* Wheaton, IL: Tyndale, 1995.

Lambert, Tony. *The Resurrection of the Chinese Church.* Wheaton, IL: Shaw, 1994.

Lawrence, Carl, and David Wang. *The Coming Influence of China.* Artesia, CA: Shannon, 2000.

McDermott, Gerald. *Jonathan Edwards Confronts the Gods.* New York: Oxford University Press, 2000.

_____. *One Holy and Happy Society.* College State: Pennsylvania State University Press, 1992.

Merwin, Wallace, and Francis Jones, eds. *Documents of the Three-Self Movement: Source Materials for the Study of the Protestant Church in Communist China.* New York: National Council of Churches, 1963.

Moore, T. M., ed. *Praying Together for Revival.* Phillipsburg, NJ: Presbyterian & Reformed, 2004.

Nee, Watchman. *Christ the Sum of All Spiritual Things.* New York: Christian Fellowship, 1973.

_____. *The Normal Christian Life.* Colorado Springs, CO: International Students, 1969.

_____. *The Spiritual Man.* New York: Christian Fellowship, 1968.

Powell, Charles R. "Spiritual Awakening in China Today: Out from, and Returning to, Jerusalem." Doctoral diss., Gordon-Conwell Theological Seminary, 2003.

Ross, Andrew C. *A Vision Betrayed: The Jesuits in Japan and China, 1542–1742.* Edinburgh: Edinburgh University Press, 1994.

Rule, Paul A. "The Chinese Rites Controversy: A Long-Lasting Controversy in Sino-Western Cultural History." *Pacific Rim Report* 32 (February 2004): 1–8.

Ryrie, Charles. *Dispensationalism.* Chicago: Moody Bible Institute, 1995.

Schaff, Philip, ed. *The Creeds of Christendom.* Vol. 3. Grand Rapids: Baker, 1993.

Svigel, Michael J. "The Apocalypse of John and the Rapture of the Church: A Reevaluation." *Trinity Journal*, n.s. 22, no. 1 (Spring 2001): 23–74.

Westbrook, Robert. "Social Criticism and the Heavenly Vision of Jonathan Edwards." *Soundings* 59 (1976): 397–409.

"Who 'Owns' Back to Jerusalem?" 2002–2006. www.backtojerusalem.com (June 19, 2006).

Whyte, Bob. "Some Reflections on Protestant Life in China." Pages 55–68 in *All under Heaven: Chinese Tradition and Christian Life in the People's Republic of China.* Edited by Alan Hunter and Don Rimmington. Kampen, Netherlands: Kok, 1992.

Wilson, John F. "History, Redemption, and the Millennium." In *Jonathan Edwards and the American Experience.* Edited by Nathan Hatch and Harry Stout. New York: Oxford University Press, 1988.

Withrow, Brandon G. "A Future of Hope: Jonathan Edwards and Millennial Expectations." *Trinity Journal*, n.s., 22, no. 1 (Spring 2001): 75–98.

Chapter 10

The Emerging Contours of Global Theology

Renaissance in Theological Scholarship

On May 24, 1738, a young John Wesley went "very unwillingly" to a society meeting held on Aldersgate Street in London. While there, at about 8:45 p.m., he was listening to someone read Martin Luther's *Preface to St. Paul's Epistle to the Romans.*[1] Wesley later wrote the following in his journal about what happened that night:

> While he was describing the change which God works in the heart through faith in Christ, I felt my heart strangely warmed. I felt I did trust in Christ, Christ alone, for my salvation; and an assurance was given me that he had taken my sins away, even mine; and saved me from the law of sin and death.[2]

I cherish this vignette from church history, which has nurtured me for many years. Church historians still debate about what exactly happened to Wesley that night, but no one can deny that this "Aldersgate experience" became a defining moment in his life.

Many of us may not be able to look back on our lives and point to a moment as dramatic as Wesley's Aldersgate experience or Augustine's garden experience when he heard those famous words of a child, "*Tolle lege, tolle lege.*"[3] Nevertheless, I am sure nearly all of us can recall hearing or reading something that dramatically changed our perspective. After we heard it, we thought differently, we prayed differently, or perhaps we preached differently. It is important to have milestones or turning points in our

---

1. Martin Luther, *Preface to St. Paul's Epistle to the Romans,* trans. Charles E. Hay (Philadelphia: United Lutheran, 1903).

2. John Wesley, *The Journal of the Rev. John Wesley,* ed. Nehemiah Curnock (London: Epworth, 1938), 1:475–76.

3. In the fourth century, while Augustine was sitting in a garden, he heard a child's voice crying out, "*Tolle lege, tolle lege*" ("Take up and read, take up and read"). He opened the Scriptures and read in silence Romans 13:13–14, "Let us behave decently, as in the daytime, not in orgies and drunkenness, not in sexual immorality and debauchery, not in dissension and jealousy. Rather clothe yourselves with the Lord Jesus Christ and do not think about how to gratify the desires of the sinful nature." Upon reading that text, Augustine writes, "All the gloom of doubt vanished away."

spiritual and intellectual journeys. I can recall a number of moments in my life as a pastor, missionary, or seminary professor when I read or heard something that became a strategic catalyst, propelling me to deeper reflection and faith.

In fact, the seed that many years later compelled me to write this book can be traced back to a single sentence spoken by one of my professors, Andrew Walls, during my doctoral studies at the University of Edinburgh. It is a statement that appeared later in an article he wrote in 1999: "Theological scholarship needs a renaissance of mission studies."[4]

At first, Walls' statement struck me as backwards and counterintuitive. In other words, many of us have long observed how desperately mission studies needs a more vigorous exposure to theological scholarship, but could the reverse also be true?[5] Could mission studies really help to stimulate a renaissance in theological scholarship? The answer is a resounding yes!

Indeed, it is increasingly becoming clear that theological scholarship in the West has largely lost its missiological moorings and often operates in isolation from the burgeoning realities of the global church. Yet, the theology of the New Testament is clearly set within the larger missiological framework of the first-century church as believers proclaimed the good news of Jesus Christ throughout a hostile Roman empire and beyond.

The gospel is inherently a gospel of action, not merely a gospel of reflection; it is not merely propositions to be believed, but a salvation to be proclaimed. Could mission studies, long the stepchild within the family of theological studies, now become the very stream God uses to stimulate new life and vitality into the very heart of evangelical theological scholarship?

This book has sought to demonstrate that the global church, which has arisen in large part because of the remarkable sacrifices of generations of faithful missionaries, is bringing many important new issues to the table for theological reflection. Furthermore, I am convinced that these represent just a small sampling of the multitude of new issues that are on the horizon of the global church and, if heeded, will help to stimulate a renaissance in theological scholarship.

Four Key Themes

In this chapter I will explore four of the more significant ways in which the rise of the Majority World church and the studies this book has modeled might help to promote such a renaissance in Western theological scholarship. First, I will reflect on how the emergence of global theological reflection is fostering a reintegration of the various branches of theological studies.

4. Andrew F. Walls, "In Quest of the Father of Mission Studies," *International Bulletin of Missionary Research* 23, no. 3 (July 1999): 98.

5. I am referring to the strong relationship between mission studies and the social sciences (especially cultural anthropology and linguistics), which has produced many valuable insights, but also its own share of challenges in keeping missiology properly grounded in theology. This same tension is apparent in the useful insights of psychology that are routinely used in the training of Christian counselors, or insights from the business sciences in training pastors in church administration, etc.

Second, I will examine in particular the discipline of systematic theology to demonstrate how a more global, integrative, and cross-disciplinary approach might influence that discipline. Theological studies in general have suffered in recent years, but systematic theology, once regarded as the "queen of the sciences," has suffered the most and has actually been eliminated from the core of required courses in many seminaries in North America. Because of the important role systematics plays not only as the firstfruits of exegetical and biblical theology but also in shaping the rest of theological studies, this study is particularly interested in how the emergence of the global church can contribute to the discipline of systematic theology.

Third, because of the rapidly expanding cultural diversity of the church, I will explore the implications of the growing cultural particularization in theological studies. For the first time since the Reformation, the center of the global Christian movement lies outside the West. In fact, we now can look around the world and see not one, but multiple centers of theological reflection. I will examine both positive implications as well as potential dangers in this trend.

Fourth, I will explore the growing interest in a more active theological engagement with ideologies of unbelief and the particular challenges that non-Christian religions pose in a post-Christendom world.

These four areas do not exhaust the implications of the rise of a growing, self-theologizing, Majority World church. However, they will serve to point out some of the defining contours of the emerging global theological discourse and, in the process, help those of us in the West more effectively to contribute to and understand the changing context of theology today.

1. Reintegration of the Theological Disciplines

Theology is our attempt to understand the biblical revelation within the framework of our particular historical and cultural setting. In the early church theological reflection was more integrated and only gradually developed into the separate subdisciplines of biblical/exegetical theology, systematic theology, historical theology, and practical theology, which are characteristic of Western theology today. *Exegetical theology* focuses on the exposition of the actual texts of Scripture and serves as the foundation for all the other theological disciplines. Because our working definition of theology refers to our attempt to understand the biblical revelation, it is assumed without argument that biblical/exegetical theology must, by definition, be fully integrated into all other branches of theology.

Systematic theology in a broad sense is really nothing more than the systematic organization of biblical answers or insights into questions we pose to the text of Scripture. In this broad usage, it is an ancient practice of the church and was barely distinguishable from biblical theology. Indeed, a healthy church carefully and systematically looks to the Scriptures, rather than to the shifting winds of culture, to answer its most perplexing questions. However, after the patristic period (second to eighth centuries), the discipline became more narrowly defined, and Western systematic theology increasingly focused on a synchronic approach that sought to organize the teachings of Scripture within a fixed structure of reality that would be "comprehensive, logically consistent and conceptually coherent."[6]

Thus, what we recognize as systematic theology today did not emerge until the publication of Peter Abelard's twelfth-century masterpiece, *Four Books of the Sentences.* This work was a dramatic departure from the more traditional approach whereby theology arose out of the work of exegesis and commentary on biblical texts, such as flourished during the Carolingian period.[7] In other words, systematic theology is a more recent discipline than the field of biblical theology.

The Protestant Reformation continued to develop systematic theology in a way that focused on questions believed to be universally relevant and sought to organize the biblical data within fixed categories and developed according to accepted notions of reason and logic. One of the earliest and best examples of Protestant systematic theology is John Calvin's masterful and influential *Institutes of the Christian Religion*, first published in 1536, but updated and expanded through 1559.

With the emergence of systematic theology as a precise discipline, *historical* and *practical theology* gradually emerged as separate subdisciplines based on a diachronic[8] approach focusing on redemptive history and specific issues pertinent to the practical issues affecting the life of the church at any given time. Eventually these areas became separate fields of study and the natural resistance to integration set in, especially between the synchronically oriented systematic theology, which focused on a fixed sacred text, and the more diachronic disciplines, which examined theology and practice within the flow of church history.

Historical theology focuses on the development of doctrine over the course of time within the context of church history. One of the most comprehensive surveys available today is Jaroslav Pelikan's five-volume *The Christian Tradition: A History of the Development of Doctrine.*[9] Practical theology emerged as a separate discipline last and included such diverse areas as mission practice, ethics, preaching, and pastoral care. The pietist Augustus Herman Francke (1663–1727), who taught at the University of Halle in Germany, is considered the first Protestant professor of practical theology.[10]

---

6. "Synchronic" refers to an analysis that is less concerned with changing historical problems the church faces. Instead, a synchronic approach strives to understand truth within universal categories and a fixed structure of reality. See Tite Tienou and Paul G. Hiebert, "From Systematic and Biblical to Missional Theology," in *Appropriate Christianity*, ed. Charles H. Kraft (Pasadena, CA: William Carey Library, 2005), 121.

7. I am thinking of such biblical scholars as Alcuin (735–804) and Hrabanus Maurus (784–856). See E. Ann Matter, "Exegesis and Christian Education: The Carolingian Model," in *Schools of Thought in the Christian Tradition*, ed. Patrick Henry (Philadelphia: Fortress, 1984), 90–105. Origen's third-century *De Principiis*, while not a full systematic theology, is an even earlier theological commentary on a wide array of Christian doctrines.

8. A diachronic approach assumes that as new, practical issues emerge, theological discourse should address these new issues. This is evident in the disciplines of ethics and pastoral theology. These disciplines never presume to work within fixed categories.

9. The five volumes are as follows: vol. 1, *The Emergence of the Catholic Tradition (100–600)*; vol. 2, *The Spirit of Eastern Christendom (600–1700)*; vol. 3, *The Growth of Medieval Theology (600–1300)*; vol. 4, *Reformation of Church and Dogma (1300–1700)*; and vol. 5, *Christian Doctrine and Modern Culture (since 1700)*—all published by the University of Chicago Press.

10. This division of theology into exegetical, systematic, historical, and practical was inspired by the nineteenth-century theologian F. Schleiermacher's *Doctrine of Faith* and is reflected in the structures of contemporary seminary education and curriculum design.

This division of theology into separate, clearly defined areas that arose out of the Western church has worked reasonably well over the centuries but is becoming increasingly difficult to maintain in the context of global Christianity. In fact, every branch of theology is being affected by the emerging global context. First, exegetical theology has benefited from the insights of Majority World Christians, especially those from social and cultural settings similar to the first century.

Second, Western systematic theology is based on certain philosophical agreements concerning the best structure of logic, understood as internally consistent and noncontradictory. But there are different kinds of logic. Aristotelian logic is known as syllogistic or term logic, which analyzes the reasonableness of certain propositions. Yet syllogistic logic does not allow for intuitively valid inferences as predicate logic does.[11] Several countries in Asia, particularly India, have a long history of philosophical arguments that are also internally consistent but do not follow the dominant conventions of Western logic. There are also different kinds of reasoning and different ideas as to the precise relationship of logic to reason.

Furthermore, there are verifiably different cognitive processes in various regions of the world that affect how information is logically structured and perceived.[12] Some people are serial learners and learn sequentially; others are trained as holistic learners and learn in a more hierarchical manner. We cannot, therefore, assume that the way systematic theology has been traditionally structured and presented throughout the history of Western civilization is the most logical, the most effective, or the only way in which theology can be systematically structured for the larger, global context.

Third, historical theology has focused almost exclusively on the development of doctrine and theology in the West, particularly after the close of the ecumenical councils. Adolph von Harnack's monumental *History of Dogma*, for example, does not take seriously theological developments in Eastern Orthodoxy after the eighth century and is virtually silent, as is Pelikan's *History of the Development of Doctrine*, about developments in Latin America, sub-Saharan Africa, and Asia. Historical developments related to the Majority World church have been traditionally delegated to specialist "mission studies," since these studies were considered ancillary to the main stream of Christian history and tradition.

The whole structure of historical theology assumes *our* Christian history as the starting point, from which everyone else eventually derives their own history. However, in light of the emergence of substantial numbers of indigenous Majority World Christians who do not see themselves as related to Roman Catholicism or Eastern Orthodoxy or Protestantism, coupled with the dramatic recession of Christian faith among Europeans, it becomes increasingly problematic to keep recounting church history and historical theology in the same way.

Andrew Walls has insightfully pointed out that there is an enormous difference between writing church history and writing *Christian* history. He writes: "Church

11. Predicate logic was finally able to solve the problem of multiple generality, a dilemma that had long eluded schemes of syllogistic logic.

12. See David Hesselgrave, "Cultural Differences and the Cognitive Process," ch. 21 in *Communicating Christ Cross-Culturally*, 2nd ed. (Grand Rapids: Zondervan, 1991).

history writing requires ecclesiological choice; it assumes, consciously or unconsciously, a specific identification of the church, or at least a particular manifestation of it."[13] When students sign up for a course in church history, what is actually being studied is a well-defined selection of themes within the history of Christianity that are relevant to a particular group of Christians who share a geographic and confessional heritage.[14]

However, as global Christianity becomes increasingly made up of peoples from Asia, Africa, and Latin America and these newly emerging indigenous expressions become normative, the whole structure of how we understand and talk about church history must also undergo a dramatic change. Historical theology today must relate to Christian history, not just church history. Church history syllabi will need to be rewritten to reflect a more global perspective on the church, particularly as African and Asian Christianity become increasingly normative and Western Christianity becomes more ancillary to the larger global movement.[15]

In the West, as noted earlier, our cultural and ecclesiastical history flows primarily from the Roman empire, so what happened in Western Europe dominates our understanding of church history. However, after having spent considerable time with Christians from various parts of Asia, I can testify that the Roman empire does not loom nearly as large from the perspective of peoples shaped by the Persian, Ashokan, or Han empires. This background, in turn, dramatically influences how Christian history is understood and told.

Fourth, practical theology has focused almost exclusively on the life and practice of the church in the West. This has influenced how we train students to preach, understand church administration, teach Christian education, and practice missions. While certain principles, broadly speaking, are applicable universally, much of practical theology in the West is not nearly as applicable to the church in the Majority World as we might suppose.

For example, Christian education in the West largely accepts without serious question the value of separating people into different age groups and placing them in separate rooms. However, in my experience in Asia, not only is this practice impossible to implement in a house church setting, but it also makes certain assumptions about learning and family dynamics that are not necessarily applicable to Majority World peoples. Mission studies in the West largely assume certain kinds of sending and support structures that are not nearly as important or relevant in the practice of Majority World-initiated missions. What is considered effective preaching in a Western setting may strike an audience outside the West as overly scholastic, polished, or rehearsed. Such examples could be multiplied many times.

---

13. Andrew F. Walls, *The Cross-Cultural Process in Christian History* (Maryknoll, NY: Orbis, 2002), 5.

14. Ibid.

15. According to the Pew Forum on Religion in Public Life, in some European countries the actual number of Muslims attending a mosque in a given week has surpassed the number of Christians attending church in a given week. See their "An Uncertain Road: Muslims and the Future of Europe" (http://pewforum.org/docs/index.php?DocID=60). See also Timothy M. Savage, "Europe and Islam," *The Washington Quarterly* 27, no. 3 (Summer 2004): 25–50.

The larger point, however, is that the very division of theology itself into separate categories that sometimes function in isolation from one another is no longer tenable. Western peoples tend to think that they *know* something when they understand the theory behind something. This is why traditional pedagogy in the West first sets forth the theory and then moves to the particular examples or application of that theory to specific contexts. However, in many Majority World cultures, something is only *known* if it has been first experienced in a concrete situation. In fact, sometimes the philosophical theory behind something is regarded as either unknowable or known only to someone after many years of praxis.[16]

One of the most common observations of Majority World Christians is the desperate need to revitalize theology by approaching the theological disciplines in a more comprehensive, integrated way. This is why Latin American theologian Gustavo Gutiérrez, in his landmark book *A Theology of Liberation*, defines theology as "critical reflection on Christian praxis in the light of the word."[17] It is a cry for greater integration between Christian reflection and Christian practice. A similar urgency can be detected in William Dyrness' *Invitation to Cross-Cultural Theology*: "We have tried to broaden the typical Western understanding of theology as sure knowledge to include the practices and symbols by which vernacular theology is articulated."[18] In both cases these leaders are calling for a more integrative approach to theology, one that brings the disciplines into a closer relationship with one another and allows for a broader understanding as to how theological formation takes place in the church around the world.

In conclusion, the emergence of a culturally diverse, global church requires a more comprehensive reintegration of the theological disciplines. While there are still considerable benefits to be enjoyed by allowing for the integrity of the various disciplines so that they can flourish in their own right, this recognition does not negate the need to encourage more active listening and interdisciplinary thought in all of the disciplines of theology.

Historical and practical theology must be forced to be more cognizant of the implications of the growth of Majority World Christianity and the particular issues these Christians are facing. We must be prepared to inhabit a world where North American and Western European Christians are no longer at the center of global Christianity. This does not mean that we no longer have a strategic role to play. It simply means that we must act in genuine partnership with Christians from around the world. We must become less ethnocentric about how theology and church history are discussed. We learn to rejoice that the church today is looking more like John's eschatological vision (Rev. 7:9–10) than at any time in history. Theological institutions in the West must step forward and train people within a larger global context because our students are more diverse, our ministry contexts are more varied, and global consciousness can no longer be expected only of our missions students.

16. Edmund Perry, *The Gospel in Dispute* (Garden City, NY: Doubleday, 1958), 99–106. See also Herman A. Witkin, *Cognitive Styles in Personal and Cultural Adaptation* (Worcester, MA: Clark Univ. Press, 1978).

17. Gustavo Gutiérrez, *A Theology of Liberation* (Maryknoll, NY: Orbis, 1988), 11.

18. William Dyrness, *Invitation to Cross-Cultural Theology* (Grand Rapids: Zondervan, 1992), 155.

2. Renaissance in Systematic Theology

The second major issue focuses specifically on the discipline of systematic theology. What would a more integrative approach to systematic theology actually look like?

In chapter 1, I expressed my conviction concerning the ongoing importance of studying systematic theology as an integral part of ministerial training. Having taught theology in North America as well as in Asia, I see training in systematic theology as an integral part of the preparation for ministry anywhere in the world. However, despite this confidence, I cannot escape the fact that as a teacher in India, I often find Western systematic theologies unhelpful when seeking to provide even a broad foundation in addressing a whole range of theological and ethical issues that my students regularly raise in class.

The systematic textbooks I had used in my own training seemed so tidy and organized and comprehensive, but when carried overseas they stared back at me with glaring weaknesses, shocking silences, and embarrassing gaps. Many of the more common questions I am asked in India have never been raised in my classes in the USA. This challenge is what, in part, led me to recognize the need for more integration between the theological disciplines. I would now like to explore how a more integrative approach will influence the discipline of systematic theology.

The renaissance in systematic theology I am advocating recognizes that before the systematicians begin their work, they must anticipate many of the practical issues that will arise in a given context. This does not mean, for example, that every ethical and cultural issue in India should somehow get integrated into an Indian systematic theology. It does not mean that the discipline of practical theology cannot flourish in India as it has flourished elsewhere or that there are not many themes in systematic theology that are universally applicable to the whole church of all ages. However, it does mean that an authentic systematic theology in India must anticipate certain issues and explore certain themes that might otherwise be neglected. In other words, merely translating Western systematic theologies into indigenous languages around the world will not be adequate.

A few examples from my experience in India will help to highlight the need for indigenous systematic theology to be done by Indian Christians. One of the questions I am regularly asked is if it is permissible or advisable for Christians to eat meat sacrificed to idols. The custom in India is to take this food, known as *prasad*, consecrate it, and offer it to the idols as an act of worship known as *puja*. The food is then taken to various homes in the village as an act of hospitality and friendship. In Indian culture, to refuse *prasad* is to reject the friendship and hospitality of your neighbor. In contrast, many Christians insist that accepting *prasad* is, at best, a tacit approval of idol worship and, at worst, an actual demonic participation in idolatry.

In responding to this dilemma, I have found exegetical commentaries on 1 Corinthians disappointing because they leave so many questions related to this issue unanswered, even though the contemporary parallel with the situation in 1 Corinthians 8 is obvious. Likewise, courses on ethics are comparatively rare in seminaries in India, and the few textbooks used are often the same textbooks used in Western seminaries.[19] For years I have wondered why Indians who were so interested in cultural and ethical questions were so slow to produce their own texts on ethics. One of the main reasons is that it takes a good grounding in systematic and historical theology to have the necessary framework to face a whole range of new and constantly changing ethical issues. My students knew these issues were important, but did not always have the theological tools to know how to respond to them, especially when issues were raised that were not explicitly addressed in the Scriptures.

Another issue I am frequently asked about by my Indian students concerns Christians with a Hindu background whose parents named them after Hindu gods, a common custom in India. These Hindu converts to Christianity often ask me if I would encourage them to take on a new, Christian name when they are baptized, or if they should retain their original name, even if they were originally named after a Hindu god. Over the years, I have spent many hours with Indian students examining the long list of Christians in Romans 16 who receive Paul's individual greeting. Several of these Christians have names with clear pagan associations, such as the household of Narcissus or Hermes or Olympas (see Rom. 16:11, 14–15). Texts such as these have encouraged Indian Christians from a Hindu background that it is not necessary to change their names when they receive Christian baptism.

In discussing these and many similar issues with my Indian students, I gradually came to see that part of their preparation in systematic theology needs a subsection under ecclesiology entitled "church and culture," which sets forth more explicitly biblical principles concerning the relationship of the church to the surrounding non-Christian world and culture, including all of the religious dimensions of culture. It is virtually impossible to have a well-informed ecclesiology in India without also having a thorough understanding of how the presence of the church relates to the larger Hindu, Islamic, and Buddhist context around them.

This is a problem not just for Indian Christians. Christians around the world face issues unique to their particular setting that require special theological reflection. For example, Japanese Christians are crying out for a better theological basis for understanding the biblical teaching regarding what it means to honor our parents, even after they are deceased.

The basic problem is that Western systematic theologies are still written with a Christendom mind-set, assuming the absence of rival theistic claims as well as rival sacred texts. They tend to be overly preoccupied with philosophical objections to the Christian message, rather than with religious objections based on sacred texts or major social traditions that contradict the claims of Scripture. This is why chapter 2 was devoted to exploring theology proper in relation to claims about Allah, and chapter 3 focused on thinking about our theology of the Bible in relation to the claims of other sacred texts. Systematic theology needs to be recast with a greater sensitivity to the larger missiological orientation of the biblical text. It is to our shame that, as Thomas Finger correctly

19. See, for example, John Jefferson Davis, *Evangelical Ethics: Issues Facing the Church Today* (Phillipsburg, NJ: Presbyterian & Reformed, 2004). This is an insightful survey of ethical issues facing the church and is used in various parts of the world. Yet it was written primarily for Western readers and is focused on issues that are of particular relevance to the Western Church.

observed, "systematic theology arose as a branch of academic study pursued in universities and not primarily as a task of the church involved in the world at large."[20]

I am convinced that the work of systematic theology is far more important and far more complex a task than I ever realized. It is important because every church in the world needs a systematic introduction to biblical themes that will best help and guide them in formulating ethical, cultural, and practical applications of theology. It is complex because theological reflection must arise out of the particularities of each new generation and within each new context. No single systematic theology can be held up as universally adequate for all Christians, even though Western theological textbooks are routinely taken, used, and accepted as normative. Theological textbooks must become more contextually sensitive without losing sight of the grand universal themes that unite all Christians through space and time. I anticipate a time, which has already begun to dawn, when theologians from around the world produce major theological works written from their own contextually sensitive perspective, yet helpful and edifying for the global church.

One example of a systematic theology that models the kind of balanced approach that needs to be replicated in various settings around the world is Wilbur O'Donovan's *Biblical Christianity in African Perspective.* O'Donovan's systematic theology is written specifically for the African context. On the one hand, he is clearly cognizant of universal themes that are applicable to all peoples. He devotes considerable space, for example, to establish the authority of Scripture and to discuss theology proper, Christology, pneumatology, ecclesiology, and eschatology. On the other hand, he has entire sections that would not be a part of a systematic text written for a Western audience. O'Donovan's thirty years of experience working and teaching in Africa helped him realize the needs of future pastors and evangelists working there.

For example, O'Donovan devotes an entire section to exploring the relationship of the Christian to the spirit world. He carefully sets forth biblical teaching regarding the origin of evil, demonology, and spiritual warfare, which is so important to effective ministry in Africa. He explores the biblical attitude towards sorcery, witchcraft, bribery, and a host of other issues that are relevant for the African context. He is not attempting to write a book on African ethics or a host of other particular cultural issues that Africans face. However, he does lay a systematic foundation that provides the necessary support for further theological work that we would more precisely categorize as ethics or practical theology. O'Donovan's *Biblical Christianity in African Perspective* is the kind of systematic work that models what I am encouraging.

O'Donovan's work is not only helpful for Africans, but it may also provide help to future systematic theologians in the West as we increasingly face challenges from movements like Wicca and from the resurgence of paganism, as well as growing questions concerning demonology in our own culture. Indeed, to be prepared for ministry as a world Christian, we all need to grapple with issues that heretofore have been reserved for missionaries in preparation for a specific contextualized ministry.

20. Thomas Finger, *Christian Theology: An Eschatological Approach* (Nashville: Nelson, 1985), 1:20–21, as quoted in Tienou and Hiebert, "From Systematic and Biblical to Missional Theology," 122.

The clear message for our times is that we must learn to practice a more engaged theology in the midst of a social and cultural landscape that is constantly changing. We must be more adaptive and contextually sensitive. We need to be reminded that the discipline of systematic theology will invariably lose its vitality if it succumbs to either or both of two problems, which, unfortunately, have persistently plagued the discipline.

First, systematic theology, regardless of its origin, loses its vitality when it becomes overly confident, thinking that its particular reflection has covered all issues for all time for the entire church. Andrew Walls has pointed out that "the world-view of Hellenistic civilization rested on the conviction that every important question had been canvassed."[21] When that happens, it loses the capacity to listen to new questions and to return to the Scripture with a fresh perspective.

This should not be taken as the relativization of the theological task, since many of the questions brought to the text are, in fact, the same for all Christians everywhere. After all, regardless of our linguistic, social, or ethnic background, we all share a common headship in the first Adam as sinners and in the second Adam as members of the redeemed community. We worship the living God, who is "the same yesterday and today and forever" (Heb. 13:8). No generation or culture will ever be exempt from the need to understand the biblical rejection of sin, the call to repentance, the redeeming power of the cross, the wonderful attributes of the Triune God, and so forth. Truths like these inevitably give the entire church in all ages a broad framework of many shared questions and affirmations. But, despite our many commonalities, we simply do not all share the same cultural and social milieu. The challenges the church faces in certain parts of the world and the proclivities toward certain sins are frequently peculiar to this setting and give rise to their own sets of questions that need to be posed to the text.

Not only are there cultural differences, but there are global realities that arise because of the particular time in which we live. Jonathan Edwards was a brilliant theologian, but he did not live at a time when theological reflection regarding the ethics of genetic engineering or an informed Christian position regarding the ethics of in-vitro fertilization was even in the range of possible questions to be posed to the text. This setting, in turn, influenced the more foundational work of systematic theology in the eighteenth-century concerning the sanctity of life within the larger doctrine of creation.

Thus, we must admit that any particular systematic theology can only, at best, be *representative* of a particular set of questions brought to the text at a particular time.[22] This is why even the greatest systematic theologies can never take the place of the Scripture. Scripture is the only inerrant guide for the faith and practice of the

21. Andrew F. Walls, *The Missionary Movement in Christian History: Studies in the Transmission of Faith* (Maryknoll, NY: Orbis, 1996), 33.

22. In reply to the objection that these are ethical issues and do not properly belong in a systematic theology, the reader must remember that the separation of ethics from systematic theology is, itself, part of the history of how theological discourse developed in the West. Patristic theologians did not accept such a sharp division of systematic theology from ethics. Nevertheless, I am not arguing for a full integration of systematic theology with ethics. I am arguing that the particular ethical issues the church faces should be anticipated and prepared for by the work of systematicians, who lay the necessary theological framework.

church in all ages and is able to reflect "God's own transcendent authority over all cultures."[23]

Second, systematic theology also loses its vitality whenever it loses its missiological focus. In other words, in an effort to systematize the details of the entire Bible, it all too easily misses the overarching message and theme of the entire Bible, which focus on God's initiative to save and redeem a people for himself who, in turn, bear witness to him through word and deed. We do not meet any "pure theologians" in the New Testament, if by that expression we mean people whose entire lives were given over solely to theological reflection. Instead, we meet people like the apostle Paul, whose lives were devoted to proclaiming the gospel and in the process produced remarkable theology.

This phenomenon was not driven by the exigencies of the early church, which had neither sufficient personnel nor the financial means to support a full time class of professional theologians. Rather, it is actually an important, biblical precedent reminding us that the best theological reflection emerges when it is the closest to the life and mission of the church. Indeed, history has demonstrated over and over again that theological reflection untethered from the broader missiological context of the New Testament quickly becomes cold rationalism. Christianity is not merely a theology to be affirmed, but a message embodied in a person who must be proclaimed.

If doctrinal purity were the sole key to spiritual vibrancy, then the church in Asia Minor (modern-day Turkey), which was at the ecclesiastical center of the world Christian movement at the time and produced the most sublime statements of Christian orthodoxy (such as the Nicene Creed and Chalcedonian Christology), should have also spawned a vibrant church. However, the people became spiritually moribund and collapsed in the face of those heralding the message of Islam. Today, Turkey is almost entirely Islamic with only a tiny Christian community.

Later, after the Reformation, the church learned, once again, that doctrinal precision does not guarantee spiritual vitality. The Reformation served an invaluable role in restoring a biblical theology to many areas that had been neglected. However, soon many of the Protestant churches found themselves with profound, accurate theological formulations, but lacking in the spiritual vibrancy that had produced the Reformation in the first place. German Pietism, which produced such remarkable people as Philip Jacob Spener (1635–1705) and Nikolaus Ludwig von Zinzendorf (1700–1760), was God's gift to the church to help restore spiritual vitality to the church and, in the process, to give birth to the Protestant missionary movement.

In chapter 7 we explored how in the twentieth century and in these opening years of our present century God has been using Pentecostalism to breathe fresh winds of renewal into the church around the world and, in the process, to produce over a half a billion new believers, many of whom are located in parts of the world that heretofore have not enjoyed a significant Christian witness. As we noted, Pentecostalism not only helped to restore the church's spiritual vitality but also became "a major force in

23. William Dyrness, *Learning about Theology from the Third World* (Grand Rapids: Zondervan, 1990), 31.

world evangelization."[24] Even though formal Pentecostal scholarship has been slow in emerging, the movement has still managed to strengthen Western theologies of the Holy Spirit and provide a corrective to the pervasive neglect of certain features of the ongoing work of the Holy Spirit in the world and in the life of the church.

Even when Pentecostals themselves were theologically imprecise, the movement was sustained because they have largely maintained a deep commitment to the Scriptures, and their reflection has been born out of a Christ-centered mission and witness. In short, church history demonstrates the truth of the phrase, *ecclesia reformata semper reformanda*.[25] Whenever we drift away from Jesus Christ and his mission in the world, he raises up better readers of the Bible, and the church is once again called back to its first love.

I am convinced that the inclusion of Majority World theological scholarship serves as a renewing influence on Western theological scholarship. Much of that scholarship is born out of the vibrancy of evangelism and the life of the church. Millions of new Christians from places like Morocco, Nepal, and China are reading the Bible for the first time. Throughout much of the Majority World church, especially in Africa and Asia, the church and not the seminary has become the center of theological instruction and discussion.

In the West, theological reflection usually finds its locus in the seminaries. This arrangement can give the impression of being more sophisticated and erudite, but, in reality, theological education too often becomes separated from the vitality of the church's mission. This is not to diminish the vital importance of seminary scholarship and training. It does, however, remind us of the importance of seminaries maintaining a close and vibrant connection with the church. Those of us who teach must never forget that we are both teachers of the church as well as learners of the church. Seminaries exist to serve the church, not merely to perpetuate their own existence.[26]

In chapter 9 we observed the remarkable theological work of Jonathan Edwards, most of which was produced while he was a pastor at Northampton and later, beginning in 1750, when he served as a pastor and missionary to the Housatonic Indians in Stockbridge. Indeed, one of the Chinese leaders of the Back to Jerusalem Movement summed it up well when he said that "the pursuit of doctrinal purity in and of itself only results in legalistic bondage if you have no intention of also obeying God's command to proclaim the gospel throughout the earth."[27] It is this reconnection between theological scholarship and the church's mission that is so vital to the future of a truly robust global Christian movement.

24. Wilbert R. Shenk, "Recasting Theology of Mission: Impulses from the Non-Western World," *International Bulletin of Missionary Research* 25, no. 3 (July 2001): 101.

25. The phrase means that a truly reformed church should always be reforming itself. In other words, the Reformation is not merely a historical event of the sixteenth century, but an ongoing reality in the life of the true church. Every generation has its own share of heresies and blind spots that need the loving rebuke of the Scriptures and the perspective of the larger global church through space and time.

26. Even though I currently teach at a large North American seminary, I continue to teach every year in India and to preach almost weekly in the church. This has proved a valuable and regular reminder of the close connection that should exist between the seminary, the church, and the mission field.

27. Paul Hattaway, *Back to Jerusalem: Three Chinese House Church Leaders Share Their Vision to Complete the Great Commission* (Carlisle, UK: Piquant, 2003), 127.

3. Particularization of Theological Discourse

The third theme for consideration is the growing emphasis on the diverse particularity of today's theological discourse. In chapter 1 we examined the shift in the center of gravity of the Christian movement that, especially since 1970, has moved dramatically southward and eastward. However, the story of the emergence of Majority World Christianity is more interesting and more complex than merely a shift in the center of gravity.

The church has, over the centuries, shifted to various cultural and geographic centers. But never before has the church gained strength, geographically and culturally, in so many different regions of the world simultaneously. The Christian message has been received by more new peoples, from more diverse cultures, than at any time in the history of the church. In fact, the church of Jesus Christ is now, without any serious rivals, the largest and most culturally and ethnically diverse movement anywhere in the world. We can no longer speak of a single Christian center. It cannot be definitively located in Africa or Latin America or Asia, for it has simultaneously moved to multiple new centers, as reflected in the title of Samuel Escobar's insightful book, *The New Global Mission: The Gospel from Everywhere to Everyone.*[28]

This dramatic shift in the center of gravity, along with the emergence of multiple new centers of Christian faith, contrasts to the formation of each of the three major Christian traditions—Roman Catholicism, Eastern Orthodoxy, and Protestantism—that each have been dominated by a single center of universality. Roman Catholicism sees Western Europe in general and Rome in particular as the center of gravity for the Christian movement. It is not surprising that every pope has been from Western Europe. Eastern Orthodoxy, throughout its history, has been dominated by the central importance of the Byzantine tradition, history, and culture. Protestantism, while far more diverse, has nevertheless been dominated by Western culture since its inception until the early decades of the twentieth century. We are now witnessing what John Mbiti has called the emergence of multiple new "centers of universality."[29]

However, despite the changing face of the church, the Western world continues to remain the dominant center for theological training and writing. We are in danger of becoming what Mbiti calls "kerygmatically universal" while remaining "theologically provincial."[30] In other words, the global centers of the church's vibrant proclamation are becoming increasingly diverse, whereas theological reflection continues to be dominated by Western scholarship.

Mbiti's point was that even though "the centers of the Church's universality are no longer in Geneva, Rome, Athens, Paris, London, or New York" but are now in "Kinshasa, Buenos Aires, Addis Ababa, and Manila," there has not been the corresponding shift towards "mutuality and reciprocity in the theological task facing the universal

28. Samuel Escobar, *The New Global Mission: The Gospel from Everywhere to Everyone* (Downers Grove, IL: InterVarsity Press, 2003).

29. As quoted in Kwame Bediako, *Christianity in Africa: The Renewal of a Non-Western Religion* (Maryknoll, NY: Orbis, 1995), 157.

30. John S. Mbiti, "Theological Impotence and the Universality of the Church," in *Mission Trends No. 3: Third World Theologies*, ed. Gerald H. Anderson and Thomas F. Stransky (New York: Paulist; Grand Rapids: Eerdmans, 1976), 6.

church."[31] Steady streams of the brightest minds in the world have made their pilgrimage to do theological studies in the West. However, the theological learning they acquired from the older churches has, argues Kwame Bediako, not been able "to cope with the new concerns in the new churches."[32]

This problem has not been lost on many Christian leaders from Africa, Asia, and Latin America. The publication of the English translation of Gustavo Gutiérrez's *A Theology of Liberation* in 1973 was for many in North America the first exposure to a sustained critique of some of the inadequacies of Western theological reflection for Christians in Latin America. However, similar concerns had already begun to emerge in Africa, as seen, for example, in the writings of John Mbiti (b. 1931) from Kenya and Kwesi Dickson (1929–2005) from Ghana.

Japanese theologians have also produced theologies that reflect the particularities of their Asian setting. For example, Kazoh Kitamori's (1916–1998) *Theology and the Pain of God* (1958) and Kosuke Koyama's (b. 1929) well-known *Waterbuffalo Theology* (1974) both focus on the sufferings of Christ on the cross as the central theme and foundation for Japanese theology.[33] Later, in his remarkable book *Mount Fuji and Mount Sinai*, Koyama has explored the whole notion of a "geographic center" of Christianity and the implications of worshiping a God who reveals himself at Mount Sinai as a mobile God.[34]

Taiwanese theologian Choan-Seng Song (b. 1929) has published several books that focus on Asian theology, including his *Third-Eye Theology: Theology in Formation in Asian Settings* (1979) and *Theology from the Womb of Asia* (1986). Asian theologian Byung-Mu Ahn (1922–1996) is representative of a number of Korean scholars promoting *minjung* theology,[35] which, like liberation theology from Latin America, seeks to explore theology from the perspective of the marginalized and the oppressed. A similar theological tradition has emerged in India (in reaction to the oppression perpetuated by high caste Brahmins in India) known as *dalit* theology, represented in the writings of Arvind Nirmal.

All of these theologians are considered major theological voices in their particular context. With the exception of Nirmal, they also received their theological training in the West.[36] The result is that these theologies are often written in response to or reaction against traditional Western theology. For example, one of the common themes in these works is the clear orientation and sensitivity to one or more of the following: religious pluralism, economic poverty, and political or social disenfranchisement. None of these themes has been central features of the dominant Western theological tradition. Therefore, these themes frequently provide a basis for critiquing Western theology. This, in turn, has helped to stimulate a dramatic diversity within

31. Ibid., 9–10; cf. also Bediako, *Christianity in Africa*, 154.

32. Bediako, *Christianity in Africa*, 155.

33. Kazoh Kitamori, *Theology and the Pain of God* (Richmond, VA: John Knox, 1958); Kosuke Koyama, *Waterbuffalo Theology* (Maryknoll, NY: Orbis, 1974).

34. Kosuke Koyama, *Mount Fuji and Mount Sinai: A Critique of Idols* (Maryknoll, NY: Orbis, 1985).

35. *Minjung* theology refers to a "people's theology" that emerged in Korea.

36. Gutiérrez (Institu Catholique in Lyons), Kosuke Koyama (Princeton), John Mbiti (Cambridge), Kwesi Dickson (Oxford), Choan-Seng Song (University of Edinburgh), and Byung Mu Ahn (University of Heidelberg).

contemporary Western theology, as found, for example, in the feminist theology of Rosemary Radford Ruether (b. 1936) and in the black theology of James Cone.[37]

One cannot help but rejoice at the growing theological contributions from Christians around the world. Indeed, Paul Hiebert is surely correct when he insists that one of the true signs of a vibrant church is when it becomes "self-theologizing."[38] Furthermore, there is no need to resist the emergence of Asian or African or Latino theology out of fear that it is unduly characterized by liberal tendencies. I have read enough theology to understand that every region of the world is now producing theologies that are representative of the entire theological spectrum and that defy being easily pigeonholed.

My concern, regardless of the theological orientation, is over the growing fragmentation of theological discourse today. There is a dangerous tendency to simply accept the growing diversity in the global church as inevitably producing an infinite number of niche theologies. This is analogous to the situation after it became clear that the King James Version was no longer the only acceptable English translation of the Bible. The result has been the emergence of dozens of translations and paraphrases, all with their own particular following—including Bibles designed for children,[39] for youth,[40] for feminists,[41] for Southerners,[42] and so forth.

Likewise, there is a dangerous tendency to embrace the notion that globalization and diversity within the church means that the Koreans should have a *minjung* theology, women a feminist theology, blacks a black theology, Indians a *dalit* theology, and so forth. The result is that Western theology continues to be the standard by which all other theologies find their departures and the emerging indigenous theologies remain ancillary subsets, or what Robert Schreiter refers to as "hyphenated theologies."[43] In my view, this trend is not a healthy way to celebrate the growing diversity in the life and experience of the global church.

Furthermore, every authentic theology must not only celebrate the insights of its own particularity, but also reflect a universalizing quality that expresses the catholicity shared by all Christians everywhere. As Andrew Walls has said, "the Lord of hosts is not a territorial Baal."[44] If Jesus is truly Lord, then he is Lord of us all and we are all members of the same body.

For those of us steeped in the Western traditions, it is not enough to simply celebrate the emergence of African indigenous theologizing; we must come to realize how much we need to learn from their theological reflections. Likewise, African

37. Rosemary Radford Ruether, *New Woman, New Earth: Sexist Ideologies and Human Liberation* (New York: Seabury, 1975); James Cone, *Black Theology and Black Power* (Maryknoll, NY: Orbis, 1969, 1999).

38. Paul G. Hiebert, *Anthropological Reflections on Missiological Issues* (Grand Rapids: Baker, 1994).

39. *The Children's Bible in 365 Stories* (Oxford, England: Lion Children's Books, 1995).

40. *The Youth Bible* (Nashville: Word [division of Nelson], 2002).

41. *The Inclusive New Testament* (Hyattsville, MD: AltaMira [Priests for Equality], 1996).

42. See Clarence Jordan, *Cotton Patch Version of Matthew and John, Cotton Patch Version of Luke and Acts, Cotton Patch Version of Hebrews and General Epistles* (El Monte, CA: New Win, 1970–1997).

43. Robert J. Schreiter, *The New Catholicity: Theology between the Global and the Local* (Maryknoll, NY: Orbis, 1997), 2.

44. Andrew F. Walls, "Eusebius Tries Again: Reconceiving the Study of Christian History," *International Bulletin of Missionary Research* 24, no. 3 (July 2000): 107.

Christians can continue to benefit from Western, Asian, and Latin American reflections. In short, the celebration of particularity should not be allowed to disintegrate into theological fragmentation. We in the West are living in the midst of the great "reverse migration," which is bringing millions of new people from Asia, Africa, and Latin America into our midst.[45] We cannot opt for *only* a localized theology. Today, all theology is becoming increasingly global.

We are also coming to recognize the local nature of all theology. Today's context must recognize and embrace the emergence of a "glocal" theology. The term *glocal* was first coined with a distinctively Christian application by Roland Robertson in 1995, but was quickly picked up and used by others.[46] The word is a conflation of "global" and "local." It reflects the need for theology to be both local and global at the same time. The greatest paradigm for this is, of course, the incarnation itself. It is Andrew Walls who has insightfully pointed out that the incarnation is not just God becoming a man, but God becoming *a particular man*. There is no generic incarnation. There is only the specific one in which God in Jesus Christ took on particular flesh and lived in a particular culture and spoke a particular language, and so forth. Yet, Jesus embodied a universal message that embraces every culture, language, and people.

We should see the mutual benefit of listening to one another as brothers and sisters in Christ, members of the same family of God. In this book we have benefited from listening to a wide number of voices, including Indian Jesuits, independent African Christians, Korean Christians, Spirit-filled Latinos, Chinese missionaries, and followers of Jesus from a Muslim background. If we engage in this kind of sustained cross-cultural theological discourse with the church around the world, the sheer diversity of global Christianity will help free the church from any one particular cultural bias. Instead, it will help to foster a greater clarity regarding the universal truths of the gospel that are integral to the Christian proclamation throughout history.

4. Theological Engagement with Ideologies of Unbelief and with Non-Christian Religions

The final theme to consider is the role ideologies of unbelief and non-Christian religions play in the formation of global theology. Theological traditions in the West arose in the post-Constantinian period within the context of Christendom. The seven ecumenical councils held between 325 and 787 focused primarily on clarifying Christian orthodoxy against heterodox proposals from *within* the church. Thus, the church's earliest theological formulations were forged during this rising tide of Christianity within the empire and the collapse of paganism.

The focus of the church was more on internal challenges posed by Arius, Pelagius, Nestorius, and Eutyches than on what must have seemed like the rather remote external challenges of Hinduism, Buddhism, and, after the seventh century, Islam. Granted,

45. The eighteenth and nineteenth century witnessed the great migrations of European peoples. The twentieth and twenty-first century will be characterized by an even greater migration of Majority World people groups into the Western world.

46. Roland Robertson, "Glocalization: Time-Space and Homogeneity-Heterogeneity," in *Global Modernities*, ed. Mike Featherstone, Scott Lash, and Roland Robertson (Thousand Oaks, CA: Sage, 1995), 25–44.

the church still faced the paganism of Britain and the Germanic tribes at the outer reaches of the empire, but at the center was the emergence of a new Christian civilization. The religions of the Hellenistic/Roman world were in a state of collapse and Christ was preached as one who triumphs over false, discredited gods. No one would have suggested that the church needed to contextualize the message by asserting that Zeus/Jupiter was just another name for the God and Father of our Lord Jesus Christ.[47]

This attitude was replicated as the church moved northward and encountered new pagan pantheons. As the church penetrated the Nordic world, no one suggested that the church proclaim Odin, Frigg, and Thor as a kind of Trinitarian *preparatio evangelica*. Christ was proclaimed over against these gods. In short, the church found its primary challenge not in the religious structures of the ancient world but in the philosophical structures of Hellenism. To the patristic fathers, Aristotle alone posed more of a challenge than the whole company of the Olympians.

This context had a deep impact on the formation of theology, which became far more concerned about philosophical objections to the Christian message than about any rival theistic claims or alternative books of revelation. In contrast, the Jesuits found in China a highly articulate faith with deep philosophical underpinnings. Thus, the early Jesuit mission to China had to be advanced along different lines. As we examined in chapter 6, Chinese Buddhism, with its highly developed conception of salvation through Amita Buddha, could not be simply swept away as crumbling primalism. The God of Christian proclamation had to somehow be related, at least in part, to what they already believed.

A similar challenge occurred in India. Hinduism in its classical form emerges from the philosophical reflections of the Upanishads. It might be tempting to regard the plethora of gods and goddesses in India as crass polytheism that will quickly collapse under the bright light of the radiant monotheism of the Christian proclamation. However, the Hindu religious structure is ultimately rooted and grounded in a whole network of highly refined, subtle philosophical thought and, as the history of Christian in India work has demonstrated, is not easily dislodged.[48]

Likewise, Islam arose after Christianity and posits, as we noted in chapter 2, a monotheistic God who is declared identical with the God of Abraham. Furthermore, from its inception Islam has developed carefully reasoned objections to key doctrines in Christianity, particularly the incarnation and the Trinity. Muslims boldly proclaim an alternative book of revelation, the Qur᾿an, which, in their view, supersedes all previous books of revelation. Far from collapsing in the face of Christianity, Islam has grown to become the second largest religion in the world and remains the fastest growing religion in the world.[49] This development puts Christian witness in the

47. Walls, *The Missionary Movement in Christian History*, 70.

48. The most influential philosophical school in India is Vedanta, especially the *advaita* philosophy of Sankara and the *visistadvaita* philosophy of Ramanuja. Ramanuja is the most explicit in demonstrating how the popular gods of village Hinduism relate to the larger structure of Hindu philosophy emerging from the Upanishads.

49. In 2006 Islam claimed 1,339,392,000 adherents as compared with 2,156,350,000 Christians. However, despite growing from 558,131,000 adherents in 1900 to the current number of 2,156,350,000 the Christian faith has decreased as an overall percentage of world population from 34.5 percent to 33 percent.

Islamic world in a very different context from that of the early Christian proclamation in the empire.

Even in Africa, which did not produce major philosophical systems of thought, monotheistic conceptions of a creator God are deeply entrenched; generally speaking, missionaries identified the creator God of African faith with the God of Christian faith.[50] Speaking theologically, one can say that missionaries believed that God preceded them into Africa. As Kwame Bediako has pointed out, this is "the reason why 'God' could not rise up against the 'gods' as he could do in the Semitic, Graeco-Roman and northern European Teutonic contexts and phases of evangelization. The God of the Bible turned out to be the God whose name has been hallowed in vernacular usage for generations. This did not happen in Europe."[51]

The gospel has flourished the most in Africa when God was presented not as an imported deity from Europe but as the God who was already there, although known and worshiped only dimly and needing the full revelation of the person and work of Christ as revealed in Scripture. What are the implications of this for theological reflection in today's context? We will briefly look at three major implications.

First, unlike the emergence of Christianity in Western Europe, Christianity in the Majority World is growing in the very heartlands of major non-Christian religions. The new Christians emerging in the global South and East do not live in a context where there is any shared Christian consensus as was characterized by the Christendom model in Europe and, by extension, the North American context, which was enculturated with Christian values shared even by most non-Christians. In the Christian North, Christianity spread without facing the challenges of any major non-Christian religion or any sacred texts.

In contrast, the new growing edge of Christianity faces a dramatically different situation. This is, of course, not a new problem. However, up to this point the percentage of Christians from these contexts was, relatively speaking, small, and it was viewed as something vaguely on the edge of a Christian movement centered in Europe and North America. It was assumed that the major contact with these Christians was from the missionaries who bravely carried the Christian message into these contexts. Quite naturally, it was expected that such missionaries needed more thorough training on the challenges of world religions and the particular obstacles they would face once they arrived on the mission field.

However, we are now in a situation where the new centers of Christianity are there, not here. Christianity is now predominantly post-Western. Thus, the need for a more explicit response to the challenges of world religions and the assertions of rival sacred books of revelation is now central, not peripheral, to the church's theological task.

It is one of the themes of this book that knowledge of and the ability to respond to the objections of world religions and the specific challenges of their sacred texts is

During the same time period Islam grew from 12 percent of world population to 17 percent. See David Barrett, Todd Johnson, and Peter F. Crossing, "Status of Global Mission: AD 1900–AD 2025," *International Bulletin of Missionary Research* 30, no. 1 (January 2006): 28.

50. Lamin Sanneh, *Whose Religion Is Christianity? The Gospel beyond the West* (Grand Rapids: Eerdmans, 2003), 10, 31–32.

51. Bediako, *Christianity in Africa*, 55.

key to the emergence of a theology relevant for the emerging Majority World church. Theology must now be written with a greater awareness of the challenges posed by other religious traditions. This is why chapter 2 focused on the identity of Allah as compared with the God proclaimed in biblical revelation. A proper theology of God for Christians can no longer be adequately discussed in isolation from the challenges of Islam. In older theologies, theism was either presuppositionally accepted or it was presented against the backdrop of various philosophical objections to it.

Chapter 3 focused on the pre-Christian sacred texts of Hindu converts to Christianity because in this new global context we no longer have the luxury of assuming that the Bible is the only sacred text known to those to whom we minister. Quite the contrary, most people in these new centers of Christian expansion are familiar with the teachings of another text they regard as sacred. This is a situation with no real parallel in the West. Furthermore, chapter 5 sought to take seriously the presence of African traditional religion and chapter 6 sought to grapple with the Japanese reverence for Amita Buddha. There are new reference points that must guide theological formulation in this new, exciting phase of post-Western Christianity.

Second, not only must we adjust to a post-Western Christianity, but we must increasingly recognize the new theological challenges of life in a post-Christian West. It is important to recognize the difference between the two phrases, post-Western Christianity and post-Christian West. Post-Western Christianity refers to the vibrant expansion of Christianity in many parts of the world outside the West. The post-Christian West refers to the equally dramatic recession of Christian faith in the West. This recession does not mean that we resign ourselves to living quietly as an ever-diminishing subculture in an increasingly secular, godless society. On the contrary, it means that the Christian faith must become far more robust in articulating how the Christian gospel is distinct from secular consumerism.

Life in a post-Christendom, post-Christian context means that we can no longer assume that the Christian faith can be well preserved in the face of continued accommodations to the surrounding culture. Rather than embracing the trend toward accelerated accommodations to the entertainment culture and the abandonment of Christian vocabulary and historical roots, we must relearn how to live out the Christian faith as a striking alternative to what is practiced in the surrounding society. This challenge has huge implications not only for a strong prophetic witness in terms of morality and personal piety, the traditional shibboleths of evangelical Christianity, but also for our commitment to justice, our understanding of community, our practice of hospitality, and our concern for the environment, to name a few. The minimalistic approach to faith as seen in much of the church growth movement, which focuses on the least one has to do or believe to be a Christian, must be abandoned and replaced with a leaner, far more robust and theologically literate Christian populace in the West.

Another important aspect of life in a post-Christian West is the increased presence of the post-Western Christians living in the West. In 1930 the United States was comprised of "110 million Whites, 12 million Blacks and just 600,000 'others,' meaning

Native Americans and Asians."[52] By the turn of the twenty-first century, America was home to over 30 million immigrants, with 12 million from various parts of Asia, including China, Japan, Philippines, Vietnam, and Korea.[53] These new Americans are far more literate about non-Christian religions and the sacred texts represented by those traditions. The questions and perceptions about Christianity are different and require a more active engagement in their worldview. Clearly, the preparation of ministers requires Bible colleges and seminaries to give their students a more missiologically focused theological education even if they never minister outside the United States.

Third, a more active engagement with world religions and ideologies of unbelief requires a more ecumenical attitude toward other Christians who share the apostolic faith. As discussed in chapter 7, I am not using the term *ecumenical* here to refer to the failed ecumenism represented by the World Council of Churches and the National Council of Churches. That kind of liberal ecumenism has modeled the very kind of uncritical accommodation to modernity that this book soundly rejects. But I refuse to allow those who have either forgotten the gospel or lost the moral courage to proclaim it to rob the rest of the church of the term *ecumenical*. The kind of ecumenism I am referring to is the deeper, older ecumenism that finds its roots in historic Christian confessions. A case for this has been effectively set forth in Thomas Oden's excellent work *The Rebirth of Orthodoxy*, as well as in the volume by J. I. Packer and Oden entitled *One Faith: The Evangelical Consensus*.[54]

We can no longer afford the kind of entrenched sectarianism that has often characterized fundamentalism and evangelicalism. This does not mean that we must relinquish our distinctive theological convictions. But it does mean that we must distinguish more explicitly and publicly between the *kerygmatic* truths that unite all true Christians and the *adiaphora*, where there are legitimate differences. The old world of Christendom may have, sadly, permitted the kind of divisions that have marred the church's witness and her obedient response to Jesus' high priestly prayer that we "may be one" (John 17:11). But in the context of global Christianity we must first and foremost see ourselves as *Christians* proclaiming the apostolic faith and only secondarily as Reformed Christians, Pentecostal Christians, Dispensational Christians, or Arminian Christians. We must learn to think of ourselves as members of a massive global Christian movement that is looking more and more like John's vision in Revelation 7:9, which encompasses people from every nation, tribe, people, and language.

CONCLUSION

One of the persistent trends in recent years in the post-Christian West has been the resurgence of gnostic claims that the gospel as proclaimed in the New Testament is a product of historical biases and political intrigue and therefore cannot be regarded as

52. Philip Jenkins, *The Next Christendom: The Coming of Global Christianity* (London: Oxford Univ. Press, 2002), 100.

53. Ibid.

54. Thomas Oden, *The Rebirth of Orthodoxy* (New York: HarperSanFrancisco, 2003). See also J. I. Packer and Thomas C. Oden, *One Faith: The Evangelical Consensus* (Downers Grove, IL: InterVarsity Press, 2004).

trustworthy. In its stead, there seems to be no end to the creative and fanciful alternative explanations and historical "correctives" being offered to an eager public. Many Western Christians are exhausted by the avalanche of shocking exposés of cover-ups and a culture of corruption in the church and the political sphere, where even the most bizarre new explanations seemed morbidly plausible.

In a "Jerry Springer" culture we have lost the capacity to be shocked, and a hermeneutic of suspicion surrounds anything that claims to be authoritative. Dan Brown is just one of many who have exploited this vulnerability with his wildly popular, multimillion bestseller, *The Da Vinci Code*, also made into a movie in 2006 starring Tom Hanks.[55] Books like Bart Ehrman's *Misquoting Jesus: The Story behind Who Changed the Bible and Why* and Michael Baigent's *The Jesus Papers: Exposing the Greatest Cover-up in History* are testimony to a culture that has grown tired and distrustful of the gospel.[56] People no longer want to sing, "Tell me the old, old story"; they want to hear something new, however bizarre, however scandalizing, however far-fetched, however remote from the New Testament.

Another 2006 bestseller to hit the book stores was *The Gospel of Judas*, which claimed to give to its readers the *real* gospel.[57] Liberal New Testament scholars were quick to hail it as the greatest breakthrough since the discovery of the Dead Sea Scrolls. This text has led some to believe that Judas Iscariot was actually Jesus' favorite disciple. Yet, to throw doubt on the Gospels in favor of a gnostic fragment hailed as the secret gospel of the betrayer Judas is analogous to the popular musical *Wicked: The Untold Story of the Witches of Oz* in contrast to the beloved Frank Baum classic, *The Wizard of Oz*. The musical throws suspicion on the actual text and claims to tell the *real* story from the perspective of the two witches. This resurgence of Gnosticism claims to reveal secret, previously hidden truths that cast doubt on the faith received from the apostles. This trend reveals much about where we are at this point in our culture. Tragically, even some sectors of the church have been swept into this downward gnostic spiral.

However, there is another story that must also be told. This story is not producing any bestselling books or blockbuster movies or musicals. Yet it is a story far bigger and broader than anything we are experiencing in the West. It is the story of the never-ending power of the gospel and the apostolic faith by people around the world. For every copy of the *Gospel of Judas* that flies off the shelves of Borders or is sent out by the warehouses of Amazon.com, there are tens of thousands of people who are reading the true gospel for the very first time. The Bible is being enthusiastically read with fresh new eyes and with a new sense of immediacy.[58]

55. Dan Brown, *The Da Vinci Code* (New York: Doubleday, 2003).

56. Bart Ehrman, *Misquoting Jesus: The Story behind Who Changed the Bible and Why* (New York: HarperCollins, 2005); Michael Baigent, *The Jesus Papers: Exposing the Greatest Cover-up in History* (San Francisco: HarperSanFrancisco, 2006). This is particularly tragic because it further reinforces for many Muslims their long-standing claim that the New Testament has been corrupted and is not trustworthy.

57. Rodolphe Kasser, Marvin Meyer, and Gregor Wurst, eds., *The Gospel of Judas* (Washington, DC: National Geographic, 2006). See also Herbert Krosney, *The Lost Gospel: The Quest for the Gospel of Judas Iscariot* (Washington, DC: National Geographic, 2006).

58. For an excellent study of this, see Philip Jenkins, *The New Faces of Christianity: Reading the Bible in the Global South* (London: Oxford Univ. Press, 2006).

It is being read by people familiar with persecution and suffering. It is being read by believers who are often a tiny minority in the midst of a climate hostile to their faith. It is being read by believers who understand the bold, revolutionary implications of the gospel. It is being read by people who take its message seriously and fully anticipate the supernatural in-breaking of the kingdom in their midst. The gospel is being read afresh as good news.

The result is that the church of Jesus Christ is growing in unprecedented ways in parts of the world once only regarded as the mission field. So, while 4,300 people may be leaving the church everyday in Europe and North America, 16,500 are coming to faith each day in Africa alone. The growth rate in China is just as dramatic. Most of these new believers have never even heard of Dan Brown or the Jesus Seminar.[59] They are too busy preaching the gospel, baptizing new believers, and planting churches to be distracted by what, in the long run, is just another fleeting, ephemeral challenge to the lordship of Jesus Christ and the authority of his Word.

The studies explored in this book are based on the premise that the expansion of global Christianity can provide a much-needed renaissance in theological studies. In a larger sense, I am convinced that the growth of Majority World Christianity, coupled with the new waves of immigration into the West, may be the only hope for a resurgence of biblical Christianity in our midst. We can no longer afford to let these new exciting realities of global Christianity be swallowed up by any kind of evangelical self-absorption or fundamentalist parochialism, or the latest theological fad of liberalism that suffers from gospel amnesia.

These new believers from around the world are bringing many new questions and issues to the text of Scripture that are helping to reenergize the whole task of theology. Their theological concerns are less theoretical and more practical and missiological. What is emerging is what Andrew Walls has called the "rethinking of the framework of theology" in a way that anchors "Christian scholarship in Christian mission."[60]

This book has just touched on a tiny sampling of issues for each of the major themes of systematic theology. We have had the opportunity to listen in on theological conversations going on in the Middle East, in India, in Africa, in Japan, in Latin America, in Korea, and in China. The theological discourse with which we have interacted is just the opening strains of a great symphony of new theological voices. That is why this book cannot pretend to be exhaustive. It can, at best, only be suggestive. The issues raised here are offered as representative examples, indicating the general direction of theological inquiry in the new context of global Christianity.

Those of us from the older northern churches of Christendom must listen attentively to these new southern Christians. We are no longer the only, or even the central,

59. The Jesus Seminar refers to a controversial group of more than two hundred scholars who, since 1985, have cast doubt on the trustworthiness of the Gospels and have developed their own criteria for determining which words of Jesus found in the New Testament are authentic. They became popular in the media because of their use of four different colors of beads in voting to express various degrees of confidence or distrust about the words of Jesus.

60. Andrew F. Walls, "Christian Scholarship and the Demographic Transformation of the Church," in *Theological Literacy for the Twenty-First Century*, ed. Rodney L. Peterson (Grand Rapids: Eerdmans, 2002), 175, 181.

players on the field. Admittedly, this is not an easy adjustment for us. We are not accustomed to living in a world where the heartlands of Christianity are located in Africa, Latin America, and Asia. Nevertheless, twenty-first-century Christianity will largely be determined by the faithfulness of those outside our primary sphere of influence. After all, the theology that matters the most is wherever the most Christians are located.

We must rejoice that in God's sovereignty he has given us the opportunity to serve in new and exciting ways alongside our brothers and sisters from around the world. As global Christians, we have "been to the mountaintop" and have captured a glimpse of some of the great things God is doing around the world today. We have listened as our brothers and sisters from around the world have responded to God's surprising work in their midst. Together with all Christians in all times and places we must surely recognize that the best theological enquiry anywhere in the world, or during any time in history, always serves to pull the entire church forward into that great eschatological fact of Jesus Christ.

BIBLIOGRAPHY

"An Uncertain Road: Muslims and the Future of Europe." The Pew Forum on Religion and Public Life: http://pewforum.org/docs/index.php?DocID=60, 6–18.

Anderson, Gerald H., and Thomas F. Stransky, eds. *Mission Trends No. 3: Third World Theologies.* New York: Paulist; Grand Rapids: Eerdmans, 1976.

Baigent, Michael. *The Jesus Papers: Exposing the Greatest Cover-up in History.* San Francisco: HarperSanFrancisco, 2006.

Barrett, David, Todd Johnson, and Peter F. Crossing. "Status of Global Mission: AD 1900–AD 2025." *International Bulletin of Missionary Research* 30, no. 1 (January 2006): 27–30.

Bediako, Kwame. *Christianity in Africa: The Renewal of a Non-Western Religion.* Maryknoll, NY: Orbis, 1995.

Brown, Dan. *The Da Vinci Code.* New York: Doubleday, 2003.

The Children's Bible in 365 Stories. Oxford, England: Lion Children's Books, 1995.

Cone, James. *Black Theology and Black Power.* Maryknoll, NY: Orbis, 1969, 1999.

Curnock, Nehemiah, ed. *The Journal of the Rev. John Wesley.* Vol. 1. London: Epworth, 1938.

Davis, John Jefferson. *Evangelical Ethics: Issues Facing the Church Today.* Phillipsburg, NJ: Presbyterian & Reformed, 2004.

Dyrness, William. *Invitation to Cross-Cultural Theology.* Grand Rapids: Zondervan, 1992.

_____. *Learning about Theology from the Third World.* Grand Rapids: Zondervan, 1990.

Ehrman, Bart. *Misquoting Jesus: The Story behind Who Changed the Bible and Why.* New York: HarperCollins, 2005.

Escobar, Samuel. *The New Global Mission: The Gospel from Everywhere to Everyone.* Downers Grove, IL: InterVarsity Press, 2003.

Finger, Thomas. *Christian Theology: An Eschatological Approach.* Vol. 1. Nashville: Nelson, 1985.

Gutiérrez, Gustavo. *A Theology of Liberation*. Maryknoll, NY: Orbis, 1988.

Hattaway, Paul. *Back to Jerusalem: Three Chinese House Church Leaders Share Their Vision to Complete the Great Commission*. Carlisle, UK: Piquant, 2003.

Hesselgrave, David. *Communicating Christ Cross-Culturally*. 2nd ed. Grand Rapids: Zondervan, 1991.

Hiebert, Paul G. *Anthropological Reflections on Missiological Issues*. Grand Rapids: Baker, 1994.

The Inclusive New Testament. Hyattsville, MD: AltaMira (Priests for Equality), 1996.

Jenkins, Philip. *The Next Christendom: The Coming of Global Christianity*. London: Oxford University Press, 2002.

Jordan, Clarence. *Cotton Patch Version of Matthew and John, Cotton Patch Version of Luke and Acts, Cotton Patch Version of Hebrews and General Epistles*. El Monte, CA: New Win, 1970–1997.

Kasser, Rodolphe, Marvin Meyer, and Gregor Wurst, eds. *The Gospel of Judas*. Washington, DC: National Geographic, 2006.

Kitamori, Kazoh. *Theology of the Pain of God*. Richmond, VA: John Knox, 1958.

Koyama, Kosuke. *Mount Fuji and Mount Sinai: A Critique of Idols*. Maryknoll, NY: Orbis, 1985.

_____. *Waterbuffalo Theology*. Maryknoll, NY: Orbis, 1974.

Kraft, Charles H. *Appropriate Christianity*. Pasadena, CA: William Carey Library, 2005.

Krosney, Herbert. *The Lost Gospel: The Quest for the Gospel of Judas Iscariot*. Washington, DC: National Geographic, 2006.

Luther, Martin. *Preface to St. Paul's Epistle to the Romans*. Trans. Charles E. Hay. Philadelphia: United Lutheran, 1903.

Matter, E. Ann. "Exegesis and Christian Education: The Carolingian Model." Pages 90–105 in *Schools of Thought in the Christian Tradition*. Edited by Patrick Henry. Philadelphia: Fortress, 1984.

Oden, Thomas. *The Rebirth of Orthodoxy*. New York: HarperSanFrancisco, 2003.

Packer, J. I., and Thomas C. Oden. *One Faith: The Evangelical Consensus*. Downers Grove, IL: InterVarsity Press, 2004.

Pelikan, Jaroslav. *The Christian Tradition: A History of the Development of Doctrine*. 5 vols. Chicago: University of Chicago Press, 1971–1991.

Perry, Edmund. *The Gospel in Dispute*. Garden City, NY: Doubleday, 1958.

Robertson, Roland. "Glocalization: Time-Space and Homogeneity-Heterogeneity." Pages 25–44 in *Global Modernities*. Edited by Mike Featherstone, Scott Lash, and Roland Robertson. Thousand Oaks, CA: Sage, 1995.

Ruether, Rosemary Radford. *New Woman, New Earth: Sexist Ideologies and Human Liberation*. New York: Seabury, 1975.

Sanneh, Lamin. *Whose Religion is Christianity? The Gospel beyond the West*. Grand Rapids: Eerdmans, 2003.

Savage, Timothy M. "Europe and Islam." *The Washington Quarterly* 27, no. 3 (Summer 2004): 25–50.

Schreiter, Robert J. *The New Catholicity: Theology between the Global and the Local*. Maryknoll, NY: Orbis, 1997.

Shenk, Wilbert R. "Recasting Theology of Mission: Impulses from the Non-Western World." *International Bulletin of Missionary Research* 25, no. 3 (July 2001): 98–107.

Tienou, Tite, and Paul G. Hiebert. "From Systematic and Biblical to Missional Theology." Pages 117–33 in *Appropriate Christianity*. Edited by Charles H. Kraft. Pasadena, CA: William Carey Library, 2005.

Walls, Andrew F. "Christian Scholarship and the Demographic Transformation of the Church." Pages 166–83 in *Theological Literacy for the Twenty-First Century*. Edited by Rodney L. Peterson. Grand Rapids: Eerdmans, 2002.

_____. *The Cross-Cultural Process in Christian History*. Maryknoll, NY: Orbis, 2002.

_____. "Eusebius Tries Again: Reconceiving the Study of Christian History." *International Bulletin of Missionary Research* 24, no. 3 (July 2000): 105–11.

_____. "In Quest of the Father of Mission Studies." *International Bulletin of Missionary Research* 23, no. 3 (July 1999): 98–105.

_____. *The Missionary Movement in Christian History: Studies in the Transmission of Faith*. Maryknoll, NY: Orbis, 1996.

Witkin, Herman A. *Cognitive Styles, Essence and Origins: Field Dependence and Field Independence*. New York: International Universities Press, 1981.

_____. *Cognitive Styles in Personal and Cultural Adaptation*. Worcester, MA: Clark University Press, 1978.

The Youth Bible. Nashville: Word (Nelson), 2002.

Glossary

Adiaphora: The nonessential elements of the gospel that may vary among Christians; in contrast with the kerygma. See *Kerygma.*

Afʾāl: According to the Ashʿarites, those predicates of Allah that relate to his actions; that is, his absolute versus his relative attributes.

African Traditional Religion: ATR refers to African religions bound together by profound similarities in their general structure and in the religious outlook of many African peoples.

Age of Mappō: The current degenerate age as described in Buddhism. This age lasts for ten thousand years, during which the practice of true dharma is impossible and enlightenment unattainable.

Al-dhā: According to the Ashʿarites, those predicates of Allah that relate to his presence, that is, his relative versus his absolute attributes.

Amida Buddha: See *Amitabha.*

Amitabha: The Bodhisattva of "unlimited light" in Pure Land Buddhism; known in China as A-mi-t'o and in Japan as Amida (Amita). According to Pure Land texts, Amitabha was once a monk named Dharmākara who, after countless lifetimes of practice, achieved enlightenment and can rescue others through the repetition of his name. See *Namu Amita Butsu* and *Nembutsu.*

Anāhata śabda: Literally, "unstruck sound," referring to the transcendental cosmic sound that Hindus regard as resonating throughout the universe and frequently characterized by the sound "OM" (pronounced "aum").

Anātman: Literally, no-self. In Buddhist thought, a denial of the Brahminical tradition, which posited an eternal self (atman). Clinging to the concept of self or atman was, for the Buddha, an attachment that impeded true enlightenment.

Aratus: A Cilician poet of the fourth century BC whom the apostle Paul quotes in Acts 17:28.

Arianism: Christological heresy named after its founder, Arius, who held that the Son of God was not eternal but was created by God before the creation. Arianism was condemned by the Council of Nicea in AD 325.

Arius: Founder of Arianism. See *Arianism.*

Arjuna: A main character in the *Bhagavad-Gita*, who is counseled by Krishna to perform the duties of his caste by killing. See *Bhagavad-Gita*.

Ascending Christology: Christological expressions concerning the person of Christ that start out "from below" and arrive at an understanding of his person through the lens of his work. Ascending Christology is typical of African Christologies and is in contrast to the traditional, ecumenical Christological formulations, which are known as "descending Christologies." See *Descending Christology*.

Ashʿarites: School of theology founded by al-Ashʿari (AD 873–935) that emphasized the superiority of revelation over reason. He taught that the Qurʾan was uncreated and eternal.

Aum: See *OM*.

Autosoteria: Self-salvation of a human being.

Aya: Literally, "signs," referring to the individual verses into which each of the 114 chapters (surahs) of the Qurʾan is divided.

Bhagavad-Gita: Literally, the "song of our Lord," widely regarded as the most famous of Hindu scriptures. It was probably composed between 150 BC and AD 250 and actually is part of a larger work known as the Māhabhārata.

Bhajan: A devotional song or hymn associated with a particular form or style, usually within the Indian context.

Bhakti: Devotion, faith, and loving surrender to a deity in Hinduism. A bhakta is one who is devoted to a particular deity.

Bhaktism: A devotional form of Hinduism. See *Bhakti*.

Bodhisattva: Literally, an "enlightened being," referring to someone who has refused liberation from the wheel of samsara and out of compassion, returns to assist all sentient beings towards perfect enlightenment.

Chain of isnad: The list of oral sources that trace the sayings or observations of the Hadith about Muhammad back to the Prophet or his immediate companions.

Chalcedon, Council of: The fourth ecumenical council held in Asia Minor in AD 451, most famous for repudiating errors in some expressions of Nestorianism and Eutychianism and establishing the orthodox Christological formula that declared Christ to be two natures united in one person without confusion, change, division, or separation.

Constantinople, First Council of: The second ecumenical council held in AD 381, which reaffirmed the Council of Nicea's (AD 325) condemnation of Arianism and safeguarded Christ's humanity by condemning Apollinarianism, which, in part, denied that Christ had a human mind.

Contextualization: To communicate in word and deed and to establish the church in ways that make sense to people within their local cultural context, presenting Christianity in such a way that it meets people's deepest needs and penetrates their worldview, thus allowing them to follow Christ and remain within their own culture. See also *Extractionism.*

CPA: The Catholic Patriotic Association, which was created by the Communist Party in China to provide oversight for Roman Catholic Christians.

Dalit: Chosen self-designation by untouchables and other noncaste (scheduled caste) peoples of India.

Dalit theology: A people's theology of liberation that originated in India in reaction to oppression by the high caste Brahmains. See *Dalit.*

Dependent arising: See *Pratitya-samutpāda.*

Depositum fidei: Deposit of faith.

Descending Christology: Christological expressions concerning the person of Christ that start out "from above" and arrive at an understanding of his person through the lens of his deity. Descending Christology is representative of the traditional, ecumenical Christological formulations and is in contrast to "ascending Christologies." See *Ascending Christology.*

Deus otiosus: Latin for "hidden" or "neutral" God.

Dharma: In Hinduism, a broad conception of duty, particularly the importance of fulfilling caste obligations (varna) and life stages (asrama). In Buddhism, the term is used to refer to the essential body of Buddhist teaching, including the Four Noble Truths, the eightfold path, pratitya-samutpāda, and other key Buddhist doctrines.

Dharmākara: Earthly name of Buddhist follower who took on the forty-eight vows and who, upon enlightenment, became known as Amitabha. See *Amitabha.* It is his eighteenth vow that is the source of the Nembutsu doctrine. See *Nembutsu.*

Diamond Sutra: A famous Mahāyāna sutra written between AD 300–700 that, like the Heart Sutra, is a condensed version of the famous Perfection of Wisdom sutras. See *Prajnaparamita Sutras.*

Diffused monotheism: A form of monotheism whereby the supreme being is manifested in a lower pantheon of lesser divinities.

Docetism: A range of doctrinal positions that downplayed the real humanity and suffering of Christ.

Ecumenical councils: The church councils that found broad acceptance in the whole body of the church. The four most widely accepted ecumenical councils are: Nicea (AD 325), Constantinople (381), Ephesus (431), and Chalcedon (451).

Eightfold Path: The spiritual path prescribed by the Buddha along which a devotee must travel to achieve enlightenment. The eight stages along the path are right understanding, right thought, right speech, right action, right livelihood, right effort, right mindfulness, and right concentration.

Ephesus, Council of: The third ecumenical council held in AD 431, which condemned tendencies in expressions of Nestorian theology that maintained two separate persons in the incarnate Christ. See *Theotokos.*

Epimenides: A semimythical seventh-century BC Cretan poet quoted by the apostle Paul in Acts 17:28.

Eshin: Literally, to "turn about." It is the language that Shinran's followers use to describe the total abandonment of human effort and the reception of Amida's unmerited grace.

Eutyches: Present at the Council of Ephesus, he strongly opposed Nestorius and the heresy of Nestorianism. See, *Ephesus, Council of.*

Extractionism: A term used in missiology for the practice of excessive separation from one's cultural context.

Four Noble Truths: Four truths promulgated by the Buddha that form the foundation of all Buddhist dharma. The giving of these four truths is generally referred to as "turning the wheel of dharma."

Glocal theology: A conflation of the two words "global" and "local." It reflects the need for theology to be both local and global at the same time.

Hadith: A collection of oral traditions (sunna) related to things the prophet Muhammad said, did, or approved of, written down in a short narrative and verified through a reliable chain of oral transmitters (isnad). The most important collections of Hadith are those by al-Bukhari (d. 870) and al-Muslim (d. 875).

Hamartiological: Pertaining to sin.

Hanifs: Literally, "one who turned away from paganism." Refers to an indigenous monotheistic movement that preceded Muhammad in Arabia.

Heart Sutra: A famous Mahāyāna sutra written between AD 300–700 that, like the Diamond Sutra, is a condensed version of the famous Perfection of Wisdom Sutras. See *Prajnaparamita Sutras.*

Hejira: Literally, "immigration," referring to the origin of the Islamic era when Muhammad and a group of followers left Mecca for Yathrib (Medina) on July 16, 622. See *Yathrib.*

Hinayana: Literally, "little vehicle." A pejorative term used by Mahāyāna (great vehicle) Buddhists to describe ancient Buddhism, which, in their view, was not privy to the full knowledge of the Buddha's revelations. See *Therevada.*

Homogenous unit principle: A principle developed by Donald McGavran, stating that people prefer to not cross social and ethnic barriers when becoming a Christian and that they prefer to worship with people who are culturally like themselves.

Hypostasis: From the middle of the fourth century this term was contrasted with "ousia" to refer to the individual reality of each person of the Trinity. The orthodox position affirms that God is one in essence (ousia), yet existing eternally in three distinctions (hypostases) known as Father, Son, and Holy Spirit.

Ilāha: Literally "The God." The Arabic form of Allah that includes the definite article. It is used in place of the capitalized English word, "God."

Ilham: Islamic concept of inspiration that can happen to any spiritual person.

Imam: For Sunni Muslims, the prayer leader in a mosque and used for the Four Rightly Guided Caliphs and the founders of the four schools of law. Among Shiʾite Muslims the term is used for special descendants of ʿAli and Fatimah, who, they believe, are the true successors of Muhammad. Shiʾites are divided over how many imams are accepted as true imams.

Injil: Islamic term for the original, uncorrupted New Testament gospel, but which does not correspond to any of the four gospels found in the Christian New Testament.

Isa: Arabic name for Jesus.

Isaya umma: Literally, "community of Jesus." A term C-4 Muslim background believers sometimes use to describe themselves.

Ishta devata: The practice in Hinduism that allows a person to worship a particular, chosen deity without necessarily denying that other gods exist.

Jiriki: Literally, "self power." Includes not only the mainstream monastic rigors of Therevada, but also the meditative schools of Mahāyāna that emphasized discipline, austerities, and strenuous technique in order to accrue the necessary merit toward enlightenment. It stands in contrast to tariki. See *Tariki.*

Jōdo path: The only path toward enlightenment that is viable in the Age of Mappō. It involves invoking the assistance of Amida Buddha. See *Age of Mappō.*

Jodo Shin Shu: The True Pure Land stream of Mahāyāna Buddhism that emphasizes salvation comes completely through the grace of Amida Buddha.

Jodo Shu: An invocational stream within Mahāyāna Buddhism known as Pure Land Buddhism that espouses the transferable merits of Amida Buddha.

Kaʾaba: Literally, "cube," referring to the holiest shrine in Islam located in the Grand Mosque in Mecca, Saudi Arabia. The Kaʿbah contains the sacred Black Stone.

Kalpa: Hindu cosmology of time that corresponds to a day and a night of Brahma, comprising approximately 8.649 billion years.

Karma: Principle of cause and effect in Hinduism and Buddhism asserting that all acts or deeds leave their influence on a future transmigration of the actor.

Kerygma: The essential elements of the gospel that unite all true Christians; stands in contrast with the adiaphora. See *Adiaphora*.

Krishna: Important avatar of Vishnu in the Vaisnava tradition of Hinduism and known in popular Hinduism for his conversation with Arjuna, which is recorded in the Bhagavad-Gita.

Lankāvatāra Sutra: Popular title of an important Mahāyāna sutra that emphasizes the importance of meditation in achieving liberation.

Larger Sutra: A major Pure Land text with the full title: *Larger Sukhāvati-yvūha Sutra,* in which the life of Amida Buddha as an early monk named Dharmākara is explored.

Logos spermatikos: An expression meaning "seed of reason" or "seed of the word," which appears in both Middle Platonist and Stoic ethical writings and is a possible source for Justin Martyr's adaptation and application of the phrase in a Christian context referring to Christ's presence in preincarnate contexts.

Lotus Sutra: Popular title of an important Mahayana sutra that is particularly revered by the Tendai and Nichiren schools of Buddhism, which emphasizes the role and assistance of bodhisattvas to assist a Buddhist in their path toward enlightenment.

Mahābhārata: One of the two great epics of Hinduism. The Bhagavad-Gita is found in this epic. The other great epic is the Rāmāyana, which extols the heroism of Rama.

Mahāyāna: Literally, "great vehicle," referring to the largest division of Buddhism and providing various means of enlightenment for the laity.

Majority World: A term referring to Africa, Asia, and Latin America where the majority of the world's Christians are now located.

Minos: Zeus's son. The poem by Epimenides that Paul quotes in Acts 17:28, which includes the words of Minos. See *Epimenides*.

Mokśa: Release or liberation from the wheel of samsara or rebirth in Hinduism.

Monophysitism: Literally, "one nature," referring to the heretical doctrine that in the incarnate Christ there is only one nature, not two. This view, held by Eutyches (378–454), was condemned by the Council of Chalcedon in AD 451.

Mukti: See *Mokśa*.

Muʿtazila: The rationalist school of Islamic theology that seeks to reconcile faith and reason.

Muʿtazilites: Followers of the Muʿtazila school of Islamic theology. See *Muʿtazila*.

Nafs-al-Rahmān: The "Divine Breath." A language formed by "the twenty-eight letters of the Arabic alphabet."

Namu Amida Butsu: Enlightenment formula that expresses homage to Amitabha or Amida Buddha. In China it is known as the Nien-fo—Namo A-mi-t'o Fo. The repetition of this formula is regarded as a necessary component for rebirth in the Pure Land.

Nembutsu: Buddhist doctrine of repeating the name of Amida Buddha as a source of enlightenment. See *Namu Amida Butsu.*

Nestorianism: A Christological position denying that the two natures of Christ were fully united into one person. Nestorianism was condemned by the Council of Ephesus in AD 431. See *Ephesus, Council of.*

Nestorius: Founder of the Christological heresy, Nestorianism. See *Nestorianism.*

Nicea, Council of: The first ecumenical council of the church, held in AD 325 and called by Emperor Constantine. This council discussed whether the nature of Jesus Christ was the same or similar in relation to the Father. The views of Arius were overwhelmingly condemned.

Noetic principle: A Christian theological principal that includes reflection, reason, propositional statements, etc. This principle must be balanced with the ontic principle. See *Ontic principle.*

Nonretrogression: A stage in Buddhism where it is no longer possible to retrogress back to an inferior realm. This stage is believed to be reached if one reaches the Pure Land.

OM (Aum): The symbol of the anāhata śabda ("unstruck sound") that embodies the true knowledge. See *Anāhata śabda.*

Ontic principle: A Christian theological principle that includes immediacy of God's presence, personal experience with God, etc. This principle must be balanced with the noetic principle. See *Noetic principle.*

Ousia: being or essence.

Padroado: The 1493 Papal decree that divided the world between Spain and Portugal, initially giving Spain exclusive rights to the New World in the West and Portugal the rights to the East. Later the line was moved to give Portugal access to the New World.

Pali canon: Title of the sacred text collection of the Therevada school of Buddhism. See *Tipitaka.*

Pelagianism: An early heresy named after the British monk Pelagius. His views did not recognize the sin nature, only particular sinful deeds individuals have committed. Pelagianism was condemned at the Synod of Carthage in 418 and, later, at the Council of Ephesus in 431. It is doubtful whether Pelagius himself actually affirmed these views.

Pitaka: "Baskets" or divisions in the Pali canon of Buddhism. The three baskets (tipitaka) are Vinaya Pitaka, Sutra Pitaka, and Abhidharma Pitaka. See *Tipitaka* and *Pali canon.*

Prajāpati: In Hinduism, a cosmic figure who sacrifices himself to create the world.

Prajnaparamita Sutras: Term for a collection of Mahāyāna texts known as the "perfection of wisdom" sutras dated around 100 BC and later condensed in such influential texts as the Diamond Sutra and the Heart Sutra.

Prasad: In Hinduism, food that has been offered to idols in the act of worship. See *Puja.*

Pratitya-samutpāda: The Buddha's theory of causality. The term, often translated as dependent arising, refers to a chain of dependent links that are used to describe the process by which something is given apparent existence. All existence is causally conditioned and there is no first cause. The doctrine is often illustrated with twelve links called nidanas.

Preparatio evangelica: Literally, "gospel preparation," referring to God's work in the pre-Christian heart that prepares a person to receive and respond to the gospel message.

Primal vow: The eighteenth vow of Amida Buddha, in which he vows to assist others by inviting them to call on his name in order to achieve enlightenment. In this vow he denies himself enlightenment in order to help others.

Puja: Image worship in Hinduism often involving the offering of flowers, incense, and food and acts of veneration.

Pundrams: Sacred marks drawn on the foreheads of Hindus indicating which particular sect of Hinduism the person follows.

Purānas: Important body of Hindu religious texts that highlights the exploits of various gods and goddesses, often used to support key sectarian beliefs and traditions in popular Hinduism.

Pure Land: Mahāyāna conception of a "Buddha-land," where a transcendent bodhisattva resides. It has no ultimate reality or existence.

Qudsi hadith: Sacred hadith, which are binding on the Islamic community.

Ramanuja: Hindu philosopher and theologian (traditionally, 1017 – 1137), who is the intellectual father of the *visistadvaitin* branch of Vedantism and widely regarded as one of the most influential thinkers in the history of India. See *Visistadvaita.*

Rāmāyana: One of the two great epics of Indian literature. The Rāmāyana extols the heroicism of Rama and Hanuman, among others, in rescuing his wife Sita from the evil King Ravana on the island of Sri Lanka.

Sacra Congregatio de Propaganda Fide: Founded by the Roman Catholic Church in 1622 to assist in training new missionaries, to oversee all Roman Catholic missionary work, and to coordinate major new missionary initiatives in non-Roman Catholic regions of the world.

Salat: Second pillar of Islam, which refers to the ritual prayers performed five times daily by Muslims.

Samhitās: A collection of the four earliest strands of the Vedas apart from the later additions of the Brahmanas, Aranyakas, and Upanishads.

Sankara: Hindu philosopher and theologian who lived from 788–820 and is widely regarded as one of the most influential thinkers in the history of India. He is the intellectual father of Advaitism and his commentary on the Brahma Sutra continues to influence the formulation of Hindu thought today.

Shahadah: The first of the five pillars of Islam known as the Confession of Faith: "I bear witness that there is no god but Allah, and Muhammad is the prophet of Allah."

Shariʿa: Literally, "path," this refers to Islamic Law. See *Sunni*.

Sharif Hadith: Noble Hadith. These are worth emulating but are not binding on the Islamic community. See *Hadith*.

Shiʾite: The sect of ʿAli that claims that the caliphate belongs exclusively to members of ʿAli's family and affirms the special role of an infallible imam. Eventually Shiʿism developed several major branches based primarily on how many imams they officially recognize. The most important branches are known as the Zaydis (also called Fivers), the Ismaʾilis (also called Seveners), and the Imamites (also called Twelvers). See *Imam*.

Shinjin: Literally, "true (sincere) heart or mind." A key term used by Shinran for the concept of "faith."

Shiva: Prominent Hindu deity associated with creation, fertility, and destruction.

Shōbō period: The golden age of the human race when the Buddha first taught the *dharma*. In the shōbō period, the dharma could be understood and obeyed.

Shōdo path: In Buddhism, the "path of the sages."

Shubha: A set of rosary-like prayer beads commonly used by Muslims to recite the ninety-nine beautiful names of Allah.

Sifāt: Literally, "attributes," it refers to the Islamic Sunni belief in seven attributes of Allah that are distinct from his essence: life, knowledge, power, will, hearing, sight, and speech. See *Sunni*.

Sikh Granth: A sacred Sikh text.

Simul iustus et peccator: The declaration propagated by Luther that reckons the believer as existing in the duality of being justified, yet remaining a sinner until he is made perfect in the end.

Smriti: Literally, "that which is being remembered," referring the lower, second-tier body of sacred texts in Hinduism. It is often contrasted with the highest level of literature, śruti. See *Śruti.*

Śruti: Literally, "that which is being heard"; it refers to the highest level of sacred literature in Hinduism, including the Vedas and the Upanishads. It is often contrasted with the smriti, a lower level of literature ("that which is remembered"). See *Anāhata śabda* and *Smriti.*

Sunna: In Islam, refers to the example of the Prophet that gives guidance to the Islamic community and eventually was written down in collections known as Hadith and informs Islamic law (Shariᶜa). See *Shariᶜa.*

Sunnat-el-faᶜil: Hadith that describe what Muhammad did.

Sunnat-el-kaul: Hadith that describe what Muhammad said/commanded.

Sunnat-et-takrir: Hadith that describe what Muhammad allowed.

Sunni: The major body of Islam comprising 80 percent of Muslims worldwide and who recognize the first four caliphs as the true successors of Muhammad.

Surah: A chapter in the Qurᵓan.

Sutras: Authoritative texts in Hinduism and Buddhism, often including aphorisms.

Tahrif: The Islamic doctrine of corruption that claims that the Jews and Christians distorted the meaning of the text of Scripture without necessarily altering the text itself.

Tanzil: Literally, "sending down." Known as the greatest form of revelation in Islam, occurring only with revelation directly transmitted from the Preserved Tablet into the mind of Muhammad and recorded in the Qurᵓan.

Tariki: Literally, "other power." The focus of Pure Land Buddhism that depended on Amida by reciting the nembutsu for enlightenment; in contrast to jiriki. See *Jiriki* and *Nembutsu.*

Tawhid: Doctrine of the unity of God that, in the Islamic context, refers to a strict non-Trinitarian monotheism.

Theanthropic: Refers to the uniting of God and man in the incarnation into one unified person, while not denying that the divine and human essence of Christ remains distinct.

Theological translatability: The ability of the kerygmatic essentials of the Christian faith to be discovered and restated within an infinite number of new global contexts.

Theotokos: Literally, "God-bearer," a term used widely as a devotional title for Mary, the mother of Jesus. See *Nestorianism.*

Therevada: Literally, "the elders," and referring to the more ancient, monastic expression of Buddhism. See *Hinayana.*

Tipitaka: Three "baskets" or divisions in the Pali canon of Buddhism: Vinaya, Sutra, and Abhidharma. See *Pali Canon* and *Pitaka.*

Translatability: The ability of the Christian faith to be discovered and restated within a number of historical, geographic, and cultural contexts.

TSPM: Three-Self Patriotic Movement organized by the Communist Party in China to provide oversight of all Protestant Churches.

Tukārām: A seventeenth-century Marati, poet-saint from Maharashtra, India. Tukārām was a devotee of the god Krishna and his poems are filled with love and adoration to Krishna. They are used as sacred texts in the bhakti tradition of Hinduism.

Upanishads: Literally, "to sit down near"; it refers to a collection of mostly philosophical and reflective writings attached to the end of the various strands of Vedic literature, which form the basis for much of the development of Hindu philosophical thought.

Vedas: A term frequently referring to the entire structure of Vedic literature including the Samhitās, the Brahmanas, the Aranyakas, and even, at times, the Upanishads. Some writers apply the term only to the Upanishads; some even use it to refer only to the Samhitās.

Visistadvaita: Literally, "modified nondualism"; it refers to another major branch of Vedanta and is often associated with the Hindu philosopher Ramanuja.

Viśnu: Hindu deity who first appears in the Rig-Veda, but gradually assumes a more prominent role and is the source of the most important avatars in Hinduism today.

Wahy: Literally, "prophetic rapture." Found, according to Islam, in the undistorted portions of the Jewish and Christian writings.

Waldensians: A heretical group organized by Peter Waldo in the twelfth century who preached apostolic poverty as the way to perfection.

Yathrib: Pre-Islamic name of Medina, the city of the Prophet. See *Hejira.*

Index

We want to hear from you. Please send your comments about this book to us in care of zreview@zondervan.com. Thank you.